I0085972

VARIETIES OF POWER

COLUMBIA STUDIES IN MIDDLE EAST POLITICS

COLUMBIA STUDIES IN MIDDLE EAST POLITICS

Marc Lynch, Series Editor

Columbia Studies in Middle East Politics presents academically rigorous, well-written, relevant, and accessible books on the rapidly transforming politics of the Middle East for an interested academic and policy audience.

For a complete list of books in the series, please see the Columbia University Press website.

MARWA SHALABY

VARIETIES OF
POWER

Women's Political Representation in
Arab Parliaments

Columbia University Press / *New York*

Columbia University Press
Publishers Since 1893
New York   Chichester, West Sussex
cup.columbia.edu

Copyright © 2025 Columbia University Press
All rights reserved

Library of Congress Cataloging-in-Publication Data
Names: Shalaby, Marwa author
Title: Varieties of power : women's political representation in
Arab parliaments / Marwa Shalaby.
Description: New York : Columbia University Press, 2025. |
Includes bibliographical references and index.
Identifiers: LCCN 2024049177 | ISBN 9780231218658 hardback |
ISBN 9780231218665 trade paperback | ISBN 9780231562393 ebook
Subjects: LCSH: Women—Political activity—Arab countries |
Women legislators—Arab countries | Legislative bodies—
Arab countries | Authoritarianism—Arab countries
Classification: LCC HQ1236.5.A65 S53 2025 |
DDC 328.082/09174927—dc23/eng/20250402
LC record available at https://lccn.loc.gov/2024049177

Cover design: Noah Arlow
Cover image: Shutterstock

GPSR Authorized Representative: Easy Access System Europe,
Mustamäe tee 50, 10621 Tallinn, Estonia, gpsr.requests@easproject.com

CONTENTS

CONTENTS

FIGURES AND TABLES

FIGURES

TABLES

ACKNOWLEDGMENTS

The idea for this book started as I was preparing my postdoctoral job applications. I was deeply interested in examining women's roles in autocratic legislatures, mainly in the Middle East and North Africa (MENA) region. While developing the project proposal, I found that research on MENA's legislatures, let alone on women in these legislatures, is almost nonexistent. Logistical issues, such as the inaccessibility of parliamentary records and security concerns, can partially explain this dearth of scholarship. However, this was not the case for other autocratic contexts. Research on MENA's legislative politics was mostly lacking due to scholars' views of these legislative bodies as inconsequential because they are not leading to democratization. These views became even stronger after the Arab uprisings. It is clear that MENA's persistent authoritarianism has drawn scholars' attention away from the region and its legislative institutions.

When I joined Rice University in 2013 as a postdoctoral fellow, I decided to study these often-overlooked institutions and was determined to open the "black box" of MENA's autocratic legislatures. Shortly after, I initiated the Governance and Elections in the Middle East Project (GEMEP).

I conducted fieldwork and collected legislative data from Tunisia, Jordan, Morocco, Lebanon, Kuwait, and Algeria. The beginning of the fieldwork and data collection was challenging, and the outcomes were often uncertain. I faced numerous security issues and logistical and institutional obstacles throughout my research trips. Soon, I started to realize the magnitude of the project and the enormous amount of effort and time needed to construct these high-quality, reliable datasets. However, I was always overwhelmed by the generosity of everyone I encountered on my trips and their willingness to support me. I remained hopeful as I felt that every research trip was getting me closer to my goals.

The data collection for this book required an army of multilingual undergraduate and graduate research assistants. I was lucky to have Ariana Marnicio as the lead research associate at Rice University's Baker Institute for Public Policy. Ariana managed the undergraduate team of researchers with professionalism and diligence. Her energy and enthusiasm carried the team through challenging times. There are many undergraduate students to thank, including Ankita Ajith, Maithili Bagaria, Naomi Eisenbeiss, Lana Elserag, Yasna Haghdoost, Lucian Li, Mackenzie Mott, Kimberly Rightor, Annum Sadana, and Laura Zhang. I am also grateful for the research assistance of the graduate researchers Luai Allarakia, Abdullah Aydogan, Adan Obeid, Khalid Saleh, and Dina Shahrokhi. I will always be thankful for the exceptional efforts of Laila Elimam, who led the data collection team for the cross-national committee membership dataset and completed it with unmatched precision. At the University of Wisconsin–Madison, I was lucky to recruit exceptional undergraduate and graduate students to continue the data collection efforts: Lojain Adly, Ghaida Edreis, June Jung, Vikrant Kamble, Monica Komer, Quincy Kroner, Jérémie Langlois, and Morgan Snyder.

Writing this book was another long journey, and I am grateful to many people who supported me and helped shape the book's main arguments and ideas. I owe my deepest thanks to all the great women I met throughout my fieldwork who always filled my heart with hope, strength, and resilience. I remember how my research trips always started with uncertainty and apprehension, but I have always left the field charged and dazzled by these magnificent women trying to make a difference despite the hardships they face and the adverse circumstances. There are so many individuals to thank who have generously shared their time, experiences, and knowledge with me. In Jordan, I thank Abla Abu Elba, Reem Abu Delbouh, Majid al-Amir, Khamis Attiya, Wafaa Ben Mustafa, Hind al-Fayez, Mohammad Sharman, Dima Tahboub, and many others who preferred to be anonymous. Furthermore, acquiring the data in this book would not have been possible without the support of the general secretary of the Jordanian Lower Chamber and Mr. Fayeq Fantool Alzaydan, the head of the monitoring unit. In Morocco, I am grateful for the insights of Lubna Amhair, Azzoha al-Arrak, Ibtissame Azzaoui, Rachida Ben Massoud, Naema Ben Yahya, Boutaina Karraouri, Mounira Rajaoui, Eman Yaqoubi, and many others who did not want their names disclosed. I am also grateful to Dr. Ahmed Mufid, the head of the Studies Unit in the Moroccan Lower Chamber, who facilitated the interviews and access to the parliamentary records. In Kuwait, I am grateful for Hamad al-Baloshi, Mohammad al-Dalal, Sheikha al-Jassim, Salwa al-Jassar, Ali al-Kandari, Alia al-Khaledi, Alnoud al-Sharekh, Ghadeer Aseri, Dalal Buresli, Asrar Hayat, and many others who preferred to be anonymous.

I am deeply grateful for the generous support and funding from various institutions, which played a significant role in bringing this book to light. Since joining the University of Wisconsin in the fall of 2019, I have been fortunate to have their unwavering support for the book's data collection and fieldwork. The financial support from Wisconsin's Alumni Research Foundation (WARF), the Office of the Provost, and the Office of the Vice Chancellor for Research and Graduate Education (VCRGE) at the University of Wisconsin–Madison was instrumental. I was also honored to receive the Anna Julia Cooper Postdoctoral Fellowship from the Office of the Vice Provost for Faculty and Staff Programs at the University of Wisconsin–Madison in 2019. The fellowship year was crucial for completing the fieldwork and preparing the datasets for analysis. Additionally, my fellowship at Harvard University's Center for Middle East Studies (CMES) during the spring of 2023, with the generous support of Melanie Cammett and Kristin Fabbe, was a significant boost to the book's progress.

I also thank the generous support of the Carnegie Corporation of New York (CCNY). CCNY funding for course buyouts at the University of Wisconsin–Madison gave me the time needed to make progress on the book and other related projects.

The feedback I received from the book workshops organized by the Project on Middle East Political Science (POMEPS) and Governance and Local Development Institute (GLD) was invaluable. The thoughtful comments by Fernando Casal Bertoa, Marc Lynch, Ellen Lust, Aili Tripp, Melody Valdini, and Lena Wängnerud significantly strengthened the book. The participants of the 2019 annual meeting of the Empirical Study of Gender Research Network (EGEN), especially Amanda Clayton and Jennifer Piscopo, and the attendees of the 2021 GLD conference on Gender and Politics in MENA and the American Political Science Association (APSA) 2021 annual meeting, including Daniela Donno and Lindsay Benstead, also provided crucial feedback on earlier versions of the book. I also thank Valeriya Mechkova for her excellent comments at the 2022 European Conference on Politics and Gender. Their contributions were instrumental in shaping the book, and I am deeply grateful for their engagement and support. The book also benefitted from conversations with Fernando Bizzarro and Allen Hicken.

* * *

Support for this research was provided by the University of Wisconsin–Madison Office of the Vice Chancellor for Research with funding from the Wisconsin Alumni Research Foundation.

VARIETIES OF POWER

INTRODUCTION

*Sit down, Hind! Sit down, Hind! May God curse the day and those who
introduced the [gender] quota system to the Jordanian Parliament.*

—MEMBER OF PARLIAMENT (MP) YEHYA AL-SAUD DURING A LEGISLATIVE SESSION
TO A FEMALE MP, HIND AL-FAYEZ, ON DECEMBER 2, 2014

I t was far from an ordinary day in the Jordanian parliament. Heated
floor discussions on political Islam and Arab nationalism had started
when a member of the Muslim Brotherhood (MB) took to the floor to
criticize the larger space given to the nationalists in Jordan as compared to
the Islamists. Hind al-Fayez, a female legislator who won a quota seat in the
2013 legislature and came from a nationalist family, dared to disagree and
criticize the divisive rhetoric of the Islamist party member. Soon, a heated
confrontation erupted between Hind and male legislator Yehya al-Saud,
who interrupted his colleague and asked her repeatedly to sit down and stop
talking. Hind continued her speech while ignoring al-Saud's requests. Right
after, he started banging aggressively on the bench and verbally assaulting
her while cursing the gender quota and those who introduced it to the
Jordanian parliament. Even after being rebuked by the head of the session

for his aggressive and sexist comments, he refused to apologize and yelled at the other female legislators, "Go back home and put some makeup on for your husbands and do some cooking."

While this incident may reflect one of the countless instances of sexism and violence against women in politics across the globe, what is remarkable about this incident is how Hind al-Fayez was verbally attacked not because of her performance or policy stances but because of the way she entered the parliament: the quota system. An institutional mechanism widely hailed as an important step toward female political empowerment was used as a weapon against her and other female legislators to demoralize them and belittle their presence and influence. In a personal interview with Hind al-Fayez three years after this incident, she expressed her frustration with the long-standing inequalities in the Jordanian political realm where "the Honorary President, the President of the King's Bureau, the Prime Minister, the President of the Senate, most of the appointees [in the Senate], the President of the General Assembly—are all men. This would make you think that men can lead and women cannot since they are absent from these positions. It has been rooted in them. . . . You need to fight this image and bring women in."[1] Despite being directly attacked for being a female legislator with a quota seat, Hind still believed that gender quotas are one of the most important mechanisms to correct inequalities and address the marginalization of women in politics.[2] A former female legislator in Morocco echoed a similar view: "Despite the shortcomings of the existing quota system, I believe that quotas are necessary to combat the systemic exclusion of women from the legislative sphere. Gender quotas are like medications that may be prescribed short-term to address specific issues or can be a long-term treatment for a chronic illness."[3]

Unquestionably, the introduction of gender quotas across the globe has transformed the political landscape for women. Since the mid-1990s, women's representation in national politics has exponentially increased—in both democracies and autocracies (figure I.1). Women's numerical presence in national legislatures has risen substantially since the implementation of gender quotas in the twenty-first century in many dictatorships, including the Middle East and North Africa (MENA).

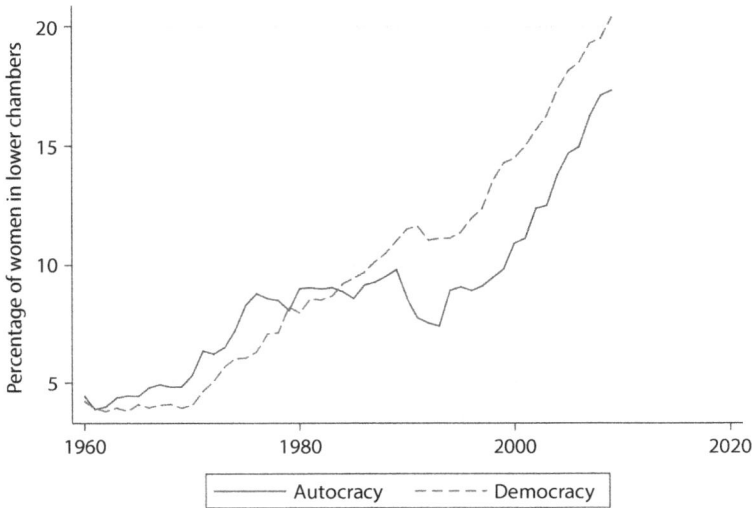

FIGURE I.1 Regime type and female representation in national legislatures

Source: Lührmann et al. (2018); V-Dem Institute V11.1. The autocracy category includes both closed and electoral autocracies. Closed autocracy: no multiparty elections for the chief executive or the legislature. Electoral autocracy: de jure multiparty elections for the chief executive and the legislature but failing to ensure those elections are free and fair, or de facto multiparty, or a minimum level of Dahl's institutional prerequisites of polyarchy as measured by V-Dem's Electoral Democracy Index (v2x_polyarchy).

The incremental increase in women's descriptive representation over the past two decades in autocracies raises two important puzzles. The first puzzle relates to whether the increased number of women in authoritarian legislatures has granted them more power and influence: How do the politics of authoritarianism shape women's political influence?[4] How does autocratic regimes' restriction of political competition, such as banning or weakening political parties to constrain the opposition, affect women's legislative behavior and priorities? Despite the proliferation of studies on authoritarian legislatures that have scrutinized the role of seemingly democratic institutions under authoritarianism and the autocrats' incentives to incorporate women in decision-making processes, we still have little notion of women's political power and legislative behavior.

The second puzzle of this book deals with the role of political parties in shaping women's legislative behavior and political power. Research investigating the link between the presence and strength of political parties and women's political representation has flourished in established and new democracies. However, our knowledge remains limited in autocratic settings where political parties vary widely in terms of their organizational strength and capacity. As figure I.2 reveals, there has been a strong association between authoritarian party-based regimes and women's numerical presence in national legislatures over the past few decades. The figure also demonstrates that women are more likely to gain greater access to national legislatures in party-based regimes compared to other authoritarian regime types, such as military and personalist regimes. Yet scholars have paid little attention to the intersection of women's political representation and political parties in autocracies.

This book offers insights into both puzzles and aims to develop a novel theory on women's political representation under authoritarianism. Thus, it focuses on three distinct yet interrelated dimensions of women's political

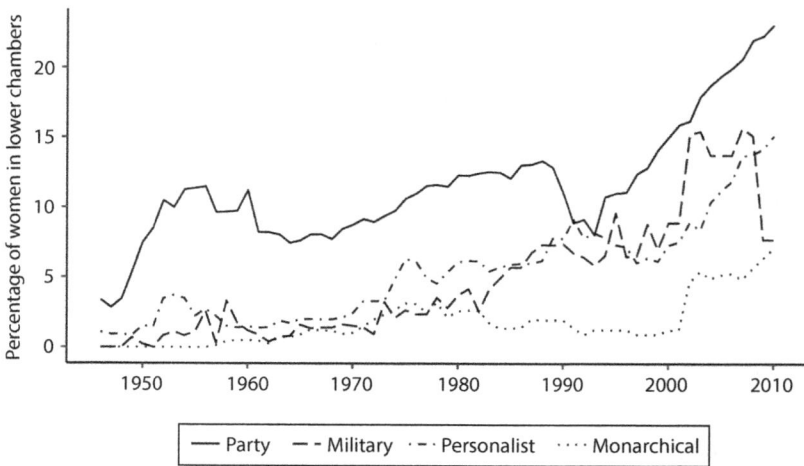

FIGURE I.2 Authoritarian regime type and women's political representation

Source: This graph is based on Geddes et al.'s (2014) classification of political regimes. It represents the four main categories of authoritarian regimes. The party category includes the party, party-military, party-personal military, party-personal, and party-based oligarchy; the military category includes indirect military and military-personal.

power in nondemocracies: presence, influence, and representation. By *presence*, I allude to the conceptualization of descriptive representation as the representative's characteristics rather than their actions and how legislatures should mirror society regarding gender, race, and other demographics.[5]

I define and measure women's *influence* as integration in high-level positions and levels of substantive representation. Women's integration into the political process involves their membership and leadership of influential decision-making bodies, such as committee membership and leadership.[6] As Anne Marie Goetz further points out, women's political effectiveness depends on whether they gain access, presence, or influence—the latter (which is most important) occurs under "accountability mechanisms" that incorporate women's concerns and preferences, such as women's participation in influential parliamentary committees and leadership positions.[7]

The *substantive representation* of women is another measure of influence within legislatures by focusing on their legislative behavior and priorities. By substantive representation, I refer to the degree to which representatives seek to advance the group's interests and preferences—or, in other words, the translation of policy preferences into legislative outcomes in favor of the represented group.[8] I argue and provide empirical evidence that women affiliated with highly institutionalized parties are more likely to gain access to influential positions within legislatures and substantively represent women's interests.

In this book, I focus on a specific aspect of political parties: the degree of party institutionalization (PI).[9] PI is conceptualized as the proportion of the parties in the system that have robust organizations and the extent to which the parties' long-term goals drive the behavior of the elites and masses within the political system, whether it is a democracy or an autocracy.[10] As I demonstrate in the following chapters, the institutionalization of individual parties (despite the absence of party system institutionalization in most autocracies) is crucial for women's exercise of political power. Research on women in politics in established democracies has paid little attention to the effect of the institutionalization of individual parties on women's political power and substantive representation. This is mainly due to the limited variation in individual parties' institutionalization in democracies, which—unlike autocracies—tend to have relatively strong, institutionalized parties and party systems. I contend that whereas gender quota systems may level the political field for women, the presence of institutionalized political parties is crucial for women's ability to exercise power and exert political influence.

Importantly, I differentiate between individual parties' institutionalization and party system institutionalization (PSI), which is often a measure of the external dimension of political parties, particularly interparty competition. PSI has developed in democratic settings and mainly focuses on the stability and predictability of the party system.[11] PSI is mostly nonexistent in autocratic regimes, given dictators' efforts to suppress political opponents and centralize power within their own hands and/or circle of regime allies. As a result, PSI plays a marginal role in explaining most political outcomes in nondemocracies.[12] This book is mainly concerned with investigating the effect of the internal features of individual parties on women's ability to gain influence and exercise political power within legislatures. PI also differs from regime institutionalization, which relates to "the creation of rules and procedures that tie the leader's hands by empowering other elites."[13] To sum up, my goal is to investigate the factors shaping women's political influence and control and the differential effect of authoritarianism on shaping legislators' behavior, with a particular focus on women in power in autocratic settings with varying levels of PI.

Investigating women's representation in autocratic legislatures is more relevant now than ever because of the rise in women's presence in elected office and the persistence of dictatorships worldwide. According to Freedom House, 2016 marks the "10th consecutive year of decline in global freedom."[14] "Partly free" and "not free" countries are increasing, composing most of the world's countries (79 percent). According to 2023 data from the V-Dem Institute, an independent research organization, about 72 percent of the world's population lives in autocracies.[15] Furthermore, multiparty monarchies, multiparty military systems, and limited multiparty regimes currently constitute the second-largest category after democracy, at 24 percent versus 42 percent of democratic systems.[16]

Addressing these questions is also essential because of the ongoing debates around the role of female politicians in nondemocracies. Recent work has problematized women's political inclusion in contexts where autocrats tend to instrumentalize women's rights to legitimize their rule and to enable them to engage in human rights abuses or consolidate authoritarian control.[17] Genderwashing—promoting gender equality with ulterior motives—may help the regime appear progressive and democratic while diverting attention away from its authoritarian practices.[18] These views often focus on the regime's motivation to include women in the political process but rarely systematically explore the agency and preferences of female politicians in these contexts. More importantly, these views tend to oversimplify the role of contextual factors in shaping women's access and exercise of power, such as the presence and strength of political parties.

AUTHORITARIAN INSTITUTIONS, WOMEN, AND POLITICAL POWER

Work in established democracies has shown that parties are the gateway for female political representation, and their presence is integral for advancing women's presence in politics.[19] Parties are crucial for female politicians' nomination, recruitment, and legislative behavior.[20] Nevertheless, the role of political parties in shaping women's access and exercise of power in autocracies remains understudied. This has created a significant gap in our understanding of representation and gender politics beyond developed democracies. Political parties and legislative institutions have been more prominent in shaping autocratic politics in the post–Cold War era.[21] Since the 1990s, about 70 percent of authoritarian regimes have introduced multiparty elections. According to 2022 data from the V-Dem Institute, more than 90 percent of dictatorships also established legislatures. To date, scholarship on the intersection of gender and autocratic institutions has focused on two main strands of research: (1) the structure and outcomes of authoritarian institutions and (2) the autocrats' motivation to adopt women's rights—with no attention paid to the intersection of these two areas.

First, research on authoritarian political institutions has proliferated to investigate the "wide and foggy" zone that exists between liberal democracies and authoritarian regimes and to understand variations across nondemocratic political structures better.[22] Furthermore, studies have assessed the likelihood of nondemocratic regimes' transition to democracy,[23] prospects for survival,[24] power-sharing strategies,[25] and the outcomes of the negotiated policy concessions between the opposition, ruling elites, and the masses.[26]

The presence of seemingly democratic institutions in autocracies is important for many reasons. Institutionalized autocracies—defined as regimes with parties and legislatures—are associated with higher levels of civil liberties and regime longevity[27] as they alleviate the issue of power sharing between the regime and the ruling elites,[28] increase the bargaining power of the ruling party vis-à-vis the dictator,[29] and provide autocrats with information to manage conflict.[30] Furthermore, maintaining a façade of representative democracy and multiparty elections is desirable for promoting economic growth[31] and improving the regimes' image in international and domestic circles.[32] Electoral authoritarian regimes, especially those with strong left-leaning parties and institutionalized party systems, are also more likely to have lower levels of inequality.[33]

In addition to investigating the structure of autocratic institutions, their outcomes came under scrutiny. While a group of scholars upheld the view that they do not necessarily produce substantive policy outcomes[34] and tend to lack decision-making power,[35] burgeoning literature challenges these views. Recently, a large body of research focusing on individual cases and large-N empirical studies[36] has attempted to open "the black box of authoritarian policymaking."[37] Most studies have found that electoral institutions have significant policy consequences, even though they may not result in executive turnover.[38] For instance, a cross-country analysis demonstrated that adverse electoral shocks to the ruling party may result in budget spending on education and social policies, whereas an increase in electoral support leads to higher military spending after elections.[39]

Focusing on the individual-level behavior of legislators within these electoral institutions, several explanations have emerged to better understand individual legislators' policy preferences and priorities. One view holds that legislators under authoritarian institutions are mainly motivated to access state resources and by rent distribution.[40] Proximity to the ruling elites provides legislators with direct benefits and an increased ability to allocate private and local public goods to their constituents with little or no influence on policymaking.[41] Contrastingly, burgeoning literature demonstrates that legislators play a crucial representative role despite the constraints imposed by the autocrat. One study indicated that political elites in China voice the issue priorities of the public, except for sensitive topics that may destabilize the incumbent regime.[42] Similarly, another study of delegates' behavior in the Vietnamese parliament demonstrated that legislators ask questions important to their local constituents; however, their behavior is highly "parameterized" within the rules delineated by the ruling regime.[43] Legislators in Morocco are also responsive to public opinion. There are consistent patterns of elite-citizen issue congruence, especially in areas that are not sensitive to the incumbent regime.[44] However, these studies have paid little attention to the gender differences in legislative behavior and/or the role of political parties in shaping women's legislative behavior in autocracies.

Second, the recent increase in women's presence in the political arena, especially in autocratic countries, has led to unprecedented scholarly attention to scrutinize autocrats' motivation to adopt women's rights. Autocrats adopt gender-related reforms, including gender quotas, for various reasons. They tend to view gender-related reforms as less politically risky than introducing reforms relating to improving the rule of law, human rights, and/or civil liberties that may threaten their survival.[45] According to Daniela Donno and colleagues, "The proliferation of gender reforms even in closed authoritarian regimes where civil society is repressed points to the complementary importance of "top-down" pressures."[46] Genderwashing may help the regime appear progressive and democratic while diverting attention away from its authoritarian practices.[47]

Autocrats may also rely on gender reforms to create a positive modernizing image for their states[48] and to signal to their citizens that the government enjoys democratic traits.[49] Furthermore, gender reforms can improve the dictator's international reputation; therefore, they may adopt such strategies to deflect pressures to democratize,[50] appease international donors,[51] and virtue signal.[52] Autocratic regimes governed by institutionalized ruling parties have a higher capacity to introduce gender reforms due to their increased ability to cultivate broader support coalitions and closer connections with society.[53]

The introduction of gender quotas in national politics that has fast-tracked women's access to power is indeed one of the most effective strategies adopted by autocrats to promote their popularity and international standing.[54] What is still missing is a deeper understanding of the tangible outcomes of such gender reforms on the link between women's numerical presence and political (and policy) outcomes under authoritarianism. Work on women's substantive representation in democracies has multiplied over the past decades. Theoretically, the increased presence in legislative institutions should benefit women because they have dissimilar priorities and preferences than men. Women's presence in such positions of power has a positive effect on the representation of women's interests as a group.[55] Furthermore, the role of political parties and partisanship in shaping women's candidacy and legislative behavior is well documented in established democracies.[56] However, do these findings hold in dictatorships where partisanship and political party systems' fragmentation dominate?

There is growing evidence from nondemocracies that gender quotas have enhanced women's substantive representation[57] and promoted women-friendly policies.[58] However, the role played by political parties and how they may shape women's political power and substantive representation remain unclear.

AUTHORITARIAN PARTIES, PARTY INSTITUTIONALIZATION, AND WOMEN'S POLITICAL POWER

Autocrats have established regime-affiliated parties to solidify power, mobilize support, and appease elite challengers.[59] Furthermore, they allow non-regime parties to contest elections and offer them some policy influence to divide the opposition and increase coordination costs among their opponents.[60] Interestingly, most research on authoritarian parties has paid significant attention to party-based regimes and their political and policy outcomes, and our knowledge of nonregime parties remains lacking.[61] Thus, a significant bias exists in the literature toward exploring the structure and outcomes of the ruling parties in autocracies rather than individual parties and how they shape governance and/or policy outputs.[62]

An often-ignored aspect in the study of the intersection of autocratic legislatures and women's political representation is the effect of political parties operating under authoritarianism on women's exercise of power. I am interested in exploring the impact of a specific aspect of political parties in autocracies: the institutionalization of individual parties and how it shapes women's political power (i.e., access to influential committee positions within the legislature) and legislative behavior (i.e., substantive representation).

I argue that women affiliated with highly institutionalized parties are more likely to have political power and influence. I distinguish between PSI and individual PI and their relationship to women's representation, which I explore in more depth in chapter 2. I focus on the institutionalization of individual parties rather than PSI because PSI in most autocratic settings is almost absent. Furthermore, recent work has shown that PSI and PI are two distinct phenomena.[63] Novel datasets with specific measures on PI in the country and party levels (e.g., 2020 V-Party dataset) offer a unique opportunity to better understand the link between the internal features and the behavior of individual parties and women's legislative behavior in autocracies.[64]

I contend that institutionalized political parties—characterized by organizational stability, continuity, and solid connections with voters and societal groups—are integral to women's ability to exercise political power. As I detail in chapter 2, parties' organizational capacity and stability may not only condition women's access to political power but also affect women's ability to gain influence and exercise political power within legislatures.[65] PI is measured along two main dimensions: the *scope* of PI, which deals with party organization, and the *depth* of institutionalization, which captures the party's linkage with the masses and elites and the party's cohesion.

Regarding the *scope* of PI, I argue that political parties' organizational capacity is essential for coordinating and channeling women's interests within and outside the legislature. Highly institutionalized parties that function as an organization with clearly defined rules and sufficient material and human resources are better able to cultivate, recruit, and support female candidacies.[66] This can be attributed to the fact that institutionalized parties have more extensive linkages to society that are essential for coalition building and the mobilization of women. In addition, highly institutionalized parties tend to have less centralized nomination processes that often occur through local branches and grassroots levels with less interference from the center. This has been defined as "organizational complexity."[67] Such complexity enables parties to implement candidate selection mechanisms that ensure female inclusion and better equip them to channel political demands.[68]

Relatedly, such "bottom-up" structures facilitate the flow of information where institutionalized parties can better identify and aggregate demands from citizens and organized interests through civil society linkages and/or local branches.[69] These organizational structures are valuable in contexts with gender quotas because they facilitate candidate recruitment and selection; however, these organizations are increasingly important in contexts with no gender quotas where women lack organized support and political experience. Furthermore, this organizational complexity matters for promoting women in male-dominated, autocratic settings as women politicians tend to be isolated from existing networks of power and lack homosocial capital.[70]

The *depth* of institutionalization also facilitates interparty collaboration between female members compared to contexts with no parties and/or when multiparty competition exists and where parties lack horizontal and vertical linkages and/or legislative cohesion. Collaboration and coalition building among women are vital components of the legislative process, especially in nondemocratic settings where women tend to be newcomers to politics and due to the opacity of policymaking processes within these institutions. Collaboration across party lines enables women to overcome structural barriers, attain political power and influence, and negotiate with higher echelons of power (e.g., government officials, ruling elites, the incumbent regime) to whom women often lack access and influence.[71]

My argument differs from extant scholarship on the link between PI and women's rights under authoritarianism in important ways. First, research has shown that dictatorships governed by institutionalized party-based regimes are positively linked with women's political and economic rights[72] and political inclusion.[73] This link is attributed to these parties' greater capacity and ability to use the inclusion of women as a tool for coalition building, regardless of the presence of multiparty elections.[74] My work builds on these views but also demonstrates that the institutionalization of individual parties in autocracies, not just the ruling party's institutionalization, matters for the promotion of women's political influence.[75] Second, studies have also shown a strong link between PI and women's descriptive representation in Brazil's national legislature[76] and subnational politics in Tunisia—even with the presence of gender quotas.[77] My analysis contributes to this stream of research, and I contend that PI matters for women's descriptive representation, especially in contexts with no quota system in place. Importantly, I view PI as crucial for women's political power and substantive representation in autocratic legislatures.

WHY THE MIDDLE EAST AND NORTH AFRICA REGION?

I focus in this book on the seventeen Arab MENA states and exclude non-Arab states, such as Turkey and Israel, due to their different trajectory of democratization in addition to cultural and linguistic differences.[78] The MENA region offers a fitting case to explore the link between the politics of authoritarianism and women's political representation for several reasons. First, the MENA region continues to endure some of the most resilient autocratic structures. According to the V-Dem 2023 democracy report, autocracy across the MENA region has remained stable over the past three decades with few exceptions.[79] The cautious opening of the political space in the 1990s has significantly reshaped the region's power dynamics. Most Arab states have formed legislative assemblies, introduced electoral reforms, and held competitive elections—mainly in response to severe economic and political crises and international and domestic pressure.[80] Nonetheless, there are wide cross-national differences regarding the structures and modes of selection and/or election of these assemblies and their degree of political competition. There are also wide variations in individual parties' institutionalization levels across the region. Whereas parties have been allowed to form and compete freely in elections in some states, dictators banned or restricted their activities in others.

By the turn of the century, the limited success of MENA states' ability to democratize and/or build more inclusive political systems led scholars to discredit these legislative institutions and their outcomes quickly. Over the past decades, research has viewed MENA's elections and/or legislatures as channels for distributing rents or the circulation of elites to strengthen incumbent regimes.[81] These elections have been viewed as significant political events for political elites and voters; however, the electoral competition is not about policymaking per se.[82] Elections are primarily about access to state resources and clientelistic networks. Others argue that the cautious introduction of multiparty systems has mainly led to the creation of several new parties that reproduce the regimes' autocratic and nepotistic practices rather than promote more liberal, democratic processes.[83] Autocrats have used elections to send signals about acceptable venues for political participation to both elites and voters, garner international and domestic support,[84] and identify the most loyal party figures to be rewarded by the ruling regime.[85] Opposition forces have viewed elections as an opportunity to gain visibility in the media and raise public awareness about the incumbent's procedural or policy-related missteps.[86]

These views on MENA's legislative politics have not only obscured the study of the region's legislative politics but also negatively impacted the systematic analyses of the policymaking processes and the role of women within and across these legislatures, especially in states where legislatures play a substantive role in the political arena. Currently, only a handful of studies have explored the inner dynamics of MENA's legislatures.[87] This is problematic given that all twenty-two Arab countries have legislative councils, most directly elected.[88] Some countries even have upper and lower chambers.[89] As I outline in chapter 3, there are variations in the legislative strength of MENA's legislatures, but they perform substantial legislative and monitoring roles. Most of MENA's legislatures approve the annual budget, discuss and ratify laws submitted by the executive, question ministers, form committees, and propose bills. Burgeoning research has uncovered patterns of responsiveness to citizens' priorities, especially in areas that are not sensitive to the incumbent regime[90] and significant variations in policy preferences between the pro-regime and opposition groups.[91]

In addition to their legislative role, most of MENA's legislatures monitor the executive and government officials. For instance, legislators asked more than 30,000 oral and written questions in Morocco's 2011 legislature. In Kuwait, notwithstanding the small assembly size (fifty MPs), legislators asked about 3,350 questions and proposed 700 bills between 2009 and 2011. Legislators asked over 3,000 parliamentary questions in Jordan's 2013 legislature and initiated dozens of investigations.

Second, MENA's autocrats have promoted women's rights since independence from colonial powers in the 1950s and 1960s. Rulers viewed these rights as an important tool to ensure the survival of their regimes and constrain the opposition. For them, women's rights were less politically risky and helped them to improve their image and reputation in the international arena and domestically. Thus, autocrats promulgated gender-focused reforms for economic (Egypt's Nasser in 1956), strategic (Tunisia's Bourgiba in 1956), and security motives (Morocco's King Mohammad V in 2002). In other cases, gender reforms resulted from international and donor pressures on the incumbent autocrats (e.g., the introduction of reserved seats for women in the case of Jordan in 2003).

MENA's dictators also introduced various forms of gender quota policies. Nevertheless, women's political representation in the MENA region remained low, with one of the lowest rates of female representation in national legislatures worldwide until the 2010s (figure I.3). The scene changed after the onset of the Arab uprisings, with many countries taking steps to increase the presence of women in formal politics.[92] As a result, women's presence in

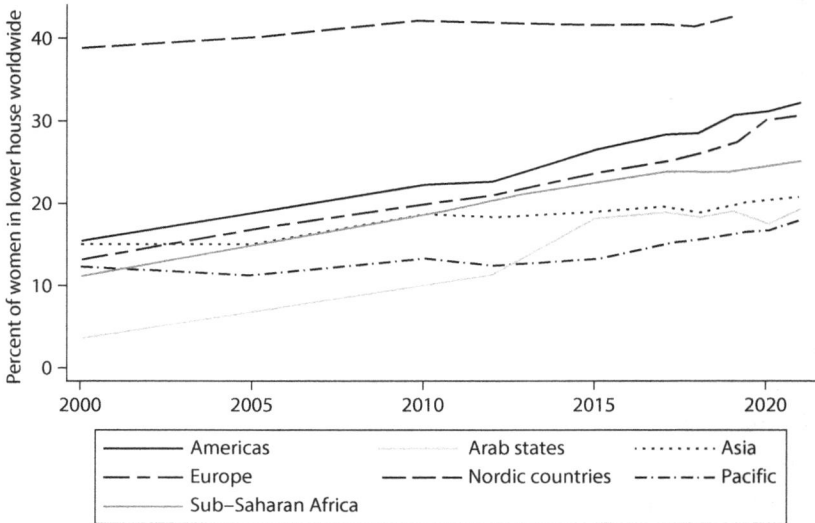

FIGURE I.3 The percentage of women in lower chambers worldwide

Source: International Parliamentary Union (IPU).

national legislatures exceeded 10 percent for the first time in 2012. Despite the recent progress, women's representation in Arab national legislatures stood at 18 percent in 2021, compared to 40 percent in Nordic countries and 27 percent in the rest of Europe.[93]

Notably, there are significant cross-national variations (table 1.1). For instance, most Arab countries have taken measures to bridge the gender gap in politics through constitutional and electoral mechanisms. Still, many countries across the region continue to lag with the lowest percentages of women in national legislatures globally. Wide variations exist regarding quota types, enforcement mechanisms, and placement mandates. For instance, the United Arab Emirates and Egypt are currently the pioneering countries in female political representation in legislative bodies, with 50 and 27 percent, respectively. Meanwhile, several countries, such as Oman, Lebanon, and Yemen, have negligible or no female presence in legislatures.

Furthermore, women face challenges in winning additional seats beyond the allocated quota.[94]

Research explicating the drivers of female (under)representation in MENA politics over the past decades was based on individual, qualitative case studies, with little attention paid toward explicating cross-national variations across the region.[95] Moreover, studies mostly centered around the effect of the sociocultural,[96] institutional,[97] and structural[98] factors on women's descriptive representation.

Third, there is a substantial gap in our understanding regarding women's substantive representation in the MENA context and autocracies more generally. In particular, research on the role of women in MENA's legislatures is lacking, and the few existing studies have yielded mixed findings. Research has found that quota women have limited capacity to initiate change due to the hegemony of the male political parties' leaders and the weakness of female alliances within the legislature.[99] Others contend that women elected through the quota system have succeeded in building alliances despite their ideological differences, allowing them to draw attention to women's issues and push for substantial women-focused legislation.[100] Similarly, Lindsay J. Benstead found that women's political inclusion in clientelistic settings is crucial for advancing women's access to services.[101] However, it is important to note that these studies, except for that by Benstead, have primarily relied on single cases and qualitative observations of legislators' behavior without systematic data collection and analysis of their actual legislative behavior and preferences.[102] In addition, these studies have paid limited attention to the varying effects of authoritarian politics, especially the impact of the constraints imposed by the autocrat on political parties on shaping women's legislative behavior and priorities.

EMPIRICAL STRATEGY

The book uses a mixed-method approach to data collection and analysis. It combines qualitative and quantitative data sources with content analysis of legislative data and other primary sources. I rely on a decade of fieldwork and original data collection across the MENA region. Obtaining reliable, high-quality data on autocratic legislatures' procedural rules and legislative activity is often challenging in authoritarian settings. However, I was able to gain access to the research sites and collect original legislative and electoral data. In 2013, I initiated the Governance and Elections in the Middle East Project (GEMEP) dataset, the only available source on the legislative activities of Arab parliaments. I led a team of multilingual researchers to systematically gather and code original data on Arab parliaments between 2013 and 2020. Data were obtained from my extensive fieldwork in the region supplemented by online sources. The GEMEP dataset has comprehensive information on parliamentary questions; legislator-level information such as age, education, party affiliation, political expertise, legislative committee appointment and leadership data, and ideological affiliation; district-level characteristics; and variations in electoral laws within and across cases. More details on the data and coding can be found in appendix A.

I gathered over three thousand cross-country legislative committee and leadership appointments (for male and female legislators). I use the committee assignment dataset in chapter 4 to measure the extent to which women gain influence and power within autocratic legislatures. Furthermore, parliamentary questions (PQs) were translated and systematically coded according to the Comparative Agenda Project (CAP) coding scheme to facilitate comparability.[103] I rely on PQs to measure women's substantive representation (chapter 5).

In addition to quantitative data, I collected data on electoral laws and procedures. I conducted content analyses of primary sources, mainly electoral laws, constitutional amendments, parties' platforms and organizational rules, parliaments' internal bylaws, laws regulating political parties' activities, and campaign information. Furthermore, my analysis builds on a wealth of interview data. I have conducted over ninety interviews with MENA-based legislators, activists, women's organizations, party officials, and leaders.

Regarding the case selection, the research design of this study relies on the most similar systems design.[104] I focus on Morocco, Jordan, and Kuwait, which are hereditary monarchies with important commonalities, such as culture, social characteristics, religion, and regime type. These countries are rated as either "not free" or "partly free" by the Freedom House and have had a long history of elected legislatures. To ensure that the countries under study capture the distinctions that are essential for my theory development, I have also selected my cases purposively based on key explanatory variables, namely the numerical presence of women in national legislatures and the implementation of gender quota policies in addition to the degree of institutionalization of political parties.[105] These cases have varying levels of female representation and PI—the two main variables I investigate in this study.

Regarding female political representation, Morocco is a strong case for women's descriptive representation. Women have been allowed to vote and run for elections in Morocco since 1963; however, it was only at the advent of the twenty-first century that women could play a substantive role in politics. In 2002, a "gentlemen's agreement" between the political parties resulted in thirty seats being reserved or allocated to women on their electoral lists. In the aftermath of the Arab uprisings, Morocco increased the number of reserved seats for women as part of the 2011 constitutional amendments that guaranteed women 60 of the 395 seats (16.7 percent) in the lower chamber. According to this electoral reform, these 60 seats (in addition to the 30 youth quota seats) are elected through closed national lists. The remaining 305 seats are elected from 92 multimember local constituencies. In the 2016 elections, women won 10 seats (about 13 percent of women's total seats) from local districts for the first time, compared to 7 and 4 seats in 2011 and 2007, respectively. Women constituted 20.5 percent and 24 percent of the 2016 and 2021 legislatures, respectively.

In Jordan, women have been allowed to vote and run for office since 1974 but could not exercise their rights until 1984, mainly due to the suspension of the legislature. Before the introduction of the quota system in 2003, female candidates ran for several elections, but only one woman could win a seat in 1993. Following female candidates' inability to win any seats in the 1997 elections, Jordan introduced its first quota system for women in 2003 by reserving 6 of 110 seats for women (5 percent). Women's political representation has fluctuated over the past decade. Women constitute 11.5 percent of the 2020 lower chamber.

The third case is Kuwait, which has no gender quota. Unlike the other two cases, women were only allowed to vote and run for office in 2005. Women ran as candidates in the 2005 elections but could not win any seats. In 2009, four female candidates gained seats (8 percent of total seats), a historic win for women following decades of marginalization. In the aftermath of the Arab uprisings, the parliament was dissolved twice in 2012. Only one woman was elected in the 2013 and 2016 legislatures, making up merely 2 percent of the parliament.

There are also significant variations across the three cases in the degree of PI. Morocco presents a strong case regarding the strength of PI as one of the first countries in the MENA to grant political parties the right to form and compete in national and local elections—as stipulated by Article 3 of the country's postindependence constitution. The regime has held multiparty elections since 1963 and granted suffrage to all segments of Moroccan society. Jordan represents a case of weak PI. Whereas political parties were allowed to participate in elections, they remained fragmented in the electoral arena and unable to mobilize and win seats running on the party ticket (except for the Islamist party). Finally, political parties are banned in Kuwait, but there are currently several parliamentary blocs with distinct demographic characteristics and ideological orientations.[106] The Islamic Constitutional Movement (ICM) remains the only institutionalized bloc with considerable continuity and a robust support base.

My findings reveal significant variations across the three cases relating to women's political influence and legislative behavior. Even with the presence of quota systems in Jordan and Morocco, there are still considerable variations regarding women's legislative behavior and priorities that I attribute to the degree of PI in the two cases. Women's political power and legislative behavior remain marginal in Jordan and Kuwait with the absence of institutionalized political parties and gender quota policies. I also find that individual-level characteristics of female legislators, such as ideological affiliation, have a limited impact on their legislative behavior. Consistent with extant research, institutional and contextual factors have a substantial effect on shaping female legislators' behavior and preferences.[107] In sum, although the introduction of quota systems has contributed to bridging the marginalization of women in national politics, the absence of institutionalized parties limits women's ability to gain influence and power across MENA's legislatures.

CONTRIBUTIONS AND OVERVIEW OF THE BOOK

CONTRIBUTIONS

This book makes several contributions to the study of gender and authoritarian politics, representation, comparative political parties, autocratic legislatures, and Middle East politics. My theory integrates diverse strands from many literatures to make a coherent case for the role of political parties in shaping women's political representation in nondemocracies. First, theoretically and empirically, it contributes to extant scholarship on the intersection of gender and authoritarianism. Studies investigating the dynamics of electoral institutions under authoritarian regimes have proliferated over the past two decades. Still, only a few studies have systematically investigated the effect of authoritarian politics on women's access to political power and/or their legislative behavior.

Second, my work contributes to existing scholarship on women's representation and gender quota implementation and draws attention to the outcomes of quota policies in nondemocratic settings. It builds on and extends existing studies on the effect of gender quotas on women's numerical presence[108] and their implications for shaping policy preferences and priorities.[109] The book sheds light on the limits of gender quotas when it comes to women's political influence and substantive representation in autocratic legislatures and demonstrates that the context under which quotas are implemented shapes not only women's access to power but also their preferences and priorities. Bringing together work on authoritarianism, comparative political parties, legislative politics in autocracies, and gender politics, this book demonstrates that the degree of institutionalization of individual parties matters for women's influence and substantive representation. This caveat remained unexplored in former work on the topic.

Relatedly, the book contributes to extant research on comparative political parties and their effects on policymaking and political outcomes in autocracies.[110] It moves beyond the existing literature, focusing on how parties contribute to regime stability and survival in autocracies. It offers the first systematic investigation of the effect of PI on gendered outcomes. Thus, my work contributes to a burgeoning literature that pays closer attention to the micro-level effects of PI in nondemocratic contexts. Extant scholarship on PI has focused on macro-level processes, mainly in democratic and transitioning contexts, such as the link between the institutionalization of political parties and democratic consolidation,[111] democratic stability,[112] welfare state development,[113] economic growth,[114] and the level of PSI.[115] However, few studies have focused on autocracies and/or the effect of PI on micro-level political processes and behavior.[116] It is also problematic that most research has often linked the concept of institutionalization to democratic contexts and/or democratization processes; as maintained by Allen Hicken and Erik Martinez Kuhonta, "eliding institutionalization with democracy inherently creates 'conceptual misinformation.'"[117]

Finally, the book contributes to the study of MENA politics in two crucial ways. First, scholarship has predominantly focused on the dynamics of MENA's legislative politics[118] or on the challenges facing women in promoting their social status,[119] with little or no cross-national research systematically investigating the intersection of both realms (i.e., the presence of women in electoral politics). Thus, substantial knowledge gaps exist in our understanding of legislative politics under authoritarianism and the role played by female legislators. It also led to scholars' overreliance on representation and legislative behavior theories developed and tested in more democratic contexts, most of which have little explanatory power in the MENA region.

Second, the book provides a wealth of original data that promise to advance scholarship on MENA's legislative and gender politics. The scarcity of reliable, high-quality data on the region has hindered MENA scholars' ability to connect with broader themes in comparative politics.[120] Previous work on legislative politics in the region has often relied on secondary sources and single-case analyses due to the difficulty of obtaining original records.[121] Such a dearth of data has limited scholars' ability to move from single-country studies to more general arguments about authoritarian institutions, pinpoint trends that might be similar to other contexts, and draw meaningful generalizations.[122] This book aims to bridge these gaps by offering one of the first systematic cross-national analyses of legislators' behavior under authoritarianism in the MENA region, relying on fine-grained, original legislative data.

OVERVIEW OF THE BOOK

The book has five chapters and a conclusion. In chapter 1, I provide an overview of women's political representation in the MENA region over the past two decades. I aim in this chapter to highlight cross-national variations relating to women in MENA's legislatures, situate the MENA regimes in comparison to other autocratic regimes, and identify the significant gaps in the scholarship on women in politics under authoritarian regimes. I present and problematize existing explanations of women's political underrepresentation in the MENA. I demonstrate that these explanations fall short when explaining the observed patterns in women's descriptive representation in these contexts.

Chapter 2 outlines the theoretical framework of the study. The first part of the chapter deals with women's political power and substantive representation in autocracies and highlights the current knowledge gaps. The second part introduces my theoretical framework and provides cutting-edge scholarship on the link between PSI and the institutionalization of individual parties. I show that whereas PSI may be nonexistent in MENA's political systems, individual parties have historically enjoyed varying levels of institutionalization. I then present my main theoretical framework: the impact of institutionalized political parties on women's political power in nondemocratic settings. I also outline the mechanisms to explain why institutionalized parties matter for women's political power and legislative influence.

Chapter 3 sheds light on the three cases of the book. I start with a discussion on the case selection. Then, I analyze the role of legislatures and the details of the policymaking process, followed by analyzing the electoral laws and rules regulating political contestation across the three cases over the past two decades. I also provide a detailed analysis of women's political representation in the three cases. I present the political and legislative context under which women operate to gain access to political power and highlight the varying challenges they face to access political power.

Chapter 4 aims to demonstrate the effect of PI on women's access to influential positions within legislatures across the three cases. I argue in this chapter that women affiliated with highly institutionalized parties are more likely to gain increased power and influence in legislatures. Thus, the chapter focuses on women's membership in legislative committees for over a decade. I build on former work and classify committees based on their prestige and visibility. Relying on an original dataset of committee assignments (N = 3000) supplemented with legislator-level data, the findings of the multivariate analyses support my argument that women's affiliation with highly institutionalized parties is positively linked to their access to influential committees. In Jordan, women have achieved inconsistent gains and were systematically marginalized from influential committees despite their increased numbers in the legislature with the gender quota in place for almost two decades. The analysis demonstrates similar results for the Kuwaiti case.

In chapter 5, I investigate the monitoring role of female legislators across the three cases using PQs to test my theoretical argument regarding the varying effects of PI on women's legislative behavior. Despite the limited legislative role of these legislatures, I argue that they perform an important oversight function and that examining legislators' PQs is one of the best available methods to understand legislators' true preferences that are often subject to less pressure from party leaders and other party members. Relying on more than twenty-one thousand PQs posed by male and female legislators supplemented with legislator-level data, I find that women in

Morocco are more likely to pose questions relating to women's issues compared to Jordan and Kuwait. I also find that female legislators' affiliation with institutionalized parties in Jordan increases their ability to represent women compared to those running as independents without party support. I attribute these variations to the nature of party competition, where women in Morocco are more "protected" by the existing institutionalized party structures. In contrast, most women in Jordan and Kuwait are on their own when running for elections and navigating the legislative arena once elected. I argue that the incentives for reelection and fear of further marginalization within the legislature push female legislatures away from focusing on gender-specific topics.

The conclusion summarizes the theoretical and practical implications of the book. It then discusses the scope conditions of my theory and the results. I then test the generalizability of my findings in other autocratic contexts to show that the theoretical framework outlined in the book may extend beyond the MENA region. The book concludes with the practical implications of the results for female political empowerment, the importance of PI in dictatorships, and directions for future research on the topic.

1

ACCESSING POLITICAL POWER

When you run for elections with a group or a party, you know who your group is, their beliefs, what to say, and what to promise. But when you are running alone, it is just you! It feels fake! This is not a democracy! This is like, "Vote for me; I am excellent. I am going to do this and that." But you know these are all lies because you cannot do anything alone! I think this is a fundamental issue for women in particular. Any woman, regardless of her age and education, wants to know. . . . How can she do this on her own? I tried it! I have been on TV and written extensively. I also have a big family, so I decided to run. But this was not enough. Female candidates must have some political party or a group that supports their ideas and policy stances. This is not the case for men, although we both do not have parties. The political arena is male-dominated. It is all about connections and networks; still, men are the strongest in economics and politics! They are the heads of the big companies, the banks, and the family. They are the heads of everything! Women continue to be in the background.

—FEMALE CANDIDATE IN KUWAIT'S 2020 NATIONAL ELECTIONS, INTERVIEW WITH
AUTHOR IN KUWAIT CITY, 2023

The past few decades have witnessed a surge in studies exploring why dictators introduce gender reforms, including promoting women's inclusion in decision-making.[1] However, in-depth analyses of the conditions under which these reforms operate and how the existing sociocultural and political contexts may affect the successful implementation of top-down gender reforms in autocracies remain scarce. Cross-national studies comparing democracies and authoritarian regimes have emphasized the strong positive link between women's numerical presence in legislatures and institutional variables, such as ruling-party institutionalization, quota mechanisms, institutionalized parties and multiparty elections, and women's positions in civil society.[2] Yet little progress has been made to systematically discern the correlates of women's descriptive representation in autocracies and how authoritarian politics, combined with the absence of effective political competition, obstruct women's path to political power. As the quote at the beginning of this chapter indicates, the absence of parties and lack of genuine political competition have a detrimental effect on women's ability to access elected office regardless of their qualifications and resources. As the quote shows, these autocratic practices have gender-differential effects. The crackdown on political competition is hurting women even more as they lack access to the existing male-dominated networks of power.

This chapter outlines the status of women's descriptive representation and the factors shaping their access to political power in the Middle East and North Africa (MENA). Whereas existing work focusing on sociocultural, structural, and institutional factors has offered invaluable insights into why women are underrepresented in MENA's politics, it fails to explain cross-national variations in women's access to political power. It also pays little attention to how autocratic regimes in MENA compare to autocratic regimes elsewhere. I start this chapter by detailing the existing sociocultural explanations, followed by a discussion and empirical testing of the effect of institutional and structural factors on women's access to political power. I also compare the MENA region to other autocracies and highlight the similarities between MENA and other authoritarian regimes. This chapter sheds light on how women enter the political arena to better understand how they exercise power and influence within these legislative assemblies—the book's main focus.

EXPLAINING VARIATIONS IN WOMEN'S POLITICAL REPRESENTATION IN MENA

SOCIOCULTURAL EXPLANATIONS

MENA's sociocultural context is often blamed for women's underrepresentation in politics. Work has mostly focused on the roles that religion, traditional and patriarchal gender norms, and variations in women's movements have played in shaping women's access to power.[3]

Investigating Islam's effect on women's political representation, some authors argue that "Islamic religious heritage is one of the most powerful barriers to the rising tide of gender equality."[4] Similarly, others claim that Islamic traditions and authoritarianism suppress women's rights in Muslim-majority countries.[5] In contrast, some researchers challenge these findings and present evidence that the suppression of women's rights is more likely to occur in Arab rather than Muslim-majority states.[6] This finding was revisited by other scholars, who found that gender-egalitarian attitudes are much lower in Arab versus non-Arab countries.[7] Relatedly, it was demonstrated in a cross-national analysis that states fare better in promoting women's rights when rulers exert control over the incursion of religion into the political sphere.[8]

Furthermore, the predominance of patriarchal and traditional power structures, mainly through the tribal systems that continue to govern gender relations and act as gatekeepers for women's political power, may hinder women's ability to access leadership positions.[9] Such patriarchal networks have weakened women's ability to compete independently in the political realm without reliance on such connections. For instance, tribes in Jordan, especially the small ones, use their female quota seats strategically: they tend to nominate women in districts where they are less likely to win seats.[10] Mounira M. Charrad provides one of the first comparative studies on the Maghreb.[11] The author attributes women's underrepresentation not to Islam or to oil production, but rather to the long history of "kin-based solidarities" in the political realm among male elites. She claims that states, like Tunisia, that have moved beyond kin-based solidarities have managed to advance women's rights further than states like Algeria and Morocco that continue to struggle to gain autonomy from tribal or kin ties. However, there is a dearth of research on how tribal and other ethnic identities interact with existing autocratic structures in the region and how they condition women's access to political power. These views also ignore the effect of international pressure and modernization forces, which I discuss in detail in the following section.

Mass attitudes may have a more direct effect on women's access to politics in several ways. Women's underrepresentation in politics is often blamed on the low demand for female politicians and voters' bias against female candidates. Thus, parties are reluctant to nominate women as they fear the loss of the seat due to the lower levels of public trust in women's capabilities as political leaders.[12] However, analyzing public opinion data over the past two decades presents a different picture. Data from the Arab Barometer show that citizens' support for women in political leadership is increasing, with wide cross-national variations.[13] Citizens view women as qualified political leaders and express support for gender quota policies. This support is even more pronounced among female voters.[14] Notably, support for women in political leadership in most countries does not translate to increased female presence in MENA's legislatures. For example, survey data show that citizens in Lebanon express the highest support for women in politics, yet women's political representation in Lebanon has not exceeded 6 percent for the past two decades (table 1.1).[15] Similarly, public support for women is currently higher in Morocco than in Tunisia; however, there are significantly more women in politics in Tunisia.

During my fieldwork and interviews with female candidates and politicians, they challenged the notion that women's underrepresentation in politics is the result of voters' bias against female politicians. A female legislator in Morocco stated, "That is not true [that voters have no confidence in female politicians]. Voters are more likely to place their trust in women than men. They know that they are less corrupt. I am not saying that they [women] are all saints. We still need to select good candidates. But no, the problem is not the voters."[16]

TABLE 1.1 Women in national legislatures in the MENA region

COUNTRY	ELECTION YEAR	TYPE OF QUOTA/YEAR INTRODUCED	% WOMEN IN LOWER CHAMBER	ELECTORAL SYSTEM	RIGHT TO VOTE NATIONAL ELECTIONS
Algeria	2012	Voluntary party (2002)/ Mandatory (2012)	31.6%	List proportional representation (PR)	1958
	2017		25.8%		
	2021		8%		
Bahrain	2010	No quota	2.5%	Two-round system (TRS)	1973
	2014		7.5%		2002 (universal)
	2018		15%		
	2022		20%		
Egypt	2010	Reserved seats	12.7%	TRS	1956
	2012	Quota revoked	2.0%	List PR	
	2015	Provisional quota	15.6%	Mixed system	
	2020		27.5%	Mixed system	
Iraq	2010	Reserved seats	25.2%	Open list PR	1980
	2014		25.0%		
	2018		26.4%		
	2021		28.8%		
Jordan	2010	Reserved seats	10.8%	Single nontransfer-rable vote (SNTV)	1974
	2013		12.0%	SNTV and PR	
	2016		15.0%	Mixed system	
	2020		12%	Mixed system	
Kuwait	2009	No quota	8.0%	SNTV	2005
	2012		4.0%		
	2016		2.0%		
	2020		0%		
	2022		4%		
	2023		2%		
Lebanon	2009	No quota	3.1%	Block vote	1952
	2018		4.7%	PR lists	
	2022		6%		

Libya	2012	Reserved seats	16.5%	Mixed	1964
	2014		16.0%		
Morocco	2011	Reserved seats	16.7%	Closed list PR	1959
	2016		20.5%		
	2021		24%		
Palestine	2006	Legislative quota	13.0%	Mixed (placement provision)	1946
Oman	2011	No quota	1.2%	First past the post (FPTP)	1994
	2015		1.2%	SNTV	Universal suffrage in 2003
	2019		2.3%		
Qatar	2021	No quota	4%	15 members are appointed/30 members are elected	2003
Saudi Arabia	2013	Reserved seats	20.0%	Appointed	2011
Syria	2012	No quota	12.4%	Block vote	1949
	2016		13.2%		
	2020		11%		
Tunisia	2011	Voluntary party	26.0%	Mixed	1959
	2014	Legislative quotas	31.0%	Closed PR lists (vertical zipper)	
	2019		26.2%		
	2022		16%		
United Arab Emirates	2011	No quota	17.5%	SNTV	2005
	2015		22.5%	20 members are appointed/20 members are indirectly elected	(Only one-quarter of population vote)
	2019	Parity law	50.0%		
Yemen	2003	Voluntary party	0.3%	Majority (FPTP)	1967
	2019	None	0%		

Sources: https://www.ipu.org/national-parliaments; https://www.electionguide.org/elections/type/upcoming; https://www.idea.int/data-tools/data/gender-quotas.

Note: Election years vary in table 1.1, as they mostly reflect when women first entered the parliament in their respective countries and/or when gender quotas were introduced. Gaps in election years, such as in Yemen and Palestine, denote no elections.

In Kuwait, the cofounder of Mudhawi List, a nongovernmental organization (NGO) dedicated to the promotion of women's political representation, stated that whereas cultural attitudes can be partially blamed for women's underrepresentation, there are more substantial obstacles facing female candidates: "Some of them [obstacles] have to do with [voters'] education, the culture, but it is mostly the lack of gateway positions. These men who are running are not running on a whim. These men started in student unions. They ran for football clubs. They were in labor unions, co-ops, and the municipality, then became candidates for parliament. For women, most of these positions are closed. . . . We do not lack women with merit! Women have experience and are qualified. We lack opportunities."[17] Another female legislator in Jordan's 2016 lower chamber echoed a similar view, emphasizing the transformation of the societal beliefs about women in politics by stating, "Sometimes people claim that voters do not support women. This issue is not true, in my opinion. On the contrary! I felt that the governorate's people supported me regardless of their backgrounds or gender."[18]

Moreover, scholarship on the link between citizens' support and female electability in MENA has provided mixed findings. On the one hand, studies have shown that voters' patriarchal attitudes may play a role in shaping gender stereotypes and contribute to the perception that women lack the necessary (i.e., masculine) traits for leadership.[19] Other studies focusing on gender stereotypes have provided further insights into mass attitudes and support for female politicians. Most of these studies have investigated the effect of trait and issue gender stereotypes and/or explored the way political gender stereotypes may shape citizens' voting behavior in transitioning and autocratic contexts.[20]

For instance, a 2015 study exploring the link between gender, religion, and electability using a survey experiment in transitional Tunisia found support for role congruity and social identity theories.[21] The study also found significant gender biases toward female candidates as religious voters—both men and women—tended to vote for female religious candidates. Other work shows significant gender-related variations in Jordan and Tunisia regarding the electability of female candidates with business-related backgrounds compared to those with civil society backgrounds.[22] The authors attribute these variations to gender-based stereotypes about women as caring and "community oriented," which are more congruent to their roles within civil society organizations. Another recent study investigated the effect of gender—and leadership-congruent political platforms—on support for female candidates in post-transition Tunisia and found that prevailing voter bias exists against female candidates, especially among voters with patriarchal views.[23] Voters also tend to favor candidates who emphasize issues congruent with issue gender stereotypes, such as security. Finally, a study exploring the link between mass attitudes toward female representation and perceived corruption in Lebanon demonstrates that women's political support is mainly driven by citizens' perceptions of corruption.[24] The analysis shows that citizens who view female politicians as more trustworthy and "clean" are more likely to express higher levels of support for gender quota policies.

On the other hand, more recent research paints a rather different picture of the link between voter bias and female electability. For instance, one study found that citizens in six MENA countries are more likely to support female candidates than male candidates (i.e., pro-female bias).[25] Similarly, another study investigated the effect that women's presence on legislative committees has on the public's perceptions of procedural legitimacy in Jordan, Morocco, and Tunisia.[26] The authors found that women's presence in decision-making positively impacts the public's perceptions of procedural legitimacy and committee decisions. Furthermore, other researchers found that gender stereotypes do not shape voters' evaluations of either male or female politicians.[27]

In sum, research on the effect of cultural attitudes on women's political representation has yielded mixed results, and many knowledge gaps persist. While sociocultural factors may partially explain women's underrepresentation, more work is needed to explain the varying levels of women's political representation across the region. As shown in table 1.1, wide intraregional variations in women's numerical presence call for closer attention to the correlates of women's descriptive representation and how they may affect women's power and influence within legislatures.

STRUCTURAL EXPLANATIONS

Comparative studies have emphasized the role of structural factors, such as female labor force participation, educational attainment, and fertility rates, in promoting women's presence in the political sphere.[28] Higher levels of economic development may reduce social inequality and contribute to higher levels of gender parity.[29] However, work assessing the impact of structural factors on women's descriptive representation in MENA has also yielded mixed results. The MENA region has witnessed remarkable achievements over the past decades in female health and education outcomes, which resulted in a substantial decrease in fertility and mortality rates and the narrowing of the gender gap in education and literacy rates.[30] Yet most recent studies have shown that this progress has not translated to more opportunities for women in the economic sphere.[31] Women's economic participation in MENA continues to be the lowest in the world, with merely 25.2 percent of women aged fifteen and older actively participating in the labor market compared to more than 50 percent worldwide.[32]

Many scholars have drawn attention to the direct and indirect effects of structural factors such as higher male-female population sex ratios, unequal family laws, and oil wealth on shaping women's access to power.[33] For instance, it has been argued that the discovery of oil in many Arab states has contributed to gender inequality in the economic and political realms.[34] Oil-based economies and their emphasis on nontradable goods have limited women's presence in the formal economy and, hence, their political influence.[35] Other studies attribute the low levels of women's labor force participation in Muslim-majority countries to interstate wars and reservations concerning the content of the Convention on the Elimination of All Forms of Discrimination Against Women (CEDAW), structural adjustment programs, and low foreign direct investments.[36]

Economic factors may also condition women's access to power in two important ways. First, the low levels of female presence in the economic realm have limited their access to male-dominated power networks. Second, the lack of financial resources has negatively impacted women's ability to fund campaigns and mobilize voters, especially given the dominant clientelistic and vote-buying practices in most parts of the region. A former female candidate and minister in Kuwait argued:

> The financial aspect is a big issue! If you want to run for parliament, you must have a lot of money to fund your campaign. Here in Kuwait, candidates can take money from either a rich person controlling the country or from the government, but you will have to be their ally once elected. I wasn't willing to choose any of these options, which was a problem. I started with a very, very small campaign run by volunteers. I didn't pay anything. Also, we don't have a law [in Kuwait] that permits candidates to raise money from their supporters. Like the donation system.[37]

A former female candidate in Lebanon echoed a similar view and stated, "I had to pay ten thousand dollars for a half-hour interview two months before the election. I had to pay twenty thousand dollars for that half an hour from two weeks onto the election day. Men spend 17 million dollars sometimes to get there. So, I could not [continue the campaign]."[38] The cofounder of an NGO in Kuwait assisting female candidates voiced similar concerns:

> The cost of running a parliamentary campaign is very high in Kuwait. Specifically, if you run in certain districts and do not belong to a de facto party paying the bill, if you are a woman, the bill will be much higher because there are so many other factors that you will have to throw money at, such as Radio talks, TV appearances, and billboards. All of that is a built-in cost. A female candidate often asks if it is worth it. It is a real shame because many quality women do these calculations, and they say no! Not in this environment![39]

Structural explanations may also intersect with individuals' patriarchal attitudes and contribute to limiting women's presence in the public domain. Mass beliefs about women as the upholders of tradition and caregivers have led to vertical (i.e., women having limited access to leadership positions in the institution) and horizontal (i.e., women being concentrated in specific professions in the labor market) gender occupational segregation. As a result, women who enter the workforce are primarily confined to socially acceptable, lower pay, and less visible professions, such as education, healthcare, agriculture, welfare, or volunteer work.[40] Thus, they may lack the clout and wealth often deemed desirable for political candidates.

Again, the intraregional variations in female labor participation and economic development levels fail to explain women's political representation patterns. Recent data on women's labor force participation and levels of socioeconomic development (i.e., per capita income, life expectancy, education) fall short of explaining the varying levels of women's presence in the political arena. For instance, whereas the United Arab Emirates (UAE) and Qatar have the highest rates of women in the workforce, Morocco and Saudi Arabia lag significantly behind. Nevertheless, as shown in table 1.1, Morocco has more women in politics than Qatar and Kuwait.

To empirically test the effect of the structural factors on women's political representation, I conduct multivariate analyses based on time-series data from sixteen Arab states (table 1.2). The unit of analysis is the country-year. The main dependent variable for Models 1–3 is the percentage of women in the lower chambers after each election between 1993 and 2021 and 1991–2010 for Model 4.[41] Models 1 through 3 present findings for the MENA region, and Model 4 presents results for all autocracies. Data are obtained from the authors' records, the World Bank, the Inter-Parliamentary Union (IPU), and the Varieties of Democracy V.13 dataset. (For more information on the coding of these variables and the data sources, refer to table A.1 in appendix A.) The MENA dataset combines election results with socioeconomic indicators such as gross domestic product (GDP) per capita constant 2000 U.S. dollars transformed to its natural logarithm to reduce skewness, female labor force participation, and life expectancy rates. The analysis also includes institutional factors (Model 2), discussed in the following section. All models include year-fixed effects to account for system-wide temporal changes or shocks. All errors are clustered at the country level in all the models.

Model 1 shows the effect of the structural factors on women's numerical presence in legislative assemblies. Specifically, I test the impact of a

TABLE 1.2 Multivariate analysis of women's representation in lower chambers

	STRUCTURAL FACTORS–MENA (1)	INSTITUTIONAL FACTORS–MENA (2)	FULL MODEL– MENA (3)	ALL AUTOCRACIES (4)
Proportional representation system		0.024 (0.028)	0.001 (0.026)	3.236 (1.962)
Mixed system		−0.038 (0.032)	−0.053 (0.022)	1.61 (1.587)
Majoritarian		−0.030 (0.026)	−0.002* (0.03)	−1.527 (1.80)
Quota		0.124*** (0.019)	0.130*** (0.032)	2.273*** (0.792)
Multiparty elections		−0.026** (0.012)	−0.008 (0.013)	−1.330** (0.613)
Female in labor force	−0.002 (0.004)		−0.004* (0.001)	0.309*** (0.072)
Life expectancy	−0.003 (0.005)		−0.006 (0.006)	0.1923* (0.102)
Logged gross domestic product per capita	−0.009 (0.021)		0.030 (0.024)	1.36 (1.051)
Constant	0.376 (0.309)	0.058 (0.038)	−0.072 (0.253)	−25.67*** (7.96)
R-squared	0.518	0.695	0.71	0.48

Standard errors are reported in parentheses; $^*p < 0.10$, $^{**}p < 0.05$, $^{***}p < 0.01$.

Note: Sixteen Arab states are included in the analysis: Algeria (1997, 2002, 2007, 2012, 2017, 2021); Bahrain (2002, 2006, 2011, 2014, 2018); Egypt (1995, 2000, 2005, 2010, 2011, 2012, 2015, 2020); Iraq (1996, 2000, 2005, 2010, 2014, 2018); Jordan (1993, 1997, 2003, 2007, 2010, 2013, 2016, 2020); Kuwait (2009, 2012, 2012, 2013, 2016, 2020); Lebanon (1996, 2000, 2005, 2009, 2018); Libya (2012, 2014); Morocco (1997, 2002, 2007, 2011, 2016, 2021); Oman (2007, 2011, 2015, 2019); Palestine (1996, 2006); Qatar (2021); Syria (1994, 1998, 2003, 2007, 2012, 2016); Tunisia (1994, 1999, 2004, 2009, 2011, 2014, 2019); United Arab Emirates (2011, 2015, 2019); and Yemen (1997, 2003). Saudi Arabia is excluded from the analysis since it does not have an elected lower chamber.

country's logged GDP per capita, women's labor force participation rates, and life expectancy rates as a proxy for the country's human development on women's access to political power. Consistent with former studies, the results demonstrate the marginal role of structural factors in shaping women's political representation.[42] Female labor force participation has a weak statistically significant effect (Model 3), albeit negative. Models 1 and 3 show no relationship between countries' levels of development and GDP per capita and women's presence in national legislatures. Notwithstanding the oil wealth and increased levels of human development in several MENA states, these factors seem to play a less substantial role.

Model 4 compares the MENA region to other autocracies. Regarding structural factors, higher levels of female labor force participation and life expectancy have a statistically significant effect on women's descriptive representation in non-MENA autocracies. Nevertheless, these factors do not impact women's access to political power in MENA, as shown in Models 1 and 3 (table 1.2).

INSTITUTIONAL EXPLANATIONS

Women are commonly perceived as "newcomers" to politics in MENA. However, they were granted the right to vote and run for office in many Arab states as early as the 1950s, even before many other established democracies (table 1.1). Following independence from colonization in the mid-twentieth century, Arab autocrats initiated wide-ranging "state feminism" policies that created a system of public patriarchy.[43] Most of MENA's postindependence constitutions granted women equal political and economic rights as part of state-sponsored feminism. For instance, in the 1950s, Egypt's Gamal Abdel Nasser promoted state feminism to increase his legitimacy and alienate opponents, including the Islamists.[44] Similarly, Tunisia's former president, Habib Bourguiba, engineered state feminism to garner support and restrain the opposition and the country's patriarchal kin-based networks.[45]

As part of their state feminism efforts, MENA autocrats also adopted gender quotas. In Egypt, gender quotas were introduced in 1979 by a decree from President Anwar Sadat.[46] The quota was canceled in 1987 because of pressure from the leftist and rightist political groups.[47] Similarly, King Abdullah II bin al-Hussein initiated women's political inclusion in Jordan. The king has been the main sponsor of gender reforms and established the Jordanian National Commission for Women (JNCW) in 1992 to advise the monarchy on issues relating to women's rights. Headed by the former king's sister, Basma bint Talal, the JNCW promoted and garnered support for gender quotas in Jordan.[48]

However, women's presence in the decision-making realm continued to lag, and top-down efforts to empower women politically had limited success compared to other gender reforms, such as the Personal Status Code (CPS) in Tunisia.[49] Thus, many Arab states had resorted to gender quotas by the advent of the twenty-first century to increase women's numerical presence in legislatures. As shown in table 1.1, reserved seats and voluntary party quotas are the most common form of gender quotas in the MENA. These reforms were introduced for several reasons: international pressure,[50] attempts to garner mass support[51] and marginalize opposing voices, mainly the Islamists,[52] and pressure from women's movements.[53]

Tunisia, Morocco, and Algeria were the first Arab states to introduce voluntary party gender quotas in 1999, 2002, and 2002, respectively. Yemen also introduced a voluntary party quota in 2003. Jordan enforced reserved seats for women in 2003, starting with six reserved quota seats that increased to twelve seats in 2010 and fifteen in 2013. Iraq introduced a minimum 25 percent legislated gender quota on the national level in the country's 2004 interim constitution. The ensuing electoral law also enforced strict placement mandates where parties must place women in every third place on their electoral lists.[54]

MENA's autocrats undertook further steps to promote women's political representation in the aftermath of the 2010 Arab uprisings. For the first time, women's presence in national legislatures exceeded 10 percent in 2012.[55] Mandatory party quotas were introduced after the Arab uprisings in Algeria and Morocco, while Tunisia introduced the parity clause in its newly drafted postrevolution constitution.[56] Egypt implemented a provisional quota system in the 2015 parliamentary elections, and its postrevolution constitution stipulated a 25 percent quota for women in local elections.[57] In 2019, constitutional amendments were ratified to introduce 25 percent reserved seats for women. In Egypt's 2020 legislative elections, women constituted about 27 percent of the lower chamber. As of 2020, eleven of seventeen Arab states have adopted some form of gender quotas in their national legislatures. However, progress remains uneven, and wide variations exist regarding quota type, enforcement mechanisms, and placement mandates (see table 1.1).

Most Arab Gulf states have no gender quotas, and/or some still lack directly elected lower chambers. Moreover, political parties are outlawed and replaced with political societies and de facto blocs, based primarily on ideology. Bahrain was the first Gulf state to grant women the right to vote in 2002, and women ran for elections in 2003. Only one woman was able to enter the council in 2006 and 2010, while three women were able to win seats in 2014. Since 2013, all members of Saudi Arabia's consultative (Shura) council have been appointed by the emir. Women ran for local elections for the first time in the 2015 municipal elections. In 2019, the UAE introduced a parity law in its lower chamber. Half of the Federal National Council's (FNC) members are indirectly elected by an electoral college (see table 1.1), while the emirates' rulers appoint the other half. Seven women won seats in the 2019 elections, and a royal decree appointed thirteen women. As a result, women currently constitute 50 percent of the FNC. Finally, Qatar held its first legislative elections in 2021. Women could not win competitive seats, and the emir appointed two women. Women's representation is also marginal in Oman and Kuwait, with women constituting around 2 percent in both legislatures elected in 2019 and 2022, respectively.

The introduction of gender quotas to "fast-track" women's political inclusion challenged existing explanations relating to Islam, culture, kinship, and oil, as the numbers of women in Arab legislatures have grown exponentially over the past two decades.[58] Table 1.1 demonstrates that gender quotas have substantially improved women's ability to gain access to political power; nonetheless, wide variations exist in the institutional and/or electoral contexts under which these quotas are implemented. As evident in table 1.1, most Arab states have majoritarian electoral systems in place. Previous studies have shown that proportional representation (PR) systems (i.e., seats are allocated in proportion to the percentage of votes received by candidate/party) are more conducive to female political inclusion,[59] especially if combined with closed party lists.[60] Placement mandates (i.e., laws that stipulate the placement of female candidates in winnable positions in party lists) are also effective mechanisms for promoting women's representation as they send powerful signals to parties about the state's commitment to women and other marginalized groups. Yet these mandates are uncommon in the MENA, mainly due to the weakness of political parties and the absence of stable party systems throughout the region.[61]

Relatedly, district magnitudes (i.e., the total number of seats allocated per electoral district) may also condition women's access to political power in both democracies and autocracies. Comparative gender and politics scholarship has shown that larger district magnitudes are linked to increased female political representation since multiple candidates may be elected from the same district so that female newcomers can win seats without displacing male candidates.[62] Furthermore, small district magnitudes may further disincentivize political parties to form and/or run for elections, given their lower chances of winning seats. As shown in table 1.1, most MENA countries implement majoritarian electoral systems that tend to have low district magnitudes that favor regime loyalists and ethnic and tribal candidates.

Small district magnitudes can disadvantage female candidates in highly conservative districts since constituents tend to vote for tribal and/or ethnic male candidates. Even in cases like Kuwait, where the district magnitude is considerably large (ten seats for five national electoral districts), the existing majoritarian electoral system, combined with the current ban on political parties, has limited women's access to power. As a result, women have never been able to win a seat in the predominantly tribal fourth and fifth districts. The tribal composition of these districts, combined with the electoral system in place, has made it almost impossible for women to disrupt the existing male-dominated networks.

I conduct a multivariate analysis in table 1.2 to explore the effect of gender quotas and the electoral system in place (i.e., PR, mixed, or majoritarian) on women's numerical presence in Arab legislatures (see table A.1 in appendix A for more details on the coding and data sources). As demonstrated in Model 2, a quota system is the strongest predictor of women's numerical representation in Arab legislatures. Unlike previous work on the link between women's representation in lower chambers and the electoral system in place, I find no statistically significant effect of the electoral system (i.e., majoritarian versus proportional representation) on women's representation in lower chambers.[63]

Model 3 presents the full model with the structural and institutional factors discussed in this section and the previous section and shows a more comprehensive picture of the status of women's descriptive representation in MENA. Again, the presence of gender quotas remains the most significant predictor of women's presence in national legislatures. The results also demonstrate that electoral laws have limited explanatory power regarding women's political access, especially in contexts with a gender quota system. Model 3 also shows a negative effect of majoritarian electoral laws on women's representation, consistent with previous work on the link between the electoral system and women's representation.[64] However, this effect is not as strong as the presence of a quota system.

An important, albeit understudied, factor in shaping women's representation is the role of political parties in promoting (or hindering) women's descriptive representation in nondemocratic settings. Recent work has shown that multiparty elections are negatively associated with higher levels of women's political rights and women's political representation in autocracies.[65] As maintained by Daniela Donno and Anne-Kathrin Kreft, "multi-party competition may, in fact, unleash political forces that only crowd out progress on women's rights and representation."[66] However, less is known about the effect of multiparty elections on women's representation in the MENA region. Most of the work exploring the link between political parties and women's access to politics has provided qualitative evidence on the adverse effects of parties' traditional and opaque internal structures and ideology on women's recruitment and nomination.[67] As I detail in chapter 2, political parties currently play a minor role in shaping regional politics more generally. As of 2022, six Arab states continue to outlaw political parties.

To test the effect of multiparty elections on women's descriptive representation in MENA, I have included a variable that measures whether the country holds multiparty national elections in Models 2 and 3 (table 1.2). Interestingly, the presence of multiple parties in national elections is only statistically significant in Model 2; however, the effect diminishes when the structural factors are introduced in Model 3. I attribute the statistically insignificant results in Model 3 to the relatively limited number of multiparty elections and the weak presence of political parties in the electoral arena in most MENA states.

Model 4 compares the MENA region to other autocratic regimes. Similar to other dictatorships, gender quotas matter for women's descriptive representation. The model also confirms findings from previous work on the negative effect of multiparty elections on women's numerical presence in national legislatures. The findings also demonstrate that the country's level of human development matters for women's presence in autocratic legislatures but not for the MENA region.

Recall that the book's main argument is that the degree of party institutionalization matters for women's influence and exercise of power. As I demonstrate in the previous analysis, gender quotas are powerful tools to break the entry barriers for women. However, recent studies have shown evidence that quotas can promote women's descriptive representation more effectively if implemented in contexts characterized by strong, institutionalized parties. Comparative work has demonstrated that party institutionalization matters for women's political inclusion in Brazil. As maintained by Kristin Wylie, "to promote women's participation, parties must have the capacity to recruit and provide female aspirants with essential psychological, organizational, and material support and the will to do so."[68]

However, work on the role of party institutionalization on women's numerical presence continues to be lacking in autocratic regimes, including the MENA region. Only one study has explored the effect of incumbent party institutionalization on women's political exclusion in autocracies.[69] The author finds a strong positive effect between the level of institutionalization of the incumbent regime's party and women's political inclusion compared to regimes in which authoritarian parties are less institutionalized.

However, this study solely focuses on ruling parties, with no attention paid to autocratic regimes with existing institutionalized parties–other than the ruling regime. Another study dealing with party institutionalization (PI) in transitioning Tunisia found that parties' organizational strength and capacity may affect their ability to comply with gender-related reforms, mainly gender quotas.[70] More work is needed to better understand how and under what conditions the relationship between PI and women's numerical presence persists in the MENA region and other autocracies.

* * *

I outlined in this chapter the existing cultural, structural, and institutional explanations for women's underrepresentation in MENA and other autocratic regimes. I argued that these explanations are lacking as they fail to incorporate the impact of authoritarianism and autocratic practices on shaping women's access to politics. Furthermore, the analyses presented in this chapter show that the MENA region is not exceptional in terms of the institutional and structural factors explaining women's numerical presence in politics compared to other autocratic regimes. Except for the relationship between women's labor force participation and women's presence in national legislatures, the determinants of women's political inclusion in national legislatures are relatively consistent. But what about the link between party institutionalization and women's substantive representation? Whereas the results throughout this chapter have consistently shown that gender quotas are powerful institutional tools for increasing women's numbers in politics, do they have similar effects on women's political power and substantive representation in dictatorships?

In chapter 2, I focus on women's substantive representation in autocratic legislatures and present the book's theoretical framework on the relationship between PI and women's legislative behavior and influence. As I discuss in more detail in the following chapter, while gender quotas are potent mechanisms to overcome women's marginalization in the political sphere, the weakness or absence of institutionalized political parties has negatively affected women's legislative behavior and preferences once in power.

2
PARTY INSTITUTIONALIZATION AND WOMEN'S REPRESENTATION

Parties are incapable of entering the parliament, except for the Muslim Brotherhood. Candidates run as individuals, and they win seats as independents. This creates an enormous burden for everyone, especially women who must manage and fund their electoral campaigns and bear the economic and political burden. This is not an easy or simple issue. It is creating significant obstacles for women [in Jordan].

—FEMALE LEGISLATOR IN JORDAN'S 2013 LEGISLATURE,
INTERVIEW WITH AUTHOR IN AMMAN, 2018

Throughout my fieldwork in the region, it was always puzzling how female legislators strongly emphasized the importance they attribute to women's issues and priorities in our interviews. However, a closer look at their legislative behavior shows wide variations in their ability to voice women's interests. What explains this puzzle? I aim to answer this puzzle and outline the book's theoretical framework in this chapter. The chapter starts with shedding light on women's political influence and substantive representation in democratic and autocratic legislatures. I then focus on authoritarian legislatures and move into the theoretically less well-charted territory: the effect of individual parties' institutionalization on conditioning women's legislative behavior and influence. Before I discuss the link between party institutionalization and women's political power, I provide an overview of the status of the Middle East and North Africa (MENA) region's political parties over the past few decades and highlight the existing knowledge gaps on the link between political parties and women's political power.

In the second part of this chapter, I develop a novel explanation for women's influence and substantive representation in autocratic legislatures. Specifically, I focus on the relationship between the institutionalization of individual parties and women's influential positions within the legislature and their policy preferences and priorities (i.e., substantive representation). It is imperative to analyze how power is exercised (i.e., committee appointments and monitoring role) to better assess their role within these legislative bodies. I argue that whereas gender quotas have substantially promoted the presence of women in autocratic legislatures, these policies have a limited effect on advancing women's substantive representation. The institutional context under which women politicians operate strongly impacts their behavior. Thus, I contend that women's political influence is conditioned by the extent to which they are affiliated with institutionalized parties. Female politicians affiliated with highly institutionalized parties are more likely to access influential committee positions and substantively represent women than those affiliated with weakly institutionalized parties and/or run as independents. The chapter concludes with a discussion of the alternative explanations and the conclusion.

WOMEN'S SUBSTANTIVE REPRESENTATION AND INTERESTS: A COMPARATIVE PERSPECTIVE

In her groundbreaking book, *The Concept of Representation*, Hanna Pitkin offers one of the most comprehensive theoretical frameworks on political representation. Pitkin defines political representation as "a public, institutionalized arrangement involving many people and groups, and operating in the complex ways of large-scale social arrangements."[1] Thus, representation is the outcome of the structure and functioning of the whole system and the patterns emerging from the multiple activities and players in the system.

Subsequent research has focused on three primary forms of representation: descriptive, substantive, and symbolic. Descriptive representation is conceptualized as "the politics of presence" and is generally considered a "mirror" for the population from which the representatives are drawn. The argument for descriptive representation is based on the premise that elected officials are more likely to represent those with whom they share personal characteristics (i.e., women)[2] and "act for" them.[3] Thus, descriptive representation is important for the legitimacy of elected bodies and to remedy the marginalization of women and other minority groups.[4] According to this view, there is a strong need for devising institutional mechanisms (such as gender quotas, legislative mandates, and proportional electoral districts) to ensure that marginalized groups are fairly represented by those who share their policy positions on important issues.[5]

Increasing the number of women in legislative assemblies may also promote substantive representation.[6] In theory, substantive representation is directly related to the degree to which representatives seek to advance the group's interests and preferences—or, in other words, the translation of policy preferences into legislative outcomes in favor of the represented group.[7] Even though the empirical relationship between substantive and descriptive representation has been debated among scholars, recent studies lend substantial support that legislators' characteristics[8] and identities have a positive impact on the types of measures prioritized, proposed, and passed on behalf of different groups.[9] Moreover, increasing the number of women in decision-making institutions may substantially impact women's substantive input in issues relating to national budgets, the ideological direction of government policies, and policy priorities to remedy the underrepresentation of women in elected office. As maintained by Jane Mansbridge, "descriptive representation by gender improves substantive outcomes for women in every polity for which we have a measure."[10]

According to the critical mass theories, for women to play a more prominent role in the decision-making process and advocate for women's issues and perspectives,[11] their numerical presence should substantially increase.[12] More recent research has questioned the critical mass theory's underlying assumptions and emphasized the theory's underspecification[13] and demonstrated that increased numerical presence is not often conducive to more attention to women's interests and priorities.[14] Furthermore, studies exploring the link between gender quotas and policy change reveal that quotas' positive effects on advancing the priorities and interests of women as a group are hardly generalizable across different contexts and institutional arrangements.[15]

Beyond numbers, research dealing with women's legislative behavior in established and developing democracies has yielded mixed results and perspectives. The numerical presence of women in legislatures may not automatically translate to the prioritization of women's issues. As Sue Thomas eloquently expressed, "One group of scholars argue that bringing more women will alter the process by which business is conducted. Articles suggest that women will reform the political procedures and make them more humane and more cooperative. Another strand of research suggests that women will keep their eyes trained on different sorts of legislative goals than men's traditional goals. A third group argues that these expectations are naïve as women have to work within the boundaries of legislative norms to succeed."[16] Institutional contexts may also significantly influence whether and how gendered legislation occurs, with one scholar maintaining that "different institutional contexts foster dissimilar amounts of feminist activity."[17]

But what constitutes women's interests and priorities? Scholars have problematized the notion of "women's interests"[18] and questioned the underlying assumptions of existing scholarship on women's substantive representation that views women as a homogenous entity with similar interests and preferences.[19] Yet research on women's substantive representation in established democracies has shown consistent gender differences in policy preferences and priorities. Female legislators are more likely to represent women's interests since they share similar life experiences and structural societal positions, which differ from men.[20] Women may also view their role in the political realm as an extension of their roles within their own families and communities[21] and are more likely to see themselves as the representatives of women.[22] Compared with their male counterparts, female legislators also tend to pay closer attention to issues related to women's rights[23] and other areas of traditional interest to women such as health, education, social welfare, and environment.[24] Relying on time-series cross-sectional data, researchers have demonstrated that substantial increases in women's numerical representation (i.e., quota shocks) are associated with more government spending on historically feminine areas, such as public health.[25]

Comparative research has shown relatively consistent findings. For example, the Argentinian lower chamber and the U.S. Congress have shown similar gender-based policy priorities, especially in women's and children's rights issues.[26] In addition, bills introduced in the Honduras Congress have been shown to hold the same female policy priorities as those in established democracies.[27] Female legislators tend to focus on women's rights, with no significant gender differences concerning children and family issues. However, studies of gender-based differences in legislators' attitudes and bill initiation behavior in Latin America uncovered significant patterns of female marginalization regarding bill initiation, particularly in women's and children's and family issues.[28] Relatedly, another study showed evidence that increased female representation in sub-Saharan Africa is associated with higher spending on health and reduced infant mortality.[29]

Regarding the role of political parties in conditioning women's substantive representation, studies have explored the effect of partisanship on women's policy preferences.[30] However, most studies examining women's influence and behavior in legislative institutions have often included party affiliation as a control variable, with no attention paid to the effect of parties' organizational strength and internal features. This gap can be mainly attributed to the dominant views in political parties' scholarship that often treat parties and party organizations as dependent variables and the absence of substantial variations relating to political parties' organizational strength in democracies.[31] Unlike most non-democratic settings, political parties in democracies are often allowed to participate in elections and are organizationally strong with more clearly defined policy platforms and support bases.

WOMEN'S LEGISLATIVE POWER IN AUTOCRACIES

Does the link between women's descriptive and substantive representation hold outside the democratic world? How does it vary across autocratic contexts? Some argue that we should expect women's substantive representation in nondemocracies to be similar to democratic settings given the fact that women's interests, such as education and health policies, as well as their "feminist" interests usually are not sensitive to the incumbent autocrat.[32] Furthermore, women's interests tend to pose little or no threat to regime stability. For instance, in transitioning Hong Kong, female and more liberal legislators are more likely to focus on feminist issues.[33] In sub-Saharan Africa, women representatives and women citizens are more likely to prioritize poverty reduction, healthcare, and women's rights. In contrast, male representatives prioritize infrastructure projects.[34]

Focusing on the MENA region, scholarship discerning the link between women's numerical and substantive representation has relied on single cases and/or the reported/stated priorities and policy preferences of female legislators. These studies had mixed and, in many cases, even contradictory findings. For instance, one study investigated the success of women's caucuses in the Iranian parliament in producing significant policy outcomes for women under authoritarianism, even without a critical mass.[35] Similarly, studies have shown that gender quotas in Morocco have enabled women to build alliances within the legislature despite their ideological differences, pay close attention to women's issues, and pass women-focused legislation.[36] Relatedly, it was found that female legislators in the Turkish parliament are more likely to sponsor bills on women's rights and equality despite the presence of highly disciplined parties and their low numerical presence (17 percent female representation).[37] The authors also uncover interesting variations relating to female legislators' ideological affiliation and their attention to different issue areas. Other studies have shown that quotas have advanced women's sustainable representation in the political realm in Morocco,[38] women's ability to access influential committee appointments within MENA's legislatures,[39] and service responsiveness to female constituents in Algeria and Morocco.[40] Researchers found similar results in a study of the 2015 Egyptian parliament that showed that female deputies tend to pay more attention to women's issues during parliamentary debates.[41]

Contrastingly, others have questioned the utility of implementing gender quotas under autocratic political regimes and their relevance for producing women-friendly outcomes. For example, a study on pretransition Tunisia finds that the authoritarian structures hindered female parliamentarians' effectiveness.[42] In Morocco, the informal gender quota, introduced in 2002, had a limited impact on advancing women's rights.[43] Quota policies are "embedded" in the fabric of the existing authoritarian structures, with a limited impact on producing genuine change.[44] Women have limited capacity to initiate change due to the hegemony of the male party leaders and the weakness of female alliances within the legislature. James Liddell echoes similar views and sheds light on the challenges facing female politicians operating under authoritarian regimes, mainly in Morocco.[45]

Similar to the shortcoming relating to the link between political parties and women's legislative behavior in democracies, there is a substantial gap in our understanding of the effect of political parties on shaping women's legislative behavior in autocracies. Former studies have paid increased attention to the link between institutionalized party-based regimes and the promotion of women's political and economic rights in dictatorships[46] and women's political inclusion;[47] however, no studies have directly investigated the effect of institutionalized political parties on women's political power. Also, no study examines women's monitoring or oversight role in autocratic legislatures and/or the issues they focus on while posing legislative questions.

Existing research on the intersection of women in politics and political parties in MENA has overlooked the role of party institutionalization (PI) in conditioning women's political influence and policy priorities. Except for one study that tackled the effect of PI on female recruitment in Morocco and Egypt, it is still unclear how features of political parties, namely their varying levels of PI, may shape women's political influence and legislative behavior.[48] These features may shape the capacity and incentives for political parties to advance women's political power regardless of the parties' ideology. I argue that whereas gender quotas are valuable mechanisms for overcoming structural and institutional inequalities by increasing women's numerical presence in politics, institutionalized political parties are essential for women's substantive representation and gaining power and influence within autocratic legislatures. Institutional mechanisms that are best for increasing women's descriptive representation may not necessarily maximize women's substantive representation.[49]

My theoretical framework aims to explain variations in women's political influence and substantive representation under authoritarianism. I outline two main mechanisms to explain why PI matters for women's political power: (1) organizational complexity related to the scope of PI and (2) the depth of PI that facilitates inter- and intraparty collaboration between female legislators. I discuss the two mechanisms in more depth in the second part of this chapter.

To measure women's political influence, I examine their access to legislative committees in autocratic legislatures. Women's political effectiveness depends on whether they gain access and power within legislatures.[50] I argue that women affiliated with highly institutionalized parties are more likely to gain access to highly desired, influential committees that confer power and prestige to individual legislators. Institutionalized parties have the capacity to support women within legislatures and provide them with the necessary resources and tools to gain influence compared to those elected without party support (i.e., independent legislators) and/or those affiliated with weakly institutionalized parties. Parties also have incentives to promote women's presence in influential legislative committees as political party leaders often deem committee appointments and leadership essential to fulfill policy goals and ensure party unity.[51] While I expect a positive association between PI and female legislators' access to influential committees, I do not expect women's affiliation with institutionalized parties to negatively affect their membership in social and women's committees as they may choose to serve on these committees to advance women's rights and policy preferences. The more crucial issue is that they are not marginalized from influential and high-prestige committees and are sidelined to less desirable, low-prestige committees.

To capture variations in women's substantive representation, I rely on Susan Carroll's conceptualization of women's interests as "those (areas) where policy consequences are likely to have a more immediate and direct impact on significantly larger numbers of women than of men."[52] Furthermore, I differentiate between what is deemed feminine/women's interests and feminist policy areas. I expect women affiliated with highly institutionalized parties to better represent women's interests and play a more substantial representative role than female legislators who run as independents and/or are affiliated with weakly institutionalized parties.

PARTY INSTITUTIONALIZATION AND WOMEN'S POLITICAL REPRESENTATION

POLITICAL PARTIES AND PARTY SYSTEMS IN THE MENA REGION

Research on party systems and parties' organizational structures in established and transitioning democracies has proliferated over the past few decades; however, research on the role and function of political parties in nondemocracies remains scarce.[53] This issue can be mainly attributed to the fact that scholarship on party system institutionalization often equates it with a democratic process[54] and political influence,[55] rather than as a unique process where organizations may gain stability and value.[56] Despite the fragmentation and/or absence of party systems in nondemocracies, political parties play an essential role—whether they actively participate in elections or not.[57] Political parties in autocracies make power-sharing deals credible,[58] contribute to authoritarian regime effectiveness,[59] and enable forms of co-optation via the hierarchical assignment of services and benefits.[60] Furthermore, stable, institutionalized parties are crucial for representing citizens' priorities and preferences and managing external opposition along with opponents from within the ruling circle.[61]

Despite the increasing importance of political parties toward understanding autocratic politics and regime survival, political parties in MENA remain mostly understudied, and their policymaking role is undertheorized.[62] One reason for this shortcoming is the lack of democratic progress in the region and the undue focus on party system institutionalization rather than the institutionalization of individual parties—an important caveat that I discuss in more detail in the following section. Furthermore, the fragmentation of MENA's political parties and their limited access to decision-making has drawn scholars away from systematically analyzing their characteristics and roles. Applying indicators often developed in democratic settings, MENA's party systems are considered irrelevant. Meanwhile, parties have remained highly fragmented with weak organizational capacity, except for the Islamist parties, which have historically been more organized with strong societal ties.

Notwithstanding their current state of fragmentation, MENA's political parties played an influential role during the first decades of the twentieth century in shaping the political processes through their active resistance to colonial powers in the pre-independence era (for instance, the al-Wafd party in Egypt, the Istiqlal party in Morocco, and the neo-Destour party in Tunisia). The communists, Baathists, and Islamists gained organizational and ideological strength in the post–World War II era and were able to spread beyond state boundaries.[63] Parties' roles receded in the postindependence period, including the nationalist and leftist parties, which incumbent regimes often perceived as a threat to their stability.[64] Pre-independence parties were soon replaced by ruling single parties, and the single-party systems prevailed.[65] These single parties were ideologically weak and reinforced alternative forms of elite-mass linkages, such as tribal, patron-client, and kinship ties.[66]

As many Arab countries ushered in a period of political liberalization during the 1990s in response to the global wave of democratization following the end of the Cold War and the rise of competitive authoritarian institutions, electoral competition became the norm despite close state supervision, vote-buying practices, and citizens' apathy toward party politics. By the advent of the twenty-first century, most of the secular and Islamist opposition parties, as well as the pro-regime parties, had mastered the rules of the game and actively participated in elections with well-defined support bases and electoral strongholds, albeit with internal fragmentation, ideological polarization, and vague electoral platforms. Parties providing services to their constituents managed to survive and garner voters' support.[67] From the regime's perspective, it was increasingly clear that parties posed minimal threat to their rule. Even more, parties have become tools for the incumbent regimes to solidify power by co-opting political opponents and appear democratic to international audiences and foreign donors.[68] As argued by Shadi Hamid, "political parties provided [the regimes] the illusion of freedom and pluralism."[69] Thus, the introduction of multiparty elections has led to the creation of parties that often reproduced the regimes' autocratic and nepotistic practices rather than promote democratic processes.[70]

Despite the intraregional commonalities in the parties' internal structures and roles, there are wide variations regarding the rules governing political parties' formation. Parties were allowed to form in some capacity in Lebanon, Egypt, Jordan, Iraq, Tunisia, and Algeria but were restricted or banned in others. In monarchies, mainly Jordan and Morocco, monarchs introduced "palace pluralism," where multiparty competition was permitted, albeit arbitrated by the monarch, who is viewed as above party politics.[71] However, political parties are still banned in all the Arab Gulf states and operate under different labels (i.e., "political societies" in Bahrain and Oman and "blocs" in Kuwait)—or are entirely outlawed (i.e., Qatar, United Arab Emirates [UAE], and Saudi Arabia).

Political parties are legalized in other contexts but lack the organizational and mobilizational capacity to compete and/or win legislative seats. Most parties in Jordan, for instance, currently play a marginal role in the electoral arena and are often replaced with political blocs with no ideological ties or coherent policy programs. A former female deputy in Jordan's

2012 legislature describes the blocs as "very fragile, fluid, and unstable and . . . not connected by a single political line, but only by interests. They come together when there are elections for the committees, and after that, that is it, they are dissolved, nothing keeps them together."[72] These conditions also led to the "independent candidate" phenomenon—candidates who run without political or ideological affiliation.[73] For instance, in Jordan's 2013 and 2016 legislative elections, independent candidates won about 82 and 77 percent of the total seats, respectively. Notably, seven out of the twenty-two Arab League member states have women politicians elected to their positions without any party affiliation or support.[74]

In the aftermath of the Arab uprisings, new parties have mushroomed in transitioning Tunisia, Egypt, and Libya.[75] However, most of these new parties encountered numerous organizational and financial challenges, especially when faced with the electoral savvy of well-funded, highly organized Islamist parties. Thus, most new parties rarely survived more than one legislative election.[76] Furthermore, the post–Arab uprising era witnessed the reemergence of the old guard, institutionalized parties that successfully rebranded and regained voters' loyalty. As maintained by Francesco Cavatorta and Lise Storm, "the average age of the top two parties in at least one of the two most recent legislative elections was above thirty years in a significant number of instances (Algeria, Egypt, Lebanon, Morocco, Palestine, and Sudan), in some countries covering cases from both the pre- and post-Arab uprisings era."[77] Multiparty elections continued to be the norm over the past two decades, especially after the Arab uprisings. However, the absence of PI has left an enduring effect on women's access to political power and their legislative behavior, especially in contexts with no gender quotas in place.

PARTY INSTITUTIONALIZATION IN THE MIDDLE EAST AND NORTH AFRICA

Consistent with extant political parties' scholarship, I differentiate between individual parties' institutionalization[78] and party system institutionalization (i.e., a stable set of parties that interact regularly).[79] One group of scholars viewed PI as an "internal dimension" of party system institutionalization,[80] while others considered party system institutionalization as the "external dimension" of parties (i.e., interparty competition) that is often conditioned by multiple factors, such as a country's electoral and institutional settings and level of economic development.[81] Furthermore, some studies considered PI as an initial step for party system institutionalization and its stabilization,[82] whereas others argued that individual PI and party system institutionalization are not necessarily identical processes and/or mutually compatible.[83] This book adopts the latter view that individual parties' institutionalization and party system institutionalization are distinct processes, especially in autocratic settings where political parties tend to be weak and/or the electoral scene is dominated by regime-affiliated parties. I conceptualize PI as the internal features and stability of individual political parties, whereas party system institutionalization involves parties' external features and relationships with other parties in a specific country.

Focusing on the "internal" characteristics of parties, research has conceptualized PI as a party-level property related to the party's operations as an organization or network,[84] degree of temporal stability, value infusion,[85] ability to mobilize new social forces in the political process,[86] and degree of internal systemness (i.e., interdependence of different sectors).[87] Thus, PI is "a process and procedures by which organizations acquire value and stability" that may apply to both democratic and nondemocratic systems.[88]

Studies have explored different aspects of PI: electoral volatility,[89] complexity (i.e., whether the party centers on one individual/personalism), adaptability (i.e., party age, generational succession and party's ability to shift role from opposition to a governing party), cohesiveness and level of fragmentation (i.e., the number of effective parties), and autonomy (i.e., independent of other social groupings, such as clan, family or class).[90] Thus, institutionalized political parties are characterized by stability, long-term goals, and stable connections with voters.[91] Contrastingly, weakly institutionalized parties "lack lasting societal ties, with limited value infusion, stability, minimal organizational cohesiveness or 'internal systemness' and are susceptible to personalist politics."[92]

To overcome difficulties associated with measuring individual parties' institutionalization and issues related to the limited temporal and spatial data on political parties, a novel country-level dataset was collected of PI in democracies and autocracies that dates to 1900.[93] The PI index measures the degree to which a party approximates an ideal type and captures patterns and variations in the organization and behavior of the political parties.[94] It measures the extent to which political parties within a polity are characterized by (1) permanent organizations at the national level, (2) permanent local party branches, (3) the most common type of linkage to constituents, (4) distinct party platforms, and (5) legislative cohesion.[95] These five indicators capture the internal characteristics of the individual parties rather than the party system. They also measure the proportion of parties with robust organizations and the extent to which "the parties' long-term goals orient the behavior of elites and masses in a political system."[96]

In addition to the country-level PI data, the V-Dem Institute has recently collected the Varieties of Party Identity and Organization (V-Party) dataset. It examines political parties' policy positions and organizational structures worldwide and highlights shifts and trends within and between parties since 1970 (V-Party 2020).[97] I rely on the PI literature and the country- and party-level measures of PI to develop and test my argument on the link between women's political power and PI. Notably, the PI index and the V-Party indicators capture parties' internal characteristics regardless of the degree of the party system institutionalization and the country's level of democracy, which are crucial for my theoretical framework. Using the V-Party dataset, I construct an index that captures variations in the organization and behavior of the individual political parties to use in my empirical analyses in chapters 4 and 5 (see table A.7 in appendix A).

Party system institutionalization is mostly absent in MENA because of the autocrats' tight control of political competition and the emergence of ruling party systems, as explained earlier. Yet MENA's states have varying levels of individual parties' institutionalization that remain unexplored. Figure 2.1 presents the PI index for different regions worldwide (V-Dem PI index 2017). What is notable about this graph is how the MENA region stands out concerning political parties' degree of institutionalization.

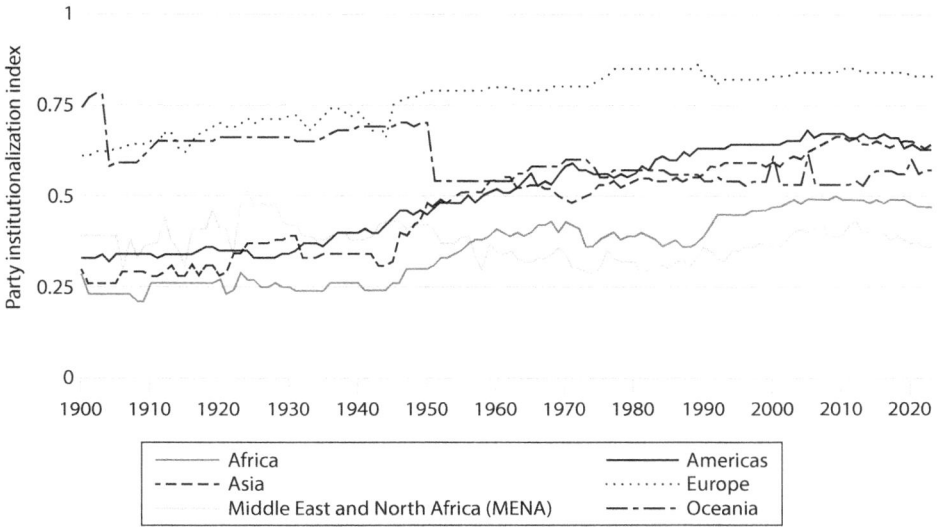

FIGURE 2.1 Regional party institutionalization index (1900–2023)

Source: Bizzarro et al. (2017). Party institutionalization ranges from 0 to 1, where higher values indicate greater institutionalization.

The figure shows that MENA's political parties enjoyed considerable levels of institutionalization until the mid-twentieth century, even compared to Asia, the Americas, and Africa. The figure also depicts the steady pattern of parties' decline since the 1950s following the independence of most MENA states from colonialism and the inception of autocratic rule, as I elucidated in the previous section. Regimes' political liberalization efforts in the 1990s resulted in a modest increase in the degree of parties' institutionalization. This increase remained largely static, leading to significant implications for women in power and the political process. The advent of the Arab uprisings has created a slight surge in PI, albeit brief.

In addition to regional variations in the PI index (figure 2.1), there are significant intraregional variations. As evident in figure 2.2, Tunisia, Egypt, Morocco, and Algeria have historically had the highest levels of PI. Contrastingly, Oman and Kuwait have the lowest levels of PI, given the

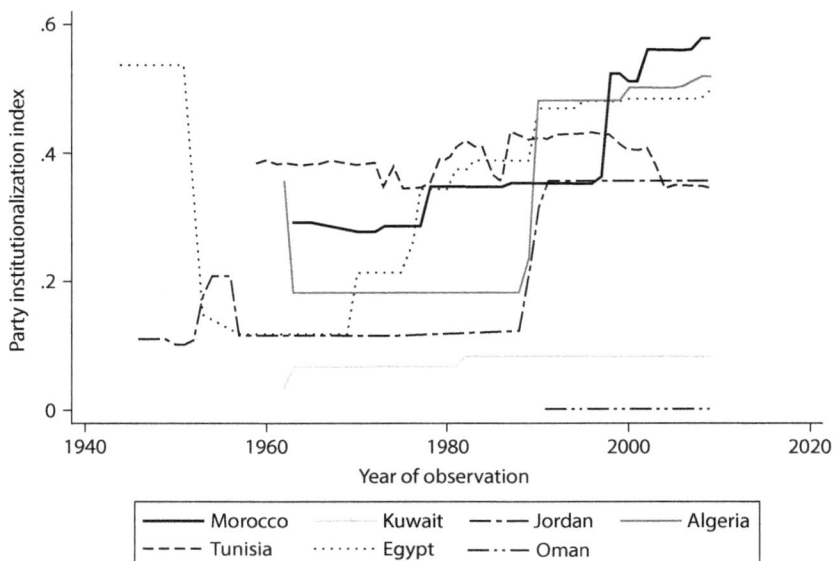

FIGURE 2.2 Party institutionalization in the Middle East and North Africa (1950–2015)

Source: Bizzarro et al. (2017). Party institutionalization ranges from 0 to 1, where higher values indicate greater institutionalization. Broken lines in the graph denote missing data points.

restrictions on political parties' formation in these countries. Finally, parties in Jordan have been allowed to compete and run for elections since 1989, as I explain in more detail in chapter 3, but they have had consistently low levels of PI over the past few decades. In the following section, I outline the effect of varying levels of PI on women's political power and influence.

POLITICAL PARTIES, PARTY INSTITUTIONALIZATION, AND WOMEN'S POLITICAL REPRESENTATION IN MENA

Decades of scholarship on the role of political parties in promoting women's political inclusion in established and new democracies have shown that parties are the gateway for female political representation and that their role is integral for advancing women's presence in politics.[98] Parties have a significant influence on the nomination, recruitment, and legislative behavior of female politicians. As maintained by Pamela Paxton and Melanie Hughes, "Parties are the real gatekeepers of office. . . . Because they play such an important role in the composition of parliament, we must understand how parties differ in encouraging or discouraging women's access to parliament."[99] Parties' patriarchal internal structures and informal procedures may curtail women's progress and sustain their subordination.[100] Furthermore, parties' organizational strength and capacity may affect their ability to comply with gender-related reforms, mainly gender quotas.[101] However, studies exploring the effect of PI on women's political power are scarce since democracies often have highly institutionalized parties (and party systems), and cross-country variations are more likely to be inconsequential for women's political representation.[102]

But what about the party link in nondemocracies? As shown in figure I.2, there is a strong association between party-based autocratic regimes and female descriptive representation since the 1990s and the surge in competitive authoritarian regimes.[103] Still, this figure tells us little about the impact of parties' levels of institutionalization on women's access to power and/or exercise of power in nondemocracies where wide variations in individual parties' institutionalization exist. Focusing on the MENA region, a burgeoning literature has addressed political parties' role in shaping women's access to power. Scholars have reflected on the adverse effects of parties' male-dominated and opaque internal structures on women's recruitment and nomination.[104] Others have questioned the utility of the supply and demand theories to explain female underrepresentation in politics and highlighted the efforts of female aspirants from within parties to push for increased representation.[105]

Despite the dearth of scholarship on women and political parties in MENA, more generally, ample studies have focused on the impact of parties' ideology on women's nominations and recruitment strategies. Researchers have shown that women's increased representation within Islamist parties in Yemen and Jordan is mainly attributed to their ability to seize windows of opportunity while party leaders are subsumed in resolving schisms within the party.[106] This study concluded that women's increased presence in these contexts may not necessarily be attributed to a shift in Islamist parties' ideologies toward women. Investigating the cases of Egypt's Muslim Brotherhood (MB) and Morocco's Justice and Development Party (PJD), Katarína Škrabáková argues that the degree of intraparty centralization and institutionalization are essential for females' candidacy and recruitment.[107] The author finds that the less centralized, more institutionalized PJD party is more likely to facilitate women's candidacy than the more centralized MB. Whereas many of these studies are primarily concerned with women's descriptive representation, others have explored the symbolic effects of gender quotas within conservative parties. Research has also investigated the significant transformation in the discourse and practices of ultraconservative parties in Palestine, Israel, and Egypt following the introduction of gender quotas.[108]

What remains missing in MENA's research on women in politics is the role of PI in conditioning women's political influence and policy priorities. It is still unclear how the internal features of political parties, namely the varying levels of PI, may shape women's political influence and legislative behavior in these settings. I posit that whereas gender quotas are important for overcoming structural and institutional inequalities by increasing women's numerical presence in the decision-making arena, the presence of institutionalized political parties is essential for women's substantive representation and for gaining power and influence within autocratic legislatures, as I detail in the following section. I build on previous work on the link between incumbent PI and women's numerical representation[109] and increased economic and political rights.[110] My book also expands existing research on autocrats' ability to use the inclusion of women as a tool for coalition-building and focuses on the link between PI more generally—not just the ruling party's degree of institutionalization—and shifts the emphasis to the effect of PI on women's legislative behavior.[111]

Importantly, I distinguish between multiparty competition and PI, an integral point often ignored in previous research. Most recent research has demonstrated that party-based regimes—usually based on the institutionalized regime party—are associated with higher levels of female political inclusion. For instance, a study that relied on data from more than 108 countries between 1946 and 2010 showed that regimes' levels of PI are positively linked with women's political inclusion.[112] Nevertheless, it is unclear whether these parties are effective because they are highly institutionalized or because of their privileged position of power. Even more, multiparty electoral competition is not directly related to PI and, in turn, female political inclusion. This is also reflected in my earlier multivariate analysis, which demonstrated that multiparty elections have a statistically insignificant effect on women's numerical presence in MENA's lower chambers. These findings are consistent with earlier work that found a strong association between institutionalized party-based regimes and greater economic and political rights for women, but not necessarily multiparty elections.[113]

In sum, the mere presence of political parties and multiparty elections is insufficient to promote women's political power. Regardless of the number of parties competing for elections, weakly institutionalized parties fail to advance women's representation as they lack the capacity and the incentives to promote women in politics, especially in contexts with no quota system.[114] This issue is more acute in autocracies, where power is concentrated with the autocrat and their allies, and political parties are often given limited space and minimal powers if allowed to operate.

But why does PI matter for women's political power? Parties have the capacity and resources to organize citizens with policy platforms and give ordinary people a voice in governance.[115] In general, political parties perform two main functions: (1) recruiting leaders and structuring political competition[116] and (2) performing a representative role to organize mass involvement[117] and craft policy preferences.[118] Institutionalized parties, in particular, have stable connections with voters, legislative cohesion, distinct policy platforms, and a physical presence through branches and organizations, both locally and nationally.[119]

As aforementioned, the institutionalization of individual parties is measured along two main dimensions: the *scope* of PI that deals with parties' organizational capacity, and the *depth* of institutionalization, which captures the party's linkage with the masses and elites and the party's legislative cohesion. Consistent with the existing conceptualization of individual parties' institutionalization, I outline the effect of these dimensions on women's political power and influence: (1) the scope of PI that is essential for promoting women's political inclusion and (2) the depth of PI that facilitates inter- and intraparty collaboration between female legislators and connects women with voters.

I posit that parties' organizational capacity and stability (i.e., the scope of PI) matter for promoting women's political inclusion and channeling women's interests within and outside the legislature. Highly institutionalized parties tend to have less centralized nomination processes that often occur through local branches and grassroots levels with less interference from the center. This has been defined as "organizational complexity." Such complexity enables parties to implement candidate selection mechanisms that ensure female inclusion.[120] Moreover, party branches and women's wings are essential for facilitating women's political candidacy and mobilizing and connecting female candidates with voters before and during elections.[121] Political parties' stability and continuity are integral to their ability to develop organizational structures to promote women's political inclusion. New parties, such as those established in the aftermath of the Arab uprisings that competed for only one election and then disappeared from the electoral arena, lack the organizational tools and ability to support women and promote their inclusion. Parties' organizational capacity matters in contexts with gender quotas in place as they facilitate candidate recruitment and selection; however, this capacity is even more crucial in contexts with no gender quotas where women lack access to male-dominated networks of power.

Additionally, institutionalized parties often function as organizations with clearly defined rules and sufficient material and human resources; thus, they are better able to cultivate, recruit, and support female candidacies.[122] These resources are crucial for women politicians in highly conservative settings where they are often sidelined from political power, and their presence in the electoral arena is a relatively new phenomenon. In these settings, women are rarely part of the existing power networks and often lack the necessary homosocial capital to advance in politics on their own.[123] Women politicians face additional challenges in autocratic settings where the political scene is often dominated by the regime's close allies and the rules of the game are ever-changing, as I detail in chapter 3.

Institutionalized parties with organizational capacity and strong links with society are better able to perform their representative role. Highly institutionalized parties have the organizational structure to "incorporate and stabilize social demands,"[124] channel political demands,[125] represent various geographical areas and social groups, and link diverse constituencies.[126] Moreover, such "bottom-up" structures facilitate the flow of information.[127] Bizzarro and his colleagues maintain that "regional party branches and stable linkages with citizen groups help strong parties to elicit information about appropriate policy design for legislation and to find policies that are adapted to local contexts, which eases the subsequent task of effective implementation."[128] These linkages enable parties to identify and aggregate demands from citizens and organized interests.[129] Importantly, institutionalized parties with a physical presence on the national and local levels and stable ties with constituents are important for coordinating with women's groups and civil society organizations and channeling their demands. This explains why institutionalized parties with local party branches and affiliated organizations can better establish local connections, represent voters' needs, and promote women's political representation.

The depth of PI may also condition women's behavior within the legislature and explain variations in the process and nature of women's political representation. Strong parties with high levels of party cohesion facilitate coordination and collaboration among party members and provide space for striking bargains.[130] They also have the tools to monitor party members, reward good behavior, and punish dissidents.[131]

As demonstrated in the comparative legislatures' scholarship, collaboration and coalition-building among women are essential for policymaking. Women's affiliation with highly institutionalized parties is necessary for promoting their power and influence within legislatures. Collaboration and coalition-building among women are vital components of the legislative process, especially in nondemocratic settings where women are newcomers to politics and due to the opacity of policymaking processes within these institutions. Collaboration across party lines enables women to overcome structural barriers, attain political power and influence, and negotiate with higher echelons of power (i.e., government officials, ruling elites, the incumbent regime) to whom women often lack access.[132]

The three cases in this study reflect significant variations in the levels of PI, as I show in figure 2.2 and explain in depth in chapter 3. Morocco is a strong case for institutionalized political parties, while Jordan represents a weak case for PI. Kuwait is an important case where political parties are banned, and women run as independents with no party support. Thus, I aim to test two main propositions in chapters 4 and 5. In chapter 4, I test my first proposition and use women's committee assignments as a proxy to measure their influence and power within legislatures. Relying on a decade of committee appointment data, I argue that women affiliated with institutionalized political parties are more likely to access influential committees. Contrastingly, women affiliated with weakly institutionalized parties or who run as independents are less likely to access such committees. I am also interested in explaining women's legislative behavior variations in these settings. I test my second proposition in chapter 5 and argue that female legislators are more likely to represent women's interests when affiliated with highly institutionalized political parties. I test my argument using parliamentary queries between 2009 and 2017 in Morocco, Jordan, and Kuwait.

ALTERNATIVE EXPLANATIONS

The main argument of this book is that PI matters for women's political power and ability to represent women in autocratic settings. However, I am not claiming that women's legislative power is dependent solely on the existence of strong, institutionalized parties. Other factors that may also condition women's legislative power and influence are equally important, such as the strength of women's movements and organizations, the electoral system in place, the country's level of democracy, and/or the competitiveness of the political system, and the prevalent gender norms. I detail these alternative explanations below and discuss how I account for their potential effect.

First, women's organizations play an integral role in women's political integration not only in democracies but also in autocratic settings.[133] This caveat is especially relevant in Morocco, where women's organizations have a long history of gender activism and have played a critical role in empowering women in the public sphere.[134] Thus, it is possible that the findings of this study can be mainly attributed to the strength of women's activism in Morocco as opposed to the less dynamic women's movements in Kuwait and Jordan. I argue that this is not the case for two main reasons.

As I elucidated earlier, highly institutionalized, organizationally strong parties facilitate the work of women's movements and magnify their impact. Institutionalized parties with stable horizontal and vertical ties to societal actors facilitate the coordination and channeling of demands. An excellent example of how institutionalized parties may amplify the work of women's organizations is evident in the adoption of the 2004 Mudawana reforms in Morocco. In this case, the socialist party (Socialist Union of Popular Forces [USFP]) promoted the reforms that the feminist movement's campaign made, demanding reform not directly to the king but to the parliament.[135] The success of these efforts in 2004 is mainly attributed to the coordination among women's movement, parliament, and the prime minister in contrast to the more modest reforms proposed in 1993 that reaped small gains.[136]

Moreover, I account for variations in the link between parties and social groups in all the models, including women's associations. I have constructed a PI index in chapters 4 and 5 that includes a measure capturing the extent to which the party maintains ties to social organizations (see table A.7 in appendix A). Therefore, variations associated with the strength of women's movements are already accounted for in all my statistical models.

Second, variations observed in women's political power and influence in the three countries may be linked to the electoral system in place. Extant scholarship on democracies has shown that proportional representation (PR) is more conducive to higher levels of women's descriptive representation,[137] especially if combined with placement mandates.[138] My data allows me to test for this specific aspect. In 2013, Jordan elected almost one-quarter of the legislature's seats via PR party lists, while the other three-quarters were elected via single nontransferable vote (SNTV), a majoritarian electoral system. I run separate analyses for women elected via the PR system. I compare them to those elected from single-member districts and find no substantive difference in their legislative behavior.

Third, variations in women's political representation can be attributed to the level of competitiveness of the legislative assembly and/or democracy in the countries under study. However, empirical data lend little evidence to this argument. Kuwait is often considered the most liberalized Arab monarchy with a powerful, democratically elected parliament.[139] Despite being constrained by regime-loyalist governments, it is still considered the region's "most empowered parliament."[140] Thus, this book confirms findings from previous research that a country's level of democracy is not a significant explanatory variable for understanding cross-national and regional variations in women's presence and influence in legislative institutions.[141] It argues that political parties' presence and degree of institutionalization may offer a more accurate explanation to understand women's political representation in autocracies.

Finally, the high levels of political power and substantive representation observed in the Moroccan context can be attributed to the country's more gender egalitarian norms. This is unlikely because of two reasons. First, as I demonstrate in chapter 1, variations in public attitudes toward women politicians across the MENA region rarely reflect the reality of women's political power. According to the Arab Barometer data, states with the most progressive gender attitudes, such as Lebanon, have one of the region's lowest numbers of women's politicians. Second, more recent research on public attitudes toward women politicians in Jordan, Tunisia, and Morocco has shown that gender norms do not explain variations in citizens' evaluations of political outcomes.[142] This is why I conclude that the context under which women politicians operate, namely the presence of institutionalized political parties, has the most substantial effect on shaping their behavior and political power.

* * *

Over the past two decades, we have accumulated significant knowledge of autocratic legislatures' functions and policy outcomes. Furthermore, studies have investigated why autocrats adopt women's reforms, including gender quota policies. Still, our understanding of women's legislative role in autocracies and how political parties condition their political power remains lacking. I address an often-overlooked aspect in gender and authoritarianism research: the link between parties' level of institutionalization and women's political power and legislative behavior.

This chapter presents the book's theoretical framework and offers insights into women's political influence and substantive representation in nondemocracies. Using party-level data from three Arab autocracies, it explores the role of PI in conditioning women's political power and legislative priorities. I discuss several alternative explanations, such as the role of women's organizations, the effect of the electoral system in place, the level of democracy and/or electoral competitiveness, and the structure of prevalent gender norms. I show why these explanations are insufficient to explain the variations in women's political power and influence detailed in chapters 4 and 5.

3

NAVIGATING POWER

Playing on an Uneven Field

The real issue [in Jordan] is the absence of democracy and the targeting of the weaknesses of political parties. This strategy [weakening the democratic process] achieves its goals through multiple ways: the electoral law, the administration of elections, and the regulatory interference in every issue in the[party]institution. . . . Parties are always targeted, and you cannot move forward, honestly. For the parties, there is no dialogue surrounding it [democracy], and it is not there at all. . . . They do not want parties in the parliament under any condition.

—FORMER FEMALE MP IN THE JORDANIAN PARLIAMENT AND FIRST FEMALE
SECRETARY GENERAL OF A LEFTIST POLITICAL PARTY, INTERVIEW WITH
AUTHOR IN AMMAN, 2016

his chapter introduces the three cases in the book: Jordan, Kuwait, and Morocco. I start by discussing the case selection and outline the role of legislatures and policymaking in each case. This discussion is followed by detailed sections on the intersection of the electoral context and women's political representation. This chapter presents three varying contexts where women access political power through mandated gender quotas and parties with a low degree of institutionalization (i.e., Jordan), a case with no gender quota system or organized party competition (i.e., Kuwait), and finally, a case with mandated gender quotas and highly institutionalized political parties (i.e., Morocco). The chapter also outlines the process of women's political representation in the three cases and the challenges they face to access political power.

WHY MOROCCO, JORDAN, AND KUWAIT? WHY MONARCHIES?

The research design of this study relies on the most similar systems.[1] I focus on Morocco, Jordan, and Kuwait, which are hereditary monarchies with important commonalities, such as cultural attitudes, religion, presence of legislative institutions, and regime type. Table 3.1 presents the three cases' political, electoral, and economic characteristics. These countries are rated as partly free.[2] Kuwait is oil dependent, whereas Morocco and Jordan are resource-poor countries. As I detail in the following section, the three monarchies have a long history of elected legislatures with varying legislative and oversight powers. According to the Parliamentary Power Index (PPI), the assembly in Kuwait enjoys the most legislative powers, followed by Morocco and Jordan.[3]

To ensure that the countries under study capture the distinctions that are essential for my theory development, I have selected these cases purposively based on key explanatory variables, namely women's numerical representation in national legislatures and the presence of gender quota policies, and party institutionalization—the two main variables I investigate in this study.[4] Regarding women's political representation, the three cases have significant variations in the number of women in their lower chambers (table 3.1). The cases also vary in their gender quota policies. Morocco has introduced voluntary gender quotas since 2002, and Jordan has reserved seats for women since 2003. In contrast, Kuwait has no gender quotas (table 3.1).

TABLE 3.1 Cases in the study

CASES	JORDAN 2010–2016	MOROCCO 2011–2016	KUWAIT 2009–2016
Freedom House	Partly free, 5	Partly free, 4.5	Partly free, 5
Parliamentary Powers Index (PPI)	0.218	0.312	0.375
Oil dependence	No	No	Yes
Quota system for women	Yes	Yes	No
Party institutionalization index (0–1)	0.3	0.55	0.1
Political parties in legislature	Limited	Yes	No
Number of parties/blocs represented in parliament	22 blocs	18 parties	7 blocs
Size of legislature	130	395	50

Sources: Freedom House scores are obtained from the Freedom House website: https:// freedomhouse.org; the Parliamentary Powers Index is obtained from: https://polisci.berkeley .edu/sites/default/files/people/u3833/PPIScores.pdf; the party institutionalization index is obtained from: https://www.v-dem.net/media/publications/v-dem_working_paper_2017_48 .pdf; the number of parties/blocs for Jordan and Morocco are obtained from the official results of Inter-Parliamentary Union, while for Kuwait, the number of blocs is based on the author's data collection.

In addition to variations relating to gender quota policies, the three countries differ in the presence and strength of political parties in their electoral arenas. Political parties are allowed to compete in elections in Jordan and Morocco but not in Kuwait and are replaced by political blocs with shared demographic characteristics and ideological orientations. Even though parties are allowed under the law to compete in Jordan, they remain weak. Most candidates run as independents, except for the Islamist party and a few other small leftist parties. Legislators form parliamentary blocs based on blurry ideological lines and/or shared policy interests, but only after being elected.[5]

Given the varying ability of parties to form and compete in elections, the three cases differ substantially in their levels of party institutionalization. According to the V-Dem party institutionalization index (PII), Morocco has had the highest level of party institutionalization since the late 1990s, followed by Jordan (figure 3.1). Contrastingly, Kuwait continued to have the lowest PI scores over the past few decades, with a slight improvement

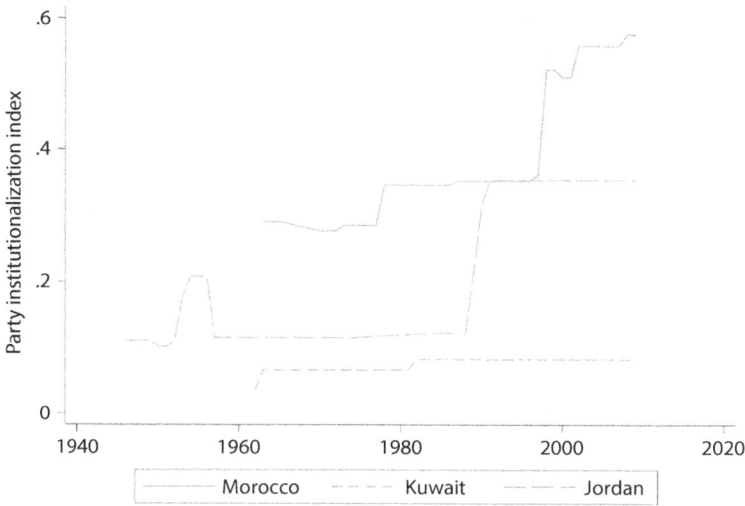

FIGURE 3.1 Party institutionalization in Morocco, Jordan, and Kuwait (1950–2015)

Source: Bizzarro et al. (2017). Party institutionalization ranges from 0 to 1, where higher values indicate greater institutionalization. Broken lines in the graph denote missing data points.

in the aftermath of the 1990 Gulf War. In 2015, Morocco's PII was 0.55 compared to 0.3 and 0.1 in Jordan and Kuwait, respectively (0 is the lowest level of party institutionalization, and 1 is the highest).

Furthermore, I focus mainly on monarchies for two reasons. First, my theory relies on investigating the role of institutionalized parties on women's influence and exercise of power. In MENA's electoral autocracies, such as Algeria and Egypt, the most institutionalized parties are those affiliated with the ruling regimes. In these contexts, separating the effects of party institutionalization on women's representation from regime power and institutionalization is challenging. Contrastingly, monarchical systems lack ruling parties. The distance between the regime and political parties in monarchies allows me to develop my theory and explore the effect of party strength on women's political power. Additionally, legislatures in the three cases under study have enjoyed decades of continuity and remained relatively stable after the 2010 Arab uprisings, unlike other electoral autocracies in the region, namely Syria, Tunisia, and Egypt.

Second, the number of closed autocracies—regimes without multiparty elections for the executive—has exceeded the number of liberal democracies in 2023 for the first time in more than two decades (V-Dem 2023). Over the past decade, the number of closed autocracies has reached thirty-three compared to twenty-two in 2012. Currently, closed autocracies constitute more than one-third of the total number globally. Our knowledge of the dynamics of women's representation in autocracies is already limited and even more so in closed autocracies. Thus, there is a pressing need to gain a deeper understanding of the legislative process in these contexts and the political parties' role in promoting women's power and influence.

LEGISLATURES AND POLICYMAKING IN JORDAN, KUWAIT, AND MOROCCO

Legislatures play several roles in authoritarian political systems: co-opt elites with rents and policy influence,[6] represent the public's preferences,[7] redirect blame,[8] and enable more credible power-sharing.[9] However, there is significant variation regarding the ability of authoritarian legislatures to perform these functions,[10] partly because some act as subordinate "rubber stamp" bodies, while others operate as a real constraint on the executive.[11] Like other autocratic regimes, there are significant variations across the three legislatures under study regarding their legislative and monitoring roles and relationship with the incumbent regimes. Temporal variations are also evident across the three regimes.

Figure 3.2 presents some of these variations over the past decades (1950–2015). Remarkably, the three legislatures have a long history with short periods of interruptions, as I outline below. The figure also shows that whereas the legislature in Kuwait possesses significant prerogatives to constrain the executive and question ministers compared to the Moroccan and Kuwaiti legislatures, the legislatures in Morocco and Jordan have substantial

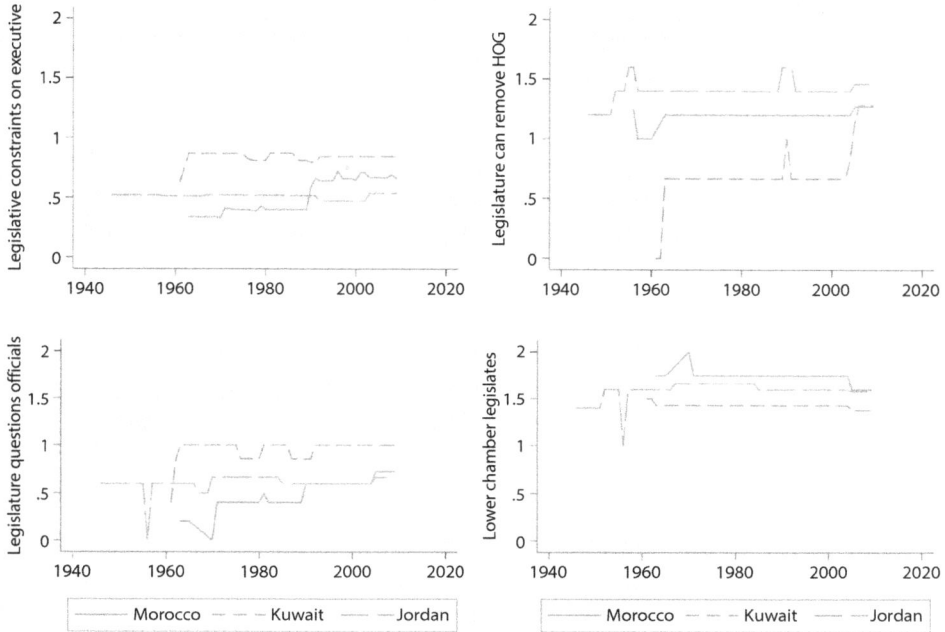

FIGURE 3.2 Assemblies and legislative powers in Morocco, Jordan, and Kuwait (1950–2015)

Source: The figure uses V-Dem's ordinal measure of whether the legislature can (1) constrain the executive, (2) remove the head of government (HOG), (3) question officials, and (4) legislate. Countries receive an annual rating of 0 (no, not at all), 1 (occasionally), and 2 (yes, for the most part). Data are between 1950 and 2016.

legislative powers. Meanwhile, the legislature in Jordan has more power to remove the head of the government than in the other two cases.

Starting with the case of Jordan, the legislative system has two main branches: the Chamber of Notables (Majlis al-Ayan) and the House of Representatives (Majlis al-Newab). While the appointment to the Chamber of Notables is exclusively by royal decree, the lower chamber is elected via direct elections. A dual executive system of the monarchy and the government dominates the decision-making process in Jordan. The king wields substantial political influence, but the government manages day-to-day decision-making and is formally responsible for all state policies. The king appoints the prime minister, and the prime minister then chooses the cabinet with informal involvement by the monarchy.

The Jordanian lower chamber possesses several formal powers that can be used to exert influence over the decision-making process.[12] MPs oversee and approve the general budget, participate in floor debates, ratify the government's proposed laws, propose legislation changes, and vote in committees and on the floor. These powers allow them to influence the cabinet's agenda as it winds through the legislative process. Notwithstanding the parliament's limited legislative role, it plays a significant monitoring role (figure 3.2). Legislators may pose parliamentary questions, interrogate ministers and the prime minister, submit petitions and complaints, establish investigative committees, and hold votes of confidence in the government.[13]

Despite the shortcomings of the legislative process, politicians and voters take the legislature and its elections quite seriously. Voter turnout was 56.6 and 36 percent in the 2013 and 2016 elections, respectively. A former female MP in the sixteenth legislature stated, "The parliament represents the highest legislative authority in the country, and we did not have a parliament in Jordan for a very long time. . . . So, the parliament is a victory for the Jordanian people, and it is no doubt a democratic victory despite the parliament's performance. We make mistakes because the parliament is a vital institution, and we must hold onto it."[14]

After the Arab uprisings, a constitutional amendment was adopted in 2012 that required the monarchy to consult with the legislature before selecting the new government. The changes also included strengthening the government's accountability to the parliament (Articles 53 and 54, 2012). Other reforms relating to the electoral system were introduced, such as establishing the Elections Commission to ensure the integrity of elections, in addition to changes to the electoral law that I detail in the next section.[15]

Kuwait has one of the longest histories of legislative politics in the Gulf Cooperation Council (GCC) and the Arab world. The first Kuwaiti legislative council was established in 1938 following a massive nationwide campaign spearheaded by wealthy merchants. The council wrote the country's first constitution that directly challenged the powers of the emir.[16] The council lasted only six months and was dissolved following disputes between the ruler and the merchants.[17] After gaining independence in 1961, Kuwait had several interrupted experiments with legislative politics and constitution writing that lasted until the end of the 1990 Gulf War.[18]

The executive-legislative relations in Kuwait have been somewhat tenuous. Kuwait has no upper chamber (senate). The Kuwaiti Parliament (also known as the National Assembly) consists of fifty directly elected members in addition to fifteen ministers appointed by the emir[19]—who should not exceed one-third of the parliament[20]—and at least one minister who is directly elected in the Assembly. The emir appoints the prime minister and cabinet members after consulting with the prime minister (Article 56, Kuwait Constitution) and has the power to veto legislation issued by the parliament and dissolve the parliament (Article 107). Members of the ruling family are not allowed to run for parliamentary elections, but they occupy the most influential cabinet positions.[21] The right of parties to form is absent from Kuwait's constitution. Parties are replaced by political groups based on ideological and sectarian orientations. Similar to the Jordanian case, parliamentary blocs are formed in the legislature. Bloc members may agree on some issues, yet their affiliation and voting behavior remain fluid and inconsistent.

The Kuwaiti parliament plays a substantial legislative role. It approves laws proposed by the government (i.e., draft laws) and the legislators (i.e., law proposals/bills). Once legislators propose a bill, it gets forwarded to the specialized committee for study. Once the Legislative Committee approves, the bill is presented to the legislature for consideration and voting. The final text of the proposed bill is referred to the emir for final approval only after it receives enough floor votes.[22] Legislators proposed 730 bills between 2009 and 2011, but only 34 were passed. The government proposed 195 bills over the same period. In addition, the parliament is responsible for approving the budget, imposing taxes, and demanding amendments to the government budget.

In addition to its legislative role, the legislature is essential for curbing the powers of the prime minister and the appointed cabinet through its oversight prerogatives. MPs can question cabinet members or the prime minister, establish investigative committees, and vote "no confidence" on individual cabinet members and the prime minister. Legislators also have the right to overturn the emir's decrees, interpellate ministers, and even impeach the prime minister and/or the ministers (Article 100).

Similar to the Jordanian case, Morocco has a bicameral legislature: Chamber of Representatives and Chamber of Councilors. The Chamber of Representatives (lower chamber) is directly elected every five years per the 1996 constitutional amendment under the reign of the former King Hassan II. Political parties have been allowed to form and compete in elections since independence. The regime held regular elections since the 1960s and used them to "provide a mechanism of elite control and renewal from above."[23]

King Mohammad VI ascended to power in 1999 following the death of King Hassan II. The king is the head of the military and the religious leader of the monarchy, "the commander of the faithful" (Article 19 of Morocco's 1962 Constitution), with a wide range of prerogatives. Some of these powers changed in the aftermath of the Arab uprisings, as I detail later in this section. Regarding executive-legislative relations, the king appoints the prime minister (changed after the 2011 constitutional amendments), and the government and the parliament are accountable to the king, who has the right to dissolve the parliament (lower and upper chambers) and call for new elections. The king may amend laws passed by the parliament with the consent of the Constitutional Council.

The lower chamber performs legislative and monitoring roles. Concerning its legislative function, it discusses and approves draft bills proposed by the MPs, Chamber of Councilors members, and the government. While any member(s) of parliament can propose a bill, it must be presented and cleared by the government twenty days before its referral to the respective committee. Bills are then sent to the committees for study before they are referred to the Chamber of Councilors for discussion and approval. However, bills must be returned to the Chamber of Representatives for final approval, ratification, or further examination and deliberation. After a bill passes the floors, the king can approve, reject, or forward it for a public referendum.[24] A bill in Morocco also becomes law with the approval of the king (Lower Chamber's Internal Bylaws 2017). Between 2011 and 2016,

195 bills were submitted to the lower chamber for approval, eight of which were proposed by the Chamber of Councilors. Only 20 of 187 bills submitted to the lower house were passed.[25]

Regarding the lower chamber monitoring role, the body can establish ad hoc committees of inquiry to investigate the government's actions. Additionally, MPs may pose oral or written questions to the members or head of government.[26] According to the constitution, cabinet members must submit their responses within twenty days (thirty days if the question is directed to the head of the government).

In 2011, the monarchy witnessed substantial instability after the Arab uprisings. Waves of protests orchestrated by the February 20 Youth Movement swept the country.[27] The movement called for establishing a parliamentary monarchy and increasing individual freedoms and rights for minorities. As a result, the monarchy introduced constitutional reforms to appease the dissenting voices while retaining the power to oversee the armed forces and control foreign policy issues.[28] The constitutional reforms introduced measures to expand political and cultural rights to Morocco's ethnic minorities and women, strengthen party discipline, and provide further protection for the rights of the parliamentary opposition (Article 10). Additionally, the reforms strengthened the legislative role of the lower chamber by granting it the final decision on draft legislation. They stipulated that the party acquiring the plurality of seats in the lower chamber appoints the prime minister. On July 1, 2011, the new constitution was passed by popular vote, and the legislative elections took place in November 2011.

THE CASE OF JORDAN

THE LEGISLATIVE AND ELECTORAL LANDSCAPE

Jordan's 1952 constitution established individual freedoms and citizens' rights. Parties were allowed to form, and nine parties competed in the

1956 parliamentary elections. For the first time in the monarchy's history, a coalition government was formed, led by Sulieman al-Nabulsi following the victory of the Communist National Party.[29] Due to the domestic unrest and war with Israel, the parliament was suspended for more than three decades (1957–1989). The period also witnessed the imposition of martial law and a strict ban on political parties' formation and activities.[30] The deterioration of the economic conditions and the decline of international and regional support for the monarchy in the 1980s were the main catalysts for King Hussein's political reforms.[31] These reforms included lifting the political parties' ban, suspending the 1977 National Consultative Council, and recalling the Jordanian parliament in 1984.[32] During this time, the influence of the Islamists and tribes also increased in the electoral arena.[33]

The first parliamentary election took place in 1989 using the block vote/proportional representation system (i.e., the number of deputies elected from each district must equal the number of votes each voter can cast).[34] Citizens could vote for individual candidates and party lists.[35] While twelve female candidates ran for office for the first time in Jordan's history, which caused severe criticism from the Islamist forces, they all lost. Even though voter turnout was relatively high (53 percent), familial relationships and tribal affiliations heavily influenced voters' choices. Islamist candidates were the absolute winners of the 1989 elections and managed to secure 40 percent of the seats in the lower chamber.[36] This victory can be attributed to their organized campaigns and on-the-ground presence since 1957 when parties had been banned. In addition, leftist parties won about 16 percent of the seats.

The political parties law, drafted and promulgated in 1992, formally legalized political parties, making 1993 the first multiparty election in the monarchy since 1956.[37] About thirty new political parties emerged with various political and ideological stances; still, most candidates ran as independents and/or tribal affiliations.[38] The 1993 elections also witnessed the shift of the voting system to voting by single nontransferable vote (SNTV), where voters can cast only one vote regardless of the district magnitude—also known as a "one-person-one-vote" system (table 3.2). These changes

TABLE 3.2 Electoral politics in Jordan (1993–2016)

ELECTION YEAR	ELECTORAL LAW AND QUOTA STATUS	SIZE OF LEGISLATURE	NUMBER OF ELECTORAL DISTRICTS
1993–1997	Single nontransferable vote (SNTV) system; no gender or minorities quota	80 seats	21 districts
1997–2001	SNTV system; no quota	80 seats	21 districts
2003–2007 14th House of Representatives	SNTV system preserved; gender (6 seats) and minorities (12 seats: 3 seats for Chechens and Circassians and 9 seats for Christians) quota was introduced	110 seats	45 districts
2007–2009 15th House of Representatives	SNTV system preserved; no change in quotas	110 seats	45 districts
2010–2012 16th House of Representatives	SNTV system preserved; number of gender quota seats increased to 12 seats, while the minorities quota remained unchanged (12 seats)	120 seats	45 districts
2013–2016 17th House of Representatives	SNTV system amended; one proportional representation (PR) closed-list national district added; increase number of quota seats for women (15 seats) in addition to the 12 ethnic and religious minority quota seats	150 seats	45 districts in addition to one national PR district
2016–2020 18th House of Representatives	SNTV system amended; open-list PR system introduced; 15 seats reserved for women and 12 seats for ethnic and religious minorities	130 seats	23 electoral districts

Source: Author's calculations based on election data obtained from the Jordanian Ministry of Interior; House of Representatives, https://www.representatives.jo/Default/En; JP: Guide to Jordanian Politics Life, Phenix: Economic and Informatics Studies, http://jordanpolitics.org /en/home.

significantly limited the electoral prospects of the Islamists and leftists, leading to the overwhelming victory of candidates with strong tribal backgrounds and close ties with the regime. For almost two decades, elections were held under the SNTV system amid harsh opposition from the leftists, nationalists, and Islamist parties who continued to boycott elections to express their dissatisfaction with the status quo. A Jordanian expert in legislative politics described this electoral system as "a political crisis that we used to call—the crisis of the single vote."[39]

The 1997 elections witnessed a substantial decrease in voter turnout (47.5 percent compared to 55 percent in the 1993 elections) along with the boycott of the Muslim Brotherhood's political arm—the Islamic Action Front (IAF), which demanded the transition to a constitutional monarchy.[40] The 2003 election—the first since the death of King Hussein in 1999 and the dissolution of the lower house at the end of its four-year term in June 2000—was also administered under the SNTV law. The Islamists participated in the elections and won 17 seats (out of 110). The 2007 elections were also administered under the SNTV system; the Islamists won only 6 seats (out of 110) in this election. The king dissolved the 2007 parliament in November 2009 following complaints of MPs' corruption and inefficiency, and new elections took place in late 2010.

The 2010 elections (sixteenth legislature) took place under temporary election law.[41] Notably, several seats were allocated to Palestinian-majority urban districts, and some subdistricts were added. Initially, the primary purpose of this electoral amendment was to mitigate the effect of tribalism, open the political arena to fair competition, and promote political inclusion across the kingdom. Dissatisfied with the electoral amendment and the persistence of the one-man-one-vote electoral law, the opposition (mainly the IAF and a few leftist parties) boycotted the 2010 elections, which eventually led to the dominance of tribal and loyalist politics.[42]

In 2012, King Abdullah dissolved the parliament for the second time in three years after massive protests in 2010 and 2011, calling for economic and political reforms and eradicating corruption. Thus, the monarchy initiated a series of reforms to appease the public and opposition forces. The most relevant of these reforms was modifying the electoral system to include one national closed electoral list elected using a proportional representation (PR) system (table 3.2). As a Jordanian legal expert maintained,

> The Arab Spring occurred in 2011, and the people had democratic demands. A new electoral law was needed to fulfill the people's aspirations. The king decided to create the "Committee of National Freedom" led by Prime Minister Taher al-Masri, also the former president of the Chamber of Notables [senate]. The committee included all the political currents—the leftist, Islamist, nationalist parties, activists, and unions. It came up with suggestions for an electoral law that was forwarded to the government of Awn al-Khasawneh. The new law reformed the existing law [the single vote] and created a mixed law that splits up Jordan into single districts with 100 individual seats elected via the single vote [SNTV], and 27 seats were elected for the national level PR list.[43]

The 2013 elections (seventeenth legislature) witnessed the boycott of the IAF and a few leftist and youth parties (i.e., National Progressive Party, Popular Unity, and the Communist Party) in opposition to the continuation of the SNTV system. Opponents of the new law claimed that the newly introduced changes would further empower the tribal candidates and independents. Despite the boycott, the 2013 election was widely hailed by most national and international observers as being fair and free under the supervision of the Independent Election Committee (IEC).[44] The Islamic Centrist Party (ICP)—Wasat—participated in the elections and won three national and fourteen individual seats (about 11 percent of the total contested seats).

Jordan's 2016 electoral law replaced the SNTV system with an open-list PR system and eliminated the closed party list. It also reduced the number of seats in Parliament from 150 to 130, and the number of electoral districts decreased from forty-five to twenty-three. Under the 2016 law, each governorate constituted a district, with the most populated governorates divided into multiple districts. Like the 2012 electoral law, the allocation of parliamentary seats favored rural areas as there were more seats per voter in rural districts than in urban ones. While the 2013 electoral law changes aimed to strengthen the role of parties by introducing the closed PR list reserved for political parties, the 2016 open-list PR system led to the opposite effect, where individuals, rather than lists, won seats. Given the small number of districts, it became clear that only candidates placed on top of the electoral list would win seats. The IAF ended its boycott of the elections and participated in the 2016 elections. About fifty political parties competed in the elections. Only twenty-two candidates on party lists could win seats, out of 215 candidates representing the fifty parties. Political parties' representation in the legislature was merely 17 percent, most of which went to the Islamists. The IAF won ten seats, while the ICP acquired only five.[45]

The previous discussion shows how party representation has remained weak since the lift of the political parties ban three decades ago. Electoral and party laws ensure that the elected lower house favors independent and tribal candidates who focus on service provision over policy agendas and are less likely to challenge the monarchy.[46] In 2001, Ellen Lust-Okar described the political landscape in Jordan: "In both the 1950 and the 1990s, the linkages between political parties and the masses appear weak, whether measured by the parties' success at the polls, their ability to mobilize the masses in the streets, or their success in establishing media outcomes."[47] This description still accurately describes the political landscape in Jordan today, where parties remain fragmented with minimal party institutionalization.

WOMEN'S POLITICAL REPRESENTATION IN JORDAN

Jordanian women were granted the right to vote and run for office in 1974; however, they could not exercise their political rights due to the suspension of parliamentary life, as previously discussed.[48] It was not until the 1990s and the onset of a brief era of political liberalization that women could fully exercise their political and legal rights (table 3.3). This period also witnessed the proliferation of civil society organizations advocating for women's issues and legal reforms, such as the Arab Women's Federation (AWF). What is unique about the Jordanian experience—directly relevant to women's political representation—is that every assembly over the past decade was elected

TABLE 3.3 Women in the Jordanian legislature (1989–2016)

ELECTION YEAR	TOTAL QUOTA	TOTAL SEATS	WOMEN*	WOMEN ELECTED*	PERCENTAGE OF WOMEN ELECTED	WOMEN CANDIDATES	PERCENTAGE OF WOMEN CANDIDATES
1989	0	80	0	0	0	12/647	1.85%
1993	0	80	1	1	1.25%	3/534	0.6%
1997	0	80	0	0	0	17/561	3.1%
2003	6	110	6	0	5.5%	54/819	7.1%
2007	6	110	7	1	6%	NA	NA
2010	12	120	13	1	11%	NA	NA
2013	15	150	18	3	12%	NA	NA
2016	15	130	19	4	15%	252	20.1%
2020	15	130	15	0	12%	360	21.5%

* "Total women" refers to the number of women elected through the quota as well as the competitive seats. "Women elected" refers only to the number of women elected to non-quota (competitive) seats.
Source: Author's calculations based on election data from the Jordanian Ministry of Interior; House of Representatives, available at http://www.representatives.jo/ar; JP: Guide to Jordanian Politics Life, Phenix: Economic and Informatics Studies, available at http://jordanpolitics.org/en/home.

based on a different electoral law (table 3.2). This reality has contributed to the marginalization of female contenders and minimized their chances of winning seats. As eloquently put by a former female legislator in Jordan, "We [female candidates in Jordan] are alone. We are not with them [ruling male elites]. Sometimes the laws, instead of supporting a party life or political reform, on the contrary, lead to a larger gap in society."[49]

Following the reopening of the parliament in 1989, women participated in the 1993 elections for the first time, with three female candidates running for office. Only one woman, Toujan al-Faisal, was able to win an ethnic quota seat and became the first female legislator in the lower house (Amman, District 3).[50] The victory of al-Faisal encouraged more women to run during the 1997 elections. Seventeen women ran for office, yet none won a single seat.[51] Notably, female candidates ran as independents under the SNTV system with minimal tribal and/or party support.

In response to the female candidates' inability to win seats in the 1997 elections—coupled with mounting pressure from international donors, women's movements,[52] and activists—a sixteen-member committee was formed in early 2003 to study the applicability of the quota system in Jordan.[53] A few months later, the committee's recommendations promulgated the 2003 Election Law No. 11.[54] According to the amended law, six seats were reserved for women regardless of the geographical distribution or electoral district.[55] Even though the quota seats were allocated as a minimum threshold so that women could still run for (and win) competitive seats, not a single woman could win beyond the mandated quota seats in the 2003 elections. This issue was mainly attributed to the persistence of the single-member (SNTV) electoral system that favored tribal candidates and independents with tribal support.[56]

Additionally, the election of women was restricted to smaller districts with the least population density, which granted the elected female legislators minimal political influence and decision-making power.[57] As one of my female interviewees maintained, "The [2003] quota system had a defect. It encouraged small districts to nominate female representatives. They were all from certain governorates with small districts versus, for example, Amman, Jerash, al-Zarqa, and Ajnoun. The North and Center did not have as much female representation as the South because these [southern governorates] were smaller."[58] Although the number of MPs increased from 80 to 110 during the 2003 elections (with the increase in the number of districts from twenty-one to forty-five), female MPs only constituted 5.5 percent of the lower chamber.[59] During the 2007 elections, women retained the six quota seats; however, for the first time, one female MP could win a competitive seat.[60] Falak Jamani, who won a quota seat in 2003, succeeded in garnering support and competing in the 2007 elections to win a competitive seat in the district of Madaba.

The number of seats reserved for women increased from six to twelve in the 2010 elections, so every governorate in Jordan had a quota seat. Several seats were added to the Palestinian-majority urban districts and some "subdistricts" to increase the total seats from 110 to 120. One female candidate, Mudar Badran, won a competitive seat for the third time ever (table 3.3).

The 2012 election law changes introduced an additional national closed-list district, with twenty-seven additional seats open for party candidates (i.e., voters would cast one vote for one candidate under the SNTV system at the district level and an additional vote for candidates competing under the proportional electoral system at the national level). The 2012 electoral changes also increased the women's quota from twelve to fifteen seats to include three Bedouin districts (fifteen seats are reserved for female candidates who acquire the largest number of votes in their district).[61] In addition, since then, women have been eligible to win a competitive seat if they receive the largest number of votes in a district. If this occurs, the quota seat is transferred to the female candidate with the second-highest number of votes. Finally, women can be nominated by a party to take one of the twenty-seven seats reserved for political parties, with no impact on the quota seats.[62] Fifteen females acquired the reserved quota seats in 2013, and three additional women succeeded in winning competitive seats. Two female candidates won seats under the SNTV system, while one female candidate, Rula Al Huroub, won a seat under the national party list (i.e., Stronger Jordan Party).[63]

As previously noted, the 2016 elections were administered under a mixed system with an open PR list that replaced the closed one. The seats reserved for women and minorities remained unchanged from the previous elections (see table 3.3). However, the new open-list system encouraged the heads of the lists to include women to acquire more votes for the lists, even if women received a modest number of votes. A former female deputy in the 2016 legislature stated, "The new electoral law encouraged the heads of electoral lists to nominate women, spend money on their campaigns, and place them in winnable positions on the list."[64] As a result, women won four competitive seats in addition to the fifteen mandated quota seats. In chapters 4 and 5, I analyze the committee assignments and the legislative behavior of the female deputies in the 2010, 2013, and 2016 legislatures.

In sum, numerous obstacles in the Jordanian electoral arena prevent women's equitable access to political power. Undeniably, several sociocultural barriers continue to negatively affect women's political representation, such as mass perceptions of women's politicians, the rivalry between women's movements, the lack of coordination between female politicians and women's organizations, and female candidates' lack of financial resources to run successful campaigns to mobilize voters and compete in male-dominant districts.[65] However, female candidates are unable to access the political realm mainly due to deep-rooted structural and institutional impediments, such as the current single-member electoral system, the disproportional electoral districts, the general mistrust in political parties and the electoral process, and the state's coordinated efforts to weaken political parties by reinforcing the ethnic divide between citizens of Transjordanian and Palestinian origin.[66]

Female politicians in Jordan are further disadvantaged by the existing political/institutional context, given their persistent marginalization from the higher echelons of power. The weakness of political parties and the lack of party support for women's candidates continue to have a detrimental impact on women's political power. One of the few female Islamist legislators who entered the 2016 parliament as part of a political party described her experience: "The party had a big role, and my family had a major role too. So if I would calculate this numerically, I received from the party about 5,000 votes, and I received around 2,000 votes from my family."[67] Another former legislator representing one of the established leftist parties responded to my question about the most important entity that led to her winning a quota seat in the 2010 legislature by asserting that it was "The party, of course! We represent a political, nationalist framework that is very important. They [party base] all helped me without asking because they had known me for so long. The NGOs did not help me at all. Nor did I request [help] from them. The Jordanian Women's Union helped me greatly, but that is it."[68] While the implementation of gender quotas in Jordan has facilitated women's access to political power, the existing political landscape has limited their success beyond the mandated quota system and their power and influence in the legislative assembly, as I demonstrate in the following chapters in this book.

THE CASE OF KUWAIT

THE LEGISLATIVE AND ELECTORAL LANDSCAPE

Kuwait is a semiconstitutional monarchy with one of the longest histories of constitutionalism dating back to the 1920s.[69] Kuwait's democratization experience is unique, and it continues to have one of the strongest legislative bodies in the Arab world. Following the discovery of oil in the 1920s, Kuwait soon became a case of extreme rentierism (i.e., oil abundance combined with high per-capita exports).[70] The country's economy depends heavily on oil revenues and significantly lacks the economic diversification evident in many other GCC countries, such as Qatar and the United Arab Emirates.[71] The oil wealth transformed the country, but most importantly, it redefined the power relations between the ruling family and the wealthy merchant class,[72] which used to play an essential role in the decision-making process during the early 1900s.[73] While the wealth accumulated from these discoveries has helped consolidate the ruling family's power as the main controller of the oil revenues, these resources have also led to an unprecedented boom in infrastructure and social development.[74]

The revival of parliamentary life in Kuwait occurred in 1962 under Emir Abdullah al-Salim al-Sabah (1950–1965). Before gaining independence from British rule, two legislative councils were dissolved,[75] mainly due to conflicts between the merchant class and the ruling family and external threats posed by the ruler of Iraq.[76] However, the country's parliamentary life was finally restored in 1961 with the ratification of Kuwait's first postindependence constitution. The electoral law was later discussed on May 22, 1962, during the seventh meeting of the Constitutional Committee of the Constituent Assembly (an elected assembly charged with writing the constitution) and was approved within six months. According to the newly enacted law (No. 35/1962), the country was divided into ten districts, and each eligible voter was required to vote for five different candidates (a total of fifty MPs) in their respective districts.[77] Importantly, this electoral arrangement was implemented during the country's first postindependence elections in 1963 and lasted until 1975. Whereas Kuwait's 1962 constitution established unprecedented civil liberties for all citizens, including the principle of equality among all citizens, it did not grant women the right to vote or participate in elections.

A major political crisis occurred in 1976, leading to the unilateral dissolution of the 1975 assembly (Fourth Legislative Assembly) and the suspension of several articles of the 1962 constitution by Emir Sabah al-Salim al-Sabah (1965–1977). While the emir justified this move as a reaction to the lack of cooperation between the executive and legislative branches, the dissolution of the assembly was mainly fueled by the rise of the opposition in the parliament that started to pose a direct threat to the monarchy.[78] During the period of dissolution—which lasted until 1981—the emir took a series of steps to consolidate power and fragment the opposition. This era also witnessed the rise of the Islamist movement. The Sabah family, hoping to curb the opposition and silence the liberal voices in the assembly, closely supported the Islamists in the 1970s and facilitated their ascendency to power in the National Assembly and across different financial and leadership positions.[79] Meanwhile, the emir sought to further weaken the opposition by enfranchising the Bedouin and tribal populations, granting them Kuwaiti citizenship—and thus voting and political rights—before the 1981 elections, a phenomenon that is widely known among scholars as the "desertization" of Kuwaiti society.[80] By the mid-1980s, the Islamists joined forces with the tribal and Bedouin figures and created a close alliance—an issue that continues to impact women's political representation today.

In addition, significant changes were introduced to the electoral system during that period of dissolution as the emir issued decree No. 99/1980, which stipulated the redrawing of the constituencies' boundaries. According to the amended law, the country was divided into twenty-five districts instead of ten, and all eligible voters were required to vote for two candidates.[81] The 1980 electoral system had numerous drawbacks that continued to mar the electoral process for over two decades until it was finally amended in 2006.[82] For example, the twenty-five-district system facilitated the process of vote transfer and vote buying, given the small district magnitude.[83] It gave the tribal primaries the power to determine who would represent the districts and control almost half of the twenty-five districts.[84] As a result, candidates were chosen based on family ties and name recognition rather than on merit and competence.[85]

Moreover, the disproportionate redrawing of the electoral districts granted many districts more electoral weight than others, and the government was later accused of fragmenting the opposition's support base to empower the progovernment and tribal candidates in the newly elected parliament. Finally, because of the small district magnitudes and the relatively small number of voters per district, the country witnessed the rise of the phenomenon of "service deputies"—deputies mainly concerned with providing services to their constituents to guarantee reelection, even if against the public good.[86]

Another crisis rocked the parliamentary life in Kuwait in 1986, ending with Emir Sheikh Jaber al-Ahmad al-Jaber al-Sabah's (1977–2006) dissolution of the parliament for the second time in a decade. This second unconstitutional dissolution occurred amid a tense political landscape on the regional level due to the Iran-Iraq War (1980–1988) and its implications for Kuwait's security.[87] On the domestic level, the country faced an escalating political crisis. Many opposition figures who failed to join the assembly in 1981 returned to the political arena in 1985, forming an imminent threat to the government and the ruling family.

After the end of the 1990 Iraqi invasion of Kuwait, the parliament was restored in 1992 under Law No. 99/1980 following an agreement brokered between the opposition and the emir while in exile. Both parties agreed to reinstate parliamentary life once the war ended if the preoccupation electoral law remained intact.[88] What was truly remarkable about Kuwait's postwar assemblies (especially the Seventh and Eighth Assemblies) was the reemergence of the Islamist and tribal figures.

Amidst mounting tension between the liberals and the Islamist forces in 1999, the Eighth National Assembly was dissolved for the third time in the country's history, and elections were scheduled within two months.[89] In contrast to the postwar assemblies, the Ninth Assembly (1999–2003) witnessed the rise of liberal forces with the victory of sixteen liberal candidates for the first time. In 2003, Islamist and tribal candidates managed to dominate the Tenth Assembly again by winning seventeen seats each.[90] In contrast, the liberal and independent candidates won seven and nine seats, respectively.[91]

Dissatisfaction with the twenty-five-district law continued to negatively impact the electoral process. Following disagreements between the opposition and the government on the proposed number of constituencies, the Tenth Assembly was dissolved in May 2006, and a new assembly (2006–2008) was elected in June, still under the twenty-five-district electoral law.[92]

Shortly afterward, a new electoral law (No. 42/2006) was passed to divide the electoral districts into five constituencies with ten seats each (table 3.4). Each voter was required to select four candidates in their respective districts instead of two. The new electoral law, implemented in the 2008 elections, did little to balance the ideological and political polarization within the assembly. In contrast, the new system reinforced the existing sectarian and tribal allegiances, worsened by the electoral districts' persistent geographical imbalance.[93] For the fourth time in less than a decade, the emir dissolved the National Assembly. This move followed a heightened political crisis between the government (mainly the prime minister) and the opposition on corruption allegations. The emir called for new elections in 2009, which opened the door for more moderate and progovernment voices in the Thirteenth National Assembly.[94]

TABLE 3.4 History of the Kuwaiti National Assembly (1963–2016)

YEAR	LEGISLATIVE ASSEMBLY	DISSOLVED	NUMBER OF ELECTORAL DISTRICTS	NUMBER OF VOTES PER CITIZEN
1963–1967	1st	No	10	5
1967–1970	2nd	No	10	5
1971–1975	3rd	No	10	5
1975–1976	4th	Yes	10	5
1981–1985	5th	No	25	2
1985–1986	6th	Yes	25	2
1992–1996	7th	No	25	2
1996–1999	8th	Yes	25	2
1999–2003	9th	No	25	2
2003–2006	10th	Yes	25	2
2006–2008	11th	Yes	25	2
2008–2009	12th	Yes	5	4
2009–2011	13th	Yes	5	4
February 2012	NA	Cancelled	5	4
December 2012	NA	Cancelled	5	1
2013–2016	14th	No	5	1

Sources: Michael Herb, Kuwait Politics Database, available at http://www.kuwaitpolitics.org/; National Assembly, Kuwait, available at https://www.kna.kw; Raqib 50, available at http://www.raqib50.com/.

Conflicts continued, with friction between the secular voices and the tribal and Islamist forces on the one hand and disputes between the government and the opposition on the other. It led to significant turmoil in the legislative arena and the dissolution of four parliaments within six years (2006–2012). After the dissolution of the Thirteenth Assembly (2009–2011), a new round of elections in February 2012 resulted in yet another opposition-dominated National Assembly (thirty-five of the fifty members were from the opposition). The 2012 assembly was revoked in July following a historic constitutional court ruling against the emir's dissolution of the 2009 assembly.[95]

During the legislative recess, a new royal decree was promulgated in October (Law No. 20/2012) to keep the number of electoral districts at five while reducing the number of votes from four to only one. It changed the election process to a SNTV system to limit voting based on blocs and weaken the opposition.[96] This royal decree sparked a massive outcry from the opposition: Islamists, liberals, and nationalists who vowed to boycott the elections. Nevertheless, the government called for elections in December 2012 amid protests and sit-ins. Both liberal and Islamist opposition members boycotted the elections, and a new legislature was elected without any traditional opposition figures.[97] In response to an appeal against the decree, the Constitutional Court invalidated the December 2012 elections on a technicality on June 16, 2013, but maintained the electoral amendment of one vote per citizen. On July 27, 2013, new elections were held with a feeble opposition presence.

WOMEN'S POLITICAL REPRESENTATION IN KUWAIT

The amendment of Election Law No. 35/1962 in 2005 granted women the right to vote and run for office, opening the door for female candidates to participate in elections for the first time. In 2006 and 2008, female candidates ran for elections but failed to win seats.[98] It was not until 2009 that women managed to make a historic victory by winning 8 percent of the seats in a highly contested election. However, women's political presence has plunged over the past decade (table 3.5). Women continue to be

TABLE 3.5 History of women in parliament in Kuwait (2005–2020)

ELECTION YEAR	TOTAL SEATS	TOTAL WOMEN	WOMEN ELECTED	PERCENTAGE OF WOMEN ELECTED	WOMEN CANDIDATES	PERCENTAGE OF WOMEN CANDIDATES
2006	50	1	0	0	28/252	11.1%
2008	50	0	0	0	27/275	9.9%
2009	50	5	4	8%	16/210	7.6%
December 2012	50	4	3	6%	15/387	3.8%
February 2012	50	0	0	0	23/286	8%
July 2013	50	1	1	2%	8/308	2.5%
2016	50	1	1	2%	14/293	4.8%
2020	50	0	0	0	33/395	8.3%

Sources: Inter-Parliamentary Union. IPU Parline Database: Kuwait (Majles Al-Ommah), http://archive
.ipu.org/parline-e/reports/2171_A.htm; National Assembly, Kuwait, November 20, 2016; Raqib 50, http://
www.raqib50.com/parliaments/8/committees.

sidelined from political power as they are not part of the dominant camps in Kuwaiti politics: the tribes, the conservative pro-regime forces, and the Islamist opposition.

In contrast to their modest gains in the electoral arena, women have made significant strides in the socioeconomic realm over the past decades. Oil wealth has created an unprecedented boom in human and social development, which had a tremendous impact on women's education and integration into the labor force.[99] Since the 1950s, Kuwaiti women have played a critical role in the public sphere by establishing charitable and social welfare organizations. Even though most women's associations in Kuwait are primarily controlled and funded by the state, they have elected boards, written constitutions, and paid membership.[100] The 1990 Gulf War with Iraq was a turning point for women, as they played a significant role during the war and in the postwar construction period.[101] Currently, females comprise almost half of the labor force, and female students outnumber males in higher education institutions in Kuwait.[102]

Middle East and North Africa (MENA) gender scholars often blame patriarchal and cultural attitudes for women's inability to access political power.[103] While these views may offer partial explanations, they fail to explain why women were able to excel in most aspects of the public sphere except for politics in Kuwait. In reality, the existing autocratic structures and the regime's persistent efforts to consolidate power and marginalize opposing voices have created an electoral landscape that is hostile to women. On the one hand, the demographic changes in the 1960s and 1970s, spearheaded by the regime to consolidate power, resulted in unbalanced gender dynamics. As scholars Yagoub Yousif Al-Kandari and Ibrahim Naji Al-Hadben maintain, Kuwait is a clear example of a "heterogeneous society that has divisions across tribal, as well as sectarian lines."[104] They argue that tribalism and sectarianism are passive concepts but harm social development.[105] Women's rights, in general, and political rights are integral parts of the social development process; however, they were negatively impacted by the clash between the different forces of modernization and tradition. This clash became even more evident following the naturalization of thousands of Bedouins in the 1960s and 1970s as part of the ruling family's attempt to broaden their electoral support base, which was threatened by growing opposition forces, and build a solid demographic network capable of confronting a possible Iraqi threat to Kuwait's internal security.[106] The desertization of politics in Kuwait (i.e., the integration of tribal and Bedouin populations into the society) brought a set of conservative norms and traditional values to the country that further contributed to the marginalization of women and limited their roles in the political sphere.[107] This is demonstrated in the inability of female candidates to win seats in the tribe-dominated fourth and fifth districts. Over the past decade, female politicians were generally elected from the less conservative districts, namely the first and second districts.

On the other hand, the impact of the Bedouin culture on Kuwait's sociopolitical landscape was also accompanied by a sharp rise in Islamist politics during the 1970s. Following the ebb of the nationalist and pan-Arab waves during the 1970s, Kuwait—like most parts of the MENA region—witnessed the surge of Islamist forces actively competing in the electoral arena. These forces assumed leadership positions and gained overwhelming grassroots support, aided by the ruling regime as it attempted to bolster its support base in the face of liberal and populist opposition.

According to Shafeeq N. Ghabra, the Islamists were the only organized group in the 1980s, and they continued to shape the political arena until the Iraqi invasion in 1990.[108] The official establishment of the Islamic Constitutional Movement (ICM)—the political wing of the Muslim Brotherhood—in 1991 in the aftermath of Kuwait's liberation from the Iraqi invasion allowed them to compete more effectively in elections and make significant gains in the National Assembly.[109] Islamists occupied about 30 percent of the 1992 and 1996 assemblies.

Interestingly, the Islamist and tribal candidates won over two-thirds of the 2003 assembly seats.[110] Most Islamist blocs rely on women's votes and support, yet these groups have never perceived women as viable political candidates and are opposed to women's political inclusion.[111] A former female candidate in the 2020 legislative elections stated, "Islamists use their [women's] votes to gain support. Women bring them votes, but they never field women for elections. They do not want to gamble because they might lose their seat if they nominate a woman. For them, women candidates are not the 'winning horse.'"[112] A similar point was made by a former female legislator in the 2009 assembly: "They [Islamists] are ok with women working for them to ensure that they [Islamists] win seats. Meanwhile, they have issues nominating women because they believe it is against religious traditions! I think this is a double standard! If you [Islamists] are against women, why do you rely on them to win? They win because of women's votes! This is based on actual numbers!"[113]

In 2006, women ran in elections for the first time under the twenty-five districts law (Decree No. 99/1980) and could not win any seats. Following the dissolution of the 2006 (i.e., eleventh) legislature in 2008, a new electoral law (No. 42/2006) was passed to divide the electoral districts into five constituencies with ten seats each. Each voter, however, was required to vote for four different candidates in their districts instead of two. The 2008 elections for the Twelfth Assembly took place under the new law. The creation of larger districts had many negative consequences that impacted the chances of candidates not being part of a renowned tribe or the considerably more organized Islamist blocs. As a result, large tribes currently control two of the five districts, drastically reducing female candidates' chances of winning (mainly the fourth and fifth districts).

The 2012 electoral law change (Law No. 20/2012) reduced the number of votes per citizen from four to one and enacted the SNTV system. While these changes aimed to limit voting based on blocs and weaken the opposition, the shift to the "one-person-one-vote" system (i.e., SNTV) has further constrained women's access to power. Voters under the new law chose to cast their votes for their preferred tribal/familial candidates but not for the female candidates in their respective districts. Only one female candidate, Safa al-Hashem, won a seat in the 2013 elections and later resigned in May 2014.[114]

The 2016 parliamentary elections further illustrate the effect of this political landscape on women's access to political power. On October 6, 2016, the emir dissolved Parliament following a confrontation between legislators and the government over a plan to enforce strict austerity measures.[115] According to the monarchy's constitution, elections must be held within sixty days of the dissolution. While fifteen female candidates ran for election, only one female candidate, Safa al-Hashem, won and became the first woman in Kuwait's history to win a seat in two consecutive rounds. Women's gains were marginal due to the limited time and resources to organize electoral campaigns and mobilize voters. It was a formidable challenge for female newcomers to build name recognition, mobilize voters, establish electoral bases, and win supporters, in addition to the other obstacles that female political contenders typically face in elections such as lack of financial resources, ongoing national challenges, as well as the prevailing negative views about the performance of MPs more generally.[116] A former female legislator in Kuwait's 2009 assembly argues,

> The frequent dissolution of the National Assembly is a major issue [for women] for many reasons. First, women do not have enough time to prepare. Women often announce their candidacy when the new elections are announced! Most women lack previous political experience, social and community ties, and connections with existing power structures. It is almost impossible for them to win! Second, the short period to run the

elections [sixty days] negatively affects even independent men with no organized support bases. The Salafis and Islamists have organized support bases. They are always ready.[117]

The frequent dissolution of the Kuwaiti Assembly, combined with the absence of gender quotas and institutionalized political parties, continues to limit women's presence in politics. Better-organized tribal groups and the highly institutionalized Islamist bloc, with their established support bases and mobilization capacity, are reaping the gains of the hastily organized elections at the expense of female and other less connected candidates. For now, the outcome of Kuwaiti women's battle for political representation remains uncertain because of the instability of the electoral landscape and the unwillingness of the male political elites to cede power and/or to allow the introduction of gender quota reforms in the lower chamber.

THE CASE OF MOROCCO

THE LEGISLATIVE AND ELECTORAL LANDSCAPE

Morocco is also one of the first MENA countries that granted political parties the right to form and compete in national and local elections— as stipulated by Article 3 of the country's postindependence Constitution. This move was motivated mainly by King Hassan II's (1961–1999) desire to avoid the concentration of power in one party, constrain political competition, and uphold ultimate power and authority. Since the postindependence era, political parties have attracted the economic and political elites[118] and the nationalists who were part of the independence movement from Spain and France.[119] However, parties were weak and detached from most Moroccan citizens. King Hassan retained the ultimate power and relied on the legislative process to select allies and political opponents. The electoral process was a means to constrain the opposition and favor the regime's allies through co-optation, gerrymandering of electoral districts, and vote-buying practices.[120]

During the 1990s, with mounting economic and social pressure, the monarchy changed its approach and adopted what Denoeux and Maghraoui call "the strategy of political dualism." This strategy focused on promoting modern forms of democratic governance, such as opening the space for civil society organizations, free press, fair and free elections, and accountable government. Meanwhile, it strengthened the monarchy's authority as the ultimate arbiter and decision-maker, given its religious authority and distance from electoral politics and "day-to-day policymaking."[121] This strategy manifested in the 1992 constitutional reforms and the 1996 constitutional referendum. In September 1996, a constitutional amendment replaced the previous unicameral legislative system with a bicameral chamber and it was approved by a popular referendum. Thus, several reforms were introduced to the 1997 elections—the last legislative elections under the reign of King Hassan II. In August 1997, the lower chamber unanimously adopted two laws that governed the administration and organization of elections for both chambers. King Hassan also recommended that electoral majorities alternate power in the lower chamber (i.e., alternance government).

Elections took place on November 14, 1997. Candidates were elected from 325 single-member districts (compared to 222 districts in 1993) via a simple majority vote.[122] Each voter cast one vote, and voter turnout was roughly 58 percent. An alternance government led by the Socialist Union of Popular Forces (USFP) leader, Abd-Alrahman al-Youssifi, assumed power in 1998. A former female legislator stated, "Being part of the opposition for more than 40 years before assuming power, Youssifi was subject to imprisonment and harassment by the regime for a long period. When he assumed power, we all believed that was a genuine move by King Hassan II to democratize the country and open the door for more genuine reforms."[123]

The accession of King Mohammad VI to power in July 1999 raised hopes of a new beginning for the democratization process in the country. A former female legislator affiliated with the USFP stated,

The death of King Hassan II and a new young king coming to power opened new opportunities for reconciliation, reform, and genuine change. When King Mohammad came to power, we had a government headed by an opposition leftist party. A series of reconciliation efforts immediately took place, a reconciliation with the past and the major violations of the 70s where opponents were detained and tortured for their [political] stances. The king sought to reconcile with the entire society and established the Committee of Justice and Reconciliation. Other steps were taken to establish the Amazigh culture and women's rights.[124]

King Mohammad continued his father's legacy and maintained a "controlled pluralism" system that combines monarchical ultimate power while opening space for political parties and a competitive electoral process.[125] The 2002 elections were the first to occur under King Mohammad VI. The lower chamber's 325 seats were open for direct elections for the first time using the closed-list PR system. Two hundred ninety-five seats were elected in 95 multimember local districts, whereas 30 of the 325 seats were reserved for women through an informal agreement between the parties and the government but not codified in law.[126] Electoral thresholds were placed for parties to be represented in parliament: 6 percent for local districts and 3 percent for national lists. Voters cast two votes: one local vote for their multimember constituency and one national vote for the reserved seats.

The alternance government—a government headed by the leader of the political party with the plurality of votes after the lower chamber's general elections—took place under Hassan II's reign but was quickly disrupted under King Mohammad VI.[127] The new king established his right to appoint the prime minister regardless of the parties' electoral gains. Thus, the 2002 elections resulted in appointing a technocrat, Driss Jettou, as the prime minister even though the USFP had won the plurality of the votes, albeit by a small margin.

Whereas elections have enabled the monarch and political elites to build alliances and broaden their clientelistic networks of power, parties continued to compete in both local and national elections under the reign of King Mohammad.[128] Morocco has about thirty-five political parties with diverse ideological and political affiliations. They can be classified into two main types: administrative and opposition parties.[129] Administrative parties are established with the palace's support and are predominantly pro-regime. They include the Popular Movement (MP), Constitutional Union/Unity (UC), National Rally of Independents (RNI), and Authenticity and Modernity (PAM).

In contrast, the opposition parties include the nationalist parties, such as Istiqlal (PI), and the Socialist Union of Popular Forces (USFP), the left-leaning Party of Progress and Socialism (PPS) in addition to the Islamist Justice and Development Party (PJD). Despite the absence of party system institutionalization, parties in Morocco are stable with considerable levels of party institutionalization (V-Party 2020). Parties have persisted over the past decades, notwithstanding the regime's attempts to weaken their presence and inhibit their ability to build alliances.

The 2007 election was deemed the fairest and most transparent in the country's history.[130] The Istiqlal Party won the plurality of seats (fifty-two seats), and its leader, Abbas al-Fassi, became the prime minister and led a coalition government that included the Socialist Union of Popular Forces (USFP), Party of Progress and Socialism (PPS), and National Rally of Independents (RNI). The Islamist PJD won 49 seats.[131]

The Islamists in Morocco gained significant power following the Arab uprisings. In the 2011 legislative elections, the Justice and Development Party (PJD) won the plurality of seats (107 of 395 seats), and the leader of the party, Abdelilah Benkirane, became the new prime minister. Benkirane led a new coalition government with the Istiqlal Party, the Party of Progress and Socialism (PPS), and the Popular Movement. In 2016, PJD won almost one-third of the seats in the 395-member Parliament with a 43 percent voter turnout. With this victory, the PJD was the first Islamist party in Morocco's modern history to lead two consecutive governments.[132]

As I illustrate in the following section, Morocco is an influential case for female political representation with considerably high levels of institutionalized parties. While I make the case in this book that Morocco's institutionalized parties (vis-à-vis the other cases in the book and the MENA region) have produced a favorable set of outcomes for women's political power and substantive representation over the past two decades, it is essential to emphasize that Morocco is an autocratic state with a "controlled pluralist" electoral system where the monarchy and its close circle of allies (i.e., the *makhzan*) hold ultimate power, which has prevented the establishment of a strong party system.[133]

WOMEN'S POLITICAL REPRESENTATION IN MOROCCO

The postindependence constitution promulgated in 1962 granted citizens fundamental civil rights, including freedom of movement, association, and speech (Chapter 1, Article 9), and granted men and women equal political and economic rights. Women have been allowed to vote and run for office in Morocco since 1963. However, parties and voters did not view them as credible political candidates. Only at the advent of the twenty-first century could women play a substantive role in politics.

Notably, Morocco has one of the region's most vibrant women's movements, with origins as early as 1946, to "feminize" and democratize the public sphere.[134] In the 1960s, women formed professional organizations and women's associations, while others joined the ranks of the leftist parties. As maintained by a prominent female leader in the leftist USFP, "We must acknowledge the important role played by political parties' female members. Most of the leaders of the women's organizations came from the parties' ranks. The movement focused on two main demands: women's empowerment in the political and decision-making realms and the introduction of far-reaching reforms to the existing gender inegalitarian laws."[135]

A transformation in gender power relations occurred in the 1990s with the rise of women's participation in politics and the flourishing of women's movements, which were influenced by the global call for women's rights and gender equity. Whereas the push for women's rights developed from within the country, the monarchy supported the demands of the feminist movement and viewed it as an opportunity to solidify power and marginalize the opposition.[136] In 1992, a coalition of women's groups (including labor unions) gathered over one million signatures on a petition calling for the reform of the Code of Personal Status (i.e., Mudawana). The conservative and Islamist factions rallied their supporters to block any change in the highly patriarchal, sharia-based laws. Morocco's political parties, even secular opposition parties, declined to support the petition campaign. Still, the movement strongly pressured King Hassan II, and he eventually backed a more modest version of the suggested reforms in 1993.[137] In 2001, King Mohammad ordered a royal commission to review the family law. Motivated by the vigor and strength of the feminist movements and the king's desire to curb the power of the Islamists in the aftermath of the 2003 Casablanca bombings, substantial reforms were introduced to the Mudawana in 2004, which was deemed a sweeping victory for the feminist movement.

Regarding women's political representation, a committee for the participation of women in political life was formed in 1993 under King Hassan II to offer recommendations to promote women's representation in elected bodies.[138] Two women from the Istiqlal Party and USFP, representing the districts of Casablanca and Fez, entered the Moroccan parliament for the first time in the 1993 elections (table 3.6).[139] In 1997, two female candidates from Casablanca affiliated with the USFP won seats.

In contrast to the cases of Jordan and Kuwait, gender quota reforms were implemented by the political parties that enjoyed established organizational and mobilization structures. In 2002, a "gentlemen's agreement" between the political parties, backed by the new king, was concluded to reserve thirty seats for women on their electoral lists. After the introduction of reserved seats in 2002, the percentage of women in parliament jumped from less than 1 percent to more than 10 percent (table 3.6). In 2009, Nouzha Skalli of Morocco's Party of Progress and Socialism and the minister of Solidarity, Women, and Social Development in El-Fassi's government (2007–2012) led the efforts to push for a gender quota on the local level.[140] In the 2009 elections, a 12 percent gender quota was introduced in local elections, which increased to 30 percent in 2015.

In the aftermath of the Arab uprisings, as part of the 2011 constitutional amendments, Morocco increased the number of reserved seats for women,

TABLE 3.6 Women in parliament in Morocco (1993–present)

ELECTION YEAR	QUOTA	TOTAL SEATS	NUMBER OF WOMEN IN THE LOWER CHAMBER	PERCENTAGE OF WOMEN IN THE LOWER CHAMBER	WOMEN CANDIDATES	PERCENTAGE OF WOMEN CANDIDATES
1993	0	222	2	0.9%	33	1.62%
1997	0	325	2	0.62%	69	2.09%
2002	30	325	35	10.77%	266	4.53%
2007	30	325	34	10.46%	269[a]/6,691	4%
2011	60	395	67	16.96%	1,626[b]/7,102	22.9%[c]
2016	60	395	81	20.50%	NA/6,992	NA
2021	90	395	96	24.05%	2,329/6,833	34.08%

Sources: Data based on author's calculation; Darhour and Dahlerup (2013); NDI Reports 2007, 2011; House of Representatives, Morocco, available at http://www.chambredesrepresentants.ma/ar/; TAFRA, available at http://tafra.ma/.

[a]This number does not include the women nominated on national lists.

[b]This number includes women who ran for national and local district lists.

[c]Only 5.24 percent of the local lists were headed by women.

which guaranteed them 60 of the 395 seats in the lower chamber. According to this electoral reform, the 60 reserved seats for women (in addition to the 30 youth quota seats reserved for candidates under age forty) are elected through closed national lists with a 3 percent threshold. The remaining 305 seats are elected from 91 multimember local constituencies with a 6 percent threshold. Remarkably, only 5.24 percent of the local districts' lists were headed by women.[141] Still, for the first time, women won ten nonquota seats (i.e., local districts' seats) in the 2016 elections (mostly elected from the PJD) compared to four and seven seats in 2007 and 2011, respectively.

Furthermore, the 2016 amendment of the organic law that stipulated the alternation of male and female candidates on the youth quota lists allowed women to win eleven additional seats. Thus, women's representation in the lower chamber reached a record of 20.5 percent (eighty-one seats total). In 2021, the youth quota list was revoked, but the number of women reserved seats increased to ninety. Furthermore, women were able to win six nonquota seats (table 3.6).

Notwithstanding their substantial gains, many challenges continue to face women in the Moroccan electoral landscape. First, the patronage-based nature of politics limits women's ability to access nonquota seats.[142] A former female legislator critiques the opaque nature of parties' nomination processes, the predominance of patronage politics, and the exclusion of women from decision-making processes within the parties' ranks and states: "Realistically speaking, the opportunities that women have are very different from the opportunities that men have."[143] Moreover, women's increased political participation continues to have a limited impact on democratizing decision-making procedures within parties.[144]

Second, the fact that women are elected on a separate national list that tends to be concentrated in major urban centers limits their ability to secure a robust electoral base necessary to build sustainable political influence and increase their reelection prospects.[145] In my interviews with female legislators from different political parties in Morocco, women often expressed frustration with parties' tight control over the candidates' nomination process in the local/competitive districts. A former female legislator who won a youth quota seat in 2011 maintains, "I think the biggest challenge is to get re-elected. I was elected on the national list, but it is difficult to come back knowing that if you want to compete for the local district, there are already one or two people ahead of you. They [party leaders] would say, 'Okay, wait for your turn; we better give this man a chance to run, not you.'"[146]

Third, while research has found that national-level quotas have successfully increased women's numerical representation, these policies have marginally challenged males' domination of the political arena.[147] Liddell claims that while gender quotas in Morocco increased women's interest in politics and access to higher-level positions more broadly, they "acted as a surface reform taking pressure off male elites to genuinely empower women in decision-making."[148]

Relatedly, gender reforms to promote women's political inclusion in Morocco had minimally affected the democratization process despite the incremental increase in women's numbers in the lower chamber. For instance, it has been argued that women's increased representation at the national level has helped legitimize the "de-democratization" of Moroccan politics.[149] While I concur with extant scholarship that Morocco's electoral and gender-related reforms have had a marginal impact on the democratization process, several knowledge gaps on the inner dynamics and the legislative outcomes of these democratically elected institutions continue to exist. Regarding critiques of women's contribution to the legislative process, it is essential to note that these studies lack systemic analysis of the impact of women's presence in the political arena and their legislative behavior. As I empirically show in chapter 5, female parliamentarians in Morocco significantly advocated for women's issues during the 2011 and 2016 legislatures compared to the other cases under study.

Political parties in Morocco have male-dominated internal structures and nomination processes. However, these parties are more institutionalized than most countries in the region (figure 2.2). I argue that the level of party institutionalization matters for women's political power and influence within the legislature. It is also important to emphasize the positive effects of the high levels of party institutionalization to facilitate the implementation of the gender quota policies and, in turn, increase female political representation. There is no doubt that women have a weak presence in Morocco's political parties, especially on the leadership level. There is a strong need for reforms to increase women's representation within parties' organizational structures and leadership ranks. For example, several reforms to the lower chamber bylaws were introduced to ensure the inclusion of women in leadership positions, including the laws to reserve one-third of positions in the General Secretary for Women and the establishment of the gender parity and equity commission during the 2011 legislature. Yet these efforts should start at the party level and not be limited to women who have won parliamentary seats.

* * *

This chapter provides the theoretical and empirical justification for the case selection. It also highlights the role of parliaments and the nature of executive-legislative relations. It presents a detailed contextual analysis of the political and legislative landscape in the three cases, the history of women's political representation, and the challenges they continue to face in accessing political power.

Importantly, this chapter demonstrates the effect of the weakness of political parties in Jordan and their absence in Kuwait on women's ability to access political power. Parties continue to play a marginal role in Jordan's political and electoral arenas. Most MPs, including women, have no party affiliation and often run as independents, apart from the IAF and a few small leftist parties. Female candidates in Kuwait primarily run as independents or are affiliated with political groups with ideological and ethnic orientations. Women's access to political power is further constrained by the frequent dissolution of the legislature in Kuwait and the instability of electoral rules in Jordan over the past few decades.

Morocco represents a strong case of political parties' presence in the electoral arena. Despite the existing shortcomings of the electoral system and the monarchy's tight control over the legislative process, parties in Morocco are highly institutionalized, have considerably stable connections with society, and are organizationally strong. In chapter 4, I test the effects of the varying levels of party institutionalization on women's access to legislative committees. In chapter 5, I test the impact of party institutionalization on their legislative behavior and priorities.

4

COMING TO POWER

Women's Committee Membership and Leadership

So, for example, in the current [Jordanian] parliament, this is the second parliamentary round where no woman holds the presidency of a committee except for the women's committee. That is it! Nothing else! And, of course, the women's committee does not have any male members except for one man, and he is the one who repeatedly insisted on joining it as he comes from a leftist background. This is really a problem!

—FEMALE LEGISLATOR IN THE JORDANIAN LOWER CHAMBER,
INTERVIEW WITH AUTHOR IN AMMAN, MARCH 2018

Membership and leadership of legislative committees are crucial for legislators' career advancement and gaining access to high-level government officials. These appointments can be particularly valuable for women to influence policymaking and gain experience and name recognition. But how do women access these committees? Are they able to join and lead influential committees in the legislature? Or are they often relegated to less desirable, low-prestige committees, as stated by my interviewee in the quote above? Who gets access to the highly visible, sought-after committees?

In this chapter, I test my theoretical expectations that higher levels of party institutionalization are conducive to increased political power and influence for women politicians in autocratic legislatures. I argued in the previous chapters that higher levels of party institutionalization are positively associated with women's power and influence because strong parties have the capacity to support women within legislatures and provide them with the necessary resources and tools to gain influence than those elected without party support (i.e., independent legislators) and/or those elected with weakly institutionalized parties. Parties also have incentives to promote women's presence in influential legislative committees as political party leaders often deem committee appointments and leadership essential to fulfill policy goals and ensure party unity.[1] Thus, women affiliated with parties with high levels of party institutionalization are more likely to access influential committees, such as the legal, finance, and foreign affairs committees. Additionally, I expect women affiliated with institutionalized parties to be members of social and women's issues committees to gain influence and the ability to substantively represent women. However, I expect women's affiliation with strong parties to promote their ability to access influential committees within the legislature. Access to these committees enables women to push for policy changes, shape political outcomes, gain visibility and prestige, and improve their reelection prospects.

To test my argument, I focus on committee assignments and leadership in Morocco, Jordan, and Kuwait. I analyze legislative committee assignments and leadership (N = 3,000) data for over a decade. Morocco's committee membership and leadership datasets extend between 2007 and 2021 (n = 1,121). The data ranges from 2010 and 2020 (n = 1,389) for Jordan and from 2009 to 2017 for Kuwait (n = 466).[2] I find variations in women's access to influential and traditionally male-dominated committees. The results confirm my theoretical expectations that women are more likely to access influential committees when affiliated with highly institutionalized political parties. Even after controlling for the legislator's ideology and political experience, the level of party institutionalization remains the strongest predictor of women's access to influential committees, namely the legislative, financial, and foreign affairs committees.

The first part of the chapter sheds light on the centrality of committees' work to the study of legislative politics, followed by a discussion on existing scholarship on committees in authoritarian contexts, including their functions, procedures, and rules across the cases under study. The second part of the chapter presents the multivariate analysis of female membership in legislative committees in Morocco, Jordan, and Kuwait, followed by an analysis of women's committee leadership and a concluding section.

LEGISLATIVE COMMITTEES: A COMPARATIVE PERSPECTIVE

Legislative committees are integral to legislative bodies.[3] They are essential not only for policymaking[4] and holding the executive and/or government accountable[5] but also for aggregating the legislators' preferences.[6] In addition, committee assignments are essential for political parties to fulfill policy goals and ensure party unity.[7] Furthermore, committee appointments are often considered crucial tools for party leaders to reward loyalists[8] and dedicated legislators[9] and they often provide insights into existing power relations within legislatures.

For individual legislators, committee assignments are essential because of the benefits accrued in terms of career advancement and reelection prospects,[10] especially for electorally vulnerable legislators in candidate-centered electoral contexts.[11] Furthermore, committee assignments grant legislators access to resources[12] and high-level government officials and are also significant for gaining political expertise[13] and visibility among constituents.

Given their centrality to the legislative process, committee assignments have been studied extensively within the U.S. Congress and state legislatures.[14] Many theoretical frameworks explicating legislative organization were developed in the U.S. context, which informed research in other settings, mainly distributive, informational, and partisan theories. More recently, comparative analysis has emerged testing these theories in different parts of the world.[15]

Extant scholarship has classified legislative committees according to their specialization, importance, and prestige. Research has uncovered interesting, albeit mixed, findings. Scholars argue that certain committees are generally considered "feminine" or deal with "soft" issues. They mirror stereotypical notions regarding women's roles in the family and society, such as education, culture, youth, environment, social welfare, and health. These types of committees are commonly perceived as "low-prestige" committees. Other committees are categorized as dealing with "hard" issues or male-dominated areas, such as agriculture, transportation, public works, labor, and energy. Scholars have also referred to these committees as "distributive" (i.e., related to policy areas that may benefit legislators' constituents).[16] Similarly, studies have classified distributive committees as "masculine," while others are categorized as "neutral," mainly environment and justice committees.[17] More powerful and influential committees such as budget and finance, defense, international affairs, and legislative committees confer the most prestige and power to their members. These are considered the most coveted "high-policy" committees[18] and tend to be controlled by party leaders due to their high prestige and visibility.[19]

LEGISLATIVE COMMITTEES IN MOROCCO, JORDAN, AND KUWAIT

Legislative committees are the backbone of legislatures, where important policy decisions are negotiated, drafted, and formulated. Thus, they are widely deemed one of the legislatures' most significant internal organizational features.[20] Furthermore, being a member of a prestigious committee is an important legislative activity, especially in legislatures where committees are given substantial prerogatives. Similar to democratic contexts, legislative committees in authoritarian lower chambers play an important role in formulating and discussing bills, advancing policy proposals from legislators (in both the lower and upper chambers), and coordinating with the government and the king/emir.[21] Committees generate reports to the assembly, including recommendations for the relevant governmental unit.

For instance, the Economy and Financial Committee is responsible for setting the annual budget, approving government and ministries' spending, and monitoring the implementation of the budget. The Palestine Committee in Jordan regulates relations with Israel and the Palestinian refugees in Jordan. The Committee of Surveillance of Public Funds—established in the aftermath of the Arab uprisings in Morocco—is responsible for monitoring and tracking government spending, scrutinizing laws relating to monitoring the general budget, and reviewing reports of the Audit Commission. The Legislative Committee in Jordan and Kuwait reviews legislation relating to election laws, constitutional amendments, and laws regulating the internal rules of the legislature. To shed light on the importance of some committees compared to others, the Finance and Legislative Committees convened forty-eight and forty-one times during the second term of the seventeenth legislature in Jordan (2014–2015). Contrastingly, the Women and Children Committee met only nine times, while the Youth and Sports Committee met only six times during the same period.[22]

There are significant cross-national variations regarding legislative committees' composition and numbers. For instance, Morocco has only permanent or standing committees. In contrast, Jordan and Kuwait have both permanent/standing and temporary committees.[23] (Refer to tables A.3–A.5 in appendix A for more details on committees' coding and responsibilities.) Standing committees are the primary policy committees and are often clearly defined by the constitution and the lower chamber's internal bylaws. Multiple committee membership is allowed in Jordan and Kuwait; however, it is not allowed in Morocco. Furthermore, the number of committee members and leaders varies across cases, legislative sessions, and terms.

Generally, committees have the authority to convene hearings and summon witnesses. Committee leaders in Jordan may summon ministers and other government officials and communicate with ministries to request specific information or documentation (Article 69, I). The standing committees' meetings in Morocco can be televised based on the request of one-third of the committee members or if the committee is discussing a topic of public interest (Article 129, Bylaws 2013). However, most of the proceedings and work of the standing committees take place without much media attention, contrary to the parliamentary questions I analyze in the following chapter.

RULES AND PROCEDURES OF PARLIAMENTARY COMMITTEES

The procedures for committee assignments differ across the three countries. The rules regulating committee appointments are outlined in the assemblies' internal bylaws; however, these bylaws tend to be vague and less institutionalized in most parts of the region. As a female deputy in the 2014 Tunisian legislature maintains, "There are no clear rules about who gets assigned to which committee. It all depends on the presidents of the bloc who get to decide who gets on the committee. We [MPs] are pushing for legislation which will regulate the rules since there are currently no clear rules."[24]

Morocco had six standing committees in the 2007 legislature and nine committees in 2012 and 2016 (see table 4.1 and table A.2 in appendix A). Permanent committees are formed when the legislative term commences (Internal Bylaws 2013, Article 58–59).[25] Legislators are required to join one committee and are not allowed to join multiple committees. Legislators state their committee preferences at the beginning of the legislative session; however, party or group leaders mostly control the selection process. Furthermore, formal rules are silent regarding the gender composition of the committees. Committee membership is distributed proportionally to the percentage of legislative teams and opposition versus governing parties.[26]

By the inception of the legislative session in Morocco, each committee elects the committee leadership via secret voting. Committees' leadership includes one president, four vice presidents, a reporter (only in 2016), a deputy reporter (only in 2016), and two secretaries (Lower Chamber

TABLE 4.1 Committees included in the analysis

COUNTRY, YEAR, AND CHAMBER	COMMITTEE NAME
Morocco House of Representatives 2007–2011 2012–2016 2016–2021 N = 1,121	• Domestic Affairs, Decentralization, and Essential Structures (2007) • Domestic Affairs, Territorial Groups, and City Policy (2012, 2016)[a] • Justice and Legislation, Human Rights—44 members (2007, 2012, 2016) • Social Sectors (2007, 2012, 2016) • Finance and Economic Development (2007, 2012, 2016) • Production Sectors (2007, 2012, 2016) • Foreign Affairs, National Defense, and Islamic Affairs (2007, 2012, 2016) • Essential Buildings, Energy, Metals, and Environment (2012, 2016) • Education, Culture, and Communication (2012, 2016) • Surveillance of Public Funds (2012, 2016)
Jordan House of Representatives—16th, 17th, 18th sessions 2010–2013 (two terms) 2013–2016 (four terms) 2016–2020 (four terms) N = 1,389	• Administrative (2010, 2013, 2016) • Legislative (2010, 2013, 2016) • Financial and Economic (2010)/Financial (2013, 2016) • Economy and Investment (2013, 2016) • Public Freedoms and Rights of the Citizens (2010); General Freedoms and Human Rights (2013, 2016) • Integrity, Transparency, and Fact Checking (2013, 2016) • Structure and Behavior (2013, 2016) • Agriculture and Irrigation (2010, 2013, 2016) • Energy and Mineral Wealth (2010, 2013, 2016) • Palestine (2010, 2013, 2016) • Arab and Foreign Affairs (2010)/Foreign Affairs (2013, 2016) • Rural Areas and Undeveloped Land (2010, 2013, 2016) • Health and the Environment (2010, 2013, 2016) • Labor and Social Development (2010)/Labor, Social Development, and Population (2013, 2016) • Public Services, Tourism, and Monuments (2010)/Public Services and Transportation (2013, 2016) • Tourism and Monuments (2013, 2016) • National Direction and the Media (2010, 2013, 2016) • Education, Culture, Sports, and Youth (2010)/Upbringing, Education, and Culture (2013, 2016) • Youth and Sports (2013, 2016) • Women and Family Affairs (2013, 2016)[b]

Kuwait	• Petitions and Appeals (2009, 2013, 2016)
National Assembly—13th,	• Internal Affairs and Defense (2009, 2013, 2016)
14th, 15th sessions	• Legislative and Legal Affairs (2009, 2013, 2016)
2009–2011	• Budgets and the Final Account (2009, 2013, 2016)
(four quarters)	• Education, Culture, and Guidance (2009, 2013, 2016)[c]
2013–2016	• Health, Social and Labor Affairs (2009, 2013, 2016)
(four quarters)	• Financial and Economic Affairs (2009, 2013, 2016)
2016–2017	• Foreign Affairs (2009, 2013, 2016)
(one quarter)	• Public Utilities (2009, 2013, 2016)
N = 466	• Protection of Public Funds (2009, 2013)
	• Prioritization (2013, 2016)[d]
	• Protection of Public Funds (T) (2016)
	• Women and the Family (T) (2009, 2013, 2016)
	• Matters for those Requiring Special Needs (T) (2009, 2013, 2016)
	• Youth and Sports (T) (2009, 2013, 2016)

Sources: Jordan's data: House of Representatives, available at https://representatives.jo/Default /Ar; The Hashemite Kingdom of Jordan: The Parliament, available at http://parliament.jo/; JP: Guide to Jordanian Politics Life, Phenix: Economic and Informatics Studies, available at http://jordanpolitics.org/en/home; Rased, available at https://www.rasedjo.com/ar. Kuwait's data: Michael Herb, Kuwait Politics Database, available at http://www.kuwaitpolitics.org/; National Assembly, Kuwait, available at http://www.kna.kw/clt-html5/index.asp; Raqib 50, available at http://www.raqib50.com/parliaments/8/committees. Morocco's data: House of Representatives, available at http://www.chambredesrepresentants.ma/ar/; TAFRA, available at http://tafra.ma/.

Notes: For full description of the responsibilities of these committees, please refer to appendix A. Committees with a "(T)" indicate temporary committees established only in select rounds to address particular issues in more detail. Investigation committees in Kuwait and Jordan are excluded from the analysis. Years in parentheses denote the year the committee was established.

[a]Formerly Domestic, Decentralization, and Essential Structures.

[b]The temporary committees in Jordan that are not included in the analysis are the response to the Speeches of the King (2010 and 2016) and the Division of Appeals (2010).

[c]Many temporary committees in Kuwait's 2009 legislature are excluded from the analysis due to their non-policy-making prerogatives and/or noncontinuity across sessions. We only included youth, sports, and matters relating to those requiring special needs under the "social committee" category.

[d]The Prioritization Committee was established in Kuwait during the fourteenth legislature and continued through the fifteenth legislature. Its responsibility was to determine the priorities for the legislature by the inception of the legislative session. Despite being a standing committee, it is not included in the analysis because its members are mostly the existing presidents of other influential committees, such as the Legislative and Financial Committees.

Internal Bylaws, Article 60). Presidents of the permanent committees can only head one committee. Members may change their committee membership or leadership only in the third year of the legislature (Internal Bylaws 2013, Article 58–59). However, switching committees is relatively rare in the Moroccan context. Opposition parties are granted at least two president positions (Chapters 10 and 69 of the Moroccan Constitution). In 2013, the Moroccan parliament introduced a temporary Equity and Parity Committee under the nineteenth article of the 2011 constitution. One of the main achievements of the committee was to ensure women's representation in leadership positions across the committees. Thus, the 2016 legislature witnessed, for the first time, the allocation of one-third of leadership positions of committees and Chamber's Council to women (Internal Bylaws 2013, Article 52).

In Jordan's lower chamber, there were sixteen committees in 2010: fourteen standing and two temporary committees. In 2013, there were twenty standing committees and no temporary committees. There were twenty standing committees and only one temporary committee in 2016 (see table 4.1 and table A.2 in appendix A). Committee membership and leadership change from one legislative term to the next. Members of the standing committees range from five to eleven (Internal Bylaws 2013, Article 6, I). Committee membership is determined by an agreement between blocs and independent members within fourteen days of the inception of the legislative term. It should be proportional to the bloc composition within the legislature (Internal Bylaws 2013, Article 61, II). MPs state their preferences by the beginning of the legislative session; however, the heads of the bloc or party make final decisions. Secret voting occurs only when the number of nominees exceeds the maximum number of committee seats. Legislators can sit on up to two permanent committees and may not combine committee and executive office appointments (Article 61, IV). Between 2010 and 2020, roughly 85 percent of legislators were members of one permanent committee and 63 percent were members of two permanent committees. There is no limit on membership in temporary committees in the Jordanian lower chamber.[27]

Each committee has an office carrying out the committee work, supervising reports, and recording minutes (Article 65, VII). Members elect the committee's president, vice president, and reporter at the beginning of the legislative session (Article 65, I and II). There were about twenty-eight committee leadership positions in each legislative term for Jordan's 2010 legislature (fourteen committees with presidents and reporters only). In 2013 and 2016, there were sixty committee leadership positions in each legislative term with the introduction of the vice president (VP) position (twenty committees with presidents, VPs, and reporters).

Kuwait had ten standing committees in the 2009 legislature and eleven in the 2013 and 2016 legislatures. However, the number of temporary committees varies by year and legislative terms.[28] This analysis only includes three temporary committees in 2009, 2013, and 2016 (see table 4.1 for more details). The assembly has the authority to form unlimited permanent and temporary committees based on need and is responsible for drafting the rules regulating new committees (Internal Bylaws, Article 44). Committee assignments are determined by floor voting during the first week of the legislative term (Internal Bylaws 2015, Article 42). Since political parties are banned, political blocs and independents are proportionally represented in committees. Legislators must join at least one committee and no more than two standing committees (excluding the membership of the assembly's executive office). Standing committees typically have five to seven members. Between 2009 and 2017, roughly 80 percent of legislators were members of one standing committee, and 28 percent were members of two. There is no limit on membership in temporary committees in Kuwait's legislature.

Like the Jordanian case, committee membership and leadership change from one legislative term to the next. Committees elect their presidents and reporters (Article 46). In 2009, there were twenty leadership positions for the standing committees (namely presidents and reporters) and twenty-two positions in 2013 and 2016. Committees have the authority to request information from the government and/or ministries within the scope of the committee's work and summon the relevant minister or government official through the head of the assembly (Article 50).

WOMEN MEMBERSHIP IN LEGISLATIVE COMMITTEES IN MOROCCO, JORDAN, AND KUWAIT

Female legislators' political power ultimately involves membership in and leadership of key decision-making bodies, particularly committees.[29] Thus, it is imperative to pay closer attention to whether female politicians are able to gain access, presence, and influence to better evaluate their effectiveness and success.[30] Despite the proliferation of cross-national research scrutinizing recent increases in female numerical presence in politics, comparative scholarship on the role of women within legislatures continues to lag.[31] Recently, studies have paid closer attention to patterns of transformation of power relations within legislatures and systematically investigated women's roles within legislative bodies, mainly committee appointments, both temporally and cross-nationally.

Studies investigating the intersection of legislative committees and legislators' gender have provided several explanations, namely marginalization, gender stereotyping, and self-selection. For instance, one study found support for marginalization in Latin America and argued that male legislators use committee assignments to exclude female parliamentarians from important committees, such as foreign affairs and financial committees.[32] Furthermore, male elites are more likely to marginalize women when they are "newcomers" to the legislative arena. Focusing on the Argentinian subnational legislative assemblies, another researcher demonstrated that the increase of female legislators through the introduction of quotas may have initially caused male parliamentarians to exclude women.[33] Still, it eventually contributed to more significant political influence. In contrast, no empirical support was found for female marginalization in committee selections in the Norwegian parliament.[34]

Other scholars unearth evidence for gender stereotyping, which may, in turn, lead to the sidelining of women from influential committee positions due to the prevalence of gendered norms within the legislature. Less desirable committees always deal with social issues such as education, youth, women's rights, and family. One scholar asserts that women are generally overrepresented in committees dealing with "compassion issues" in Argentina, Costa Rica, and Colombia.[35] Moreover, research on U.S. state legislatures that used committee leadership data for 1993–1994 demonstrated similar trends.[36] In contrast, other research has shown that women's marginalization has diminished over time and that, whereas women were appointed to a limited set of committees in U.S. state legislatures in the 1970s, their representation has increased over time.[37]

Finally, women can be overrepresented in committees dealing with social and women's issues because of self-selection rather than deliberate marginalization from influential committees.[38] For instance, one study showed that women's committee placements in Danish municipalities are frequently driven by their preferences to be in committees dealing with children's issues instead of other male-dominated, technical committees.[39] In addition, according to an analysis of female representation in Mexico's Chamber of Deputies, women are not marginalized in terms of substantial representation (i.e., bill sponsorship, leadership positions, and committee assignments); however, the analysis depicts significant variations over time in women's presence across influential committees.[40] Consistent with this view, the marginalization of women may be due to their lack of confidence to request membership in powerful committees rather than explicit discrimination by their male colleagues and party leaders.

Based on the former discussion and my previous work on women in legislative committees across the region,[41] I focus on six main committee types that represent a wide range of specialization and levels of prestige: Women's Issues, Legislative, Economy and Financial, Foreign Affairs, Transportation, and Social Affairs. Table 4.2 details the classification of the different committees across the three cases. (The detailed committee coding is in appendix A.) I have exerted substantial effort to create spatially and temporally comparable categories while maintaining the study's theoretical expectations and underpinnings. I aim to discern the relationship between party institutionalization, women's access to power, and their role in legislatures operating under authoritarian rule. I expect female legislators affiliated with institutionalized parties to have more access to higher levels of political power compared to contexts with weak or less institutionalized

TABLE 4.2 Classification of legislative committees in Morocco, Jordan, and Kuwait

	WOMEN'S ISSUES COMMITTEE	LEGISLATIVE COMMITTEE	ECONOMY AND FINANCIAL COMMITTEE	FOREIGN AFFAIRS COMMITTEE	TRANSPORTATION COMMITTEE	SOCIAL AFFAIRS COMMITTEE
Morocco	None (included in the Social Affairs Committee)	Justice, Legislation, and Human Rights	Finance and Economic Development	Foreign Affairs, National Defense, Islamic Affairs and Moroccans Abroad	Essential Buildings, Energy, Metals, and Environment	Social Sectors; Education, Culture, and Communication
Jordan	Women and Family Affairs (2013, 2016)	Legislative Committee	Financial Committee; Economy and Investment	Foreign Affairs; Palestine	Public Services and Transportation	Labor, Social Development, and Population; Youth and Sports; Upbringing, Education, and Culture
Kuwait	Women and the Family (2009) (T)	Petitions and Appeals; Legislative and Legal Affairs	Budgets and the Final Account; Financial and Economic Affairs	Internal Affairs and Defense; Foreign Affairs	Public Utilities	Health, Social, and Labor Affairs; Education, Culture, and Guidance; Matters for Those Requiring Special Needs (T); Youth and Sports (T)

Note: Years in parentheses indicate the year the committee was established. Committees with a "(T)" indicate temporary committees established only in select rounds to address particular issues in more detail.

parties. Thus, I expect to find less marginalization of female legislators from influential committees and leadership roles when they are part of institutionalized parties.

DESCRIPTIVE ANALYSIS OF WOMEN'S COMMITTEE MEMBERSHIP

The analysis is based on an original dataset on committee assignments and leadership in Morocco, Kuwait, and Jordan that I collected, translated, and coded. The dataset covers three legislative terms for each country in the analysis (table 4.1). Data were collected from my fieldwork and the websites of the lower chambers and independent monitoring organizations in Morocco, Kuwait, and Jordan. Quantitative data are supplemented by qualitative semi-structured interviews with female legislators, current and former MPs, parliamentary staff, and top officials in Jordan, Morocco, and Kuwait (see appendix C for the detailed legislators' questionnaires). These interviews included questions on the procedures of committee appointments and the importance and prestige of specific committees. Furthermore, data on the prestige and importance of committees were obtained and verified by country experts whom I contacted. Primary data sources such as lower chambers' internal bylaws, archival data, and news articles were also analyzed and included.

I mainly focus on standing committees since much of the legislative work (discussing and approving bills) occurs in committees acting as gatekeepers.[42] As for Morocco, the dataset includes committee assignments and leadership for three legislative sessions from 2007 to 2021. Committee membership tends to be stable throughout the legislative session, but committee leadership may change by the inception of the second and third legislative terms. For instance, merely 3 percent of legislators changed their committee assignment across the three legislative terms.

In Kuwait, the data span three legislative sessions: four legislative terms for the 2009 and 2013 sessions and one term for the 2016 legislature (table 4.1). The 2020 legislature is excluded from the analysis since female candidates could not win seats. Committee assignments may change from one term to another within the same legislative session; therefore, each legislator is treated as an individual observation across terms. For example, although there are only fifty legislators in the Kuwaiti assembly, we have two hundred observations for the 2009 session, given the changes in the committee assignments across the four quarters.

Finally, the analysis includes data from Jordan's lower chamber from 2010 to 2020 (n = 1,400). While the 2010 legislature had only two terms, the 2013 and 2016 legislatures had four legislative terms.[43] Like Kuwait, committee assignments and leadership positions change across legislative terms. Before shifting attention to the statistical analysis, I provide descriptive analyses on women's committee membership—figures 4.1 through 4.3 detail female committee membership across legislative sessions for the three cases.

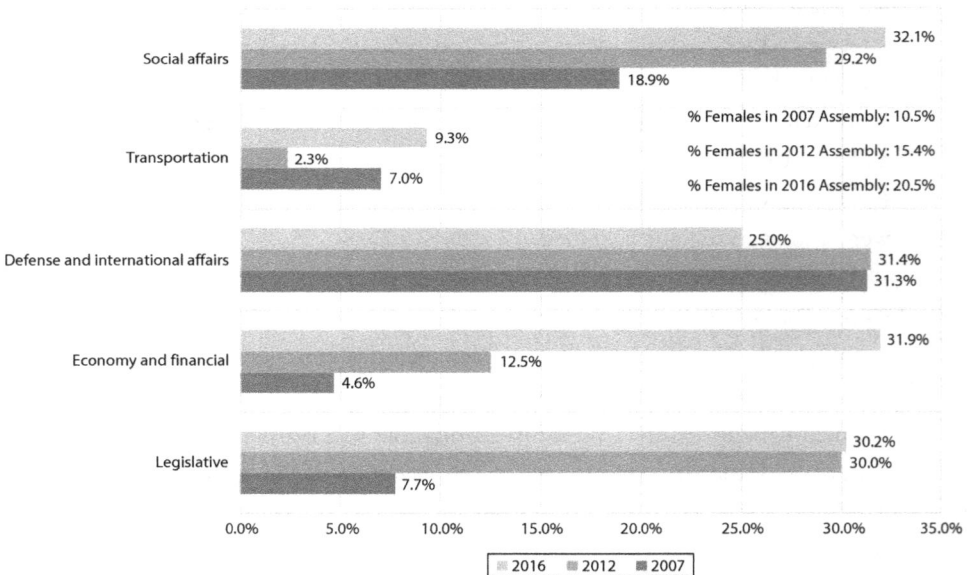

FIGURE 4.1 Percentage of females' seats in legislative committees in Morocco (2007–2021)

Source: Author's data.

Figure 4.1 shows significant temporal variations in Morocco. In 2007, women constituted only 8 and 5 percent of the Legislative and Economy and Financial Committees. However, by 2016, they constituted about 30 percent of both committees. While women continue to be heavily represented in Social Issues Committees (about 30 percent of total seats in 2012 and 2016), there is little evidence of marginalization from influential committees, especially in more recent sessions.[44]

Figure 4.2 visualizes data for the Jordanian case. It is important to reiterate that, unlike Morocco, legislators in Jordan can join two permanent or standing committees, and their membership changes every legislative term. Nearly 90 percent of female legislators in Jordan's 2016 legislature held two committee positions. This may explain why the percentage of women may denote women being overrepresented in committees compared to their numerical presence. The Women and Children Committee was established

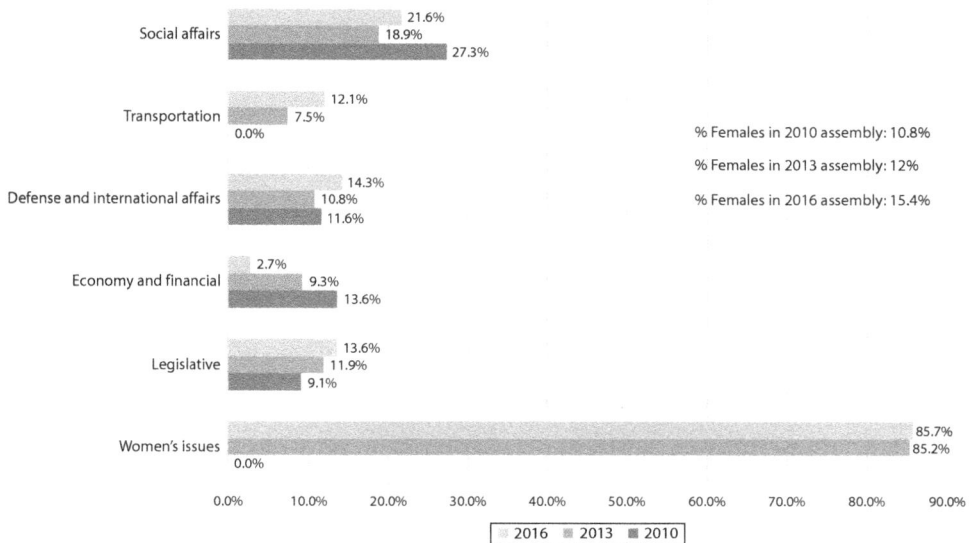

FIGURE 4.2 Percentage of females' seats in legislative committees in Jordan (2010–2020)

Source: Author's data.

as a permanent committee at the beginning of the 2013 legislature. Women constituted about 85 percent of the total membership of the Women and Children Committee, as well as 27, 19, and 22 percent of the Social Affairs Committees in 2010, 2013, and 2016, respectively.

It also shows that women's representation in influential committees, such as the Economy and Legislative, has oscillated. While women represented 14 percent of the Economy and Financial Committee in 2010, they constituted less than 3 percent on average in the 2016 legislature despite the increase in women's representation from 10 percent to 15 percent of the total parliament in 2016. While still underrepresented, women's representation on the Legislative and other male-dominated committees, such as Transportation, has grown over the past decade.

Figure 4.3 presents data on female legislators' committee membership in Kuwait. Similar to the Jordanian context, legislators can join

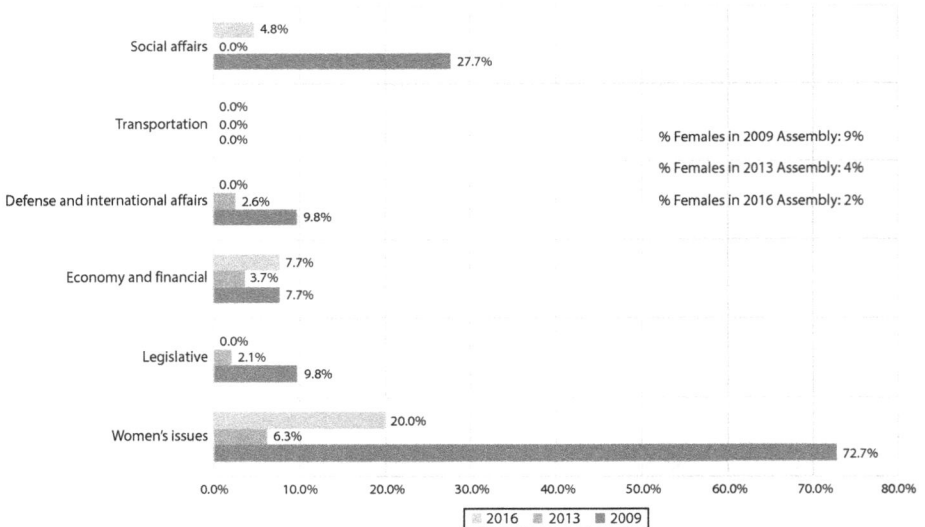

FIGURE 4.3 Percentage of females' seats in legislative committees in Kuwait (2009–2017)

Source: Author's data.

up to two standing committees and an unlimited number of temporary committees. All female legislators held at least three committee membership positions, while few held up to six positions in 2009. Even though women constituted 8 percent of the legislature (four of fifty legislators in 2009), they all had membership or leadership of the Women and Children Committee, which has been a temporary committee since 2009. Furthermore, women constituted only 6.3 and 20 percent of the Women and Children Committees in 2013 and 2016, respectively, since two women won seats in the 2013 legislature while only one female candidate was reelected in 2016.[45] Women are also heavily concentrated in the Social Affairs Committees (categories are broken down in table 4.2).

As evident from figure 4.3, women never gained access to male-dominated committees, mainly Transportation, since joining the legislature in 2009. Furthermore, the deteriorating levels of their representation over the past two legislative sessions have further contributed to women's marginalization from important committees such as the Defense and International Affairs and the Legislative. Even when women were most represented in the Kuwaiti legislature in 2009, they were underrepresented in prestigious committees, such as the Economy and Financial Committee.

It is worth noting that whereas the inclusion of female legislators in influential committees may not automatically translate into broader gender policy gains in some contexts, gender-sensitive policymaking and legislation can contribute to formulating more effective policies that address the needs of women.[46] For instance, having more women on the Economy and Financial Committee, which is one of the most influential committees across chambers and countries, may lead to the allocation of funds that address gender gaps among women and girls in areas such as education, health, and employment.[47] This caveat is particularly relevant in contexts like the Middle East and North Africa (MENA), which continue to witness glaring gender inequalities, both structural and institutional.

WOMEN'S COMMITTEE MEMBERSHIP
AND PARTY INSTITUTIONALIZATION

I run logistic regression models for the three countries in the analysis to determine the probability of female membership in each committee. I visualize the results in figures 4.4 through 4.8. The models are estimated using robust standard errors clustered around individual legislators. All models include year fixed effects to address common time shocks and country-specific developments.

The main dependent variables are binary variables that measure membership in each of the five categories of legislative committees: Legislative; Economy and Financial; Foreign Affairs; Women and Family; and Social Affairs.[48] (Refer to appendix A for more details on committee coding across the three countries.) The Transportation Committee was excluded from the multivariate analyses because women had no committee seats for the last decade in Kuwait, as shown in figure 4.3. The categories included in the analyses are chosen based on my fieldwork, detailed discussions, and consultations with country experts. It also relies on existing literature on committees in developed and developing contexts that have uncovered significant gender differences in committee assignments. The unit of analysis is the individual legislator. A legislator is coded as 1 if they sit on the committee and as 0 otherwise.

The independent variables include several legislator-level variables (table A.6 in appendix A has complete information on the variables' coding). To measure the effect of the main independent variable in this study—party institutionalization—on women's committee memberships, I constructed an additive index based on six main measures that capture the strength of political parties. The index includes the standardized scores acquired from the Varieties of Party Identity and Organization (V-Party) dataset that V-Dem (2020) collected. I have included in the index measures of parties' local organizational strength, continuation, presence of local offices, processes of candidates' nominations, cohesion, and stable links with social organizations. The index ranges between 0 and 1, with

1 being the highest level of party institutionalization and 0 denoting the absence of any party institutionalization. (See table A.7 in appendix A for more details.) This index mirrors the country-level party institutionalization index used in previous work.[49]

I created interaction terms for legislators who are females and members of an institutionalized party. Moreover, I included a variable that captures the number of committee memberships each legislator holds per legislative session to account for the fact that some chambers allow legislators to sit on more than one committee.[50] Intuitively, the more committees a legislator sits on, the greater the likelihood they will serve on any given committee.[51]

Furthermore, previous research has shown that women are disadvantaged during their first term in office.[52] Political experience may also impact women's substantive representation[53] and committee assignments.[54] Thus, I have included a binary measure of whether the legislator was reelected.

Finally, legislators' partisanship and ideology may influence their access to powerful legislative positions.[55] The analyses include a measure that captures their ideology—whether the legislator is an Islamist. In Morocco, members of the Justice and Development Party (PJD) in the three legislative sessions are coded as "Islamist" and made up 14, 27, and 31 percent in the 2007, 2012, and 2016 sessions, respectively. As for Kuwait, fifteen members (out of fifty) were affiliated with the Islamist bloc in the 2009 assembly. In 2013, the Islamic Constitutional Movement (ICM) boycotted the elections, gaining only three seats for the Islamist Salafi Alliance. In the 2016 assembly, I coded eight legislators affiliated with the ICM or the Salafists as Islamists. Finally, I code members of the Islamist Centrist Party and the Islamic Alliance Front (IAF) in Jordan as Islamists.

I present the results for the aggregate models for the three countries; I include the country specific models in tables A.8, A.9 and A.10 in appendix A. To facilitate the interpretation of the aggregate models, I present below the predicted probabilities of women's membership in the Legislative, Economy and Financial, Foreign Affairs, Women's Issues, and Social Affairs Committees in figures 4.4 through 4.8. As shown in figure 4.4, when women politicians are affiliated with an institutionalized party, their probability of being members of the Legislative Committee

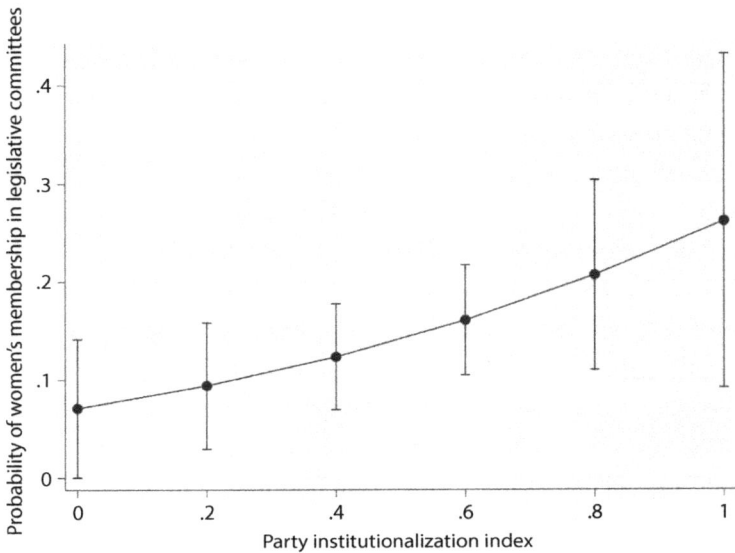

FIGURE 4.4 Probability of women's membership in legislative committees in Jordan, Kuwait, and Morocco

Source: Author's data.

significantly increases. Specifically, women are only 8 percent likely to join the Legislative Committee when they lack a party affiliation (i.e., running as independents) or are affiliated with a weakly institutionalized party. The likelihood of women's access to the Legislative Committee increases to more than 25 percent when they are affiliated with highly institutionalized parties.

Similar patterns are evident in the models exploring the correlates of women's membership in the Economy and Financial Committee. Figure 4.5 indicates that women with no party affiliation and/or who are part of weakly institutionalized parties have less than a 10 percent probability of being members of the Economy and Financial Committee. Women's affiliation with a highly institutionalized party is associated with a 10 percent increase in their likelihood of being members of the Economy and Financial Committee.

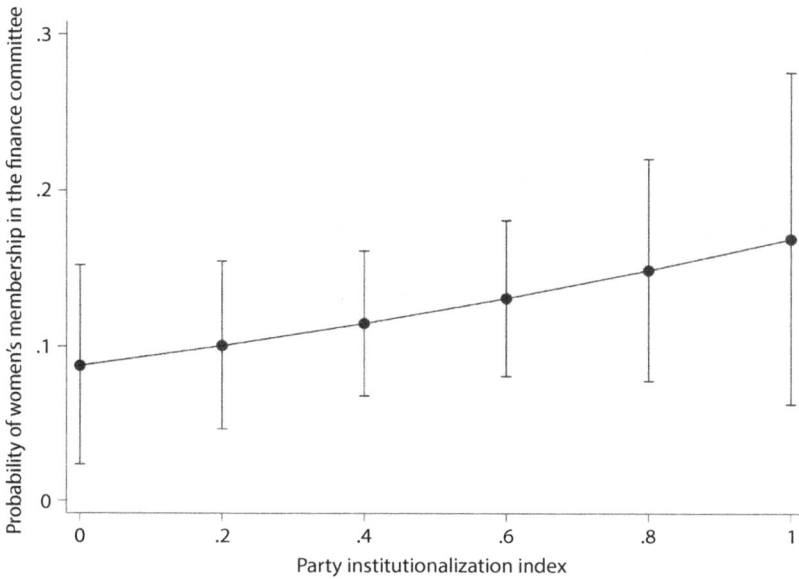

FIGURE 4.5 Probability of women's membership in the Economy and
Financial Committees in Jordan, Kuwait, and Morocco

Source: Author's data.

Figure 4.6 demonstrates the predicted probabilities of women's membership in Foreign Affairs Committees across the three cases. Again,
women's affiliation with highly institutionalized parties is associated with a
roughly 8 percent increase in their likelihood of being members of the Foreign Affairs Committees in Jordan, Morocco, and Kuwait. This is a substantial increase since women are only 13 percent likely to join the Foreign
Affairs Committees as independents.

Figure 4.7 presents the predicted probabilities of women's membership in the Social Affairs Committees in Jordan, Kuwait, and Morocco.
As expected, women affiliated with institutionalized parties are 50 percent
more likely to join the Social Affairs Committees compared with about 30
percent when they run as independents and/or with weakly institutionalized parties. These results are consistent with the theoretical argument that

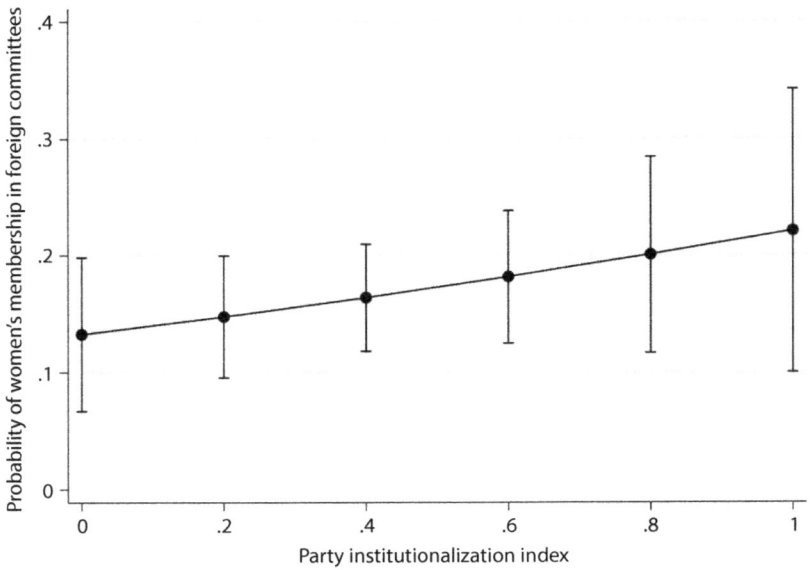

FIGURE 4.6 Probability of women's membership in the Foreign Affairs Committees in Jordan, Kuwait, and Morocco

Source: Author's data.

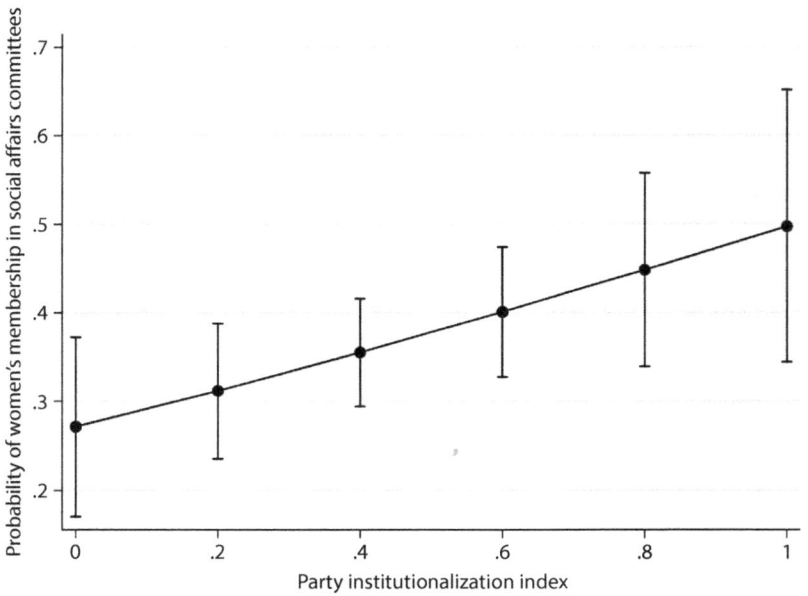

FIGURE 4.7 Probability of women's membership in the Social Affairs Committees in Jordan, Kuwait, and Morocco

Source: Author's data.

whereas party institutionalization may increase the likelihood of women's access to influential committees, it shouldn't negatively impact their choice to access Social Affairs Committees, which tend to be aligned with their careers and priorities to serve women and other marginalized groups.

Finally, figure 4.8 demonstrates the predicted probability of women's membership in Women's Issues Committees in Jordan and Kuwait. As noted in table 4.2, Morocco has no Women's Issues Committee. The marginal effect of party institutionalization on women's membership in the Women's Issues Committees is evident in figure 4.8. There is a relatively flat line compared to other committee memberships. These results are consistent with my argument that levels of party institutionalization may strengthen their ability to join influential committees; however, it may have little effect on shaping their preferences to join committees that may serve women and other social groups.

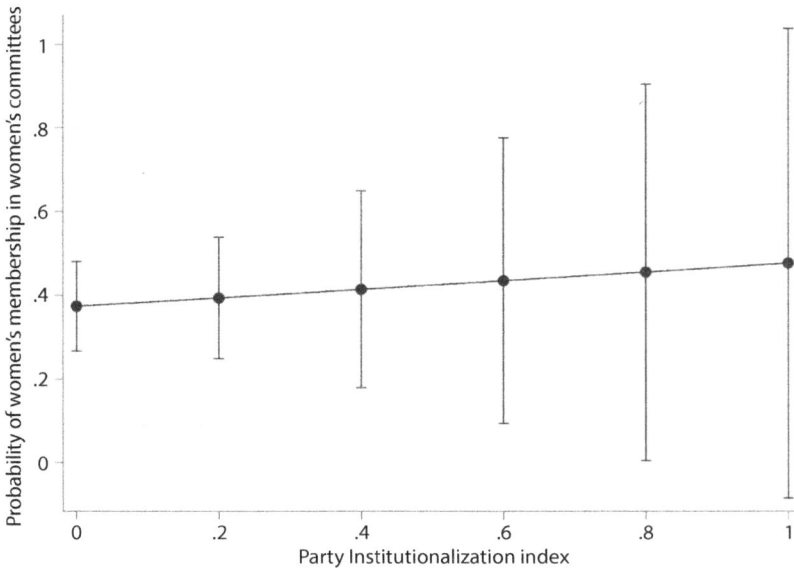

FIGURE 4.8 Probability of women's membership in the Women's Issues Committees in Jordan, Kuwait, and Morocco

Source: Author's data.

Table A.8 presents the correlates of membership in the Legislative, Economy and Financial, Foreign Affairs, Social Affairs, and Women's Issues Committee in Jordan. Models 1, 3, 5, 7, and 9 show the results with the party institutionalization variable included, whereas Models 2, 4, 6, 8, and 10 show the results for the interaction between the party institutionalization variable and the female legislator. As demonstrated in figure 4.2 and these results, the legislator's gender plays a considerable role in the type of their committee assignment. Females are overrepresented in the Women's Issues and the Social Affairs Committees and underrepresented in influential committees, namely the Economy and Financial Committees. Furthermore, they are less likely to be members of other prestigious committees, such as the Legislative and Foreign Affairs Committees, albeit this difference is statistically insignificant.

Legislators' political experience has a statistically positive effect on their membership in the Legislative Committee. First-time legislators are more likely to join the Social Affairs Committee than their senior counterparts. The legislator's ideology has a marginal effect on their membership in different committees in the analysis. Being an Islamist is positively associated with Women's Issues Committee membership. As I show in Models 9 and 10, this result mainly depends on the legislator's gender, where female legislators who are part of the only institutionalized party in the legislature (i.e., the Islamist party) are more likely to join the Women's Issues Committee.

Furthermore, the number of committees is statistically significant in all models, meaning that legislators with multiple committee assignments are more likely to sit on these committees. Finally, party institutionalization has a limited effect on committee membership in Jordan overall. Since only the Islamist parties are weakly institutionalized (the IAF and the ICM), they play a minor role in advancing women's access to influential committees, as outlined in my theory. As shown in table A.8, the weakly institutionalized Islamist parties have little power to access influential committees and enhance women's ability to join them. It is also important to note that the IAF boycotted the 2010 and 2013 elections and only participated in the 2016 and 2020 elections. The less organized ICM party competed in all elections between 2010 and 2020.

Table A.9 presents the correlates of membership in Morocco's Legislative, Economy and Financial, Foreign Affairs, and Social Affairs Committees. I did not include the Women's Issues Committee since it does not exist in Morocco (see table 4.2). To begin, the legislator's gender has a strong effect on the probability of being a member of all committees in the analysis, except for the Economy and Financial Committee. Based on the findings, there is little evidence that female legislators are marginalized from influential or high-policy committees in the Moroccan case, such as the Legislative and Foreign Affairs Committees. However, the results also show that female legislators are less likely to be members of the Economy and Financial Committee (although not statistically significant), which can be mainly attributed to their acute underrepresentation in this type of committee when their numbers started to increase. As shown in figure 4.1, recent legislative sessions have witnessed a remarkable surge in women's representation in this committee.

Another unexpected finding relates to legislators' political expertise and the probability of committee membership. Political experience does not affect legislators' probability of joining specific committees. Similarly, the legislator's ideology plays no role in their committee membership. Islamist MPs are not less likely to enter one type of committee than others. Because of the limited within-country variation in the level of party institutionalization in Morocco, the PI variable is statistically insignificant in all the models, as well as the interaction with the gender of the legislator. In other words, women are able to access influential social affairs committees in Morocco since they are all affiliated with highly institutionalized parties, unlike Jordan and Kuwait.

Table A.10 presents the correlates of membership in Kuwait's Legislative, Economy and Financial, Foreign Affairs, Social Affairs, and Women's Issues Committees. The results are presented in models 1 through 5. I do not include the interaction terms for the legislator's gender and level of party institutionalization, given that none of the women elected in the Kuwaiti lower chamber were affiliated with the Islamist party and mostly ran as independents. Focusing on the results associated with the legislator's gender, it becomes clear that the only statistically significant results are related to female membership in the Women's Issues Committee. Akin to the Jordanian case, women are less likely to be members of the Legislative and Economy and Financial Committees. There is no statistically significant relationship between the legislator's political experience in the Kuwaiti lower chamber and the likelihood of joining a specific committee. This is an interesting finding since the Kuwaiti legislature has one of the highest reelection rates in the entire region.

Furthermore, the number of committees is statistically significant in all models, meaning that legislators with multiple committee assignments are more likely to sit on these committees. This variable is statistically significant in Jordan and Kuwait, in particular, since legislators can join multiple committees, unlike the Moroccan case. Islamist legislators are less likely to join the Social Affairs and Women's Issues Committees. Like the Jordanian case, party institutionalization is marginal in explaining committee memberships in Kuwait. As previously noted, the only institutionalized parties or blocs in Kuwait are the Islamist parties that have never fielded any women candidates.

The previous analysis supports my hypotheses and reveals that women are less represented in influential and traditional male committees, especially in the cases of Jordan and Kuwait, where parties are weakly institutionalized. There is a consistent pattern of females accessing only committees aligned with "feminine" roles, such as the Social Affairs and Women's Issues Committees. While I concur that women's membership in these committees may be based on their own choice, the more critical issue is that they are not marginalized from influential and high-prestige committees and sidelined by less desirable, low-prestige committees. This is particularly relevant when legislators are allowed to join more than one committee (i.e., Jordan and Kuwait) but are still underrepresented.

Results also show that party ideology is not a strong predictor for explaining the patterns of women's committee assignments, consistent with research in other contexts.[56] I present the results for the Islamist ideology in the models, but I find similar findings when I control for blocs and parties' leftist ideology (not included in the tables). Only in Kuwait are Islamist legislators (all males since Islamists never had a female deputy) less likely to serve on the

Social Affairs Committee. Unsurprisingly, the number of committees legislators join is a strong predictor of their membership in most cases in Jordan and Kuwait (multiple committee membership is not allowed in Morocco).

Consistent with my expectation that women affiliated with institutionalized parties are more likely to gain more power and influence within legislatures, the results show that women could access influential committees in Morocco—mainly the Legislative and Foreign Affairs Committees. But what about committee leadership? Would we observe similar patterns across the three cases? I focus on female committee leadership in the following section.

WOMEN'S COMMITTEE LEADERSHIP IN KUWAIT, JORDAN, AND MOROCCO

Extant research has shown that most of the influential leadership positions in both national and local decision-making bodies are dominated by men. Even more, scholars found an inverse relationship between female representation and access to leadership positions in legislatures.[57] Women only get access to less prestigious and influential areas of policymaking that are always deemed an extension of their traditional roles.[58] However, much less is known about women's committee leadership in autocracies with varying levels of party institutionalization.

Focusing on women's leadership in our cases, findings reveal a completely different picture of women's vertical integration in MENA's legislatures. Women are generally more marginalized when it comes to the leadership of committees, especially the influential ones. Table 4.3 compares women's leadership (i.e., vertical integration) and membership (i.e., horizontal integration) positions. It is important to note that the numbers presented in the table are average percentages across legislative sessions and terms included in the analysis (table 4.1). The data shed light on women's shares of seats, as well as their committee leadership assignments: president and "other" leadership positions. The "other positions" category includes

TABLE 4.3 Average percentages of female committee membership
and leadership

		MOROCCO (2007–2016)	JORDAN (2010–2016)	KUWAIT (2009–2016)
Women, Family, and Children Committee	Seats	NA	85.5%	41.9%
	Presidents	NA	100.0%	50.0%
	Other positions	NA	100.0%	50.0%
Legislative Committee	Seats	21.5%	12.0%	5.0%
	Presidents	0.0%	0.0%	11.1%
	Other positions	34.8%	29.4%	5.6%
Economy and Financial Committee	Seats	15.0%	7.1%	5.9%
	Presidents	0.0%	0.0%	0.0%
	Other positions	40.9%	17.9%	5.6%
Foreign Affairs Committee	Seats	28.8%	12.4%	5.6%
	Presidents	12.5%	0.0%	0.0%
	Other positions	50.0%	12.5%	0.0%
Transportation Committee	Seats	6.3%	7.4%	0.0%
	Presidents	0.0%	0.0%	0.0%
	Other positions	12.5%	7.7%	0.0%
Social Affairs Committee	Seats	27.9%	21.5%	12.1%
	Presidents	61.5%	3.8%	11.1%
	Other positions	56.4%	32.5%	2.8%

VPs (only existed in Morocco's 2007 and 2016 legislatures[59] and Jordan's 2013 and 2016 legislatures), secretaries (only Kuwait and Morocco in 2007 and 2016), and reporters (Jordan and Morocco in 2007 and 2016).

Table 4.3 demonstrates wide disparities between women's membership and leadership assignments across the six committees. There are considerable gender differences relating to the level of committee leadership assignments; few women are appointed to top leadership positions, with more concentration in VP, reporter, and secretary positions (i.e., "other" category). Furthermore, women often get appointed to less influential committees focusing on women's and social issues.

In Morocco, women had no access to the committee president positions in the Legislative, Economy and Financial, and Transportation Committees. In contrast, they held about 60 percent of all the presidency positions in the Social Affairs Committee.[60] Only one female presided over the Foreign Affairs Committee for the 2007 legislative term. A more equitable distribution is observed across leadership positions in the 2007 and 2016 sessions. Female legislators occupied one-third of the Legislative Committee's VP, secretary, and reporter positions. They also occupied almost half of these positions in the Foreign and Social Affairs Committees. (See table A.5 in appendix A for a detailed description of these committees.) Finally, they held merely 12.5 percent of the other leadership positions in the Transportation Committee and about 40 percent in the Economy and Financial Committee.[61]

In contrast, the VP and reporter positions were considerably more open and accessible to female deputies in Jordan. Female legislators occupied even fewer top leadership positions across the six committees analyzed in this chapter than their already low numerical representation over the past decade (table 4.3). They could also not access committee presidents' positions except for the Women and Children and the Social Affairs Committees. They occupied all committee president positions for the Women and Family Committee over the past decade and about 4 percent of the Social Affairs Committee president positions. (See table A.4 in appendix A for a detailed description of these committees.) The quote at the beginning of the chapter that describes women's marginalization from committee leadership positions in Jordan, except for the Women's Issues Committee, confirms this finding.

Since the introduction of the VP position in 2013, sixteen women acquired twenty-five positions, twelve of which were in 2013 and thirteen in 2016. As maintained by a female legislator who served in Jordan's lower chamber for three consecutive terms: "They [male legislators] give us vice president positions very easily. They give away the vice presidencies or reporters [of committees] as exit awards. Even though it has nothing to do with the qualifications [of the female MPs] for the most part."[62]

Similarly, women gained easier access to secretary positions. Over three legislative sessions, twenty-seven women acquired about thirty-eight reporter positions. Focusing on the six categories under study, women attained all VP (in 2013 and 2016) and reporter (2010, 2013, and 2016) positions in the Women and Children Committee and almost one-third of positions in the Legislative and Social Affairs Committees. Furthermore, women assumed about 12 percent of the VP and reporter positions in the Foreign Affairs and Economy and Financial Committees.

Finally, the results for the Kuwaiti case are presented in the last column in table 4.3. It is rather challenging to interpret the results given the significantly small number of females elected to the lower chamber over the past decade. Again, women were presidents of the Women and Children and Social Affairs Committees. One woman—Massouma al-Mubarak—was elected once during the first legislative term of the 2009 session as the reporter of the Legislative Committee and then as the president during the third and fourth legislative terms. (See table A.3 in appendix A for a detailed description of these committees.) Since then, women have not assumed top leadership positions in highly influential committees, mainly the Economy and Financial and Foreign Affairs Committees.

* * *

This chapter offers original insights on female committee membership and leadership in Jordan, Kuwait, and Morocco. The analysis delves deeper into female representation beyond examining their increasing numbers in MENA's parliaments and uncovers significant variations in female membership and leadership of legislative committees. By focusing on women's vertical (i.e., leadership) and horizontal (i.e., membership in committees dealing with specific policy areas) divisions, this study sheds important light on the role of women within legislatures and speaks directly to existing comparative scholarship on women's political power in autocracies. Most importantly, this analysis sheds light on the micro-level implications of the varying levels of party institutionalization in the three cases. It demonstrates that female legislators affiliated with institutionalized parties are more likely to gain access to influential committees than those who run as independents or are affiliated with weakly institutionalized parties. However, the analysis also demonstrates clear patterns of female marginalization from committee leadership positions across all cases.

In addition to the quantitative analyses presented in this chapter, semi-structured interviews with female legislators confirmed most of the patterns observed in the analyses and shed important light on the institutional challenges facing women in accessing influential committees.

As I previously noted, committee assignments in Jordan are proportional to the parliamentary blocs, where members state their preferences by the beginning of the legislative session; however, the head of the bloc makes final decisions. Secret voting occurs only when the number of nominees exceeds the maximum number of committee seats. However, the absence of parties and the fragility of blocs in the parliament have left women in a precarious position. A former female legislator in the Jordanian lower chamber stated, "The blocs are very fragile, fluid, and unstable! Only interests connect them. They come together when there are elections for the committees, and after that, that's it; they are dissolved. Nothing keeps them together."[63]

In contrast, female legislators in Morocco described the committee selection process as relatively straightforward: "We [party] hold a meeting at the beginning of the legislative session, and you tell the party which committee you would like to join. You often get what you select, but there will be a vote if the number of nominees exceeds the party's share in the committee. But they [party leaders] don't force you to choose a specific committee."[64]

With the absence of strong political parties in Jordan, the regime has more direct power to manage the legislature's internal affairs and bring in their close allies and supporters, who tend to be males. In the interviews, most of my female legislators emphasized the effect of the undemocratic procedures aimed at constraining political parties by sidelining women to less influential committees. A former female legislator in the Jordanian lower chamber maintains: "The Legislative and the Financial Committees are the most important committees in Jordan's lower chamber. These committees are the system! They are the government! The government prefers that its closest allies control these committees! They will not allow the representatives of the opposition, for example, to lead these committees."[65]

In addition to the existing institutional barriers, female deputies running as independents expressed frustration with the prevalent discrimination and gender stereotyping in the assembly. A female legislator who served three legislative terms in Jordan's legislature and won a non-quota seat in 2013 stated, "I always nominate myself to different committees, not only the Women's Committee—notwithstanding its importance. But unfortunately, it's not easy! Men always put many obstacles in our way, although they are very aware and sure about our capabilities and qualifications."[66]

Interestingly, male legislators were unable to see this bias. In an interview with the first deputy of Jordan's 2016 legislature, he stated, "They [female deputies] speak on the floor, participate [in sessions], travel, hold lectures, [form] blocs, and even lead committees! They are in every position of power. Internal bylaws and the constitution govern our [parliamentary] work! We are a country of institutions! We have the constitution, which gives the rights for the representative . . . it's not the rights of the male representative or the rights of the female representative . . . a representative is a representative."[67]

In addition to blunt discrimination and gender stereotyping within legislatures, bias can be subtle or less visible. In my interviews, male deputies expressed their support for women's leadership and membership in influential committees because they viewed them as "qualified" and "competent." In contrast, qualification was not an issue for men to access such prestigious committees. A former male legislator in Jordan's 2013 legislature argues, "When we vote for the committee memberships in the Chamber, we all support women! For example, I will tell you about myself; I would prefer Reem Abu Dalbouh to be on the Legislative Committee because she is a legal expert! She holds a doctorate in law!"[68] This is consistent with recent research on the gendered qualifications gap that holds female politicians to higher qualifications standards, a subtle yet pernicious source of bias that often limits women's success in the political realm.[69]

I argue in this chapter that whereas party institutionalization may have a substantial effect on women's access to influential committees, women's affiliation with institutionalized parties may have a marginal effect on their preferences to join the Social Affairs and Women's Issues Committees. Women politicians may choose to serve on these committees since they align with their careers and/or enable them to help women and other marginalized social groups. Previous research has also identified women's self-selection to committees that conform to their personal and/or professional backgrounds. I find evidence for this argument in my interviews, especially in settings with no institutionalized parties. Women tend to rely on their previous experiences when they enter the assembly without party support or training. Indeed, several female legislators in Jordan and Kuwait mentioned in the interviews that they selected their committee memberships based on their education or professional experience: "There are committees which we call the important ones: the Legislative, and the Economy and Financial. These are the highest in the assembly, but if I respect myself as XX, I will not enter the Legislative Committee—why? Because this [committee] requires specialized people. For example, I can enter the Committee on Integrity and Transparency because I know the rules. I read every file I receive and familiarize myself with it. So, I can be a committee member because it doesn't require a scientific background."[70]

My interviewees also discussed the challenges that women faced to serve on prestigious committees when they first joined the parliament and how the landscape had gradually changed for women as they gained influence and clout: "When women first entered the parliament in 2002 and 2007, most women were relegated to the Social Affairs Committee. Soon, the female deputies realized that all the important laws relating to women are decided in the Legislative Committee, where laws are formulated and discussed. Since 2011, there has been a substantial increase in women's presence in important committees in Morocco, such as the Legislative and the Financial Committees."[71]

Finally, female deputies highlighted women's inability to access leadership positions in the lower chamber. A female legislator in Jordan's 2013 lower chamber stated, "There is a perception of supremacy or manliness in the assembly! They [male deputies] think that they are more deserving to lead the blocs and the committees. They view us [female deputies] as smart and active but believe we will be satisfied with non-leadership positions! We will be satisfied with the secondary positions! I was the first woman to head an elected team in the first parliament I entered! Now, after two more assemblies, I am the head of a parliamentary bloc! I am the only woman who is the president of a bloc."[72]

5

DISCERNING THE LINK BETWEEN DESCRIPTIVE AND SUBSTANTIVE REPRESENTATION

Posing Parliamentary Questions

Posing parliamentary questions (PQs) is an essential [legislative] tool. It allows legislators to question ministers and put them in really uncomfortable positions. First, people are following them [PQs] on TV, so it's also a way to show that you [MPs] are following up and raising questions that matter to them. Secondly, you are questioning the executive power and the government. They have to come and answer, and it's the only way MPs can force that. Thirdly, of course, it is also good for your image because the people will know you and see your face, how you speak, and defend their interests.

—FEMALE LEGISLATOR ELECTED FROM THE YOUTH QUOTA LIST IN MOROCCO'S 2011 LEGISLATURE, INTERVIEW WITH AUTHOR IN RABAT, 2019

Studies exploring the link between women's numerical presence in legislative bodies (i.e., descriptive representation) and their policy contributions to the groups they represent (i.e., substantive representation) have flourished over the past decades. While most studies have found evidence that women's interests and priorities differ from their male counterparts and advocated the need for increased political representation for women and other marginalized groups, other research has highlighted the role played by external factors such as the political context,[1] partisanship, internal power dynamics, and electoral incentive structures[2] that may complicate the nature or substance of representation. Interestingly, despite the proliferation of studies exploring the relationship between women in power in established and developing democracies, research on the role played by women in the legislative arena in the Middle East and North Africa (MENA) and other undemocratic settings remains scarce. More importantly, little is known about the effect of party institutionalization on women's legislative behavior and policy priorities.

In the first part of the book, I argue that while gender quotas are important mechanisms for overcoming structural inequalities by increasing women's numerical presence in the decision-making arena, being part of institutionalized parties matters for women's substantive representation and for gaining power and influence within autocratic legislatures. My goal in this chapter is to investigate the effect of varying levels of party institutionalization on women's substantive representation in Morocco, Jordan, and Kuwait.

I contend that institutionalized parties have the capacity and resources to promote female legislators' ability to represent women and play a more substantial representative role. Organizationally strong parties with strong links with constituents are essential for coordinating and channeling women's interests within and outside the legislatures. Institutionalized parties' strong ties with society are also crucial for coalition-building, facilitating information flow, and identifying citizens' demands. They provide the organizational structure to "incorporate and stabilize social demands,"[3] channel political demands,[4] represent various geographical areas and social groups, and link diverse constituencies.[5] These organizational structures are increasingly important for women in male-dominated, autocratic settings as women politicians tend to be isolated from existing power networks and lack homosocial capital.[6] Finally, party institutionalization facilitates interparty collaboration between female members compared to contexts with no parties and/or when multiparty competition does not exist. Collaboration across party lines enables women to overcome structural barriers, attain political power and influence, and negotiate with higher echelons of power (i.e., government officials, ruling elites, the incumbent regime) to whom women often lack access and influence.[7]

To reiterate, the three cases offer a unique opportunity to examine the impact of party institutionalization through a comparative lens and uncover interesting patterns of females' legislative behavior. As previously noted, the cases present different degrees of party institutionalization, with Morocco being the case with the most institutionalized political parties, followed by the Jordanian case. Party institutionalization is almost nonexistent in the case of Kuwait, except for the Islamist party that has competed in elections for the past two decades and sustained a significant level of organization and linkage with constituents. However, they have never fielded any women candidates and continue to oppose women's inclusion in politics.

To measure women's substantive representation, I rely on Susan Carroll's conceptualization of women's interests as "those (areas) where policy consequences are likely to have a more immediate and direct impact on significantly larger numbers of women than of men."[8] Furthermore, I differentiate in this chapter between what is widely deemed as feminine or women's interests and feminist policy areas, such as education, health, and social welfare. I expect women politicians affiliated with institutionalized parties to represent women's interests better and to play a more decisive representative role than female legislators who run as independents and/or are affiliated with weakly institutionalized parties.

To test my argument, I rely on a substantial aspect of women's substantive representation: posing parliamentary questions (PQs). I have constructed an original dataset of PQs (N = 21,960) posed by legislators in Jordan, Morocco, and Kuwait between 2009 and 2017. The dataset is supplemented by interview data with incumbent and former legislators and analyses of legislative records, electoral laws, and internal bylaws to better understand women's legislative behavior.

My results show significant variations across the three cases. Female legislators affiliated with highly institutionalized parties are more likely to pay more attention to areas related to women's "feminist" interests and "feminine" areas, such as education and health. Women in the Moroccan parliament are more likely to ask questions about women's interests. Party institutionalization also matters for women's ability to pose women-focused questions in Jordan. Only women affiliated with institutionalized parties represent women's interests. My findings also highlight the limited role of the legislator's ideology and seniority in shaping their legislative behavior and policy priorities.

The first part of the chapter provides a comparative overview of parliamentary questions as a valuable legislative tool. Then, I outline the rules and procedures across the three legislatures and present my data and coding scheme. The chapter proceeds by discussing the quantitative analyses. I conclude by providing qualitative evidence for the quantitative findings and conclusion.

PARLIAMENTARY QUESTIONS: A COMPARATIVE PERSPECTIVE

Parliamentary questions (PQs) are valuable parliamentary tools for both male[9] and female[10] legislators in most legislatures. PQs play an essential monitoring and oversight role over the executive branch and are necessary to hold the government accountable. Thus, legislators can monitor government activities by directing oral or written questions to cabinet members and/or the prime minister[11] and extracting information.[12] Moreover, legislative questions are one of the best and most visible legislative activities. They connect voters and legislators and shed important light on legislators' relationship with the regime and their true policy preferences and priorities.[13] PQs can also be instrumental in cultivating relationships with constituents[14] and as a vote-earning strategy,[15] where legislators can demonstrate their competency by bringing up more constituency-focused questions and concerns.

Given the concentration of power with the autocrat and the relative absence of checks and balances on the executive branch in most parts of the MENA region, legislatures in such settings play an increasingly important role in holding government officials accountable and voicing citizens' demands. For instance, the first legislative term in Jordan's seventeenth legislature dedicated almost thirty sessions to government oversight and monitoring (out of sixty-five sessions).[16] Research has also shown considerable levels of issue congruence between the public and political parties in authoritarian contexts, mainly in Morocco, even when compared to more democratic settings.[17] Relying on a systematic analysis of parliamentary questions, the study demonstrates that governing parties in Morocco's lower chamber are responsive to their support base and supporters of other parties, especially in policy areas that are not sensitive to the incumbent regime.

In addition to their significance as a monitoring tool, relying on PQs to understand legislators' preferences and policy priorities is valuable for several reasons. One researcher, for instance, maintains that using actual records of legislators provides a more accurate and objective account of legislators' behavior than relying on their reported priorities and preferences, which tend to be more subjective.[18] Furthermore, compared to roll call votes and bill sponsorship, PQs are less likely to be influenced by the party leadership and, thus, may provide a more valid measure of the individual preferences of MPs and their role orientation.[19]

PARLIAMENTARY QUESTIONS IN MOROCCO, JORDAN, AND KUWAIT

The function and process of posing PQs vary across different contexts. For example, legislators in Morocco may pose either oral or written questions to the members or head of the government (Internal Bylaws 2013, Articles 184 and 202).[20] All questions are submitted to the head of the parliament in writing, and their office is responsible for notifying the government.

Individual legislators, as well as teams, are allowed to pose questions. A session is dedicated to answering the members' questions proportional to blocs and teams' representation. Cabinet members should respond within twenty days according to the constitution (thirty days if the question is directed to the head of the government). These sessions are aired live on national television (Article 189). Highly controversial and timely topics are often discussed during these sessions, and the debates receive significant public attention.[21]

According to the chamber bylaws, the government is not obliged to answer the questions. Unanswered questions are transferred to the next session until they receive an answer (Article 192). As a result, the nonresponse rate in the Moroccan legislature is significantly high, even when compared to other parliaments in the region. Roughly 35 percent of the questions in the 2011 legislature received an answer. Written questions are even less likely to be answered by the government. As a former female deputy in Morocco maintained, "I waited so long to receive a response on a written question that I submitted to one of the ministers. After weeks of nonresponse, I posted the question on my Facebook page, and immediately, everyone started to pay attention! I got so much media attention, and I also got my response in less than a week!"[22]

In my interviews with female legislators, they repeatedly highlighted the importance of this legislative mechanism as an essential tool to promote legislators' profiles and reputations and hold the government accountable, which is also demonstrated in the quote stated at the beginning of the chapter. Furthermore, a female legislator in Morocco's 2016 legislature asserted, "The oral questions are fundamental despite the short time allocated to each legislator. These sessions are recorded and televised, and the ministers must provide a substantive and objective response; otherwise, they would have to face the public's discontent."[23]

Legislative questions in Jordan must be submitted in writing to the head of the parliament (except in budget discussions, draft bills, and government spending, where direct questions and responses are allowed). Only one legislator can sign the question, which may not be directed to more than one minister. The head of the parliament must inform the minister of the content of the question. The government official must respond to the question in writing within eight days (Lower Chamber Internal Bylaws 2013, Article 117). The head of parliament then informs the MP with the answer and files both the answer and question. The question is then discussed in the following questions session (Articles 128 and 129). The MP has the right to accept the answer if satisfied with the response, respond briefly to the minister's response, or request an investigation if they are unsatisfied with the response (Article 129). The MP can also request an investigation if they do not receive a response within a month (Article 132b). The government responded to about 90 percent of questions posed between 2013 and 2016 in Jordan.

In Kuwait, the procedures are similar. Questions can be submitted only by one legislator. Oral questions directly posed to the government are only allowed during budget and other open discussions (Lower Chamber Internal Bylaws 2009, Article 128). The head of parliament notifies the minister or the head of the government of the question and includes the question in the next session to be answered (Article 123, 2009). The minister or the head of the government has two weeks to answer the question (Article 124). In the following section, I discuss variations in the number and content of questions asked across the three cases.

DESCRIPTION OF THE DATASET, TOPICS, AND CODING OF QUESTIONS

This chapter analyzes legislative questions posed by legislators in Morocco, Jordan, and Kuwait. I rely on the Comparative Agendas Project (CAP) coding scheme to create a unique dataset on the policy agenda in the three countries.[24] The CAP studies made important contributions to the legislative politics literature and our understanding of the level of congruence between the issue priorities of the public and politicians in both developed and developing settings.[25] Each legislative question is coded according to one of the twenty-five topic areas.[26] Table 5.1 lists the twenty-five topic areas used throughout the analysis.[27] The dataset from Morocco includes 14,079 hand-coded parliamentary oral questions introduced in the 2011 and

TABLE 5.1 Comparative Agendas Project (CAP) topic areas and percentage of questions

1.	Education	9.6%
2.	Government operations/budget	9.3%
3.	Health	9%
4.	Banking, finance, domestic commerce	7.3%
5.	Transportation	7.3%
6.	Labor and employment	6.9%
7.	Law and crime	5.5%
8.	Agriculture	4.7%
9.	Community development and housing	4.2%
10.	International affairs and foreign aid	4.1%
11.	Energy	3.9%
12.	Macroeconomics	3.3%
13.	Environment	3.2%
14.	Public land and water management	2.9%
15.	Space, science, technology, communications	2.6%
16.	Social welfare	2.5%
17.	**Women/child/family***	2.4%
18.	Religion	2%
19.	Sports and recreation	2%
20.	Foreign trade	1.6%
21.	**Corruption/fact checking***	1.4%
22.	Civil rights and minority issues	1.3%
23.	Immigration/citizenship issues	1.1%
24.	Arts and entertainment	1%
25.	Defense	0.9%

Source: Comparative Agendas Project, https://www.comparativeagendas.net, and author's added categories.

Note: The percentage column is the number of questions asked in the specific category divided by the total number of questions asked.

2016 legislatures.[28] Morocco's dataset contains all the years of the 2011 legislature and the first year of the 2016 legislature. Kuwait's dataset includes the 2009–2011 session (n = 3,346). I only include one session of the Kuwaiti lower chamber since the 2013 legislature had only one female legislator who resigned shortly after the inception of the parliament. Jordan's dataset extends from 2010 to 2017 (n = 4,535). It has the questions posed by legislators from the inception of the eighteenth legislature in November 2016 until July 2017. A question is coded as women specific if it refers to a topic that affects women disproportionally more for biological or social reasons than men or addresses a social condition in which women are disadvantaged compared to men.[29] It may also address areas relating to violence against women, citizenship rights to children from foreign fathers, gender wage gaps, assistance programs for widows and single mothers, women's health, and benefits for working mothers.

About 23 percent of legislators in Morocco (95 of 395) did not pose any questions during the 2011 session. However, 60 of 67 female legislators asked questions during the same session. In Jordan, 124 of the 150 members posed questions in the 2013 legislature. Seventeen female legislators (out of 18) asked questions, whereas only 107 of the 132 male legislators posed questions. Forty-eight legislators (out of 50) in Kuwait asked questions in 2009.[30]

There are wide variations in the number of questions legislators ask in the three cases. Legislators asked between 1 and 463 questions in Jordan. In Kuwait, lower chamber members posed between 1 and 291 questions (median = 35). As for Morocco, legislators asked between 1 and 2,229 questions. Kuwait has the highest average of questions per legislator (average of 68 questions) compared to Jordan (12 questions) and Morocco (18 questions). Table 5.1 presents the percentages of each topic aggregated across the three countries.[31]

As shown in table 5.1, legislators in the three countries primarily focused on education (9.6 percent of the total questions asked), government operations (9.3 percent), health (9 percent), transportation (7.3 percent), economy and finance (7.3 percent), and labor and employment (7 percent). The least frequent questions were on civil rights (1.3 percent), corruption (1.4 percent), defense (0.9 percent), and immigration/citizenship (1.1 percent)—areas that are often controlled by the regime. This is consistent with extant scholarship that shows that legislators in autocratic legislatures tend to avoid sensitive issues that may threaten the regime's stability.[32] The following section details the distribution of questions by gender in the three countries.

REPRESENTING WOMEN'S INTERESTS THROUGH LEGISLATIVE QUESTIONS: DESCRIPTIVES

This section provides information on the distribution of the average number of questions across the top categories. Table 5.2 presents the top five question categories in the three countries by gender and illustrates clear commonalities between the policy priorities of male and female legislators in the three cases. As shown in table 5.2, female legislators focus on education (13.5 percent of the total questions asked by women), health (9.6 percent), government operations and budget (8 percent), labor and employment (6.4 percent), and law and crime (6.1 percent). Questions on agriculture and transportation received the least attention from the female legislators in the three countries.

TABLE 5.2 Top five categories asked by male and female legislators

MALE LEGISLATOR TOP FIVE CATEGORIES		FEMALE LEGISLATOR TOP FIVE CATEGORIES	
QUESTION TOPIC	PERCENTAGE OF TOTAL QUESTIONS ASKED BY ALL MALE LEGISLATORS	QUESTION TOPIC	PERCENTAGE OF TOTAL QUESTIONS ASKED BY ALL FEMALE LEGISLATORS
Government operations	9.6%	Education	13.5%
Health	8.7%	Health	9.6%
Education	8.6%	Government operations	8%
Banking and commerce	7.6%	Labor and employment	6.4%
Labor and employment	6.9%	Law and crime	6.1%
Total questions asked by male legislators	17,526	Total questions asked by female legislators	4,091

Source: Author's data.

Male legislators also focused on government operations and budget (9.6 percent of total questions asked by men), education (8.6 percent), health (8.7 percent), banking and commerce (7.6 percent), and labor and employment (6.9 percent). The most significant gap between male and female legislative behavior is in agriculture, education, and women, child, and family issue areas.

In tables 5.3, 5.4, and 5.5, I detail the percentages of PQs across gender in the three countries. Starting with Morocco, sixty of the sixty-seven female legislators asked 2,602 questions in the 2011 legislature (of 9,592 questions, about 27 percent of the total questions). Additionally, all women elected in the 2016 legislature posed 885 questions in the first legislative term of the 2016 legislature (of 4,487 total questions; table 5.3, column 1). The questions mainly focused on education (13 percent of total questions asked by female legislators), health (10 percent), social welfare and community development (7.3 percent), and finance and economics (7.4 percent). Additionally, questions about transportation, law and crime, labor and employment, and women's issues were among female legislators' priorities. The lowest number of questions were about corruption, defense, energy, environment, religion, civil rights, and immigration.

As demonstrated in the last column of table 5.3, the most significant gender differences in Morocco are in the areas of agriculture, education, foreign affairs, women and children, economy and finance, and transportation. Women are more likely than men to ask questions about education, health, women and children, and foreign affairs. In contrast, male legislators' priorities are agriculture, finance and economy, and transportation. Male and female legislators' priorities are almost similar in the areas of social welfare, law and crime, labor and employment, religion, civil rights and immigration, corruption, and defense.

Female legislators submitted 456 questions in Jordan's 2010, 2013, and 2016 legislatures (table 5.4). They submitted 120 questions in 2016 (of 915 questions), 280 questions in 2013 (of 2,869 questions), and 56 questions in 2010 (of 619 total questions). Their top priorities were education (12.5 percent of the total questions posed by female legislators), finance and economy (13.5 percent), social welfare and community development (9 percent),

TABLE 5.3 Questions asked by male and female legislators in Morocco (2011–2017)

MOROCCO[a]	FEMALE LEGISLATORS	MALE LEGISLATORS	DIFFERENCE IN PERCENTAGE
Education	459/13.2%	941/8.9%	4.3
Social welfare/community development[b]	265/7.3%	787/7.4%	−0.1
Health	365/10.5%	978/9.2%	1.3
Finance/economics[c]	260/7.4%	1031/9.7%	−2.3
Transportation	206/5.9%	846/8%	−2.1
Law and crime	209/6%	581/5.4%	0.6
Labor/employment	213/6.1%	595/5.6%	0.5
Women/children/family	181/5.2%	266/2.5%	2.7
Foreign affairs	39/5.2%	143/1.35%	3.85
Agriculture	143/4.1%	898/8.5%	−4.4
Energy	63/1.8%	328/3.1%	−1.3
Religion	58/1.6%	186/1.7%	−0.1
Civil rights and immigration	95/2.7%	230/2.2%	0.5
Environment	67/1.9%	402/3.8%	−1.9
Corruption	33/0.9%	106/1%	−0.1
Defense	18/0.5%	47/0.4%	0.1
Total questions/percentage of total questions asked[d]	3,487/24.8%	10,592/75.2%	N = 14,079

[a]Women constituted 17 and 20 percent of the 2011 and 2016 legislatures, respectively.

[b]This category combines the social welfare and community development categories.

[c]This category combines questions on the economy and the banking and commerce categories.

[d]The percentages are calculated based on the total questions male or female legislators pose. They do not add up to 100 percent because I have excluded categories with few observations, such as foreign trade; space, science, technology, and communication; sports and recreation; arts and entertainment; and public land and water management.

transportation (6.8 percent), law and crime (5 percent), and labor and employment (7.2 percent). The issues that received the least attention were defense, religion, corruption, and women and children. There was only one question related to women and family in Jordan's 2013 legislature. Female legislators did not ask questions about women's issues in the 2010 legislature.

TABLE 5.4 Questions asked by male and female legislators in Jordan (2010–2017)

JORDAN[a]	FEMALE LEGISLATORS	MALE LEGISLATORS	DIFFERENCE IN PERCENTAGE
Education	57/12.5%	268/6.8%	5.7
Finance/economics	62/13.5%	616/15.5%	−2.0
Social welfare/community development	41/9%	249/6.3%	2.7
Health	23/5%	141/3.6%	1.4
Law and crime	23/5%	134/3.4%	1.6
Transportation	31/6.8%	312/7.9%	−1.1
Labor/employment	33/7.2%	300/7.6%	−0.4
Energy	20/4.4%	221/5.6%	−1.2
Agriculture	12/2.6%	97/2.5%	0.1
Foreign affairs	10/2.2%	96/2.4%	−0.2
Environment	13/2.8%	84/2.1%	0.7
Corruption	4/0.9%	53/1.3%	−0.4
Civil rights/immigration	9/2.0%	89/2.2%	−0.2
Religion	4/0.9%	84/2.1%	−1.2
Defense	2/0.4%	42/1.1%	−0.7
Women/children/family	2/0.4%	24/0.6%	−0.2
Total questions/percentage of total questions asked[b]	456/10%	3,953/90%	N = 4,535

[a]Women constituted 11 percent of the 2010 legislature. In 2013 and 2016, they constituted 12 and 15 percent, respectively.

[b]The percentages are calculated based on the total questions male or female legislators pose. The percentages do not add up to 100 percent because I have excluded categories with few observations, such as foreign trade; space, science, technology, and communication; sports and recreation; arts and entertainment; and public land and water management.

The most significant gender differences were in the areas of education, economy and finance, social welfare and community development, law and crime, and health. Women tend to ask more questions about education, social welfare and community development, health, and environment. Contrastingly, male legislators focused more on the economy and finance, transportation, and energy. Male and female legislators' priorities are

TABLE 5.5 Questions asked by male and female legislators in Kuwait (2009–2011)

KUWAIT[a]	FEMALE LEGISLATORS	MALE LEGISLATORS	DIFFERENCE IN PERCENTAGE
Education	17.7%	9.6%	8.1
Health	9.7%	12.9%	–3.2
Corruption	9.7%	2.8%	6.9
Environment	8.3%	3.2%	5.1
Law and crime	7.9%	6.9%	1.0
Labor/employment	6.9%	10%	–3.1
Energy	5.1%	5.9%	–0.8
Social welfare/community development	4.6%	2.6%	2.0
Finance/economics	4.6%	9.5%	–4.9
Transportation	3.7%	4.9%	–1.2
Civil rights/immigration	3.7%	2.4%	1.3
Defense	2.3%	2.4%	–0.1
Women/children/family	1.8%	0.9%	0.9
Religion	0.9%	3.5%	–2.6
Foreign affairs	0.9%	2.8%	–1.9
Agriculture	0.46%	1.6%	–1.14
Total questions/percentage of total questions asked[b]	215/6.5%	3,131/93.5%	N = 3,346

[a]Female representation was 8 percent of the 2009 legislature.

[b]The percentages are calculated based on the total questions male or female legislators pose. The percentages do not add up to 100 percent because I have excluded categories with few observations, such as foreign trade; space, science, technology, and communication; sports and recreation; arts and entertainment; and public land and water management.

almost similar in the areas of foreign affairs, labor and employment, agriculture, women and children, corruption, and civil rights and immigration.

In Kuwait, 3,346 total written questions were posed between 2009 and 2011. Table 5.5 shows the distribution of questions in the 2009 legislature. All female legislators posed questions during the 2009 session and asked 215 questions (6.5 percent of total questions). Most questions focused on issues related to education (17.7 percent of all questions posed by female legislators), health (9.7 percent), corruption (9.7 percent), environment (8.3

percent), and legal issues (7.9 percent). The issues that received the least attention were agriculture, foreign affairs, religion, defense, and women and children.

As demonstrated in table 5.5 (column 3), the most substantive gender differences are in the areas of education, corruption, environment, finance and economics, and health. Male legislators are more likely to focus on health, labor and employment, finance and economics, religion, and foreign affairs. Male and female legislators' priorities are almost similar in the areas of defense, energy, women and children, and law and crime.

To summarize, females across the three cases under study are generally interested in asking questions about "feminine" domains, which are mainly education, health (except for Kuwait), environment (except for Morocco), community development, and social welfare. Female legislators are also more likely to ask questions about "feminist" issues and issues relating to children and family, especially in Morocco. Significant gender differences exist in PQs related to education, economy and finance, transportation, energy, and religion. Interestingly, the findings are mixed regarding traditional "male" domains, such as finance and economics, labor and employment, foreign affairs, agriculture, and defense. The following section focuses on the link between party institutionalization and female legislative behavior while controlling for different legislature and legislator-level covariates.

WOMEN'S SUBSTANTIVE REPRESENTATION AND PARTY INSTITUTIONALIZATION

To construct the dependent variables for the multivariate analysis, I define four thematic categories to compare women's and men's legislative behavior. These categories are women and family, foreign affairs, education, and health. Similar to previous studies, a wide range of policy areas is included to account for male (i.e., foreign affairs) and female domains and issues (i.e., education, health, and women and children). Importantly,

I do not intend to impose specific policy interests on male or female legislators, but I am mainly interested in discerning female legislators' behavior toward women's issues.

To measure the effect of the main independent variable in this study—party institutionalization—on women's legislative behavior, I constructed an additive index based on six main measures that capture the strength of political parties. The index includes the standardized scores acquired from the Varieties of Party Identity and Organization (V-Party) dataset V-Dem (2020) collected. I have included in the index measures of parties' local organizational strength, continuation, presence of local offices, processes of candidates' nominations, cohesion, and stable links with social organizations. The index ranges between 0 and 1, with 1 being the highest level of party institutionalization and 0 denoting the absence of party institutionalization. (See table A.7 in appendix A for more details.)

Interaction terms were created for legislators who are women and members of an institutionalized party. I also created a binary measure that captures the level of party institutionalization. Parties with 0.5 or more are coded as institutionalized, whereas parties with scores less than 0.5 are coded as 0.

To better understand gender differences relating to legislators performing their monitoring role in Arab parliaments, I control for various factors that may affect their priorities and preferences in the multivariate models. These factors include legislators' seniority (political expertise), which is measured by whether they were reelected or new to office. This variable was obtained from parliamentary records and my coding of previous sessions in the three countries. I also added a variable that captures ideology—if the legislator is an Islamist in Kuwait, Jordan, and Morocco. MPs affiliated with Morocco's Justice and Development Party (PJD) are coded as Islamists. In Kuwait, legislators affiliated with the Islamic Salafi Alliance, the Constitutional Islamic Movement, the National Islamist Alliance, and the Justice and Peace Alliance are coded as Islamists.[33] I code the Islamic Alliance Front (IAF) and the Islamic Centrist Party (al-Wasat) as Islamists in Jordan. The IAF boycotted the 2010 and 2013 elections, and only the Islamic Centrist Party competed for seats. The Centrist party constituted about 11 percent of the 2013 legislature. This parliament also witnessed the addition of twenty-seven national seats for the first time to promote the participation of political parties. The national list seats were removed in the 2016 elections (see table 3.2). The IAF participated in the 2016 elections and won ten seats, whereas the Islamic Centrist Party acquired only five.[34]

I also control for relevant committee membership and leadership.[35] Analysis has shown that the nature of questions or bills posed by legislators can be related to their policy specialization (as indicated by their committee assignment and leadership).[36] Legislators who are members or leaders of a specific legislative committee are more likely to pose questions falling within the issue area of their committee assignment since they gain expertise and specialization. Relevant committee membership or leadership is a dummy variable coded as 1 if a legislator serves on a committee related to the issue area of the dependent variable. Committee membership and leadership data were collected from the websites of the lower houses of these countries and the websites of independent monitoring organizations in Morocco, Kuwait, and Jordan. (A detailed description of the coding of committees' leadership and membership can be found in appendix A, tables A.3–A.5).[37] Moreover, the models include a variable measuring the total number of questions posed by legislators (total questions) to illustrate the link between legislators' propensity to ask questions generally and their interest in a specific policy area.[38]

Figures 5.1 through 5.4 visually represent the results for the female-only models for the three countries. The aggregate results for the three countries are presented in appendix A, table A.12. Tables 5.6 through 5.8 outline the results explaining the variance in legislators' behavior in posing PQs in the three countries. I used negative binomial regression model (NBREG) specification to estimate all models.[39] The unit of analysis is the individual legislator. For all the models, the dependent variable is a count variable— the number of PQs a legislator asks. Given the nature of the dependent variables, negative binomial models are the most appropriate for this type of data compared to other count models, such as Poisson, due to overdispersion. Overdispersion occurs when a significantly larger number of legislators pose a small number of questions compared to those who ask a larger number. Robust standard errors clustered at the individual legislator level are used in all model specifications to account for unobserved factors that may influence legislators' behavior. I have included year/session fixed effects in all the models to account for any temporal shocks.

Figures 5.1 through 5.4 are estimated using the female legislators' sub-sample to better visualize the effect of party institutionalization on their legislative behavior. I also report the interaction effects in table A.12 in the appendix for the aggregate data. The figures were estimated using the margin command in STATA after estimating the negative binomial models. These figures are rather challenging to interpret since the dependent variable is a count variable. However, the figures provide the most effective way to present the outcomes of interest. They show the predicted count of questions at each level of the main independent variable, the level of party institutionalization, holding all other variables in the model at their means.

Figure 5.1 presents the predicted count of questions on women and family posed by female legislators in the three countries. The graph shows that

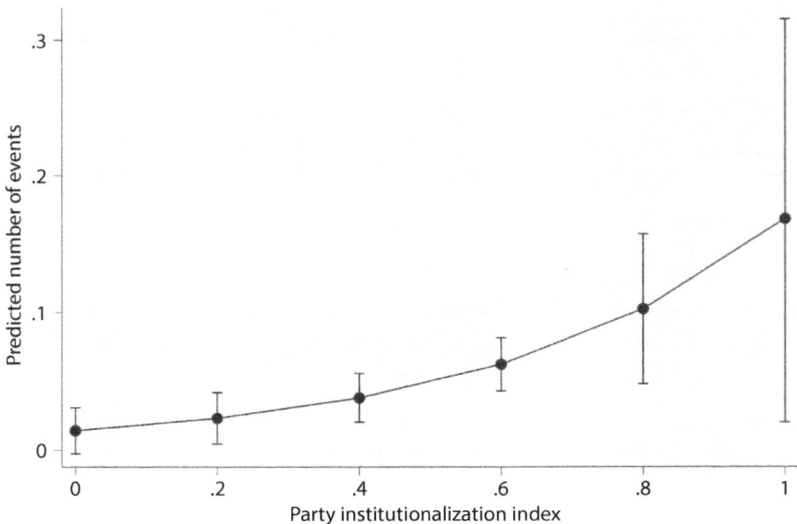

FIGURE 5.1 Female legislators posing questions on women and family in Morocco, Kuwait, and Jordan

Source: Author's data.

the number of questions relating to this area increases with party institutionalization. Similar results are present for questions focusing on foreign affairs (figure 5.2) and feminine areas, namely education (figure 5.3) and health (figure 5.4). These results support my argument that party institutionalization matters, especially for women's substantive representation in autocratic legislatures. It is also clear from table A.12 that party institutionalization particularly matters for women's ability to pose questions that relate to feminine (i.e., education and health) and feminist areas (i.e., women and children) (columns 2, 6, and 8 in table A.12) but not necessarily male-dominated issue areas, such as foreign affairs where there is statistically insignificant difference between men and women affiliated with highly institutionalized parties (column 4 in table A.12). Furthermore, columns 5, and 7 in table A.12 show that party institutionalization has a statistically insignificant effect on male legislators' posing questions on education and health. However, the interaction between party institutionalization and

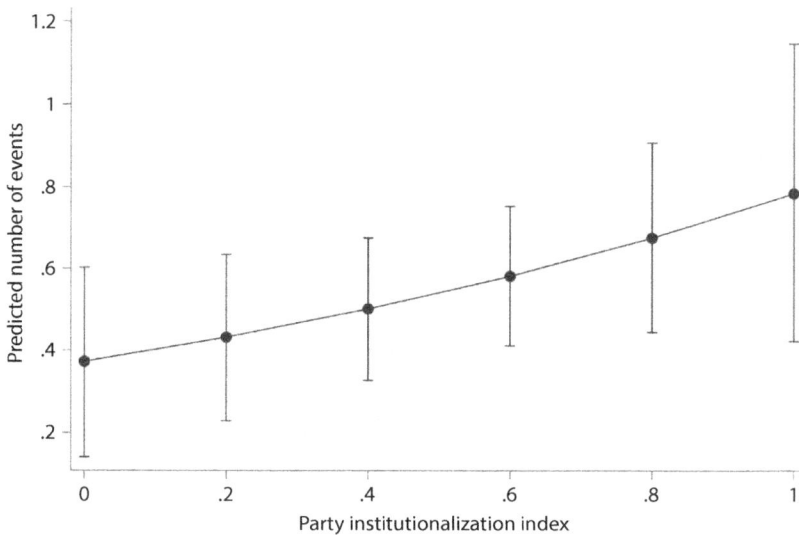

FIGURE 5.2 Female legislators posing questions on international affairs in Morocco, Kuwait, and Jordan

Source: Author's data.

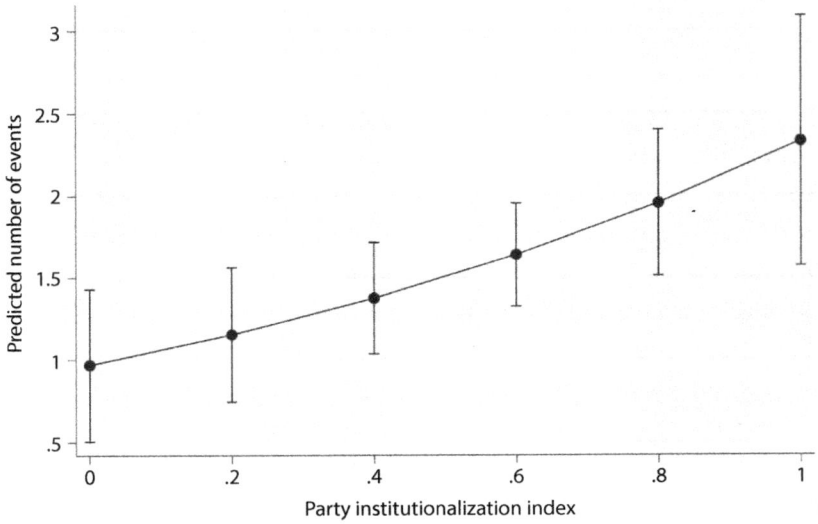

FIGURE 5.3 Female legislators posing questions on education in Morocco, Kuwait, and Jordan

Source: Author's data.

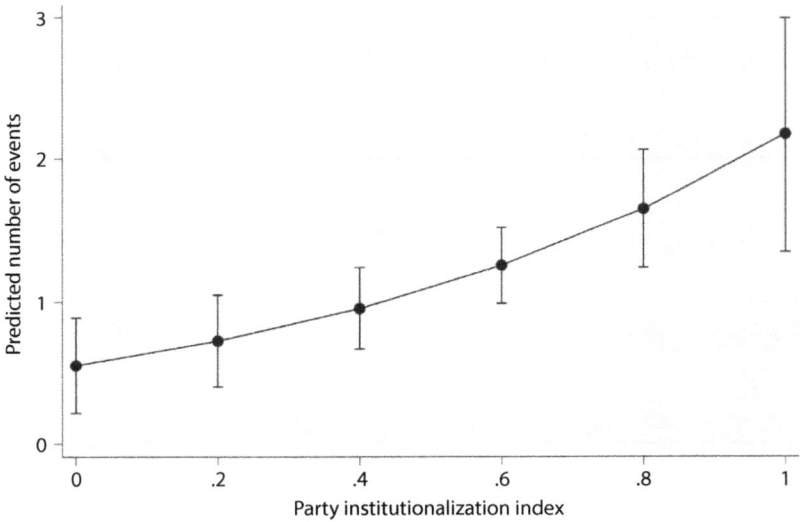

FIGURE 5.4 Female legislators posing questions on health in Morocco, Kuwait, and Jordan

Source: Author's data.

a female legislator posing questions on education and health is highly statistically significant, as presented in columns 6 and 8 in table A.12.

Despite the stark cross-national evidence on the link between party institutionalization and women's ability to represent women's interests, within-country variations are less pronounced given the fact that all parties are highly institutionalized in Morocco and not institutionalized in Kuwait (except for the Islamists, who never field women candidates). Thus, I expect to find the most pronounced within-case variations in Jordan, where considerable variations in party institutionalization are present. Women may run with the more institutionalized Islamist and leftist parties, and they may also run as independents without any party affiliation or support.

Table 5.6 shows the correlates of posing PQs in Jordan by topic. Columns 1, 3, 5, and 7 show the results with the party institutionalization variable, whereas columns 2, 4, 6, and 8 show the results for the models with the interaction between the female legislator and party institutionalization. Notably, female legislators are significantly less likely to pose questions relating to women, children, and family. Legislators' seniority is generally associated with less likelihood of posing questions about education and has no statistically significant effect on any other topic area. Furthermore, data show that posing questions in the lower chamber regarding a specific policy area is strongly associated with legislators' propensity to ask PQs generally, rather than having strong interest or priorities in one particular policy area. The models also indicate that committee membership has a modest positive effect on posing questions related to women and family.[40] Like the Kuwaiti case, multiple committee memberships are allowed in Jordan. MPs can join up to two permanent committees and as many temporary committees as they prefer. However, less than 10 percent of legislators hold more than two committee assignments (both permanent and temporary).

The results also show that Islamist party members pose fewer questions pertinent to foreign affairs. Party institutionalization has a modest effect on shaping legislators' behavior in Jordan, given the weakness of political parties. Party institutionalization only matters when posing questions related to foreign affairs. However, party institutionalization has a strong effect on women legislators. Women affiliated with an institutionalized

TABLE 5.6 Posing parliamentary questions (PQs) in Jordan's Lower House (2010–2017) (N = 4,535 PQs)

	(1) WOMEN/FAMILY	(2) WOMEN/FAMILY	(3) FOREIGN AFFAIRS	(4) FOREIGN AFFAIRS	(5) EDUCATION	(6) EDUCATION	(7) HEALTH	(8) HEALTH
Female	-2.35*	-174.27***	0.20	0.12	0.27	-0.19	0.20	-0.31
	(1.14)	(19.60)	(0.28)	(0.32)	(0.24)	(0.26)	(0.29)	(0.37)
Political experience	-1.55	-1.47	0.00	-0.01	-0.47*	-0.53*	0.07	-0.09
	(1.24)	(1.18)	(0.26)	(0.26)	(0.19)	(0.20)	(0.26)	(0.26)
Total questions	0.03**	0.03**	0.04***	0.04***	0.03**	0.02**	0.03**	0.03**
	(0.01)	(0.12)	(0.01)	(0.01)	(0.00)	(0.00)	(0.01)	(0.01)
Member of committee	2.60*	-12.05***	0.29	0.29	0.11	0.03	0.25	0.23
	(1.27)	(1.16)	(0.26)	(0.26)	(0.22)	(0.21)	(0.35)	(0.34)
Islamist	-6.10	-1.80	-10.75*	-10.23*	0.19	0.60	0.94	-0.49
	(9.30)	(7.22)	(4.24)	(4.06)	(0.92)	(0.69)	(0.69)	(0.41)
Party institutionalization (PI)	10.94	3.74	17.53**	16.58**	0.37	-1.08	-1.42	-2.59*
	(14.34)	(11.30)	(6.58)	(6.14)	(1.63)	(1.17)	(1.13)	(1.20)
Female*PI		270.20***		0.66		2.75***		3.51***
		(29.50)		(1.12)		(1.02)		(1.19)
Constant	-4.08***	-4.05***	-2.40***	-2.38***	-1.79***	-1.72***	-2.83***	-2.74***
	(0.89)	(0.88)	(0.42)	(0.42)	(0.24)	(0.23)	(0.42)	(0.41)
Year/session fixed effects	Yes	Yes	Yes	Yes	Yes	Yes	Yes	Yes
N	380	380	380	380	380	380	380	380

Standard errors in parentheses; * $p < 0.05$, ** $p < 0.01$, *** $p < 0.001$.

party pose more questions about education, health, and women and children. However, we must interpret this finding with caution given the very few questions on women and children, as demonstrated in table 5.4.[41]

Table 5.7 presents the results of Morocco's legislature between 2011 and 2017. Columns 1, 3, 5, and 7 show the results with the party institutionalization variable, whereas columns 2, 4, 6, and 8 show the results with the interaction between the female legislator and party institutionalization. Focusing on females' legislative priorities, it is evident that they prioritize women, children, and family issues compared to their male counterparts. PQs relating to feminine issues, such as education and health, are top priorities for female legislators. Foreign affairs issues received much attention from female legislators in Morocco.

While seniority tends to play an insignificant role in the questions legislators pose, legislators' membership in a relevant committee is crucial in almost all areas.[42] The ideology of legislators plays a minor role in shaping legislators' priorities, as demonstrated in table 5.7. Being an Islamist legislator has a statistically significant effect on asking questions about foreign affairs, and education. The party institutionalization variable is statistically insignificant in all models due to the lack of substantial variations across Moroccan political parties concerning their degree of institutionalization. Similarly, the interaction term between party institutionalization and female legislators is statistically insignificant in all the interaction models. All female legislators are affiliated with highly institutionalized parties and unlikely to run as independents or without party support. Consistent with my theory, women's affiliation with the highly institutionalized parties in Morocco is associated with better representation of women's interests, particularly in "feminine" areas, such as education and health, and "feminist" areas, namely women and family.

Results for Kuwait are shown in Table 5.8. I do not include the interaction models due to the absence of female legislators affiliated with institutionalized parties in Kuwait. Interestingly, being a female legislator is not associated with directing women and family-related questions. However, females are less likely to ask questions relating to foreign affairs. Seniority is negatively associated with posing questions about health. Moreover, data

TABLE 5.7 Posing parliamentary questions (PQs) in Morocco's Lower House (2011–2017) (N = 14,079 PQs)

	(1) WOMEN/FAMILY	(2) WOMEN/FAMILY	(3) FOREIGN AFFAIRS	(4) FOREIGN AFFAIRS	(5) EDUCATION	(6) EDUCATION	(7) HEALTH	(8) HEALTH
Female	1.43***	5.00	0.57**	1.18	0.64***	0.79	0.41**	-0.79
	(0.21)	(2.29)	(0.19)	(2.17)	(0.13)	(1.51)	(0.13)	(1.69)
Political experience	-0.11	-0.12	0.31	0.32	-0.22	-0.22	-0.03	-0.03
	(0.21)	(0.21)	(0.18)	(0.18)	(0.15)	(0.15)	(0.12)	(0.12)
Total questions	0.02**	0.02**	0.02**	0.02**	0.01**	0.01**	0.02**	0.02**
	(0.00)	(0.00)	(0.01)	(0.00)	(0.00)	(0.00)	(0.00)	(0.00)
Member of committee	0.43*	0.43*	1.57***	1.57***	0.81***	0.81***	0.63***	0.62***
	(0.21)	(0.21)	(0.28)	(0.28)	(0.14)	(0.14)	(0.14)	(0.14)
Islamist	-0.11	-0.11	0.44*	0.45*	0.23*	0.23*	-0.03	-0.04
	(0.19)	(0.19)	(0.17)	(0.17)	(0.11)	(0.11)	(0.13)	(0.13)
Party institutionalization (PI)	-0.01	0.59	0.50	0.57	-0.70*	-0.70*	-0.53	-0.58
	(0.64)	(0.62)	(0.66)	(0.66)	(0.40)	(0.41)	(0.36)	(0.36)
Female*PI		-5.01		-0.84		-0.21		1.67
		(3.18)		(3.04)		(2.10)		(2.32)
Constant	-2.09***	-2.50***	-1.93***	-1.98***	0.07	0.07	0.07	0.11
	(0.49)	(0.47)	(0.54)	(0.26)	(0.32)	(0.32)	(0.31)	(0.30)
Year/session fixed effects	Yes	Yes	Yes	Yes	Yes	Yes	Yes	Yes
N	692	692	692	692	692	692	692	692

Standard errors in parentheses; * $p < 0.05$, ** $p < 0.01$, *** $p < 0.001$.

TABLE 5.8 Posing parliamentary questions (PQs) in Kuwait's Lower House (2009–2011) (N = 3,346 PQs)

	(1) WOMEN/FAMILY	(2) FOREIGN AFFAIRS	(3) EDUCATION	(4) HEALTH
Female	1.08	−1.00*	0.36	−0.40
	(0.94)	(0.51)	(0.36)	(0.45)
Political experience	−0.78	−0.66	−0.46	−0.79*
	(0.59)	(0.43)	(0.28)	(0.38)
Total questions	0.01***	0.01**	0.00***	0.01***
	(0.00)	(0.00)	(0.00)	(0.00)
Member of committee	−0.16	1.29**	0.96*	0.14
	(0.83)	(0.46)	(0.38)	(0.34)
Islamist	1.14**	0.86	0.59*	0.37
	(0.41)	(0.47)	(0.24)	(0.38)
Party institutionalization (PI)	−0.07	0.67*	0.08	0.42
	(1.27)	(0.27)	(0.31)	(0.49)
Constant	−1.45**	−1.02*	0.93***	1.37***
	(0.47)	(0.43)	(0.25)	(0.34)
Year/session fixed effects	Yes	Yes	Yes	Yes
		Yes	Yes	Yes
N	48	48	48	47

Standard errors in parentheses; * $p < 0.05$, ** $p < 0.01$, *** $p < 0.001$.

show that posing questions in the Kuwaiti context regarding a specific policy area is strongly associated with legislators' propensity to ask parliamentary questions generally. Committee membership is not a strong predictor of issues raised by legislators in Kuwait.[43] As shown in table 5.8, membership or leadership of a relevant committee has a positive, statistically significant effect on posing questions about foreign affairs and education. This finding can be partly attributed to the fact that multiple committee memberships are allowed in the Kuwaiti lower chamber (legislators must join at least one permanent committee but can join up to two permanent committees, unlike Morocco, where legislators are only allowed to join one committee). Switching committee membership is also permissible in Kuwait

(Internal Bylaws 2015, Article 45). In Kuwait, most legislators change their committee appointment every legislative term, whereas in Morocco, changing committees is uncommon and limited to the third year of the legislature (Internal Bylaws 2013, Article 59).

Being an Islamist male in the Kuwaiti legislature is associated with posing more questions on women and family and education. Party institutionalization has a statistically significant effect on posing questions on foreign affairs. The interaction between party institutionalization and female legislators is unavailable in Kuwait since the Islamic Constitutional Movement—the only institutionalized bloc—has never nominated a female candidate, and the four women who won seats in the 2009 legislature ran as independents.

* * *

The results presented in this chapter demonstrate wide variations in women's legislative behavior. As argued throughout the book, varying levels of party institutionalization may significantly shape legislators' behavior and priorities and, thus, impact the introduction of gendered legislation. Data presented in tables 5.3, 5.4, and 5.5 shed light on women's policy priorities across different topics in Morocco, Jordan, and Kuwait compared to their male counterparts—without controlling for any factors that may affect their legislative priorities and preferences. The tables depict clear gender differences in issues relating to education, health, economy, and women and children-related issues, especially in Morocco and Kuwait. Education and foreign and legal affairs receive the most attention from female legislators in Jordan.

Tables 5.6 through 5.8 outline the correlates of women's legislative behavior across the three cases. The results are remarkable because of the limited attention paid to women's issues in Jordan and Kuwait. Female legislators in Kuwait and Morocco tend to focus on "feminist" areas such as education; however, the results vary across cases even after controlling for legislators' ideology, seniority, and other legislator-level variables. Data show that females are equally interested in asking questions about foreign affairs (Morocco), typically viewed as a male-dominated area. Another important pattern that emerges in Kuwait and Jordan is the absence of legislators' policy priorities, which is also evident in the fact that the total number of questions asked is one of the strongest predictors of their propensity to ask questions in a specific policy area. In addition, legislators' membership in a relevant committee is not necessarily related to the type of questions asked in Jordan and Kuwait, with few exceptions.

Even though Morocco and Jordan have institutional mechanisms (i.e., reserved seats) to promote women's political representation, there are clear variations across the two cases regarding women's substantive representation. Whereas all women in Morocco are able to represent women's interests, only women affiliated with institutionalized parties in Jordan are able to represent women. I attribute these variations to political parties' degree of institutionalization, which is critical for women's substantive representation. As I argue at the beginning of the book, institutionalized parties promote women's ability to represent women through two important mechanisms: facilitating inter- and intraparty collaboration and coordinating and channeling women's interests.

Throughout my fieldwork, female legislators in Morocco highlighted the importance of collaboration with other female legislators to formulate women-friendly policies and legislation:

> We [female legislators] established in the 2011 legislature the Commission of Justice and Equity. Eight women representing the parliamentary groups came together to work on women-specific legislation. It was a spectacular experience! I was the commission's coordinator, and every political party and ideology was represented! In our first meeting, we agreed to put the controversial issues aside, mainly abortion and inheritance. We were able to work on the internal bylaws of the lower chamber, and one of our biggest achievements was the enforcement of the gender quota in all leadership positions in the lower chamber. Women are now guaranteed one-third of all leadership positions within the legislature.[44]

Women's expertise and involvement in parties' women's branches were also crucial factors for their success within the legislature. In my interviews in

Morocco, female MPs often described their long involvement with the party branches and how it facilitated their communication with women's organizations and informal associations:

> I was a member of Istiqlal's women's branch/organization. We had direct contact with all party branches and were expected to establish more branches and recruit as many as possible. We also had strong ties with women's organizations. I believe the collaboration between the parties' women's branches and women's organizations was crucial for women's gains in Morocco, such as the Mudawana. It was an invaluable experience for me to be part of the party's women's branch and learn from this experience. Women's branches were also coordinating and learning from other parties outside Morocco on how to enact change.[45]

In addition, female legislators' concerns about reelection—especially given the absence of any party/bloc and/or tribal support to their nomination and selection—may lead to more focus on service provision and individualized demands to guarantee reelection. A study on PQs in Germany's mixed electoral system maintains that "female MPs represent women's issues more strongly compared with male MPs if their reelection is secured and the electoral incentive structure does not force them to represent the local interests of the constituency in their districts."[46] This caveat was evident in my fieldwork and interviews with female MPs in Morocco and Jordan. On the one hand, being part of a political party facilitates collaboration and coordination with other female politicians, as I previously explained. On the other hand, female legislators rely on the party's ticket to gain access to voters and connect with constituents without the constant need to focus on service provision and other constituency-specific demands that may distract them from representing women's interests. Female candidates running for election and/or reelection must undertake all these tasks to gain voters' trust and votes. In an interview with a former female legislator in Jordan, she explained why she chose not to focus on women's issues: "When you focus on women's issues, many people will say 'don't talk to her because she is just concerned with women's issues.'"[47]

Thus, women tend to focus on broader concerns and navigate the electoral landscape on their own, which poses a tremendous burden on their time and personal lives. A female legislator who was reelected multiple times in the Jordanian parliament explained in our interview how she must keep close contact with her constituents to maintain their support: "I live in the area [where I was elected], so connecting [with constituents] occurs around the clock. It is not easy or simple, especially in a society of villagers or farmers. I tried different ways to connect; I would meet people in my house day and night and in my office. Now, I dedicate the weekends to my district. I welcome people to my house and receive their requests. In addition, of course, to the phone that never stops. Because of the tribal nature of our society, people also connect with my relatives, my husband, and my husband's relatives!"[48]

CONCLUSION

I ran for the presidency of the assembly, and they asked me: What makes you think you can win? I said I just wanted to run, and I'd like to lose. I want to encourage all those [women] who come after me until a woman succeeds. I only got eight votes! Imagine the loss. They wanted to make sure to discourage any woman from running again. If I lost by forty votes and the president of the assembly won by sixty votes, there's a comparison, but I got eight votes, and he got maybe seventy!! They thought that they broke me. . . . No. You have to take on these setbacks to break the fear. This taboo has passed through generations and generations; you build a wall of fear, and it's imaginary. You only need one person to break it.

—FEMALE LEGISLATOR IN JORDAN'S 2013 PARLIAMENT,
INTERVIEW WITH THE AUTHOR IN AMMAN, 2018[1]

OVERVIEW

Women's numerical presence in autocratic legislatures is surging, yet many questions remain: Are they powerful actors? Can they change the gendered power networks within decision-making processes and push for women-friendly outcomes? What are the barriers women face in achieving power and influence? Would the mere presence of women in these male-dominated legislative bodies lead to a shift in citizens' and elites' attitudes toward women in politics, as implied by my interviewee in the quote above? Or is women's marginalization more structural than often assumed?

The main argument of this book is that authoritarianism has negatively impacted women's representation across the region. I focus primarily on the effect of party institutionalization on shaping women's influence and substantive representation within autocratic legislatures. Unlike former work that focused on the sociocultural factors to explain women's political representation in the MENA region, this book explores one central aspect of authoritarian rule and its effect on women's political representation: the degree of individual parties' institutionalization.

The book's introduction outlines the main research questions and the empirical puzzle. I posit that while research on legislative politics and women's political inclusion in autocracies has flourished, several knowledge gaps persist. For instance, we know little about the inner dynamics of autocratic legislatures, women's legislative behavior, and the consequences of their numerical presence. I contend that these gaps can be mainly attributed to the dearth of high-quality data and the lack of transparency in these legislative bodies.

In addition, voluminous research has explored the role of political parties in regime survival, rent distribution, and curbing the opposition. Still, the link between political parties' strength and women's political power and influence in autocracies remained unexplored and undertheorized. On the one hand, scholarship has focused on the inner workings of individual political parties and/or the party system as a whole. On the other hand, a burgeoning literature has explored women's descriptive and substantive representation in nondemocracies and the conditions under which political parties may condition women's access to power. No research has explored the intersection between women's substantive representation and individual parties' internal characteristics, namely the degree of party institutionalization. This book aims to bridge these gaps based on original legislative, electoral, and legislator-level data.

For many reasons, the Middle East and North Africa (MENA) region is a valuable case to test my arguments on the link between party institutionalization and women's legislative behavior and influence. First, the region has some of the world's most enduring authoritarian regimes. Second, most MENA states have elected national assemblies with substantive monitoring and legislative roles. Third, women's presence in national legislatures has substantially increased over the past few decades. Finally, there are wide interregional disparities in the rules governing political parties' formation and their degree of institutionalization.

I test my argument using three monarchies: Morocco, Kuwait, and Jordan. I chose these cases because they have varying levels of women's numerical representation, quota policies, and party institutionalization. I show that higher levels of party institutionalization are positively linked to women's political influence and substantive representation in legislative bodies.

To measure women's political influence, I analyze committee membership and leadership data to examine the effect of women's affiliation to highly institutionalized parties on their access to prestigious committees, such as the Financial and Legal Committees. I highlight the fact that women may choose to join committees that better serve women's interests (such as the women's and social affairs committees); however, I am more interested in capturing whether women are more likely to be sidelined from influential committees when they are affiliated with weakly institutionalized parties and/or running as independents. I find evidence that women affiliated with highly institutionalized parties in Morocco are more likely to access influential committees compared to their counterparts in Kuwait and Jordan.

To capture women's substantive representation, I examine their legislative behavior in autocratic legislatures while acknowledging the diversity of women as a group. Previous studies have established that women's substantive representation is a multidimensional concept and is often context specific. Thus, instead of predetermining the nature of women's interests, I examine areas where policy consequences are likely to impact more women than men directly.[2] I analyze the parliamentary queries women posed in the three countries but differentiate between feminine/women's interests and feminist policy areas. Feminist policy areas include education, health, and social welfare issues. Feminine/women's interests are issue areas that deal directly with women and family issues, such as the gender wage gap, child custody, and violence against women. My findings support my main argument that women affiliated with highly institutionalized parties are more likely to represent women's interests.

SCOPE CONDITIONS

A few scope conditions are worth noting. First, while we gain analytical leverage by limiting the study to monarchies with varying levels of party institutionalization and women's numerical representation, the particularities of the cases may raise issues of what would change as the theory travels. The nature and strength of the autocratic legislatures in question may also affect the scope conditions of my theory. This book examines authoritarian regimes in which elections and legislatures play a significant role in monitoring the autocrat and facilitating the power-sharing mechanisms among the ruling elites. Despite the weak legislative role of the assemblies in my cases, legislatures and elections are viewed by the autocrat and the public as credible institutions and continue to play a substantial monitoring function. Furthermore, autocrats, in my cases, have historically instrumentalized women's issues for domestic and international gains. Thus, I expect my theory's implications to travel to other autocratic contexts with functioning electoral institutions and regimes supporting women's rights and inclusion.

Second, although I argue that party institutionalization is important for shaping women's political power and influence, I do not claim that their legislative behavior depends solely on the presence of strong, institutionalized parties. In other words, my argument does not presuppose that other features are inconsequential. As I outline in chapter 1, many factors may condition women's access to and exercise of political power, such as structural factors, patterns of historical development, foreign pressure, intersectional identities, and political culture. Moreover, while I argue that women's substantive representation may well be unlikely in the absence of institutionalized parties, their presence hardly guarantees it. Although parties are not the sole predictor of women's legislative power and influence in autocracies, an examination of the evidence concerning the various features of party institutionalization and their impact on women's legislative behavior is crucial as it paves the way for more research on the effect of party institutionalization on other aspects of the legislative process in different settings.

Finally, this book focuses on the legislative behavior of women's deputies who entered the parliament through the quota system for the most part. Given the few women who won nonquota seats, it is difficult to systematically analyze variations in women's legislative representation across quota and nonquota seats. More data are still needed to better understand variations in women's legislative behavior across different types of seats. This is a significant limitation to note, given that burgeoning scholarship in democracies has found that female MPs elected through a gender quota seat are more likely to pay increased attention to social welfare and education issues.[3]

GENERALIZABILITY OF THE FINDINGS: CROSS-NATIONAL MODELS OF PARTY INSTITUTIONALIZATION ACROSS AUTHORITARIAN REGIMES

In the previous section, I outlined the scope conditions of this book's theory and empirical findings. Moreover, I am interested in testing the generalizability of my findings. In this section, I rely on cross-national data to test the effect of party institutionalization on various political and substantive outcomes relating to women in autocracies. Whereas acquiring detailed legislative data similar to those analyzed in chapters 4 and 5 is infeasible, I analyze outcomes that deal directly with advancing women's rights in autocracies, such as women's political empowerment, access to justice, and life expectancy. Similar to the models in chapter 1, I rely on the classification of political regimes by Barbara Geddes and her colleagues and include only regimes classified as autocracy between 1963 and 2010.[4]

I expect to find a positive link between the degree of individual parties' institutionalization and increased women's rights—both within and outside the political realm.

Table C.1 presents the results for the three dependent variables. The first dependent variable (Model 1), the women's political empowerment index (V-Dem Institute 2023 data), is coded based on the averages of three main

TABLE C.1 The effect of party institutionalization on women's rights in autocracies (1963–2010)

	(1) POLITICAL EMPOWERMENT	(2) WOMEN'S ACCESS TO JUSTICE	(3) FEMALE LIFE EXPECTANCY
Party institutionalization index	0.143** (0.05)	0.712* (0.340)	3.977* (2.33)
Multiparty elections	−0.002 (0.007)	0.0428 (0.055)	0.494 (0.555)
Civil conflict	−0.0191* (0.09)	−0.183** (0.0613)	−0.328 (0.60)
Legislature	−0.001 (0.006)	0.100 (0.062)	0.952 (0.643)
Log GDP per capita	−0.014 (0.011)	0.0644 (0.126)	1.956 (1.085)
GDP growth	−0.000 (0.000)	−0.000 (0.002)	0.040 (0.028)
CEDAW ratification	0.027* (0.010)	0.115 (0.090)	−1.678* (0.737)
Gender quota		0.0239 (0.037)	−0.074 (0.318)
Region fixed effects	Yes	Yes	Yes
Year fixed effects	Yes	Yes	Yes
Constant	0.423*** (0.088)	0.394** (0.123)	41.06*** (7.733)
N	2,300	2,330	2,330

Standard errors in parentheses; * $p < 0.05$, ** $p < 0.01$, *** $p < 0.001$. CEDAW, Convention on the Elimination of All Forms of Discrimination Against Women; GDP, gross domestic product.

dimensions: women's civil liberties, civil society participation, and political participation. A high score indicates higher levels of women's political empowerment. The second dependent variable is women's access to justice (Model 2), an interval measure coded based on whether women enjoy equal, secure, and effective access to justice.[5] The third dependent variable is female life expectancy, coded based on women's life expectancy at birth (V-Dem Institute 2023 data).

The models are estimated using ordinary least squares regression models because all the dependent variables are continuous, covering the period between 1963 and 2010. The unit of analysis is the country-year. I use random effects to account for the panel structure of the data. I have also included region and year fixed effects to account for different average levels of women's rights across regions and potential temporal shocks. The main independent variable is the degree of individual parties' institutionalization, as measured by the V-Dem Institute. The variable is an index between 0 and 1, where 1 denotes the highest level of party institutionalization. Recall that the index is based on measures relating to distinct attributes of political parties in a specific country, namely the level of the party's national and local organization, linkage to constituents, party legislative cohesion, and coherence of party platforms. The second main independent variable is whether the regime holds multiparty elections. Similar to the study by Daniela Donno and Anne-Kathrin Kreft,[6] I use the National Elections Across Democracy and Autocracy (NELDA) project coding of multiparty elections as those occurring when at least one opposition group is allowed to exist, political parties are allowed to exist, and the ballot has a choice between more than one party or candidate.[7] Donno and Kreft code whether a competitive election was held within the previous six years under the regime.[8] I also control for whether the country has recently experienced civil conflict, the presence of a legislature, GDP, GDP growth, and CEDAW ratification.

Model 1 presents the results of the political empowerment dependent variable. The party institutionalization variable has a strong statistically significant effect ($p < 0.01$) on women's civil rights, political participation, and civil society participation (i.e., political empowerment index). The effect holds after controlling for the presence of multiparty elections. However, the presence of a legislature, multiparty elections, economic growth, and gross domestic product (GDP) per capita do not affect women's political empowerment. Civil conflicts have a statistically significant negative effect on women's political empowerment. Expectedly, countries that experienced less civil conflict are more likely to have higher levels of women's political empowerment. Countries that ratified the Convention on the Elimination of All Forms of Discrimination Against Women (CEDAW) are more likely to grant women political and civil rights. Finally, I did not include a control for the presence of gender quotas in Model 1 because the dependent variable already captures women's political participation relying on their numerical presence in the lower chambers and power distributed by gender (V-Dem Institute 2023 data) (see table A.13 in appendix A for more information on the coding).

Model 2 outlines the results for our second dependent variable: women's access to justice. Similar to Model 1, the level of party institutionalization is a strong predictor of women's access to justice, even after controlling for the presence of multiparty elections. Again, civil conflicts have a statistically significant negative effect on women's access to justice ($p < 0.01$). Furthermore, the presence of a legislature, multiparty elections, economic growth, GDP per capita, and CEDAW ratification had no statistically significant effect on women's access to justice in autocracies between 1963 and 2010. Finally, the presence of gender quotas in these contexts does not affect women's access to justice.

Finally, the dependent variable in Model 3 is female life expectancy. Again, I find strong evidence that the degree of party institutionalization matters for female life expectancy ($p < 0.05$). Other variables included in the model have a statistically insignificant effect on the dependent variable. Moreover, the impact of the degree of party institutionalization remains significant when I run alternative measures for women's rights (not reported here), such as women's freedom of discussion as well as women's civil society participation. To sum up, the results of the multivariate analysis conducted on autocracies worldwide confirm my argument that party institutionalization matters for women's political empowerment as well as their access to justice, increased life expectancy, and freedom of discussion.[9]

IMPLICATIONS

The findings of this book have several implications for the study of women's substantive representation, comparative political parties, gender quotas, and autocratic legislatures. First, this book moves beyond women's numerical presence and focuses on their legislative activities and policy outcomes. It emphasizes that "access," or presence, is distinct from "voice."[10] It demonstrates that women's substantive representation in autocracies is possible even without fully democratic institutions and pathways to power. Previous work on autocratic contexts has been scarce and provided mixed evidence. For instance, researchers found that electoral autocracies are associated with increased healthcare spending and women's health outcomes.[11] However, these results do not hold in closed autocracies. Moreover, research on sub-Saharan Africa has shown that women in Rwanda and Botswana substantively represent women and have achieved considerable progress.[12] I contribute to this work by focusing on the inner dynamics of autocratic legislatures to better understand women's legislative priorities and policy preferences and the role of parties in conditioning women's behavior and influence. My findings demonstrate that highly institutionalized parties facilitate substantive representation and enable women politicians to gain power within nondemocratic legislatures.

Furthermore, contrary to previous work that mostly viewed women's presence in politics as a tool to empower the autocrat and/or for gender-washing purposes, this study sheds new light on the role played by women when they access political power in autocratic settings. It demonstrates that women supported by institutionalized parties can perform their representative role even within the confines of authoritarianism. Thus, it expands the findings from previous studies that emphasize the strong link between party-based regimes and the promotion of women's political and economic rights.[13] I show that institutionalized parties, whether ruling parties or not, are associated with higher levels of women's rights in autocracies. These findings are further confirmed in the cross-national analysis included in this chapter (table C.I).

Moreover, consistent with previous work, multiparty elections are not the key predictor of women's political inclusion and/or other political and social rights. As I show in chapter 1, multiparty elections are negatively associated with women's numerical presence in the MENA region (table 1.2). Similar patterns exist when we expand our analysis to all autocratic regimes (table 1.2). The presence of multiparty elections is also insignificant in explaining women's political empowerment (table C.1, Model 1) or other women-related outcomes, such as access to justice or life expectancy (table C.1, Models 2 and 3) in autocracies.

Additionally, this study has implications for the study of comparative political parties. It examines the adverse effects of the absence of strong political parties in nondemocracies. Former studies have closely examined the link between political parties and democratization prospects.[14] However, no work has explained the implications of political parties' absence and/or organizational weakness on women's access to and exercise of power in dictatorships. Throughout my fieldwork in the region, women politicians often expressed frustration with the ongoing marginalization of political parties and other organized political groups. Both female politicians and candidates expressed concerns that only women loyal to the regime would likely gain access and win elections. A former female candidate in Kuwait stated, "All minorities in Kuwait, even the Shia, are always with the government. Women feel weak, so they cannot stand against the government. They are always with the government!"[15] My interviewees have also expressed concerns that female MPs' affiliation with the government may affect their legislative priorities and policy preferences. Being a former minister or high-ranking government official leaves a strong imprint on women's legislative behavior, especially in contexts where women rely on the government to get (re)elected. This issue is exacerbated by the absence of gender quotas and political parties, as in the case of Kuwait. Cross-national data on the opposition's legislative behavior in MENA's legislatures lend strong evidence to these claims.[16] Compared to their male counterparts, female legislators are significantly less likely to pose sensitive questions aligned with the opposition's agenda, such as those relating to corruption, civil liberties, and defense. Work on other autocratic contexts has provided similar insights.[17]

Relatedly, extant research has demonstrated that political parties' ideologies matter. Studies in developed democracies have shown that political parties[18] and party ideology play substantive roles in promoting women to power.[19] Parties with leftist ideologies are more likely to encourage women's political representation.[20] In comparison, parties with conservative ideologies tend to marginalize women by emphasizing women's traditional roles within the family.[21] Work focusing on the link between women's access to political power and political parties in MENA has also emphasized the role of parties' ideologies.[22] In contrast to these views, I find a weak relationship between party ideology and women's substantive representation in the MENA region. In other words, party ideology is marginal in explaining variations in women's legislative behavior and policy priorities across my cases.

Furthermore, this study has important implications for the study of gender quotas beyond established democracies.[23] Most recent scholarship has provided ample evidence of the rise of softer, nonideological autocracies that rely less on violent, repressive means to maintain power.[24] Thus, autocrats introduced high-visibility gender reforms, such as political gender quotas, over the past few decades. Women's political inclusion has become an important strategy for autocrats to maintain power by improving their domestic and international standing. Whereas a voluminous literature has investigated the correlates of quota adoption and implementation in nondemocracies, few studies have provided cross-national evidence on their outcomes and/or the conditions under which they promote women's political power and women-friendly policy outcomes. This book offers some of the first systematic evidence on the conditions under which gender quotas are more likely to translate into substantive gains for women.

Building on cross-national evidence of three autocratic cases with varying levels of quota implementation and party institutionalization, I demonstrate that highly institutionalized parties (even without party system institutionalization) matter for women's ability to gain power and influence within autocratic legislatures. Gender quotas implemented in a context marked by the lack of and/or fragmented political parties, such as the case of Jordan, are less likely to yield favorable outcomes for women. The numerical presence of women within autocratic legislatures is insufficient to ensure that they wield political power and clout. This issue becomes even more evident when we compare the Jordanian case with other contexts with no gender quota, such as Kuwait. Moreover, consistent with previous research that emphasizes the marginal role of gender quotas in promoting the conditions of democracy,[25] I find no evidence across my cases that increasing women's numerical presence has led to the promotion of the democratic processes and I concur with authors Gretchen Bauer and Jennie E. Burnet that "deepening democracy is a task that electoral gender quotas and the women elected on them cannot be expected to accomplish on their own."[26]

Finally, this book has implications for the study of autocratic legislatures. It provides one of the first insights into the inner dynamics of MENA's parliaments. My findings challenge the dominant views relating to the "window dressing" role of legislatures in autocracies and provide evidence that they matter. It calls attention to the importance of paying closer attention to variations across legislatures and the myriad ways they may shape legislators' access to power and policy preferences. Moreover, the results of this book also shed light on the legislative process in MENA's legislatures before and after the Arab uprisings. My data show ample evidence that the Arab uprisings invigorated the legislative process, albeit short-lived. In all my cases, legislative activity, such as the number of parliamentary questions and investigations, increased exponentially in the aftermath of the Arab uprisings. Additionally, this book has implications for the more recent studies on the limits of representation in nondemocratic assemblies.[27] Similar to extant scholarship that finds that legislators' behavior in autocracies is limited to issues that are less likely to threaten the incumbent's regime stability and survival, I find that both male and female deputies are less likely to pose parliamentary questions or interrogate cabinet members on sensitive issues, such as those relating to corruption, civil liberties, defense, and other sensitive issues that may threaten the regime and/or draw citizens' attention to its weaknesses.

NEW DIRECTIONS FOR GENDER AND AUTHORITARIAN POLITICS RESEARCH

This book focuses primarily on women's political power and substantive representation within autocratic legislatures. It aims to answer a few questions on the intersection of authoritarian politics and women's legislative power and behavior, but many other questions remain unanswered. In this section, I detail the remaining knowledge gaps in the study of gender and legislative politics in the MENA region and autocracies more generally. I focus on three specific areas for future research: the role of gendered norms in conditioning women's legislative behavior, women's political behavior in contexts with fragmented and/or absent political parties, and the outcomes of women's presence in elected legislatures.

Legislatures are gendered workplaces.[28] More work is needed to examine how the prevailing norms within male-dominated legislative institutions may condition women's legislative behavior. Formal deliberations and decisions occur within institutions, and a primary function of institutions is to impose rules on their members. Rules set norms—the set of tacit expectations groups place on individuals' behavior—in motion.[29] For instance, a study investigating female MPs' parliamentary speeches in twenty-four democracies showed that women adopt a more masculine style the longer they stay in office.[30] Similar dynamics exist in autocratic legislatures. On the one hand, women—relatively newcomers to the legislative arena—lack the political experience and knowledge of these norms and, thus, are often relegated to less prominent leadership roles.[31] On the other hand, women are expected to adhere to the male norm and other rules of "appropriateness"; otherwise, they may face retribution.[32] Hind Al-Fayez, a female MP in Jordan's 2013 lower chamber, is a prominent example. Al-Fayez was scolded, intimidated, and prevented from reentering parliament for publicly challenging her male counterparts.

Relatedly, violence against women, in both democracies and autocracies, remains a critical issue, and its effect on women's power and influence within autocratic legislatures remains understudied. Women encounter

considerable levels of discrimination and hostility within these historically male-dominated institutions. Male politicians have been verbally
aggressive and controlling in both committee hearings[33] and parliamentary
debates, especially as the proportion of women in the legislature increases.[34]
This marginalization and hostility can further disadvantage women. Violence against women is an increasingly pressing issue for women's access
and exercise of power in highly conservative contexts where patriarchal
norms prevail. During my interviews throughout the region, female candidates and politicians expressed concerns about the abuse and violence they
face, especially on the different online media platforms. My interviewees
in Kuwait described how female politicians' legislative behavior and issue
priorities transformed after joining such male-dominated assemblies where
"they would get physically attacked and verbally abused."[35]

Furthermore, we need to better understand women's political behavior
in contexts with fragmented and/or absent political parties. Women's status
and ability to counter discrimination and push for policy changes are further curtailed in contexts with fragmented or absent political parties. First,
female MPs' minority status, coupled with the absence of party support, may
lead to competition rather than coalition building.[36] Second, in the absence
of political parties to support women's access to political power, female candidates mostly rely on their existing connections with the government and
the incumbent regime to get (re)elected. As previously mentioned, women
who gain access to power tend to support the government and its policies, or
as maintained by a former female candidate in Kuwait, "They [the govern-
ment] prefer to have those [women] who are silent. Who only do what the
government wants. They stay longer in their positions if they are silent!"[37]
More work is needed to understand better the link between women's pathways to political power and their legislative behavior and priorities. Beth
Reingold argues, "As almost every study makes clear, sex differences pale in
comparison to party differences. Among political elites, party affiliation is a
much stronger predictor of policy preferences than is sex."[38] But what about
contexts with no party systems or clear ideological demarcations?

Another critical area of research that directly speaks to women's legislative behavior in both autocracies and democracies is the effect of the

electoral system on shaping female legislators' policy preferences and priorities. Legislative studies scholars have emphasized the centrality of institutional arrangements—and the electoral system in particular—in shaping politicians' legislative behavior.[39] MPs adapt their parliamentary activities to the electoral system's incentives to increase their reelection chances.[40] In autocratic settings, extant research has overlooked the consequences of the ruling elites' manufacturing and manipulation of the electoral rules to ensure their survival. Thus, many questions remain unanswered: What is the effect of the opacity and volatility of the electoral rules on women's access and exercise of political power? Do women elected in quota seats legislate differently from those elected through competitive seats? How does a woman's running as an independent affect their legislative behavior and priorities?

Additionally, scholars should explore when and under what conditions women get reelected and how this relates to their legislative behavior. Women across MENA have limited incumbency advantage. The author's data show that women's reelection rate in MENA's legislatures is as low as 2 percent (compared to 15 percent for their male counterparts), even after the introduction of gender quota policies.[41] Although women entering the lower chamber through a quota system may be unable to run for reelection on quota lists, such as in the case of Morocco since 2011, women can still run for nonquota seats.

Furthermore, there is a strong need to explore intersectionality and how it impacts women's legislative behavior. It is often assumed that because gender quotas benefit female politicians, they are more likely to promote women's issues once in power. Yet thinking about women as a homogenous entity with one unifying identity is simplistic. Women politicians in MENA may have intertwined identities as they relate to their tribal or ethnic group, sexual orientation, and/or religious affiliation. For instance, it has been shown that electing female Islamist deputies improves service beyond electing women in general.[42] However, no existing research examines how women's intersecting identities may shape their legislative behavior and preferences.

The role of women's caucuses within autocratic legislatures is another crucial research area that remains overlooked. Scholars argue that women's caucuses with organizational resources and institutional clout may help promote women's substantive representation.[43] For instance, Morocco's Groupe de Travail des Parlementaires pour l'Egalité (GTPPE) has not only been successful at pushing legislation but also supports female legislators against harassment from other members of parliament. The cultivation and maintenance of such caucuses offer an opportunity to change the masculine culture of parliamentary institutions beyond the policy-driven structure of quotas, and their impact should be studied more systematically.[44]

Several knowledge gaps remain on the outcomes of women's presence in elected bodies in nondemocracies. In addition to understanding variations in men's and women's policy outcomes and priorities (i.e., substantive representation),[45] the effect of women's presence on public goods provision and individualized service provision (i.e., service representation) remains understudied. Additionally, scholars should pay closer attention to the link between women's presence in national assemblies and the quality of governance. Also related is the debate about whether electing women in nondemocracies reduces clientelism and corruption. Finally, there is no research on the symbolic effect of women's presence on female citizens' political attitudes and behavior (i.e., symbolic representation). Most importantly, it is imperative to understand how electing women can decrease gender-based biases and sexism, increase women's participation in elections as voters and candidates, and enhance their overall political engagement.

APPENDIX A

TABLE A.1 Codebook for datasets used in table 1.2

VARIABLE NAME	CODING	SOURCE
Year	Year of election. Models 1–3 (1993–2021); Model 4 (1991–2010)	Author's data V-Dem data
Percentage of women in the lower house	The percentage of women elected in parliamentary elections	https://www.ipu.org
Electoral system	Type of electoral system	https://www.electionguide.org/elections/type/upcoming/
Majoritarian	If electoral system is majoritarian = 1, otherwise = 0	
Proportional representation (PR) system	If electoral system is PR = 1, otherwise = 0	
Mixed system	If the electoral system is mixed = 1, otherwise = 0	

(continued)

VARIABLE NAME	CODING	SOURCE
Quota	Coded as 1 if there is a quota in place	For parliamentary elections up until 2015, these data are in the QAROT dataset. For the most recent elections, we use the quota database: https://www.idea.int/data-tools/data/gender-quotas.
Multiparty elections	v2elmulpar	Coded according to the Vdem11.1 dataset (v2elmulpar); indicates whether the national election is multiparty (on a relative scale)
Females in labor force	The percentage of female labor force participation	https://data.worldbank.org/indicator/SL.TLF.TOTL.FE.ZS?locations=DZ
Logged GDP per capita	e_migdppc (logged)	World Bank data
Life expectancy	Life expectancy refers to expected longevity at birth based on current age-specific mortality rates.	Vdem11.1 dataset

TABLE A.2 Committees' composition in Morocco, Jordan, and Kuwait

COUNTRY AND CHAMBER	NUMBER OF COMMITTEES[a]
Morocco House of Representatives 2007–2011	6
Morocco 2012–2016	9
Morocco 2016–2021	9
Kuwait National Assembly—13th session 2009–2011 (four quarters)	19–26 (10 standing and 9–16 temporary)
Kuwait 14th session 2013–2016 (four quarters)	11–22 (10–11 standing and temporary)
Kuwait 15th session 2016 (one quarter)	20 (11 standing and 9 temporary)
Jordan House of Representatives—16th session 2010–2013 (one round)	16 (14 standing and 2 temporary)
Jordan 17th session 2013–2016 (three rounds + nonordinary session)	20 (all standing)
Jordan 18th session 2016–2020 (four rounds)	21 (20 standing and 1 temporary)

[a]For some countries, the numbers of committees are in ranges because they differ across legislative rounds/quarters.

Kuwait	Protection of public funds–2009, 2013, 2016 (Corruption)	Reviews the accounting office report on funds invested nationally and internationally and those that have not been invested. Investigates the misuse of public funds and other related matters if requested by the assembly.
Kuwait	Prioritization (2013, 2016)	Defines the national assembly's priorities, cooperates and coordinates with government agencies, deals with laws not overseen by other committees, and assists in implementing the government's and assembly's priorities.
Kuwait	Petitions and appeals–2009, 2013, 2016 (Legislative)	Reviews the petitions and appeals referred to the committee, reports to the national assembly, or refers them to the responsible ministry or the specialized national committee or propose a decision or recommendation.
Kuwait	Legislative and legal affairs (Legislative)	Reviews matters associated with the legal affairs of the national assembly and ministries, and interests associated with the Ministry of Justice, religious endowments, the administration of Fatwas, and legislation. This committee is also responsible for all matters that do not fall within the prerogatives of other committees.
Kuwait	Financial and economic affairs (Economy and financial)	Deals with the economic and financial affairs related to the work of ministries, government administration, public facilities, and matters related to the ministries of finance, trade, production, and the offices of public services, accounting, and the higher council for planning, the bank of Credit and Savings, the Central Bank of Kuwait, and public institutions associated with financial and economic nature and public sector companies and plans for economic and social development.
Kuwait	Public utilities (Transportation)	Deals with matters associated with the facilities of the ministries of transport and public works, electricity, water, and municipal.
Kuwait	Affairs related to education, culture, and guidance (Education; social affairs)	Deals with issues associated with education, guidance, matters associated with the Ministries of Education and Higher Education, issues associated with education and cultural factors, and guidance associated with the Ministry of Communication.
Kuwait	Budgets and accounting (Economy and financial)	Deals with matters associated with budgets, accounting and credits, the coordination between the government's departments and administrative governance and independent agencies, and reports to the financial office.
Kuwait	Health, social, and labor affairs (Health; labor; social affairs)	Deals with matters associated with the Ministries of Health, Social, and Labor Affairs.
Kuwait	Internal affairs and defense (Defense)	Deals with matters associated with the Ministries of Internal Affairs/Interior and Defense, the general leadership, and the national guard.

Kuwait	Foreign affairs (Foreign affairs)	Deals with matters associated with establishing bilateral treaties signed between Kuwait and other countries as well as studying Kuwait's joining international agreements or organizations. The committee also reviews the foreign policy and the discussion of the latest developments at the local, regional, and international levels, and the coordination of political discourse in cooperation with the Foreign Ministry and all stakeholders in the state.
Kuwait	Women and the family—T (Women's issues)	Supports the role of women politically, economically, and socially. Monitors the implementation of the strategic plans prepared by the state regarding women and discussion of these plans with different institutions, and improves them. Oversees the implementation of national legislation that harms Kuwaiti women in a specific or general manner and the amendments that are in contradiction with the stipulations of international agreements that the state has signed and ratified in several areas. Studies the legal, judicial, educational, informational, administrative, and social aspects related to women and improves them through legislation. Establishes closer relations with organizations and bodies of local, regional, and global feminism for the exchange of information and experiences and follows developments to improve the role of women in society. The committee is expected to hold seminars and conferences in the field of women's empowerment and the development of their role in society.
Kuwait	Housing (2013 and 2016)	Deals with matters associated with housing projects and proposals in addition to solving problems related to housing.
Kuwait	Developing human and national resources (2013)	Deals with matters associated with developing procedural and substantive grounds to select the leadership roles in Kuwait.
Kuwait	Special needs—T (Social affairs)	Deals with matters associated with overseeing and implementing the eight articles of the 2010 law regarding the employment of no fewer than 4 percent of people with disabilities in the government and private sector.
Kuwait	Youth and sports—T (Social affairs)	Deals with youth and sports issues and the means of improving this sector while taking into consideration its importance in social development.
Kuwait	Human rights—T (Human rights)	Deals with the investigation of employment disputes.

ªThe committees of population affairs, treatment of unspecified conditions related to nationality, studying negative internal phenomena affecting Kuwaiti Society (2009), and committees in Kuwait data (temporary/ investigation committees [indicated by "T" in the table]) are not coded in the dataset in addition to the shared committees in Kuwait. Investigative committees in Jordan or Kuwait are not included in the analysis, as well as the environment and nuclear energy committee (Kuwait). The agriculture committee coding was removed from Kuwait as it only occurred in 2016.

Jordan—House of Representatives	Finance committee (Economy and financial)	Reviews the general budget and the government units' laws and proposals and oversees their implementation. Reviews the final reports of the ministries, the government units, and accounting office and makes recommendations to the assembly. Reviews the financial laws associated with the increase in the imports, expenses, or decreases. Monitors the public debt and makes recommendations. Reviews the Greater Amman Municipality's budget and the budgets of municipalities.
Jordan—House of Representatives	Economy and investment (Economy and financial)	Reviews the economic, financial, tax, and investment policies and laws associated with provisions, trade and industry, companies, banks, insurance, currency, banking, investment, financial, and taxes. Monitors provisional matters, markets, consumer protection, economic forecasts, growth rates, inflation, and deflation.
Jordan—House of Representatives	Foreign affairs (Foreign affairs)	Deals with matters associated with foreign affairs. Reviews foreign treaties and agreements; coordinates relations with other parliaments, unions, and parliamentary organizations; and prepares projects passed by the assembly.
Jordan—House of Representatives	Administrative (Administrative)	Reviews laws and proposals related to public and local administration, the administration of municipalities, laws and reports related to civil servants and hiring criteria, the termination of employment, retirement, and compensation.
Jordan—House of Representatives	Legislative committee (Legislative)	Deals with legal studies and proposals associated with the constitution, general elections, and legislation on civil, criminal, rights, and courts. Deals with the judicial organization, agreements, laws, personal matters, nationality, acquisitions, rent, defense, general amnesty, drugs and their psychological effects, the functioning of unions, the judicial decisions made to these legislations, and in the governance of the legislation and any laws that do not fall within the jurisdiction of the commission and any other matters referred to it by the president or the MPs. Reviews the internal structure of the assembly and reform proposals and cases associated with the representatives' immunity. Assists other parliamentary committees in drafting legislative texts.
Jordan—House of Representatives	Upbringing, education, and culture (Education; social affairs)	Reviews laws and proposals associated with upbringing, higher education, scientific research, and culture.
Jordan—House of Representatives	Youth and sports (Social affairs)	Reviews laws and proposals associated with youth, unions, committees, clubs, youth centers, and sports.
Jordan—House of Representatives	**National direction and the media**	**Deals with laws and proposals relating to the media, press, broadcasting, journalism, religious preaching, guidance, and endowments.**
Jordan—House of Representatives	Health and the environment (Health and social affairs)	Deals with laws and proposals associated with general health, health services, insurance, and environmental matters.

Jordan—House of Representatives	Agriculture and irrigation (Agriculture)	Deals with laws and proposals associated with irrigated agriculture, agricultural land watered by rain and protecting it from desertification, livestock, water and its uses, dams, and sewage. Reviews agricultural farming and protection of farmers' laws.
Jordan—House of Representatives	Energy and mineral wealth (Energy)	Deals with laws and proposals associated with electricity, oil, gas, sources of renewable and alternative energy, mineral resources, and related agreements. Reviews and monitors the pricing of petroleum and other energy policies.
Jordan—House of Representatives	Palestine (Foreign affairs)	Monitors developments associated with Palestine, the assembly's ability to take appropriate measures, Jerusalem, and the Islamic and Christian holy sites in Palestine. Monitors and solves the issue of the Palestinian refugees and displaced individuals with the objective of returning them to their country. Deals with the affairs of Palestinian exiles and deportees. Deals with strengthening the relations between Jordan and Palestine across the political, cultural, social, educational, and economic domains.
Jordan—House of Representatives	Rural and undeveloped land	**Reviews issues and proposals associated with the development of the countryside and the desert.**
Jordan—House of Representatives	Labor, social development, and population (Labor; social affairs)	Deals with laws and proposals associated with business, labor issues, vocational training, social security, charity unions, social development issues, national funds used in national development aid and employment, and related areas. Reviews laws and affairs associated with housing, development, housing opportunities, and related reports. Reviews policies for organizing the labor market and recruitment of foreign labor.
Jordan—House of Representatives	Public services and transportation (Transportation)	Deals with laws and proposals associated with public services, transportation, traffic on roads, mail, telecommunications, and related matters. Reviews and improves policies in the general transportation sector.
Jordan—House of Representatives	Tourism and monuments	**Deals with laws and proposals associated with tourism and its development as well as the monuments and their preservation. Reviews and develops plans for promoting tourism as one of the main sources of national income.**
Jordan—House of Representatives	General freedoms and human rights (Human rights)	Reviews the laws and proposals associated with the rights and general freedoms stipulated by the constitution and laws. Monitors rehabilitation and temporary detention centers, social care, and their related areas. Reviews complaints and grievances associated with the violation of human rights and general freedoms.
Jordan—House of Representatives	Integrity, transparency, and fact checking (Corruption)	Investigates financial and administrative corruption in the public and government's institutions and oversees the steps for fighting it.
Jordan—House of Representatives	Structure and behavior	**Oversees the application of the code of conduct in the lower chamber and reviews proposals associated with it. Investigates complaints filed by MPs, violations of the code of conduct, and any behavior or activity that may damage the assembly's reputation and prestige regardless of whether these complaints are internal or external.**

(continued)

Jordan—House of Representatives	Women and family issues (Women's issues)	Deals with laws and matters associated with women's issues, family and children, and monitoring the policies, plans, and programs necessary for improving the place of women socially, culturally, economically, and politically. Monitors maternal and childcare programs.

Note: Items in bold not included in the committee coding, but I include them here for completeness.

TABLE A.5 Detailed committee description in Morocco (2007–2021)

Morocco—House of Representatives	Foreign affairs, national defense, Islamic affairs, and Moroccans living abroad (Foreign affairs; defense)	Deals with foreign affairs, cooperation, the affairs of Moroccans living abroad, national defense and the defense of colonized areas and its borders, historical resistance, religious endowments, and Islamic issues.
Morocco—House of Representatives	**Domestic affairs, territorial groups, and city policy**	**Deals with domestic affairs, territorial and regional groups, construction, housing, and city/urban policy.**
Morocco—House of Representatives	Justice, legislation, and human rights (Legislative; human rights)	Deals with issues relating to justice, human rights, General Secretariat of the Government, administrative affairs, the relationship with the parliament and civil society, the supreme council, and regional councils.
Morocco—House of Representatives	Finance and economic development (Economy and financial)	Deals with finance, investment, economic preparation, privatization, public institutions, public affairs, and socioeconomic affairs.
Morocco—House of Representatives	Social sectors (Health; social affairs; women's issues; labor)	Deals with issues relating to health, youth and sports, employment, social affairs, vocational training, women and children and family and solidarity, and disability.
Morocco—House of Representatives	Production sectors (Agriculture)	Deals with issues relating to agriculture, rural development production, fishing, tourism, traditional industries, domestic and international business, and modern technology.
Morocco—House of Representatives	Essential buildings, energy, metals, and the environment (Transportation; energy)	Deals with issues relating to transportation, water, environment, transportation, energy and metals, forests, and sustainable development.
Morocco—House of Representatives	Education, culture, and communication (Education; social affairs)	Deals with issues relating to education, culture, communication, and media.
Morocco—House of Representatives	Surveillance of public funds (Corruption)	Monitors and tracks public spending. Reviews reports of the supreme council for financial accounts and the reports prepared according to Chapter 148 of the constitution. Monitors the legislative provisions related to the surveillance of public funds.

Note: Items in bold not included in the committee coding, but I include them here for completeness.

VARIABLE NAME	DESCRIPTION	CODING
Legislative committee	Whether MP is a member of the legal committee (see tables A.2–A.5 for detailed committee description)	0/1
Economy and finance committee	Whether MP is a member of the economic/finance committee	0/1
Foreign affairs	Whether MP is a member of the foreign/international affairs committee	0/1
Social affairs	Whether MP is a member of the youth/sports/disability/social welfare/affairs committee	0/1
Women's issues committee membership	MP is member of committee(s) that falls under the category of women's issues committees	0/1
Female	Gender of MP	0/1
Political experience	Reelection of MP from legislative session directly preceding current session	0/1
Number of committees	Number of committees that an individual MP is a member of	Continuous; 1 or 0 for Morocco, up to 6 in Jordan and Kuwait
Islamist	MP is member of Islamist-leaning party or bloc	Morocco (PJD); Jordan (Islamic Centrist Party in 2010, 2013, and 2016; and Islamic Front in 2016); Kuwait (Islamic Salafi Alliance, Islamic Constitutional Movement in 2009; Islamic Salafi Alliance in 2013; and Islamic Constitutional Movement, Islamist, Salafist in 2016)
Party institutionalization	Index of party institutionalization	The index includes the standardized scores acquired from the Varieties of Party Identity and Organization (V-Party) dataset collected by V-Dem (2020). I have included in the index measures of parties' local organizational strength, continuation, presence of local offices, processes of candidates' nominations, cohesion, and stable links with social organizations. The index ranges between 0 and 1, with 1 being the highest level of party institutionalization and 0 denoting the absence of party institutionalization (see table A.7 for more details).

VARIABLE NAME	PARTY-LEVEL INSTITUTIONALIZATION, V-DEM PARTY DATASET	DESCRIPTION	CODING
v2paactcom	Local organizational strength	To what degree are party activists and personnel permanently active in local communities?	0: There is negligible permanent presence of party activists and personnel in local communities. 1: There is minor permanent presence of party activists and personnel in local communities. 2: There is noticeable permanent presence of party activists and personnel in local communities. 3: There is significant permanent presence of party activists and personnel in local communities. 4: There is widespread permanent presence of party activists and personnel in local communities.
v2paelcont	Party continuation	Did the party participate in the previous election under its current name?	0: Yes, the party participated in the previous election under the same name. 1: No, the party did not participate in the previous election. 2: No, but the party participated in the previous election under a different name.
v2palocoff	Local party office	Does the party maintain permanent offices that operate outside of election campaigns at the local or municipal level?	0: The party does not have permanent local offices. 1: The party has permanent local offices in few municipalities. 2: The party has permanent local offices in some municipalities. 3: The party has permanent local offices in most municipalities. 4: The party has permanent local offices in all or almost all municipalities.
v2padisa	Party cohesion	To what extent do the elites in this party display disagreement over party strategies?	0: Party elites display almost complete disagreement over party strategies and many party elites have left the party. 1: Party elites display a high level of visible disagreement over party strategies and some of them have left the party. 2: Party elites display some visible disagreement over party strategies, but none of them have left the party. 3: Party elites display negligible visible disagreement over party strategies. 4: Party elites display virtually no visible disagreement over party strategies.

v2pasoctie	Affiliate organizations	To what extent does this party maintain ties to prominent social organizations?	0: The party does not maintain ties to any prominent social organizations. 1: The party maintains weak ties to prominent social organizations. 2: The party maintains moderate ties to prominent social organizations. 3: The party maintains strong ties to prominent social organizations. 4: The party controls prominent social organizations.
v2panom	Candidate nomination	Which of the following options best describes the process by which the party decides on candidates for the national legislative elections?	0: The party leader unilaterally decides on which candidates will run for the party in national legislative elections. 1: The national party leadership (i.e., an executive committee) collectively decides which candidates will run for the party in national legislative elections. 2: Delegates of local/regional organizations decide which candidates will run for the party in national legislative elections. 3: All party members decide on which candidates will run for the party in national legislative elections in primaries/caucuses. 4: All registered voters decide on which candidates will run for the party in national legislative elections in primaries/caucuses.
PI	Party institutionalization (PI)	Index of party institutionalization	To measure the effect of the main independent variable in this study—party institutionalization—on women's committee memberships and substantive representation, I constructed an additive index based on six main measures that capture the strength of political parties. The index includes the standardized scores acquired from the Varieties of Party Identity and Organization (V-Party) dataset collected by V-Dem (2020). I have included in the index measures of parties' local organizational strength, continuation, presence of local offices, processes of candidates' nominations, cohesion, and stable links with social organizations. The index ranges between 0 and 1, with 1 being the highest level of party institutionalization and 0 denoting the absence of party institutionalization.

TABLE A.8 Multivariate analysis of committee membership in Jordan (2010–2020) (N = 1,389)

	(1) LEGISLATIVE	(2) LEGISLATIVE (WITH INTERACTION)	(3) ECONOMY AND FINANCIAL	(4) ECONOMY AND FINANCIAL (WITH INTERACTION)	(5) FOREIGN AFFAIRS	(6) FOREIGN AFFAIRS (WITH INTERACTION)	(7) SOCIAL AFFAIRS	(8) SOCIAL AFFAIRS (WITH INTERACTION)	(9) WOMEN'S ISSUES	(10) WOMEN'S ISSUES (WITH INTERACTION)
Female	-0.25	-0.25	-0.96*	-0.91	-0.32	-0.34	0.60*	0.58*	3.97***	3.89***
	(0.70)	(0.70)	(0.55)	(0.55)	(0.34)	(0.35)	(0.28)	(0.29)	(0.45)	(0.48)
Political experience	0.80**	0.80**	0.42	0.43	-0.08	-0.07	-0.73*	-0.76*	0.26	0.27
	(0.30)	(0.30)	(0.29)	(0.29)	(0.30)	(0.30)	(0.30)	(0.30)	(0.62)	(0.62)
Number of committees	1.03***	1.03***	0.92***	0.93***	1.04***	1.03***	1.13***	1.14***	2.05***	2.06***
	(0.15)	(0.15)	(0.11)	(0.10)	(0.11)	(0.11)	(0.11)	(0.11)	(0.45)	(0.44)
Party institutionalization (PI)	0	0	-0.70	-0.43	-0.19	-0.29	-1.60	-1.57	0.72	-0.19
	(.)	(.)	(1.45)	(1.51)	(1.27)	(1.42)	(0.98)	(1.23)	(0.48)	(1.66)
Islamist	-0.47	-1.07	-0.21	-0.37	0.28	0.28	0.23	0.22	0.90*	0.93*
	(0.77)	(0.76)	(0.58)	(0.60)	(0.69)	(0.70)	(0.45)	(0.46)	(0.34)	(0.48)
Female*PI		0		0		0.36		-0.08		1.30
		(.)		(.)		(1.54)		(1.56)		(1.84)
Constant	-4.28***	-4.30***	-3.90***	-3.34***	-3.35***	-3.31***	-3.50***	-3.50***	-8.25***	-8.22***
	(0.36)	(0.36)	(0.40)	(0.23)	(0.24)	(0.24)	(0.31)	(0.29)	(1.06)	(1.06)
Year/session fixed effects	Yes	Yes	Yes	Yes	Yes	Yes	Yes	Yes	Yes	Yes
N	1,311	1,369	1,385	1,369	1,385	1,385	1,385	1,385	1,385	1,385

Standard errors in parentheses; *** $p < 0.01$, ** $p < 0.05$, * $p < 0.1$.

TABLE A.9 Multivariate analysis of committee membership in Morocco (2007–2021) (N = 1,123)

	(1) LEGISLATIVE	(2) LEGISLATIVE (WITH INTERACTION)	(3) ECONOMY AND FINANCIAL	(4) ECONOMY AND FINANCIAL (WITH INTERACTION)	(5) FOREIGN AFFAIRS	(6) FOREIGN AFFAIRS (WITH INTERACTION)	(7) SOCIAL AFFAIRS	(8) SOCIAL AFFAIRS (WITH INTERACTION)
Female	0.50*	0.58	-0.05	-0.03	0.87***	2.55	0.87***	-0.40
	(0.23)	(0.85)	(0.24)	(0.98)	(0.25)	(0.92)	(0.18)	(0.98)
Political experience	0.03	0.03	-0.21	-0.21	0.07	0.05	-0.21	-0.21
	(0.22)	(0.22)	(0.20)	(0.20)	(0.23)	(0.22)	(0.17)	(0.17)
Number of committees	2.35***	2.34***	-1.11	-0.80	1.09	0.92	0.39	0.51
	(0.59)	(0.60)	(1.04)	(1.04)	(0.68)	(0.81)	(0.62)	(0.65)
Party institutionalization (PI)	-0.22	-0.21	0.19	0.19	0.08	0.49	-0.24	-0.37
	(0.41)	(0.43)	(0.39)	(0.40)	(0.51)	(0.62)	(0.39)	(0.40)
Islamist	0.04	0.04	-0.16	-0.16	0.04	0.05	0.22	0.22
	(0.25)	(0.25)	(0.25)	(0.25)	(0.25)	(0.25)	(0.19)	(0.19)
Female*PI		-0.13		-0.02		-2.50*		1.84
		(1.23)		(1.40)		(1.34)		(1.38)
Constant	-4.02***	-4.02***	-0.17	-0.17	-3.54***	-3.51***	-1.93**	-1.96**
	(0.67)	(0.67)	(1.08)	(1.07)	(0.79)	(0.93)	(0.68)	(0.70)
Year/session fixed effects	Yes	Yes	Yes	Yes	Yes	Yes	Yes	Yes
N	1,081	1,081	1,081	1,081	1,081	1,081	1,081	1,081

Standard errors in parentheses; *** $p < 0.01$, ** $p < 0.05$, * $p < 0.1$.

TABLE A.10 Multivariate analysis of committee membership in Kuwait (2009–2017) (N = 466)

	(1) LEGISLATIVE	(2) ECONOMY AND FINANCIAL	(3) FOREIGN	(4) SOCIAL AFFAIRS	(5) WOMEN'S ISSUES
Female	−0.525 (1.112)	−0.317 (1.152)	0.508 (1.035)	0.477 (0.659)	4.251*** (0.723)
Political experience	−0.526 (0.395)	0.167 (0.388)	0.300 (0.477)	0.165 (0.343)	0.234 (0.609)
Number of committees	0.430*** (0.0876)	0.554*** (0.0949)	0.233* (0.101)	0.713*** (0.0976)	0.835*** (0.137)
Party institutionalization (PI)	−1.272 (1.550)	0 (.)	0 (.)	1.844* (0.803)	0 (.)
Islamist	0.793 (0.480)	0.503 (0.460)	−0.779 (0.814)	−0.847* (0.429)	−1.250 (0.703)
Constant	−2.196*** (0.296)	−2.438*** (0.300)	−2.81*** (0.446)	−2.40*** (0.273)	−4.763*** (0.467)
Year/session fixed effects	Yes	Yes	Yes	Yes	Yes
N	466	459	459	466	459

Standard errors in parentheses; *** $p < 0.01$, ** $p < 0.05$, * $p < 0.1$.

VARIABLE NAME	DESCRIPTION	CODING
Female	Gender of the MP	0/1
Political experience	Reelection of the MP from legislative session directly preceding current session	0/1
Total questions	The number of questions posed by a specific MP	Continuous
Islamist	MP is member of Islamist-leaning party or bloc	Morocco (PJD); Jordan (Islamic Centrist Party in 2010, 2013, and 2016; and Islamic Front in 2016); Kuwait (Islamist, Islamic Salafi Alliance, Constitutional Islamic Bloc in 2009; Islamic Salafi Alliance in 2013; and ICM, Islamist, Salafist in 2016)
Member of committee	Whether the MP is a member/leader of the women and family committee	0/1
	Whether MP is a member/leader of the foreign/international affairs committee	0/1
	Whether the MP is a member/leader of the education committee	0/1
	Whether the MP is a member/leader of the health committee	0/1
Party institutionalization (PI)	Index of party institutionalization	The index includes the standardized scores acquired from the Varieties of Party Identity and Organization (V-Party) dataset collected by V-Dem (2020). I have included in the index measures of parties' local organizational strength, continuation, presence of local offices, processes of candidates' nominations, cohesion, and stable links with social organizations. The index ranges between 0 and 1, with 1 being the highest level of party institutionalization and 0 denoting the absence of party institutionalization (see table A.7 for more details).

TABLE A.12 Posing parliamentary questions in Morocco, Jordan, and Kuwait (N = 21,960)

	(1) WOMEN/FAMILY	(2) WOMEN/FAMILY (WITH INTERACTION)	(3) FOREIGN AFFAIRS	(4) FOREIGN AFFAIRS (WITH INTERACTION)	(5) EDUCATION	(6) EDUCATION (WITH INTERACTION)	(7) HEALTH	(8) HEALTH (WITH INTERACTION)
Female	1.24***	−0.29	0.50**	0.06	0.52***	−0.04	0.35**	−0.27
	(0.21)	(0.55)	(0.17)	(0.30)	(0.11)	(0.22)	(0.11)	(0.28)
Political experience	−0.24	−0.25	0.14	0.14	−0.33***	−0.32***	−0.08	−0.08
	(0.19)	(0.19)	(0.16)	(0.15)	(0.10)	(0.10)	(0.10)	(0.10)
Total questions	0.20***	0.02***	0.02***	0.02***	0.02***	0.02***	0.01***	0.02***
	(0.00)	(0.22)	(0.00)	(0.00)	(0.00)	(0.00)	(0.00)	(0.00)
Member of committee	0.27	0.38*	1.06***	1.04***	0.64***	0.66***	0.49***	0.49***
	(0.20)	(0.20)	(0.19)	(0.20)	(0.11)	(0.11)	(0.12)	(0.12)
Islamist	−0.04	−0.07	0.38*	0.39*	0.26**	0.26**	−0.00	−0.01
	(0.00)	(0.18)	(0.17)	(0.17)	(0.10)	(0.09)	(0.11)	(0.12)
Party institutionalization (PI)	1.14***	0.94**	0.78*	0.71*	−0.11	−0.19	−0.07	−0.13
	(0.43)	(0.43)	(0.30)	(0.30)	(0.21)	(0.21)	(0.43)	(0.22)
Female*PI		1.66***		0.54		0.71***		0.73***
		(0.57)		(0.36)		(0.23)		(0.30)
Constant	−2.11***	−1.80***	−2.21***	−2.17***	0.30	0.38	0.48	0.54*
	(0.41)	(0.38)	(0.45)	(0.45)	(0.27)	(0.27)	(0.30)	(1.79)
Country fixed effects	Yes	Yes	Yes	Yes	Yes	Yes	Yes	Yes
Year fixed effects	Yes	Yes	Yes	Yes	Yes	Yes	Yes	Yes
N	1,120	1,120	1,120	1,120	1,120	1,120	1,120	1,120

Standard errors in parentheses; * $p < 0.05$, ** $p < 0.01$, *** $p < 0.001$.

TABLE A.13 Coding of variables in table C.1

VARIABLE NAME	CODING	SOURCE
Political empowerment	The index is constructed by taking the average of women's civil liberties index (v2x_gencl), women's civil society participation index (v2x_gencs), and women's political participation index (v2x_genpp). A high score indicates higher levels of women's political empowerment.	Sundström et al. (2017, V-Dem Working Paper Series 2017:19); V-Dem Codebook
Women's access to justice	Do women enjoy equal, secure, and effective access to justice? 0: Secure and effective access to justice for women is nonexistent. 1: Secure and effective access to justice for women is usually not established or widely respected. 2: Secure and effective access to justice for women is inconsistently observed. Minor problems characterize most cases or occur rather unevenly across different parts of the country. 3: Secure and effective access to justice for women is usually observed. 4: Secure and effective access to justice for women is *almost always observed.*	Pemstein et al. (2023, V-Dem Working Paper Series 2023:21); V-Dem Codebook
Female life expectancy	Life expectancy refers to expected longevity at birth based on current age-specific mortality rates.	Clio Infra (clio-infra.eu)
Party institutionalization index	The index measures the extent to which political parties within a polity are characterized by (1) permanent organizations at the national level, (2) permanent local party branches, (3) the most common type of linkage to constituents, (4) distinct party platforms, and (5) legislative cohesion.	https://v-dem.net/data/v-party-dataset/
Multiparty elections	Multiparty elections occur when at least one opposition group is allowed to exist, political parties are allowed to exist, and the ballot has a choice between more than one party or candidate.	NELDA project: https://nelda.co
Civil conflict	A dichotomous variable that codes whether the country has presently experienced civil conflict.	UCDP/PRIO
Legislature	A dichotomous variable that codes for the presence of any legislature.	Cheibub, Gandhi, & Vreeland, 2010
Log gross domestic product (GDP) per capita	e_migdppc (logged)	World Bank data
GDP growth	Rate of GDP growth	World Bank Development Indicators

(continued)

VARIABLE NAME	CODING	SOURCE
CEDAW ratification	A dichotomous variable that captures whether the country has ratified the CEDAW (Convention on the Elimination of All Forms of Discrimination Against Women) convention.	https://www.ohchr.org/en/ countries
Gender quota	Coded as 1 if there is a quota in place.	For parliamentary elections up until 2015, these data are in the QAROT dataset.

APPENDIX B

COMPARATIVE AGENDA PROJECT (CAP) CODING SCHEME AND GOVERNANCE AND ELECTIONS IN THE MIDDLE EAST PROJECT (GEMEP) ADDED CATEGORIES

1. Macroeconomics	2. Civil rights, minority issues, and civil liberties
• General domestic macroeconomic issues (includes combinations of multiple subtopics) • Inflation, prices, and interest rates • Unemployment rate • Monetary supply, federal reserve board, and the treasury • National budget and debt • Taxation, tax policy, and tax reform • Industrial policy • Price control and stabilization	• Ethnic minority and racial group discrimination • Age discrimination • Handicap or disease discrimination • Voting rights, participation, and related issues • Freedom of speech and religion • Right to privacy and access to government information • Antigovernment activities
3. Health	**4. Agriculture**
• Comprehensive healthcare reform • Insurance reform, availability, and cost • Regulation of drug industry, medical devices, and clinical labs • Facilities construction, regulation, and payments • Provider and insurer payment and regulation • Medical liability, fraud, and abuse	• General (includes combinations of multiple subtopics) • Agricultural trade • Government subsidies to farmers and ranchers, agricultural disaster insurance • Food inspection and safety (including seafood) • Agricultural marketing, research, and promotion • Animal and crop disease, pest control, and domesticated animal welfare

(continued)

- Health manpower and training
- Prevention, communicable diseases, and health promotion
- Infants and children
- Mental illness
- Long-term care, home health, terminally ill, and rehabilitation services
- Prescription drug coverage and costs
- Other or multiple benefits and procedures
- Tobacco abuse, treatment, and education
- Alcohol/controlled and illegal drug abuse, treatment, and education

- Fisheries and fishing
- Agricultural research and development

5. Labor and employment	6. Education
• General (includes combinations of multiple subtopics) • Worker safety and protection, occupational and safety health administration • Employment training and workforce development • Employee benefits • Employee relations and labor unions • Fair labor standards • Youth employment, youth job corps programs, and child labor • Migrant and seasonal workers, farm labor issues	• Higher education • Elementary and secondary education • Education of underprivileged students • Vocational education • Special education • Educational excellence • Arts and humanities • Research and development

7. Environment	8. Energy
• Drinking water safety • Waste disposal • Hazardous waste and toxic chemical regulation, treatment, and disposal • Air pollution, global warming, and noise pollution • Recycling • Indoor environmental hazards • Species and forest protection • Pollution and conservation in coastal and other navigable waterways • Land and water conservation • Research and development	• General (includes combinations of multiple subtopics) • Nuclear energy and nuclear regulatory commission issues • Electricity and hydroelectricity • Natural gas and oil (including offshore oil and gas) • Coal • Alternative and renewable energy • Energy conservation • Research and development

9. Immigration	10. Transportation
• Immigration and refugee issues	• General (includes combinations of multiple subtopics) • Mass transportation and safety • Highway construction, maintenance, and safety • Airports, airlines, air traffic control and safety • Railroad transportation and safety • Truck and automobile transportation and safety • Maritime issues, including safety and security • Public works (infrastructure development) • Research and development
11. Women and family issues**	**12. Law and crime**
• Gender-related laws and legislations • Violence against women • Honor killings • Inheritance laws • Child custody and child support • Gender wage gap • Financial support for unemployed and single mothers • Gender and sexual orientation discrimination • Parental leave and child care	• Executive branch agencies dealing with law and crime • White collar crime and organized crime • Illegal drug production, trafficking, and control • Court administration • Prisons • Juvenile crime and the juvenile justice system • Police, fire, and weapons control • Criminal and civil code • Riots, crime prevention, and crime control
13. Social welfare	**14. Community development and housing**
• Food assistance, and nutrition monitoring programs • Poverty and assistance for low-income families and individuals • Elderly issues and elderly assistance programs (including social security administration) • Assistance to the disabled and handicapped • Social services and volunteer associations	• Housing and community development • Urban economic development and general urban issues • Rural housing and housing assistance programs • Rural economic development • Low- and middle-income housing programs and needs • Veterans housing assistance and military housing programs • Elderly and handicapped housing • Housing assistance for homeless and homeless issues

15. Banking, finance, and domestic commerce	16. Defense
• Banking system and financial institution regulation • Securities and commodities regulation • Consumer finance, mortgages, and credit cards (real estate) • Insurance regulation • Bankruptcy • Corporate mergers, antitrust regulation, and corporate management issues • Small business issues and the small business administration • Copyrights and patents • Domestic disaster relief • Tourism • Consumer safety and consumer fraud • Sports and gambling regulation	• Defense alliances • Military intelligence, espionage • Military readiness, coordination of armed services air support and sealift capabilities, and national stockpiles of strategic materials • Arms control and nuclear nonproliferation • Military aid and weapons sales to other countries • Manpower, military personnel and dependents (army, navy, air force, marines), military courts • Veteran affairs and other issues • Military procurement and weapons system acquisitions and evaluation • Military installations, construction, and land transfers • National guard and reserve affairs • Military nuclear and hazardous waste disposal, military environmental compliance • Civil defense and homeland security • Civilian personnel, civilian employment by the defense industry, military base closings • Oversight of defense contracts and contractors • Direct war-related issues and foreign operations
17. Space, science, technology, and communications	**18. Foreign trade**
• Commercial use of space, satellites • Science technology transfer, international scientific cooperation • Telephone and telecommunication regulation • Broadcast industry regulation (TV, cable, radio) • Weather forecasting and related issues, oceanography • Computer industry, computer security, and general issues related to the internet • Research and development	• Trade negotiations, disputes, and agreements • Export promotion and regulation, export-import bank • International private business investments, overseas private investment corporation (OPIC) • Productivity and competitiveness of business, balance of payments • Tariff and import restrictions, import regulation • Exchange rates and related issues

19. International affairs and foreign aid	20. Government operations
• Foreign aid • International resources exploitation and resources agreement • **Palestine/Arab Israeli conflict** • International finance and economic development • Other country/region specific issues • Human rights • International organizations other than finance: United Nations (UN), UNESCO, international Red Cross • Terrorism, hijacking • Diplomats, embassies, citizens abroad, passports	• General (includes budget requests and appropriations for multiple departments and agencies) • Intergovernmental relations • Postal service issues (including mail fraud) • Government employee benefits, civil service issues • Nominations and appointments • Currency, commemorative coins, medals • Government procurement • Government property management • Contractor management • Income tax administration • Impeachment and scandal • Government branch relations and administrative issues, lower chamber operations • Regulation of political campaigns, political advertising, government ethics • Census • Relief of claims against the government • Federal holidays
21. Public lands and water management	**22. Corruption and fact checking****
• National parks, memorials, historic sites, and recreation • Natural resources, public lands, and forest management • Water resources development and research • Dependencies and territorial issues	• Monitoring the government's spending • Investigating corruption allegations in ministries • Investigating corruption of the representatives • Government efficiency and bureaucratic oversight • Government procurement fraud
23. Arts and entertainment	**24. Sports and recreation**
25. Religion	

Note: Asterisks and bolded items denote the added GEMEP categories and issue areas.

APPENDIX C

LEGISLATORS' INTERVIEWS QUESTIONNAIRE

Name:

Gender:

Male	Female

Age:

Under 35	36–45	46–55	56+

Highest level of education attained:

Some high school	High school diploma	Some college	Bachelor's degree	Master's degree	PhD

Marital status:

Married	Unmarried	Divorced	Widowed

Children:

No	Yes	If yes, how many?

I. General Questions

1. When were you first elected to parliament? Why did you decide to run?
2. Before your current position, did you have any previous political experience?
3. What was your primary occupation before getting elected?

4. From which district were you elected?

5. How many terms have you served as a deputy?

6. What are your views on gender quotas as a mechanism for selecting female candidates?

7. Do gender quotas affect how female candidates are perceived within the parliament and among the public, either positively or negatively? Do you have concrete examples?

8. Do you think the most recent changes in the electoral system in Jordan/ Kuwait have benefited minority and female candidates?

9. How does the frequent dissolution of the parliament affect the election of women and other minority groups?

II. Running for Elections: Candidacy

10. What obstacles (cultural, social, or institutional) did you face as a woman running for political office? Do you think female candidates face particular challenges while running for office compared to their male counterparts? (*Female interviewees only*)

11. Did you have volunteers working on your campaign?

12. Did you attend any training programs as a candidate before your election? Who organized the training? Did you attend any of these programs after being elected?

13. Please indicate the importance of the following organizations to your election:
    a) Political party (Jordan and Morocco only)
    b) Women's organizations
    c) Government-sponsored organizations
    d) NGOs
    e) Tribe (Kuwait and Jordan only)
    f) Labor unions
    g) Religious groups

III. Entering Parliament

Constituency Service

14. How many hours do you spend on constituency service per week?

15. What are the top three requests that you receive from your constituents?

16. How do you mainly communicate with your constituents?
    a) Face-to-face meetings
    b) Emails
    c) Other written communication
    d) Phone
    e) Regular group meetings? (If yes, how often?)
    f) Social media

17. How important are the following constituents to your legislative work?
    a) Women
    b) Lower classes
    c) The middle class
    d) Laborers and agricultural workers
    e) Professionals
    f) Your family and/or tribe

Legislative Behavior

18. As an MP, do (did) you receive any support from the party, tribe, or parliamentary bloc?

19. How many staff members do you currently have?

20. Do you work directly with female members of parliament? Is your work together based on party lines (ideology) or issue based?

21. Are you involved with the work of the women's caucus? Why or why not? What type of work does it do? Does it have any formal links with civil society? In your view, is it an effective body? How could it be made stronger? (*Female interviewees only*)

22. Based on your experience, do you think female MPs face more challenges in parliament than their male counterparts? Can you give concrete examples?

23. How many times do you get to speak in an average week . . .
    a) During open discussion sessions?

Very frequently	Frequently	Sometimes	Rarely	Never

    b) During committee deliberations?

Very frequently	Frequently	Sometimes	Rarely	Never

24. What type of issues do you focus on? *Please list your top three priorities.*
    a) Economy
    b) Environment
    c) Citizenship and immigration
    d) Education
    e) Labor and employment
    f) Energy
    g) Women's issues
    h) Fighting corruption
    i) Health
    j) Agriculture

Legislative Committees

25. Which legislative committees are you a member of?
26. How did you receive your committee assignment? Were these committees your first choice?
27. Which committees are considered the most prestigious to sit on within the assembly? Why? Which committees are perceived as the least prestigious?

Posing Parliamentary Questions

28. Why do deputies ask parliamentary questions (PQs)? Do you think posing PQs is a useful legislative tool?
29. Do you ask PQs? How often? Are there constraints on posing PQs?
30. Do you think the opposition poses more sensitive PQs?
31. Which ministry/cabinet member receives the most PQs?

Political Ambition

32. Do you plan to run for reelection? Why or why not?
33. Do you aspire to achieve higher office? If yes, which offices?
34. Do you consider yourself a role model for any of the following?
    a) Youth
    b) Women
    c) Minorities
    d) Other politicians

NOTES

INTRODUCTION

1. Personal interview, Amman, 2017.
2. Personal interview, Amman, 2017.
3. Personal interview, Rabat, 2020.
4. I use the terms "nondemocracies," "dictatorships," "authoritarian regimes," and "autocracies" interchangeably.
5. Hanna Fenichel Pitkin, *The Concept of Representation* (Berkeley: University of California Press, 1969).
6. Devin K. Joshi and Rakkee Thimothy, "Long-Term Impacts of Parliamentary Gender Quotas in a Single-Party System: Symbolic Co-Option or Delayed Integration?," *International Political Science Review* 40, no. 4 (September 2019): 591–606.
7. Anne Marie Goetz, "Women's Political Effectiveness: A Conceptual Framework," in *No Shortcuts to Power: African Women in Politics and Policy Making*, ed. Anne Marie Goetz and Shireen Hassim (London: Zed, 2003), 40.
8. Anne Phillips, *The Politics of Presence* (New York: Oxford University Press, 1995), 65.
9. Similar to Fernando Bizzarro et al., "Party Strength and Economic Growth," *World Politics* 70, no. 2 (April 2018): 275–320. I use party "strength" and "institutionalization" interchangeably in this book.
10. Fernando Bizzarro, Allen Hicken, and Darin Self, "The V-Dem Party Institutionalization Index: A New Global Indicator (1900–2015)," *SSRN Electronic Journal*, 2017, https://www.v-dem.net/media/publications/v-dem_working_paper_2017_48.pdf.

11. Giovanni Sartori, *Parties and Party Systems: Volume 1: A Framework for Analysis* (Cambridge: Cambridge University Press, 1976); Scott Mainwaring and Timothy Scully, eds., *Building Democratic Institutions: Party Systems in Latin America* (Stanford, CA: Stanford University Press, 1995).

12. Vicky Randall and Lars Svåsand, "Party Institutionalization in New Democracies," *Party Politics* 8, no. 1 (January 2002): 5–29.

13. Anne Meng, *Constraining Dictatorship: From Personalized Rule to Institutionalized Regimes* (New York: Cambridge University Press, 2020), 3.

14. Freedom House, "Anxious Dictators, Wavering Democracies: Global Freedom Under Pressure," 2016, https://freedomhouse.org/sites/default/files/FH_FITW_Report_2016.pdf.

15. Evie Papada, David Altman, Fabio Angiolillo et al., "Defiance in the Face of Autocratization. Democracy Report 2023," *Democracy Report*, 2023, https://www.v-dem.net/documents /29/V-dem_democracyreport2023_lowres.pdf.

16. Authoritarian Regimes Dataset, https://sites.google.com/site/authoritarianregimedataset/ data; Jan Teorell et al., "The Quality of Government Standard Dataset, Version Jan16," University of Gothenburg: The Quality of Government Institute, 2016, http://www.qog .pol.gu.se doi:10.18157/QoGStdJan16.

17. Sarah Sunn Bush and Pär Zetterberg, "Gender Quotas and International Reputation," *American Journal of Political Science* 65, no. 2 (April 2021): 326–41; Daniela Donno and Anne-Kathrin Kreft, "Authoritarian Institutions and Women's Rights," *Comparative Political Studies* 52, no. 5 (April 2019): 720–53; Melody Ellis Valdini, *The Inclusion Calculation: Why Men Appropriate Women's Representation* (New York: Oxford University Press, 2019).

18. Elin Bjarnegård and Pär Zetterberg, "How Autocrats Weaponize Women's Rights," *Journal of Democracy* 33, no. 2 (April 2022): 60–75.

19. Pippa Norris and Joni Lovenduski, *Political Recruitment: Gender, Race, and Class in the British Parliament* (New York: Cambridge University Press, 1995); Miki Caul, "Women's Representation in Parliament: The Role of Political Parties," *Party Politics* 5, no. 1 (January 1999): 79–98; Sheri Kunovich and Pamela Paxton, "Pathways to Power: The Role of Political Parties in Women's National Political Representation," *American Journal of Sociology* 111, no. 2 (2005): 505–52.

20. Caul, "Women's Representation in Parliament"; Tracy L. Osborn, *How Women Represent Women: Political Parties, Gender, and Representation in the State Legislatures* (New York: Oxford University Press, 2012).

21. Daniel Koss, *Where the Party Rules: The Rank and File of China's Communist State* (Cambridge: Cambridge University Press, 2018).

22. While the operation and structure of electoral institutions vary substantially in these regimes, what is common among them is their tendency to practice authoritarianism under the façade of representative democracy; see Andreas Schedler, *The Politics of Uncertainty: Sustaining and Subverting Electoral Authoritarianism* (New York: Oxford University Press, 2013), 1. Most of these regimes allow a certain degree of political competition and electoral contestation by providing a viable space for the opposition to play a role in the political

arena. See also Larry Jay Diamond, "Thinking About Hybrid Regimes," *Journal of Democracy* 13, no. 2 (2002): 21–35; Steven Levitsky and Lucan Way, "The Rise of Competitive Authoritarianism," *Journal of Democracy* 13, no. 2 (2002): 51–65; Andreas Schedler, "The Menu of Manipulation," *Journal of Democracy* 13, no. 2 (2002): 36–50.

23. Juan J. Linz and Alfred C. Stepan, *Problems of Democratic Transition and Consolidation: Southern Europe, South America, and Post-Communist Europe* (Baltimore: Johns Hopkins University Press, 1996).

24. Barbara Geddes, "What Do We Know About Democratization After Twenty Years?," *Annual Review of Political Science* 2, no. 1 (June 1999): 115–44; Barbara Geddes, *Paradigms and Sand Castles: Theory Building and Research Design in Comparative Politics* (Ann Arbor: University of Michigan Press, 2003).

25. Milan W. Svolik, *The Politics of Authoritarian Rule* (Cambridge: Cambridge University Press, 2012).

26. Vineeta Yadav and Bumba Mukherjee, *The Politics of Corruption in Dictatorships* (New York: Cambridge University Press, 2016).

27. Jennifer Gandhi, *Political Institutions Under Dictatorship* (Cambridge: Cambridge University Press, 2008).

28. Carles Boix and Milan W. Svolik, "The Foundations of Limited Authoritarian Government: Institutions, Commitment, and Power-Sharing in Dictatorships," *Journal of Politics* 75, no. 2 (April 2013): 300–316.

29. Beatriz Magaloni, "Credible Power-Sharing and the Longevity of Authoritarian Rule," *Comparative Political Studies* 41, no. 4–5 (April 2008): 715–41.

30. Svolik, *The Politics of Authoritarian Rule*.

31. Joseph Wright, "Do Authoritarian Institutions Constrain? How Legislatures Affect Economic Growth and Investment," *American Journal of Political Science* 52, no. 2 (April 2008): 322–43.

32. Levitsky and Way, "The Rise of Competitive Authoritarianism."

33. Terence K. Teo, "Inequality Under Authoritarian Rule," *Government and Opposition* 56, no. 2 (April 2021): 201–25.

34. Jennifer Gandhi and Ellen Lust-Okar, "Elections Under Authoritarianism," *Annual Review of Political Science* 12, no. 1 (June 2009): 403–22; Schedler, "The Menu of Manipulation"; Andreas Schedler, "The Nested Game of Democratization by Elections," *International Political Science Review* 23, no. 1 (January 2002): 103–22.

35. Dawn Brancati, "Democratic Authoritarianism: Origins and Effects," *Annual Review of Political Science* 17, no. 1 (May 2014): 313–26.

36. Edmund Malesky and Paul Schuler, "Nodding or Needling: Analyzing Delegate Responsiveness in an Authoritarian Parliament," *American Political Science Review* 104, no. 3 (August 2010): 482–502; Melanie Manion, *Information for Autocrats: Representation in Chinese Local Congresses* (Cambridge: Cambridge University Press, 2015); Michael K. Miller, "Elections, Information, and Policy Responsiveness in Autocratic Regimes," *Comparative Political Studies* 48, no. 6 (May 2015): 691–727; Rory Truex, "The Returns to Office in a 'Rubber Stamp' Parliament," *American Political Science Review* 108, no. 2 (May 2014):

235–51; Rory Truex, *Making Autocracy Work: Representation and Responsiveness in Modern China*. Cambridge Studies in Comparative Politics (New York: Cambridge University Press, 2016); Rory Truex, "Authoritarian Gridlock? Understanding Delay in the Chinese Legislative System," *Comparative Political Studies* 53, no. 9 (August 2020): 1455–92; Paul Schuler, "Position Taking or Position Ducking? A Theory of Public Debate in Single-Party Legislatures," *Comparative Political Studies* 53, no. 9 (August 2020): 1493–524; Ben Noble, "Authoritarian Amendments: Legislative Institutions as Intraexecutive Constraints in Post-Soviet Russia," *Comparative Political Studies* 53, no. 9 (August 2020): 1417–54.

37. Scott Williamson and Beatriz Magaloni, "Legislatures and Policy Making in Authoritarian Regimes," *Comparative Political Studies* 53, no. 9 (August 2020): 1525–43.

38. Jennifer Gandhi, Ben Noble, and Milan Svolik, "Legislatures and Legislative Politics Without Democracy," *Comparative Political Studies* 53, no. 9 (August 2020): 1359–79.

39. Miller, "Elections, Information, and Policy Responsiveness in Autocratic Regimes."

40. Gandhi and Lust-Okar, "Elections Under Authoritarianism"; Lisa Blaydes, *Elections and Distributive Politics in Mubarak's Egypt* (Cambridge: Cambridge University Press, 2010).

41. Barbara Geddes, Joseph Wright, and Erica Frantz, *How Dictatorships Work: Power, Personalization, and Collapse* (Cambridge: Cambridge University Press, 2018).

42. Truex, *Making Autocracy Work*.

43. Malesky and Schuler, "Nodding or Needling."

44. Marwa Shalaby and Abdullah Aydogan, "Elite-Citizen Linkages and Issue Congruency Under Competitive Authoritarianism," *Parliamentary Affairs* 73, no. 1 (January 1, 2020): 66–88.

45. Donno and Kreft, "Authoritarian Institutions and Women's Rights."

46. Daniela Donno, Sara Fox, and Joshua Kaasik, "International Incentives for Women's Rights in Dictatorships," *Comparative Political Studies* 55, no. 3 (March 2022): 452.

47. Bjarnegård and Zetterberg, "How Autocrats Weaponize Women's Rights."

48. Bjarnegård and Zetterberg, "How Autocrats Weaponize Women's Rights"; Aili Mari Tripp, *Seeking Legitimacy: Why Arab Autocracies Adopt Women's Rights* (Cambridge: Cambridge University Press, 2019).

49. Valdini, *The Inclusion Calculation*.

50. María José Henríquez and Tatiana Rein-Venegas, "The Resignification of the Chilean Dictatorship's International Discourse: Decolonisation, Religious Tolerance and Women's Rights," *Women's Studies International Forum* 82 (September 2020): 102389; Bush and Zetterberg, "Gender Quotas and International Reputation."

51. Assaf David and Stefanie Nanes, "The Women's Quota in Jordan's Municipal Councils: International and Domestic Dimensions," *Journal of Women, Politics and Policy* 32, no. 4 (October 2011): 275–304.

52. Aili Mari Tripp, "How African Autocracies Instrumentalize Women Leaders," *Politics and Gender* 20, no. 1 (2024): 217–22.

53. Donno and Kreft, "Authoritarian Institutions and Women's Rights."

54. Aili Mari Tripp and Alice Kang, "The Global Impact of Quotas: On the Fast Track to Increased Female Legislative Representation," *Comparative Political Studies* 41, no. 3 (March 2008): 338–61.

55. Karen Beckwith, "Plotting the Path from One to the Other," in *Representation*, ed. Maria C. Escobar-Lemmon and Michelle M. Taylor-Robinson (New York: Oxford University Press, 2014), 19–40; Beth Reingold, "Women as Officeholders: Linking Descriptive and Substantive Representation," in *Political Women and American Democracy*, ed. Christina Wolbrecht, Karen Beckwith, and Lisa Baldez (Cambridge: Cambridge University Press, 2008), 128–47; Lena Wängnerud, "Testing the Politics of Presence: Women's Representation in the Swedish Riksdag," *Scandinavian Political Studies* 23, no. 1 (March 2000): 67–91; Lena Wängnerud, "Women in Parliaments: Descriptive and Substantive Representation," *Annual Review of Political Science* 12, no. 1 (June 2009): 51–69.

56. Kira Sanbonmatsu, "Political Parties and the Recruitment of Women to State Legislatures," *Journal of Politics* 64, no. 3 (August 2002): 791–809; Michele L. Swers, *The Difference Women Make: The Policy Impact of Women in Congress* (Chicago: University of Chicago Press, 2002); Tracy L. Osborn, *How Women Represent Women: Political Parties, Gender, and Representation in the State Legislatures* (New York: Oxford University Press, 2012).

57. Gretchen Bauer, "'Let There Be a Balance': Women in African Parliaments," *Political Studies Review* 10, no. 3 (September 2012): 370–84; Gretchen Bauer and Jennie E. Burnet, "Gender Quotas, Democracy, and Women's Representation in Africa: Some Insights from Democratic Botswana and Autocratic Rwanda," *Women's Studies International Forum* 41 (November 2013): 103–12.

58. Valeriya Mechkova and Amanda B. Edgell, "Substantive Representation, Women's Health, and Regime Type," *Comparative Political Studies* 57, no. 14 (2024): 2449–81.

59. Beatriz Magaloni and Ruth Kricheli, "Political Order and One-Party Rule," *Annual Review of Political Science* 13, no. 1 (May 2010): 123–43; Koss, *Where the Party Rules*.

60. Ellen Lust-Okar, *Structuring Conflict in the Arab World: Incumbents, Opponents, and Institutions* (Cambridge: Cambridge University Press, 2005); Beatriz Magaloni, *Voting for Autocracy: Hegemonic Party Survival and Its Demise in Mexico* (Cambridge: Cambridge University Press, 2006); Gandhi, *Political Institutions Under Dictatorship*.

61. Koss, *Where the Party Rules*; Donno and Kreft, "Authoritarian Institutions and Women's Rights."

62. Magaloni, *Voting for Autocracy*; Jason Brownlee, *Authoritarianism in an Age of Democratization* (Cambridge: Cambridge University Press, 2007); Scott Gehlbach and Philip Keefer, "Investment Without Democracy: Ruling-Party Institutionalization and Credible Commitment in Autocracies," *Journal of Comparative Economics* 39, no. 2 (June 2011): 123–39; Svolik, *The Politics of Authoritarian Rule*.

63. Fernando Casal Bértoa, Zsolt Enyedi, and Martin Mölder, "Party and Party System Institutionalization: Which Comes First?," *Perspectives on Politics* 22, no. 1 (March 2024): 194–212.

64. This book relies on the party institutionalization data collected by the V-Dem Party Institutionalization Index that measures party institutionalization in both democracies and autocracies. The country-level indicators give aggregate scores across all major parties in the system. The index is constructed based on three main dimensions: the scope of party institutionalization (i.e., number of party organizations, number of party branches, and

presence of party platforms); the proportion of parties that reach a threshold of minimal institutionalization; and the depth of the institutionalization (i.e., the linkages the party establishes with the masses and elites, and party legislative cohesion). M. Coppedge et al., "V-Dem Codebook v6," Varieties of Democracy (V-Dem) Project, 2016.

65. Kristin N. Wylie, *Party Institutionalization and Women's Representation in Democratic Brazil* (Cambridge: Cambridge University Press, 2018); Lars Pelke, "Party Institutionalization, Authoritarian Regime Types and Women's Political Equality," *Contemporary Politics* 27 (April 2021): 461–86.
66. Wylie, *Party Institutionalization and Women's Representation in Democratic Brazil*, 2.
67. Robert H. Dix, "Democratization and the Institutionalization of Latin American Political Parties," *Comparative Political Studies* 24, no. 4 (January 1992): 499.
68. Aldo F. Ponce and Susan E. Scarrow, "Party Institutionalization and Partisan Mobilization," *Government and Opposition* 58 (February 2022): 745–64.
69. Magnus B. Rasmussen and Carl Henrik Knutsen, "Party Institutionalization and Welfare State Development," *British Journal of Political Science* 51, no. 3 (July 2021): 1203–29.
70. Elin Bjarnegård, *Gender and Politics: Explaining Male Dominance in Parliamentary Representation*. Gender and Politics Series (London: Palgrave Macmillan, 2013).
71. Tiffany D. Barnes, *Gendering Legislative Behavior: Institutional Constraints and Collaboration* (New York: Cambridge University Press, 2016), 3.
72. Donno and Kreft, "Authoritarian Institutions and Women's Rights."
73. Lars Pelke also argues that there are wide variations in the levels of party institutionalization across authoritarian regime types and views regime types as an unsuitable approach to model institutionalized party rule. Pelke, "Party Institutionalization, Authoritarian Regime Types and Women's Political Equality," 466.
74. Donno and Kreft, "Authoritarian Institutions and Women's Rights."
75. The main dependent variables in Donno and Kreft's study are the levels of women's economic and political rights, which differ from the scope of this book, which deals mainly with women's legislative priorities and political influence.
76. Wylie, *Party Institutionalization and Women's Representation in Democratic Brazil*.
77. Jana Belschner, "Electoral Engineering in New Democracies: Strong Quotas and Weak Parties in Tunisia," *Government and Opposition* 57, no. 1 (January 2022): 108–25.
78. These countries are Algeria, Bahrain, Egypt, Iraq, Jordan, Kuwait, Lebanon, Libya, Morocco, Palestine, Oman, Qatar, Saudi Arabia, Syria, Tunisia, United Arab Emirates, and Yemen.
79. These exceptions include the autocratization taking place in Tunisia since Said's autocratic tendencies since 2020. The changes also include Syria and Yemen becoming closed autocracies since 2012 and 2016, respectively.
80. Abdo I. Baaklini, Guilain Denoeux, and Robert Springborg, *Legislative Politics in the Arab World: The Resurgence of Democratic Institutions* (Boulder, CO: Lynne Rienner, 1999).
81. Holger Albrecht, "The Nature of Political Participation," in *Political Participation in the Middle East*, ed. Ellen Lust-Okar and Saloua Zerhouni (Boulder, CO: Lynne Rienner, 2008), 15–32; James N. Sater, "Changing Politics from Below? Women Parliamentarians in Morocco," *Democratization* 14, no. 4 (August 2007): 723–42.

82. Ellen Lust-Okar, "Elections Under Authoritarianism: Preliminary Lessons from Jordan," *Democratization* 13, no. 3 (June 2006): 456–71; Ellen Lust, "Competitive Clientelism in the Middle East," *Journal of Democracy* 20, no. 3 (2009): 122–35.

83. As'ad AbuKhalil, "Gender Boundaries and Sexual Categories in the Arab World," *Feminist Issues* 15, no. 1–2 (March 1997): 91–104; Sater, "Changing Politics from Below?"; Joseph Sassoon, *Anatomy of Authoritarianism in the Arab Republics* (Cambridge: Cambridge University Press, 2016).

84. Ellen Lust-Okar and Amaney Ahmad Jamal, "Rulers and Rules: Reassessing the Influence of Regime Type on Electoral Law Formation," *Comparative Political Studies* 35, no. 3 (April 2002): 337–66.

85. Blaydes, *Elections and Distributive Politics in Mubarak's Egypt*.

86. Bryce Loidolt and Quinn Mecham, "Parliamentary Opposition Under Hybrid Regimes: Evidence from Egypt: Parliamentary Opposition Under Hybrid Regimes," *Legislative Studies Quarterly* 41, no. 4 (November 2016): 997–1022.

87. Marwa Shalaby, "Women's Political Representation and Authoritarianism in the Arab World," Project on Middle East Political Science, 2016, https://pomeps.org/womens-political-representation-and-authoritarianism-in-the-arab-world; Shalaby and Aydogan, "Elite-Citizen Linkages and Issue Congruency Under Competitive Authoritarianism"; Marwa M. Shalaby and Laila Elimam, "Examining Female Membership and Leadership of Legislative Committees in Jordan," in *Double-Edged Politics on Women's Rights in the MENA Region*, ed. Hanane Darhour and Drude Dahlerup (Cham, Switzerland: Palgrave Macmillan, 2020), 231–55; Marwa M. Shalaby and Laila Elimam, "Women in Legislative Committees in Arab Parliaments," *Comparative Politics* 53, no. 1 (October 2020): 139–67; Daniel L. Tavana and Erin York, "Cooptation in Practice: Measuring Legislative Opposition in an Authoritarian Regime," Preprint, Open Science Framework, November 2020, https://osf.io/preprints/osf/fjdw5_v1.

88. Except for several Gulf monarchies with appointed Shura councils, such as Saudi Arabia and Qatar.

89. Ali Sawi, "State of Parliament in the Arab States," *SSRN Electronic Journal*, 2018, https://papers.ssrn.com/sol3/papers.cfm?abstract_id=3294968.

90. Shalaby and Aydogan, "Elite-Citizen Linkages and Issue Congruency Under Competitive Authoritarianism."

91. Marwa Shalaby and Scott Williamson, "Executive Compliance with Parliamentary Powers Under Authoritarianism: Evidence from Jordan," *Governance* 37, no. 4 (2024): 1163–82; Marwa Shalaby and Scott Williamson, *How Parliaments Matter: Policy and Opposition in the Middle East's Authoritarian Legislatures* (unpublished manuscript, 2023).

92. Bozena C. Welborne and Gail J. Buttorff, "Gender Quotas in the Arab World—20 Years On," *Digest of Middle East Studies* 31, no. 4 (October 2022): 340–58. A mandatory gender quota was enacted in Algeria in 2012, whereas in Morocco, party lists were expanded to include sixty reserved seats for women compared to thirty seats prior to 2011. Furthermore, a provisional quota system was implemented in Egypt's 2015 elections, and Tunisia introduced constitutional reforms mandating gender parity in all legislative bodies in 2014.

93. Inter-Parliamentary Union (IPU), "Women in National Parliaments," Inter-Parliamentary Union, September 2021, https://www.ipu.org/women-in-politics-2021.

94. Carolyn Barnett and Marwa Shalaby, "Success Beyond Gender Quotas: Gender, Local Politics, and Clientelism in Morocco," GLD Working Paper (Program on Governance and Local Development, University of Gothenburg, 2021), https://gunet.sharepoint.com /sites/sy-grp-gld---external-communications/Shared%20Documents/Forms/AllItems .aspx?id=%2Fsites%2Fsy%2Dgrp%2Dgld%2D%2D%2Dexternal%2Dcommunications%2 FShared%20Documents%2FPDFs%20for%20website%20%28external%29%2FGLD%20 Working%20Paper%20Series%2FWP%2048%2Fgld%2Dworking%2Dpaper48%2Epdf& parent=%2Fsites%2Fsy%2Dgrp%2Dgld%2D%2D%2Dexternal%2Dcommunications%2F Shared%20Documents%2FPDFs%20for%20website%20%28external%29%2FGLD%20 Working%20Paper%20Series%2FWP%2048&p=true&ga=1.

95. Haya al-Mughni, *Women in Kuwait: The Politics of Gender* (London: Saqi, 1993); Helen Mary Rizzo, *Islam, Democracy, and the Status of Women: The Case of Kuwait*. Middle East Studies (New York: Routledge, 2005); Meshal Al-Sabah, *Gender and Politics in Kuwait: Women and Political Participation in the Gulf* (London: I. B. Tauris, 2013); Madawi Al-Rasheed, *A Most Masculine State: Gender, Politics and Religion in Saudi Arabia*, vol. 43 (New York: Cambridge University Press, 2013); Eve Sandberg and Kenza Aqertit, *Moroccan Women, Activists, and Gender Politics* (Lanham, MD: Lexington Books, 2017).

96. Leila Ahmed, *Women and Gender in Islam: Historical Roots of a Modern Debate* (New Haven, CT: Yale University Press, 1993); Mounira M. Charrad, *States and Women's Rights: The Making of Postcolonial Tunisia, Algeria, and Morocco* (Berkeley: University of California Press, 2001); Suad Joseph and Susan Slyomovics, eds., *Women and Power in the Middle East* (Philadelphia: University of Pennsylvania Press, 2001); Eleanor Abdella Doumato and Marsha Pripstein Posusney, eds., *Women and Globalization in the Arab Middle East: Gender, Economy, and Society* (Boulder, CO: Lynne Rienner, 2003); Valentine M. Moghadam, *Modernizing Women: Gender and Social Change in the Middle East*, 3rd ed. (Boulder, CO: Lynne Rienner, 2013).

97. Gehan Abou-Zeid, "In Search of Political Power: Women in Parliament in Egypt, Jordan, and Lebanon," in *Women in Parliament: Beyond Numbers*, ed. Azza Karam (Stockholm, Sweden: International Institute for Democracy and Electoral Assistance, 1998), 43–54; Gehan Abou-Zeid, "The Arab Region: Women's Access to the Decision-Making Process Across the Arab Nation," in *Women, Quotas and Politics*, ed. Drude Dahlerup (New York: Routledge, 2006), 179–204; Abla Amawi, "Against All Odds: Women Candidates in Jordanian Elections," in *From Patriarchy to Empowerment*, ed. Valentine M. Moghadam (Syracuse, NY: Syracuse University Press, 2007), 40–57.

98. Michael L. Ross, "Does Oil Hinder Democracy?," *World Politics* 53, no. 3 (April 2001): 325–61; Michael L. Ross, "Oil, Islam, and Women," *American Political Science Review* 102, no. 1 (February 2008): 107–23.

99. James Liddell, "Gender Quotas in Clientelist Systems: The Case of Morocco's National List," *Al-Raida Journal* 126–27 (2009): 79–86; Sater "Changing Politics from Below?"; James N. Sater, "Reserved Seats, Patriarchy, and Patronage in Morocco," in *The Impact of*

Gender Quotas, ed. Susan Franceschet, Mona Lena Krook, and Jennifer M. Piscopo (New York: Oxford University Press, 2012).

100. Hanane Darhour, "L'Autonomisation politique des femmes: Les implications de l'usage du gender quotas dans le Parlement Marocain" (unpublished PhD diss., University of Sidi Mohammed Ben Abdellah, Morocco, 2008).

101. Lindsay J. Benstead, "Why Quotas Are Needed to Improve Women's Access to Services in Clientelistic Regimes: Why Quotas Improve Women's Access to Services," *Governance* 29, no. 2 (April 2016): 185–205.

102. Benstead, "Why Quotas Are Needed to Improve Women's Access to Services in Clientelistic Regimes."

103. See appendix B for detailed information on the Comparative Agenda Project (CAP), coding procedures, and categories. The studies of the CAP made important contributions to the understanding of the level of congruence between the issue priorities of the public and politicians in more developed and democratic settings; see Laura Chaqués Bonafont and Anna M. Palau Roqué, "Comparing Law-Making Activities in a Quasi-Federal System of Government: The Case of Spain," *Comparative Political Studies* 44, no. 8 (August 2011): 1089–119; Alper T. Bulut, "Measuring Political Agenda Setting and Representation in Turkey: Introducing a New Approach and Data Set," *Party Politics* 23, no. 6 (November 2017): 717–30; Gert-Jan Lindeboom, "Public Priorities in Government's Hands: Corresponding Policy Agendas in the Netherlands?," *Acta Politica* 47, no. 4 (October 2012): 443–67.

104. Jason Seawright and John Gerring, "Case Selection Techniques in Case Study Research: A Menu of Qualitative and Quantitative Options," *Political Research Quarterly* 61, no. 2 (June 2008): 294–308.

105. Gary King, Robert O. Keohane, and Sidney Verba, *Designing Social Inquiry: Scientific Inference in Qualitative Research* (Princeton, NJ: Princeton University Press, 2021).

106. Marwa Shalaby, "Women's Political Representation in Kuwait: An Untold Story," James A. Baker III Institute for Public Policy, 2015, http://www.bakerinstitute.org/research/womens-political-representation-kuwait/.

107. Ana Catalano Weeks and Jonathan Homola, "How Can We Measure Women's Substantive Representation," *Comparative Politics Newsletter* 32, no. 2 (2022): 16–21, https://www.comparativepoliticsnewsletter.org/wp-content/uploads/2022/12/APSA-CP_32_2_Dec_2022.pdf.

108. Drude Dahlerup, ed., *Women, Quotas and Politics*. Routledge Research in Comparative Politics 10 (London: Routledge, 2006); Tripp and Kang, "The Global Impact of Quotas"; Mona Lena Krook, *Quotas for Women in Politics: Gender and Candidate Selection Reform Worldwide* (New York: Oxford University Press, 2009).

109. Sue Thomas, *How Women Legislate* (New York: Oxford University Press, 1994); Susan Franceschet, Mona Lena Krook, and Jennifer M. Piscopo, eds., *The Impact of Gender Quotas* (New York: Oxford University Press, 2012).

110. Brownlee, *Authoritarianism in an Age of Democratization*; Gandhi, *Political Institutions Under Dictatorship*; Gehlbach and Keefer, "Investment Without Democracy"; Magaloni, *Voting for Autocracy*; Svolik, *The Politics of Authoritarian Rule*; Koss, *Where the Party Rules*.

111. Dix, "Democratization and the Institutionalization of Latin American Political Parties"; Şebnem Yardımcı-Geyikçi, "Party Institutionalization and Democratic Consolidation: Turkey and Southern Europe in Comparative Perspective," *Party Politics* 21, no. 4 (July 2015): 527–38.

112. Michael Bernhard et al., "Institutional Subsystems and the Survival of Democracy: Do Political and Civil Society Matter?," *SSRN Electronic Journal*, 2015, https://doi.org/10.2139/ssrn.2613824.

113. Rasmussen and Knutsen, "Party Institutionalization and Welfare State Development."

114. Bizzarro et al., "Party Strength and Economic Growth."

115. Randall and Svåsand, "Party Institutionalization in New Democracies."

116. Except for Ponce and Scarrow, "Party Institutionalization and Partisan Mobilization"; Eduardo Alemán, Aldo F. Ponce, and Iñaki Sagarzazu, "Legislative Parties in Volatile, Nonprogrammatic Party Systems: The Peruvian Case in Comparative Perspective," *Latin American Politics and Society* 53, no. 3 (2011): 57–81.

117. Allen Hicken and Erik Martinez Kuhonta, eds., *Party System Institutionalization in Asia: Democracies, Autocracies, and the Shadows of the Past* (Cambridge: Cambridge University Press, 2014), 574.

118. Ellen Lust-Okar, "Elections Under Authoritarianism: Preliminary Lessons from Jordan," *Democratization* 13, no. 3 (June 2006): 456–71; Nathan J. Brown, *When Victory Is Not an Option: Islamist Movements in Arab Politics* (Ithaca, NY: Cornell University Press, 2012).

119. Ahmed, *Women and Gender in Islam*; Charrad, *States and Women's Rights*; Joseph and Slyomovics, eds., *Women and Power in the Middle East*; Doumato and Posusney, eds., *Women and Globalization in the Arab Middle East*; Moghadam, *Modernizing Women*.

120. Janine A. Clark and Francesco Cavatorta, eds., *Political Science Research in the Middle East and North Africa*, vol. 1 (New York: Oxford University Press, 2018), 9.

121. These issues can also be logistical and technical, such as low budgets allocated to parliaments, understaffing, and the absence of archival and/or research units to maintain continuous, high-quality records for researchers to analyze.

122. Gandhi et al., "Legislatures and Legislative Politics Without Democracy."

1. ACCESSING POLITICAL POWER

1. Elin Bjarnegård and Pär Zetterberg, "How Autocrats Weaponize Women's Rights," *Journal of Democracy* 33, no. 2 (April 2022): 60–75; Sarah Sunn Bush, "International Politics and the Spread of Quotas for Women in Legislatures," *International Organization* 65, no. 1 (January 2011): 103–37; Aili Mari Tripp, *Seeking Legitimacy: Why Arab Autocracies Adopt Women's Rights* (Cambridge: Cambridge University Press, 2019); James N. Sater, "Changing Politics from Below? Women Parliamentarians in Morocco," *Democratization* 14, no. 4 (August 2007): 723–42; James N. Sater, "Parliamentary Elections and Authoritarian Rule in Morocco," *Middle East Journal* 63, no. 3 (July 1, 2009): 381–400.

2. On ruling-party institutionalization, see Daniela Donno and Anne-Kathrin Kreft, "Authoritarian Institutions and Women's Rights," *Comparative Political Studies* 52, no. 5 (April 2019):

720–53. On quota mechanisms, see Aili Mari Tripp and Alice Kang, "The Global Impact of Quotas: On the Fast Track to Increased Female Legislative Representation," *Comparative Political Studies* 41, no. 3 (March 2008): 338–61. On institutionalized parties and multiparty elections, see Lars Pelke, "Party Institutionalization, Authoritarian Regime Types, and Women's Political Equality," *Contemporary Politics* 27 (April 2021): 461–86. On women's positions in civil society, see Frank C. Thames, "Women's Legislative Representation in Authoritarian Regimes," *SSRN Electronic Journal* (July 2017), https://doi.org/10.2139/ssrn.3001247.

3. On religion, see Azza Karam, "Women in Politics Beyond Numbers," IDEA: Stockholm, 1998, https://www.idea.int/publications/catalogue/women-parliament-beyond-numbers; M. Steven Fish, "Islam and Authoritarianism," *World Politics* 55, no. 1 (October 2002): 4–37; Ronald Inglehart and Pippa Norris, *Rising Tide: Gender Equality and Cultural Change Around the World* (New York: Cambridge University Press, 2003); Daniela Donno and Bruce Russett, "Islam, Authoritarianism, and Female Empowerment: What Are the Linkages?," *World Politics* 56, no. 4 (July 2004): 582–607; Pippa Norris, "Why Do Arab States Lag the World in Gender Equality?," *SSRN Electronic Journal*, 2009, https://papers.ssrn.com/sol3/papers.cfm?abstract_id=1474820. On traditional and patriarchal gender norms, see Gehan Abou-Zeid, "In Search of Political Power: Women in Parliament in Egypt, Jordan, and Lebanon," in *Women in Parliament: Beyond Numbers*, ed. Azza Karam (Stockholm, Sweden: International Institute for Democracy and Electoral Assistance, 1998), 43–54; Gehan Abou-Zeid, "The Arab Region: Women's Access to the Decision-Making Process Across the Arab Nation," in *Women, Quotas and Politics*, ed. Drude Dahlerup (New York: Routledge, 2006), 179–204; Mounira M. Charrad, *States and Women's Rights: The Making of Postcolonial Tunisia, Algeria, and Morocco* (Berkeley: University of California Press, 2001); Mounira M. Charrad, "Kinship, Islam, or Oil: Culprits of Gender Inequality?," *Politics and Gender* 5, no. 4 (December 2009): 546; Amal Sabbagh, "Overview of Women's Political Representation in the Arab Region: Opportunities and Challenges," *Arab Quota Report: Selected Case Studies*, 2007, https://www.idea.int/sites/default/files/publications/the-arab-quota-report-selected-case-studies.pdf; Amy C. Alexander and Christian Welzel, "Islam and Patriarchy: How Robust Is Muslim Support for Patriarchal Values?," *International Review of Sociology* 21, no. 2 (July 2011): 249–76. On variations in women's movements, see Laurie A. Brand, *Women, the State, and Political Liberalization: Middle Eastern and North African Experiences* (New York: Columbia University Press, 1998); Nadine Sika and Yasmin Khodary, "One Step Forward, Two Steps Back? Egyptian Women Within the Confines of Authoritarianism," *Journal of International Women's Studies* 13, no. 5 (2012): 91–100; Valentine M. Moghadam, *Modernizing Women: Gender and Social Change in the Middle East*, 3rd ed. (Boulder, CO: Lynne Rienner, 2013).

4. Inglehart and Norris, *Rising Tide*, 49.

5. Fish, "Islam and Authoritarianism."

6. Donno and Russett, "Islam, Authoritarianism, and Female Empowerment."

7. Helen Rizzo, Abdel-Hamid Abdel-Latif, and Katherine Meyer, "The Relationship Between Gender Equality and Democracy: A Comparison of Arab Versus Non-Arab Muslim Societies," *Sociology* 41, no. 6 (December 2007): 1151–70.

8. Neilan S. Chaturvedi and Orlando Montoya, "Democracy, Oil, or Religion? Expanding Women's Rights in the Muslim World," *Politics and Religion* 6, no. 3 (September 2013): 596–617.

9. Sabbagh, "Overview of Women's Political Representation in the Arab Region"; Muhamad S. Olimat, "Women and the Kuwaiti National Assembly," *Journal of International Women's Studies* 12, no. 3 (2011): 76–95, https://vc.bridgew.edu/jiws/vol12/iss3/6; Ahlam Khalfan Al Subhi and Amy Erica Smith, "Electing Women to New Arab Assemblies: The Roles of Gender Ideology, Islam, and Tribalism in Oman," *International Political Science Review* 40, no. 1 (January 2019): 90–107.

10. Sarah Sunn Bush and Eleanor Gao, "Small Tribes, Big Gains: The Strategic Uses of Gender Quotas in the Middle East," *Comparative Politics* 49, no. 2 (January 2017): 149–67.

11. Charrad, *States and Women's Rights*; Charrad, "Kinship, Islam, or Oil."

12. Jamal Al Shalabi and Tareq Al-Assad, "Political Participation of Jordanian Women," *Égypte/Monde Arabe* 3, no. 9 (2012): 211–30, https://doi.org/10.4000/ema.3033.

13. Bozena C. Welborne and Gail J. Buttorff, "Gender Quotas in the Arab World—20 Years On," *Digest of Middle East Studies* 31, no. 4 (October 2022): 340–58.

14. Yuree Noh and Marwa Shalaby, "Who Supports Gender Quotas in Transitioning and Authoritarian States in the Middle East and North Africa?," *Comparative Political Studies* 57, no. 14 (2024): 2313–47.

15. Arab Barometer 2018.

16. Personal interview, Rabat, 2020.

17. Personal interview, Kuwait City, 2023.

18. Personal interview, Amman, 2018.

19. Lindsay J. Benstead, "Why Quotas Are Needed to Improve Women's Access to Services in Clientelistic Regimes: Why Quotas Improve Women's Access to Services," *Governance* 29, no. 2 (April 2016): 185–205.

20. On voting behavior in transitioning contexts, see Lindsay J. Benstead, Amaney A. Jamal, and Ellen Lust, "Is It Gender, Religiosity, or Both? A Role Congruity Theory of Candidate Electability in Transitional Tunisia," *Perspectives on Politics* 13, no. 1 (March 2015): 74–94; Lindsay Benstead and Ellen Lust, "Why Do Some Voters Prefer Female Candidates? The Role of Perceived Incorruptibility in Arab Elections," in *Gender and Corruption: Historical Roots and New Avenues for Research*, ed. Helena Stensöta and Lena Wängnerud (New York: Palgrave Macmillan, 2018), 83–104; Alexandra Domike Blackman and Marlette Jackson, "Gender Stereotypes, Political Leadership, and Voting Behavior in Tunisia," *Political Behavior* 43, no. 3 (2021): 1037–66. On voting behavior in autocratic contexts, see Marwa Shalaby, "Support for Gender Quotas and Perceived Corruption in Developing Democracies: Evidence from Lebanon," in *Corruption and Informal Practices in the Middle East and North Africa*. Corruption and Anti-Corruption Studies (New York: Routledge, 2019); Carolyn Barnett, Alexandra Blackman, and Marwa Shalaby, "Gender Stereotypes in Autocracies: Experimental Evidence from Morocco," *Journal of Politics* (forthcoming), https://www.journals.uchicago.edu/doi/10.1086/733000.

21. Benstead et al., "Is It Gender, Religiosity, or Both?"

22. Benstead and Lust, "Why Do Some Voters Prefer Female Candidates?"

23. Blackman and Jackson, "Gender Stereotypes, Political Leadership, and Voting Behavior in Tunisia."

24. Shalaby, "Support for Gender Quotas and Perceived Corruption in Developing Democracies."

25. Ellen Lust and Lindsay J. Benstead, "Is the Future Female? Lessons from a Conjoint Experiment on Voter Preferences in Six Arab Countries," *Comparative Political Studies* 57, no. 14 (2024): 2376–413.

26. Kristen Kao et al., "Female Representation and Legitimacy: Evidence from a Harmonized Experiment in Jordan, Morocco, and Tunisia," *American Political Science Review* 118, no. 1 (2024): 495–503.

27. Barnett et al., "Gender Stereotypes in Autocracies."

28. Wilma Rule, "Why Women Don't Run: The Critical Contextual Factors in Women's Legislative Recruitment," *Western Political Quarterly* 34, no. 1 (March 1981): 60; Donley T. Studlar and Ian McAllister, "Does a Critical Mass Exist? A Comparative Analysis of Women's Legislative Representation Since 1950," *European Journal of Political Research* 41, no. 2 (March 2002): 233–53; Pippa Norris and Joni Lovenduski, *Political Recruitment: Gender, Race, and Class in the British Parliament* (New York: Cambridge University Press, 1995); Richard E. Matland, "Enhancing Women's Political Participation: Legislative Recruitment and Electoral Systems," in *Women in Parliament: Beyond Numbers*, ed. Julie Ballington and Azza Karam (Stockholm, Sweden: International Institute for Democracy and Electoral Assistance, 2005), 93–111.

29. Leslie A. Schwindt-Bayer, "Making Quotas Work: The Effect of Gender Quota Laws on the Election of Women," *Legislative Studies Quarterly* 34, no. 1 (February 2009): 5–28.

30. World Bank, *Capabilities, Opportunities and Participation: Gender Equality and Development in the Middle East and North Africa Region* (Washington, DC: World Bank, 2011).

31. United Nations Development Programme (UNDP), *Human Development Report, 2005* (New York: UNDP, 2005), https://hdr.undp.org/content/human-development-report-2005; World Bank, *Opening Doors: Gender Equality and Development in the Middle East and North Africa* (Washington, DC: World Bank, 2013), https://documents1.worldbank.org/curated/en/338381468279877854/pdf/Main-report.pdf.

32. World Bank, *Opening Doors.*

33. On higher male-female population sex ratios, see Fish, "Islam and Authoritarianism." On unequal family laws, see Zahia Smail Salhi, "Algerian Women, Citizenship, and the 'Family Code,'" *Gender and Development* 11, no. 3 (November 2003): 27–35. On oil wealth, see Michael L. Ross, "Oil, Islam, and Women," *American Political Science Review* 102, no. 1 (February 2008): 107–23.

34. Ross, "Oil, Islam, and Women."

35. Ross, "Oil, Islam, and Women."

36. On the effect of CEDAW on women's labor force participation, see Michele Angrist, "War, Resisting the West, and Women's Labor: Toward an Understanding of Arab Exceptionalism," *Politics and Gender* 8, no. 1 (March 2012): 51–82. On low foreign direct investments, see Moghadam, *Modernizing Women.*

37. Personal interview, Kuwait City, 2023.

38. Personal interview, Beirut, 2015.

39. Personal Interview, Kuwait City, 2023.

40. Organisation for Economic Co-operation and Development, "Women in Business: Policies to Support Women's Entrepreneurship Development in the MENA Region," OECD, 2012, https://www.oecd.org/en/publications/women-in-business_9789264179073-en.html.

41. To construct Model 4, I rely on Barbara Geddes, Joseph Wright, and Erica Frantz, "Autocratic Breakdown and Regime Transitions: A New Data Set," *Perspectives on Politics* 12, no. 2 (June 2014): 313–31.

42. Kathleen M. Fallon, Liam Swiss, and Jocelyn Viterna, "Resolving the Democracy Paradox: Democratization and Women's Legislative Representation in Developing Nations, 1975 to 2009," *American Sociological Review* 77, no. 3 (June 2012): 380–408; S. Kimberly Adams, "The Significant Influence of Proportional Representation and Democratization on the Share of Female Parliamentarians in Middle Eastern and North African (MENA) Countries," *International Journals of Arts and Sciences* 11, no. 1 (2018): 237–52.

43. Brand, *Women, the State, and Political Liberalization*, 10, refers to state feminism as "policies directed from (as well as generally formulated at) the state leadership level, which aim at mobilizing or channeling women's (re) productive capabilities and coopting them into support for the state through such programs as raising literacy, increasing access to the labor market, establishing state-sponsored women's organizations, generally along the lines of the single-party model."

44. Mervat F. Hatem, "Economic and Political Liberation in Egypt and the Demise of State Feminism," *International Journal of Middle East Studies* 24, no. 2 (May 1992): 231–51.

45. Mounira M. Charrad and Amina Zarrugh, "Equal or Complementary? Women in the New Tunisian Constitution After the Arab Spring," *Journal of North African Studies* 19, no. 2 (March 2014): 230–43; Andrea Khalil, "Tunisia's Women: Partners in Revolution," *Journal of North African Studies* 19, no. 2 (March 2014): 186–99; Moghadam, *Modernizing Women*.

46. Sadat's aim was to salvage his popularity, which had plummeted because of the peace accords with Israel.

47. Hatem, "Economic and Political Liberation in Egypt and the Demise of State Feminism."

48. Brand, *Women, the State, and Political Liberalization*.

49. The comparison is even starker when we examine female representation in the upper houses of parliament. Women hold only 7.3 percent of the seats in the Arab world, compared to 25.5 percent in the Americas, 24.3 percent in the non-Nordic Organization for Security and Co-operation in Europe, 20.3 percent in sub-Saharan Africa, 13.3 percent in Asia, and 36 percent in the nations of the Pacific (Inter-Parliamentary Union [IPU], "Women in National Parliaments," Inter-Parliamentary Union, September 2021, https://www.ipu.org/women-in-politics-2021).

50. Bush, "International Politics and the Spread of Quotas for Women in Legislatures"; Bozena Welborne, "The Strategic Use of Gender Quotas in the Arab World," William and Kathy Hybl Democracy Studies Fellowship Paper (Washington, DC: IFES, 2010), https://aceproject.org/ero-en/regions/africa/MZ/ifes-the-strategic-use-of-gender-quotas-in-the; Aili Mari

Tripp, "Legislative Quotas for Women: Implications for Governance in Africa," in *African Parliaments*, ed. M. A. Mohamed Salih (New York: Palgrave Macmillan, 2005), 48–60.

51. Tunisia in 1956 and 1989, Morocco in 2002, Saudi Arabia in 2015, and Egypt in 1979 and 2015 are important examples of this specific point.

52. Tripp, *Seeking Legitimacy*.

53. Abou-Zeid, "The Arab Region"; Abla Amawi, "Against All Odds: Women Candidates in Jordanian Elections," in *From Patriarchy to Empowerment*, ed. Valentine M. Moghadam (Syracuse, NY: Syracuse University Press, 2007), 40–57; Drude Dahlerup, "Women in Arab Parliaments: Can Gender Quotas Contribute to Democratization?," *Al-Raida Journal* 126, no. 27 (2009): 28–38; Hanane Darhour and Drude Dahlerup, "Sustainable Representation of Women Through Gender Quotas: A Decade's Experience in Morocco," *Women's Studies International Forum* 41 (November 2013): 132–42; Assaf David and Stefanie Nanes, "The Women's Quota in Jordan's Municipal Councils: International and Domestic Dimensions," *Journal of Women, Politics and Policy* 32, no. 4 (October 2011): 275–304.

54. Andrew Reynolds, Ben Reilly, and Andrew Ellis, *Electoral System Design: The New International IDEA Handbook*. Handbook Series (Stockholm, Sweden: International Institute for Democracy and Electoral Assistance, 2005).

55. Inmaculada Szmolka, "Political Change in North Africa and the Arab Middle East: Constitutional Reforms and Electoral Processes," *Arab Studies Quarterly* 36, no. 2 (2014): 128.

56. Article 46 of Tunisia's 2014 constitution stipulates: "The state shall commit to the protection and support of women's accrued rights. The state should also guarantee equal opportunities for men and women in carrying different responsibilities. The state will seek to guarantee gender equality in legislative assemblies. The state will take the necessary measures to eradicate violence against women." According to Article 46, not only are women and men guaranteed equal representation in the legislative arena, but also women will be able to run for the presidency—a right never granted to women in any other country in the MENA region in the past.

57. Although Egypt set the laws governing local elections in its postrevolution constitution, the country has not held any local election since the overthrow of Mubarak's regime in 2011.

58. Aili Mari Tripp, "Do Arab Women Need Electoral Quotas?," *Foreign Policy*, January 19, 2012, https://foreignpolicy.com/2012/01/19/do-arab-women-need-electoral-quotas/.

59. Richard E. Matland and Donley T. Studlar, "The Contagion of Women Candidates in Single-Member District and Proportional Representation Electoral Systems: Canada and Norway," *Journal of Politics* 58, no. 3 (August 1996): 707–33; Gregory D. Schmidt and Kyle L. Saunders, "Effective Quotas, Relative Party Magnitude, and the Success of Female Candidates: Peruvian Municipal Elections in Comparative Perspective," *Comparative Political Studies* 37, no. 6 (August 2004): 704–34.

60. Mark P. Jones, "Gender Quotas, Electoral Laws, and the Election of Women: Lessons from the Argentine Provinces," *Comparative Political Studies* 31, no. 1 (February 1998): 3–21.

61. Tunisia was the first country to introduce a zipper quota in its postrevolution constitution in 2014 (Quota Project, *Global Database of Quotas for Women*, 2021, www.quotaproject.org).

In 2017, Tunisia introduced zipper and vertical quota systems to ensure women are placed in winnable positions on party lists. Noncompliance measures were introduced in Algeria in 2012, which mandate that political parties are required to place women on their lists in proportion to the number of seats in the district (between 20 and 50 percent), which led to a dramatic increase in women's political representation, as depicted in table 1.1.

62. Leslie A. Schwindt-Bayer, *Political Power and Women's Representation in Latin America* (New York: Oxford University Press, 2010), 46.

63. Adams, "The Significant Influence of Proportional Representation and Democratization."

64. Matland and Studlar, "The Contagion of Women Candidates in Single-Member District and Proportional Representation Electoral Systems"; Schmidt and Saunders, "Effective Quotas, Relative Party Magnitude, and the Success of Female Candidates."

65. On higher levels of women's political rights, see Donno and Kreft, "Authoritarian Institutions and Women's Rights." On women's political representation in autocracies, see Pelke, "Party Institutionalization, Authoritarian Regime Types, and Women's Political Equality."

66. Donno and Kreft, "Authoritarian Institutions and Women's Rights," 721.

67. On internal structures, see Margaret El-Helou, "Women and Parliamentary Elections in Lebanon," in *Arab Women and Political Participation*, ed. Hussein Abu Rumman (Amman, Jordan: al-Urdon al-Jadid Research Centre, 2000), 200–220. On ideology, see Lihi Ben Shitrit, "Authenticating Representation: Women's Quotas and Islamist Parties," *Politics and Gender* 12, no. 4 (December 2016): 781–806; Janine Astrid Clark and Jillian Schwedler, "Who Opened the Window? Women's Activism in Islamist Parties," *Comparative Politics* 35, no. 3 (April 2003): 293; Katarína Škrabáková, "Islamist Women as Candidates in Elections: A Comparison of the Party of Justice and Development in Morocco and the Muslim Brotherhood in Egypt," *Die Welt Des Islams* 57, no. 3–4 (October 2017): 329–59.

68. Kristin N. Wylie, *Party Institutionalization and Women's Representation in Democratic Brazil* (Cambridge: Cambridge University Press, 2018), 3.

69. Pelke, "Party Institutionalization, Authoritarian Regime Types, and Women's Political Equality." The author's dependent variable is an index of women's political exclusion, not women's numerical presence in legislatures per se. The index consists of five main items: power distributed by gender, gender equality in respect for civil liberties, access to public services distributed by gender, access to state jobs by gender, and access to state business opportunities by gender. The power distributed item is an ordinal measure of whether political power is distributed according to gender.

70. Jana Belschner, "Electoral Engineering in New Democracies: Strong Quotas and Weak Parties in Tunisia," *Government and Opposition* 57, no. 1 (January 2022): 108–25.

2. PARTY INSTITUTIONALIZATION AND WOMEN'S REPRESENTATION

1. Hanna Fenichel Pitkin, *The Concept of Representation* (Berkeley: University of California Press, 1969), 221.

2. David T. Canon and Richard A. Posner, *Race, Redistricting, and Representation: The Unintended Consequences of Black Majority Districts* (Chicago: University of Chicago Press, 1999).

3. Joni Lovenduski and Pippa Norris, "Westminster Women: The Politics of Presence," *Political Studies* 51, no. 1 (March 2003): 84–102.

4. Susan A. Banducci, Todd Donovan, and Jeffrey A. Karp, "Minority Representation, Empowerment, and Participation," *Journal of Politics* 66, no. 2 (May 2004): 534–56.

5. Jane Mansbridge, "Should Blacks Represent Blacks and Women Represent Women? A Contingent 'Yes,'" *Journal of Politics* 61, no. 3 (August 1999): 628–57.

6. Sarah Childs, *New Labour's Women MPs: Women Representing Women* (London: Routledge, 2004).

7. Anne Phillips, *The Politics of Presence* (New York: Oxford University Press, 1995), 65.

8. Kathleen A. Bratton, "Critical Mass Theory Revisited: The Behavior and Success of Token Women in State Legislatures," *Politics and Gender* 1, no. 1 (2005): 97–125.

9. Katherine Tate, *Black Faces in the Mirror: African Americans and Their Representatives in the U.S. Congress* (Princeton, NJ: Princeton University Press, 2004).

10. Jane Mansbridge, "Quota Problems: Combating the Dangers of Essentialism," *Politics and Gender* 1, no. 4 (December 2005): 622.

11. Ayşe Güneş Ayata and Fatma Tütüncü, "Critical Acts Without a Critical Mass: The Substantive Representation of Women in the Turkish Parliament," *Parliamentary Affairs* 61, no. 3 (July 2008): 461–75.

12. Drude Dahlerup, "From a Small to a Large Minority: Women in Scandinavian Politics," *Scandinavian Political Studies* 11, no. 4 (December 1988): 275–98; Mona Lena Krook, *Quotas for Women in Politics: Gender and Candidate Selection Reform Worldwide* (New York: Oxford University Press, 2009).

13. Sarah Childs and Mona Lena Krook, "Should Feminists Give Up on Critical Mass? A Contingent Yes," *Politics and Gender* 2, no. 4 (December 2006): 522–30; Karen Beckwith and Kimberly Cowell-Meyers, "Sheer Numbers: Critical Representation Thresholds and Women's Political Representation," *Perspectives on Politics* 5, no. 3 (September 2007): 553.

14. Jocelyn Elise Crowley, "When Tokens Matter," *Legislative Studies Quarterly* 29, no. 1 (February 2004): 109–36; Susan J. Carroll, ed., *The Impact of Women in Public Office* (Bloomington: Indiana University Press, 2001); Fiona Mackay, "'Thick' Conceptions of Substantive Representation: Women, Gender and Political Institutions," *Representation* 44, no. 2 (July 2008): 125–39; Donley T. Studlar and Ian McAllister, "Does a Critical Mass Exist? A Comparative Analysis of Women's Legislative Representation Since 1950," *European Journal of Political Research* 41, no. 2 (March 2002): 233–53.

15. Amanda Clayton, "How Do Electoral Gender Quotas Affect Policy?," *Annual Review of Political Science* 24, no. 1 (May 11, 2021): 235–52.

16. Sue Thomas, *How Women Legislate* (New York: Oxford University Press, 1994), 9–10.

17. Beth Reingold, "Women as Officeholders: Linking Descriptive and Substantive Representation," in *Political Women and American Democracy*, ed. Christina Wolbrecht, Karen Beckwith and Lisa Baldez (Cambridge: Cambridge University Press, 2008), 128.

18. Karen Celis et al., "Rethinking Women's Substantive Representation," *Representation* 44, no. 2 (July 2008): 99–110; Ana Catalano Weeks and Jonathan Homola, "How Can We Measure Women's Substantive Representation," *Comparative Politics Newsletter* 32, no. 2 (2022): 16–21, https://www.comparativepoliticsnewsletter.org/wp-content/uploads/2022/12/APSA-CP _32_2_Dec_2022.pdf.

19. Drude Dahlerup, "From a Small to a Large Minority: Women in Scandinavian Politics," *Scandinavian Political Studies* 11, no. 4 (December 1988): 279.

20. Anne Phillips, *The Politics of Presence* (New York: Oxford University Press, 1995); Karen Celis, "Substantive Representation of Women: The Representation of Women's Interests and the Impact of Descriptive Representation in the Belgian Parliament (1900–1979)," *Journal of Women, Politics and Policy* 28, no. 2 (July 2006): 85–114.

21. Elsa M. Chaney, *Supermadre: Women in Politics in Latin America*. Latin American Monographs 50 (Austin: University of Texas Press, 1979).

22. Debra L. Dodson et al., *Voices, Views, Votes: The Impact of Women in the 103rd Congress*, Center for the American Woman and Politics (CAWP) (New Brunswick: Eagleton Institute of Politics, Rutgers, State University of New Jersey, 1995).

23. Thomas, *How Women Legislate*; Michele L. Swers, "Are Women More Likely to Vote for Women's Issue Bills Than Their Male Colleagues?," *Legislative Studies Quarterly* 23, no. 3 (August 1998): 435; Debra L. Dodson and Susan J. Carroll, *Reshaping the Agenda: Women in State Legislatures* (New Brunswick: Eagleton Institute of Politics, Rutgers, State University of New Jersey, 1991); Mala Htun, Marina Lacalle, and Juan Pablo Micozzi, "Does Women's Presence Change Legislative Behavior? Evidence from Argentina, 1983–2007," *Journal of Politics in Latin America* 5, no. 1 (April 2013): 95–125.

24. Sue Thomas and Susan Welch, "The Impact of Gender on Activities and Priorities of State Legislators," *Political Research Quarterly* 44, no. 2 (June 1991): 445–56.

25. Amanda Clayton and Pär Zetterberg, "Quota Shocks: Electoral Gender Quotas and Government Spending Priorities Worldwide," *Journal of Politics* 80, no. 3 (July 2018): 916–32.

26. Mark P. Jones, "Legislator Gender and Legislator Policy Priorities in the Argentine Chamber of Deputies and the United States House of Representatives," *Policy Studies Journal* 25, no. 4 (December 1997): 613–29.

27. Michelle M. Taylor-Robinson and Roseanna Michelle Heath, "Do Women Legislators Have Different Policy Priorities Than Their Male Colleagues? A Critical Case Test," *Women and Politics* 24, no. 4 (January 2003): 77–101.

28. Leslie A. Schwindt-Bayer, "Still Supermadres? Gender and the Policy Priorities of Latin American Legislators," *American Journal of Political Science* 50, no. 3 (July 2006): 570–85.

29. Valeriya Mechkova and Ruth Carlitz, "Gendered Accountability: When and Why Do Women's Policy Priorities Get Implemented?," *European Political Science Review* 13, no. 1 (February 2021): 3–21.

30. Miki Caul, "Women's Representation in Parliament: The Role of Political Parties," *Party Politics* 5, no. 1 (January 1999): 79–98; Tracy L. Osborn, *How Women Represent Women: Political Parties, Gender, and Representation in the State Legislatures* (New York: Oxford University Press, 2012).

31. Thomas Poguntke et al., "Party Rules, Party Resources and the Politics of Parliamentary Democracies: How Parties Organize in the 21st Century," *Party Politics* 22, no. 6 (November 2016): 661–78.

32. Aliza Forman-Rabinovici and Udi Sommer, "Can the Descriptive-Substantive Link Survive Beyond Democracy? The Policy Impact of Women Representatives," *Democratization* 26, no. 8 (November 2019): 1513–33.

33. Waikeung Tam, "Do Female Legislators Have Different Policy Priorities Than Their Male Colleagues in an Undemocratic/Semi-Democratic Legislature? The Case of Hong Kong," *Journal of Legislative Studies* 23, no. 1 (January 2017): 44–70.

34. Amanda Clayton et al., "In Whose Interest? Gender and Mass–Elite Priority Congruence in Sub-Saharan Africa," *Comparative Political Studies* 52, no. 1 (January 2019): 69–101.

35. Valentine M. Moghadam and Fatemeh Haghighatjoo, "Women and Political Leadership in an Authoritarian Context: A Case Study of the Sixth Parliament in the Islamic Republic of Iran," *Politics and Gender* 12, no. 1 (March 2016): 168–97.

36. Hanane Darhour, "L'Autonomisation politique des femmes: Les implications de l'usage du gender quotas dans le Parlement Marocain" (unpublished PhD diss., University of Sidi Mohammed Ben Abdellah, Morocco, 2008).

37. Eda Bektas and Esra Issever-Ekinci, "Who Represents Women in Turkey? An Analysis of Gender Difference in Private Bill Sponsorship in the 2011–15 Turkish Parliament," *Politics and Gender* 15, no. 4 (December 2019): 851–81.

38. Hanane Darhour and Drude Dahlerup, "Sustainable Representation of Women Through Gender Quotas: A Decade's Experience in Morocco," *Women's Studies International Forum* 41 (November 2013): 132–42.

39. Marwa M. Shalaby and Laila Elimam, "Women in Legislative Committees in Arab Parliaments," *Comparative Politics* 53, no. 1 (October 2020): 139–67.

40. Lindsay J. Benstead, "Why Quotas Are Needed to Improve Women's Access to Services in Clientelistic Regimes: Why Quotas Improve Women's Access to Services," *Governance* 29, no. 2 (April 2016): 185–205.

41. Hala Abdelgawad and Mazen Hassan, "Women in the Egyptian Parliament: A Different Agenda?," *Review of Economics and Political Science* 8, no. 6 (October 2019): 558–76, https://www.emerald.com/insight/content/doi/10.1108/reps-06-2019-0076/full/html.

42. Kristine Goulding, "Unjustifiable Means to Unjustifiable Ends: Delegitimizing Parliamentary Gender Quotas in Tunisia," *Al-Raida Journal* 126–27 (2009): 76.

43. James N. Sater, "Changing Politics from Below? Women Parliamentarians in Morocco," *Democratization* 14, no. 4 (August 2007): 723–42; James N. Sater, "Reserved Seats, Patriarchy, and Patronage in Morocco," in *The Impact of Gender Quotas*, ed. Susan Franceschet, Mona Lena Krook, and Jennifer M. Piscopo (New York: Oxford University Press, 2012).

44. Sater, "Reserved Seats, Patriarchy, and Patronage in Morocco," 73.

45. James Liddell, "Gender Quotas in Clientelist Systems: The Case of Morocco's National List," *Al-Raida Journal* 126–27 (2009): 79–86.

46. Daniela Donno and Anne-Kathrin Kreft, "Authoritarian Institutions and Women's Rights," *Comparative Political Studies* 52, no. 5 (April 2019): 720–53.

47. Lars Pelke, "Party Institutionalization, Authoritarian Regime Types, and Women's Political Equality," *Contemporary Politics* 27 (April 2021): 461–86.

48. Katarína Škrabáková, "Islamist Women as Candidates in Elections: A Comparison of the Party of Justice and Development in Morocco and the Muslim Brotherhood in Egypt," *Die Welt Des Islams* 57, no. 3–4 (October 2017): 329–59.

49. Tiffany D. Barnes, *Gendering Legislative Behavior: Institutional Constraints and Collaboration* (New York: Cambridge University Press, 2016).

50. Anne Marie Goetz, "Women's Political Effectiveness: A Conceptual Framework," in *No Shortcuts to Power: African Women in Politics and Policy Making*, ed. Anne Marie Goetz and Shireen Hassim (London: Zed, 2003), 40.

51. Daniela Giannetti, Andrea Pedrazzani, and Luca Pinto, "Personal Ambitions, Expertise and Parties' Control: Understanding Committee Assignment in the Italian Chamber of Deputies," *Parliamentary Affairs* 72, no. 1 (January 2019): 119–40.

52. Susan J. Carroll, *Women as Candidates in American Politics* (Bloomington: Indiana University Press, 1994), 15.

53. Scott Mainwaring and Timothy Scully, eds., *Building Democratic Institutions: Party Systems in Latin America* (Stanford, CA: Stanford University Press, 1995); Scott Mainwaring, *Rethinking Party Systems in the Third Wave of Democratization: The Case of Brazil* (Stanford, CA: Stanford University Press, 1999); Vicky Randall and Lars Svåsand, "Party Institutionalization in New Democracies," *Party Politics* 8, no. 1 (January 2002): 5–29; Allen Hicken and Erik Martinez Kuhonta, eds., *Party System Institutionalization in Asia: Democracies, Autocracies, and the Shadows of the Past* (Cambridge: Cambridge University Press, 2014).

54. Mainwaring and Scully, eds., *Building Democratic Institutions*.

55. Francesco Cavatorta and Lise Storm, eds., *Political Parties in the Arab World: Continuity and Change* (Edinburgh, United Kingdom: Edinburgh University Press, 2018).

56. Hicken and Kuhonta, eds., *Party System Institutionalization in Asia*.

57. Beatriz Magaloni, *Voting for Autocracy: Hegemonic Party Survival and Its Demise in Mexico* (Cambridge: Cambridge University Press, 2006); Jennifer Gandhi, *Political Institutions Under Dictatorship* (Cambridge: Cambridge University Press, 2008); Milan W. Svolik, *The Politics of Authoritarian Rule* (Cambridge: Cambridge University Press, 2012).

58. Beatriz Magaloni, "Credible Power-Sharing and the Longevity of Authoritarian Rule," *Comparative Political Studies* 41, no. 4–5 (April 2008): 725.

59. Daniel Koss, *Where the Party Rules: The Rank and File of China's Communist State* (Cambridge: Cambridge University Press, 2018).

60. Svolik, *The Politics of Authoritarian Rule*, 193.

61. Allen Hicken and Erik Martinez Kuhonta, "Shadows from the Past: Party System Institutionalization in Asia," *Comparative Political Studies* 44, no. 5 (May 2011): 572–97; Hicken and Kuhonta, eds., *Party System Institutionalization in Asia*.

62. Except for Michele Penner Angrist, *Party Building in the Modern Middle East* (Seattle: University of Washington Press, 2006); Lise Storm, *Party Politics and Prospects for Democracy in North Africa* (Boulder, CO: Lynne Rienner, 2014); Cavatorta and Strom, eds., *Political Parties in the Arab World*.

63. Raymond A. Hinnebusch, "Political Parties in MENA: Their Functions and Development," *British Journal of Middle Eastern Studies* 44, no. 2 (April 2017): 159–75.

64. Valeria Resta, "Leftist Parties in the Arab Region Before and After the Arab Uprisings: 'Unrequited Love'?," in *Political Parties in the Arab World*, ed. Francesco Cavatorta and Lise Storm (Edinburgh, United Kingdom: Edinburgh University Press, 2018), 21–48.

65. Siavush Randjbar-Daemi, Eskandar Sadeghi-Boroujerdi, and Lauren Banko, "Introduction to Political Parties in the Middle East: Historical Trajectories and Future Prospects," *British Journal of Middle Eastern Studies* 44, no. 2 (April 2017): 155–58.

66. James A. Bill and Robert Springborg, *Politics in the Middle East*, 4th ed. The HarperCollins Series in Comparative Politics (New York: HarperCollins, 1994); Hinnebusch, "Political Parties in MENA."

67. Ellen Lust-Okar, *Structuring Conflict in the Arab World: Incumbents, Opponents, and Institutions* (Cambridge: Cambridge University Press, 2005); Ellen Lust, "Competitive Clientelism in the Middle East," *Journal of Democracy* 20, no. 3 (2009): 122–35.

68. Lisa Blaydes, *Elections and Distributive Politics in Mubarak's Egypt* (Cambridge: Cambridge University Press, 2010).

69. Shadi Hamid, *Islamic Exceptionalism: How the Struggle Over Islam Is Reshaping the World* (New York: St. Martin's, 2016), 133.

70. As'ad AbuKhalil, "Gender Boundaries and Sexual Categories in the Arab World," *Feminist Issues* 15, no. 1–2 (March 1997): 91–104; Joseph Sassoon, *Anatomy of Authoritarianism in the Arab Republics* (Cambridge: Cambridge University Press, 2016).

71. Hinnebusch, "Political Parties in MENA."

72. Personal interview, Amman, 2018.

73. Bozena Welborne, "On Their Own? Women Running as Independent Candidates in the Middle East," *Middle East Law and Governance* 12, no. 3 (September 2020): 251–74.

74. Welborne, "On Their Own?"

75. Marwan Muasher, "The Path to Sustainable Political Parties in the Arab World," Sada (Washington, DC: Carnegie Endowment for International Peace, 2013), https://carnegie endowment.org/posts/2013/11/the-path-to-sustainable-political-parties-in-the-arab -world?lang=en; Ellen Lust and David Waldner, "Parties in Transitional Democracies: Authoritarian Legacies and Post-Authoritarian Challenges in the Middle East and North Africa," in *Parties, Movements, and Democracy in the Developing World*, ed. Nancy Bermeo and Deborah J. Yashar. Cambridge Studies in Contentious Politics (Cambridge: Cambridge University Press, 2016), 157–89.

76. Lise Storm, "Parties and Party System Change," in *Political Change in the Middle East and North Africa: After the Arab Spring*, ed. Szmolka Inmaculada Szmolka (Edinburgh, United Kingdom: Edinburgh University Press, 2017), 63–88.

77. Cavatorta and Storm, eds., *Political Parties in the Arab World*, 10.

78. Samuel P. Huntington, *Political Order in Changing Societies* (New Haven, CT: Yale University Press, 1968); Fernando Bizzarro, Allen Hicken, and Darin Self, "The V-Dem Party Institutionalization Index: A New Global Indicator (1900–2015)," *SSRN Electronic Journal*, 2017, https://www.v-dem.net/media/publications/v-dem_working_paper_2017_48.pdf;

Fernando Casal Bértoa, "Political Parties or Party Systems? Assessing the 'Myth' of Institutionalisation and Democracy," *West European Politics* 40, no. 2 (March 2017): 402–29.

79. Scott Mainwaring, ed., *Party Systems in Latin America: Institutionalization, Decay, and Collapse* (New York: Cambridge University Press, 2018).

80. Hicken and Kuhonta, eds., *Party System Institutionalization in Asia.*

81. Hicken and Kuhonta, eds., *Party System Institutionalization in Asia.*

82. Mainwaring and Scully, eds., *Building Democratic Institutions*; Mainwaring, ed., *Party Systems in Latin America.*

83. Fernando Casal Bértoa, Zsolt Enyedi, and Martin Mölder, "Party and Party System Institutionalization: Which Comes First?," *Perspectives on Politics* 22, no. 1 (March 2024): 194–212; Randall and Svåsand, "Party Institutionalization in New Democracies."

84. Aldo F. Ponce and Susan E. Scarrow, "Party Institutionalization and Partisan Mobilization," *Government and Opposition* 58 (February 2022): 745–64.

85. Kenneth Janda, *Political Parties: A Cross-National Survey* (New York: Free Press, 1980).

86. Huntington, *Political Order in Changing Societies.*

87. Angelo Panebianco, *Political Parties: Organization and Power.* Cambridge Studies in Modern Political Economies (Cambridge: Cambridge University Press, 1988).

88. Huntington, *Political Order in Changing Societies*, 12.

89. Mogens N. Pedersen, "The Dynamics of European Party Systems: Changing Patterns of Electoral Volatility," *European Journal of Political Research* 7, no. 1 (March 1979): 1–26; Scott Mainwaring and Edurne Zoco, "Political Sequences and the Stabilization of Interparty Competition: Electoral Volatility in Old and New Democracies," *Party Politics* 13, no. 2 (March 2007): 155–78; Hicken and Kuhonta, eds., *Party System Institutionalization in Asia.*

90. Huntington, *Political Order in Changing Societies*; Panebianco, *Political Parties*; Robert H. Dix, "Democratization and the Institutionalization of Latin American Political Parties," *Comparative Political Studies* 24, no. 4 (January 1992): 488–511. Relatedly, Randall and Svåsand, "Party Institutionalization in New Democracies," provide four main elements (structural/attitudinal and internal/external) for the party institutionalization process: (1) systemness: scope, density, and regularity of interactions within the party; (2) value infusion: the extent to which party actors and supporters identify with and are committed to the party for more than instrumental reason; (3) decisional autonomy: the party's ability to set its policies without interference; and (4) reification: presence in the public imagination.

91. Bizzarro et al., "The V-Dem Party Institutionalization Index."

92. Mainwaring, *Rethinking Party Systems in the Third Wave of Democratization*; Kristin N. Wylie, *Party Institutionalization and Women's Representation in Democratic Brazil* (Cambridge: Cambridge University Press, 2018), 2. On limited value infusion, see Janda, *Political Parties.* On stability, see Huntington, *Political Order in Changing Societies.* On minimal organizational cohesiveness, see Panebianco, *Political Parties.*

93. Bizzarro et al., "The V-Dem Party Institutionalization Index."

94. Bizzarro et al., "The V-Dem Party Institutionalization Index," 3. The party institutionalization index (PII) is a country-level index developed by the Varieties of Democracy project (M. Coppedge, J. Gerring, S. I. Lindberg et al., "V-Dem Codebook v6," Varieties of

Democracy (V-Dem) Project, 2016). The PII constitutes the first global index that covers 173 countries for up to 115 years (1900–2015). It is more comprehensive than many existing indicators in terms of geographical coverage, time span, and conceptual reach (Bizzarro et al., "The V-Dem Party Institutionalization Index"). It focuses on parties' patterns of long-term stability and incorporates variations in their degree of institutionalization that are not necessarily time bound, namely party cohesion and connections with constituents.

95. M. Coppedge, J. Gerring, S. I. Lindberg et al., "V-Dem Codebook v9," Varieties of Democracy (V-Dem) Project, 2019, 281.

96. Bizzarro et al., "The V-Dem Party Institutionalization Index," 8.

97. The V-Party dataset was coded by 665 country experts who have assessed the identity of the political parties in their country of expertise with a vote share of more than 5 percent in a legislative election between 1970 and 2019 across 169 countries. This generates a dataset on 1,955 political parties across 1,560 elections—or in total, 6,330 party-election year units with 183,570 expert-coded data points. Typically, at least four locally based experts contributed to each question. Coder responses were aggregated using V-Dem's custom-built statistical model to ensure comparability across countries and time. More information is available at https://www.vdem.net/documents/8/vparty_briefing.pdf.

98. Pippa Norris and Joni Lovenduski, *Political Recruitment: Gender, Race, and Class in the British Parliament* (New York: Cambridge University Press, 1995); Caul, "Women's Representation in Parliament"; Sheri Kunovich and Pamela Paxton, "Pathways to Power: The Role of Political Parties in Women's National Political Representation," *American Journal of Sociology* 111, no. 2 (2005): 505–52.

99. Pamela Paxton and Melanie Hughes, *Women, Politics, and Power: A Global Perspective* (Thousand Oaks, CA: Sage, 2014), 270.

100. Tània Verge and Maria de la Fuente, "Playing with Different Cards: Party Politics, Gender Quotas and Women's Empowerment," *International Political Science Review* 35, no. 1 (January 2014): 67–79.

101. Jana Belschner, "Electoral Engineering in New Democracies: Strong Quotas and Weak Parties in Tunisia," *Government and Opposition* 57, no. 1 (January 2022): 108–25.

102. Bizzarro et al., "The V-Dem Party Institutionalization Index."

103. Barbara Geddes, Joseph Wright, and Erica Frantz, "Autocratic Breakdown and Regime Transitions: A New Data Set," *Perspectives on Politics* 12, no. 2 (June 2014): 313–31.

104. Margaret El-Helou, "Women and Parliamentary Elections in Lebanon," in *Arab Women and Political Participation*, ed. Hussein Abu Rumman (Amman, Jordan: al-Urdon al-Jadid Research Centre, 2000), 200–220.

105. Mona Tajali, "Protesting Gender Discrimination from Within: Women's Political Representation on Behalf of Islamic Parties," *British Journal of Middle Eastern Studies* 44, no. 2 (April 2017): 176–93; Katarína Škrabáková, "Islamist Women as Candidates in Elections: A Comparison of the Party of Justice and Development in Morocco and the Muslim Brotherhood in Egypt," *Die Welt Des Islams* 57, no. 3–4 (October 2017): 329–59.

106. Janine Astrid Clark and Jillian Schwedler, "Who Opened the Window? Women's Activism in Islamist Parties," *Comparative Politics* 35, no. 3 (April 2003): 293.

107. Škrabáková, "Islamist Women as Candidates in Elections."
108. Lihi Ben Shitrit, "Authenticating Representation: Women's Quotas and Islamist Parties," *Politics and Gender* 12, no. 4 (December 2016): 781–806.
109. Pelke, "Party Institutionalization, Authoritarian Regime Types, and Women's Political Equality."
110. Daniel Stockemer, "Women's Parliamentary Representation: Are Women More Highly Represented in (Consolidated) Democracies Than in Non-Democracies?," *Contemporary Politics* 15, no. 4 (December 2009): 429–43.
111. Donno and Kreft, "Authoritarian Institutions and Women's Rights."
112. Pelke, "Party Institutionalization, Authoritarian Regime Types, and Women's Political Equality."
113. Donno and Kreft, "Authoritarian Institutions and Women's Rights."
114. Wylie, *Party Institutionalization and Women's Representation in Democratic Brazil.*
115. Hinnebusch, "Political Parties in MENA."
116. Dix, "Democratization and the Institutionalization of Latin American Political Parties"; Storm, "Parties and Party System Change."
117. Huntington, *Political Order in Changing Societies.*
118. Dix, "Democratization and the Institutionalization of Latin American Political Parties."
119. Bizzarro et al., "The V-Dem Party Institutionalization Index."
120. Dix, "Democratization and the Institutionalization of Latin American Political Parties," 499.
121. Dono and Kreft, "Authoritarian Institutions and Women's Rights," found that at least half of all party-based autocracies have established official women's wings.
122. Wylie, *Party Institutionalization and Women's Representation in Democratic Brazil,* 2.
123. Elin Bjarnegård, *Gender and Politics: Explaining Male Dominance in Parliamentary Representation.* Gender and Politics Series (London: Palgrave Macmillan, 2013).
124. Hicken and Kuhonta, eds., *Party System Institutionalization in Asia,* 573.
125. Ponce and Scarrow, "Party Institutionalization and Partisan Mobilization."
126. Bizzarro et al., "Party Strength and Economic Growth," *World Politics* 70, no. 2 (April 2018): 275–320.
127. Michael K. Miller, "Democratic Pieces: Autocratic Elections and Democratic Development Since 1815," *British Journal of Political Science* 45, no. 3 (July 2015): 501–30.
128. Bizzarro et al., "Party Strength and Economic Growth," 279.
129. Magnus B. Rasmussen and Carl Henrik Knutsen, "Party Institutionalization and Welfare State Development," *British Journal of Political Science* 51, no. 3 (July 2021): 1203–29.
130. Bizzarro et al., "Party Strength and Economic Growth."
131. Edmund Malesky and Paul Schuler, "The Single-Party Dictator's Dilemma: Information in Elections Without Opposition: Single-Party Dictator's Dilemma," *Legislative Studies Quarterly* 36, no. 4 (November 2011): 491–530.
132. Barnes, *Gendering Legislative Behavior,* 3.
133. Mala Htun and S. Laurel Weldon, "The Civic Origins of Progressive Policy Change: Combating Violence Against Women in Global Perspective, 1975–2005," *American Political Science Review* 106, no. 3 (August 2012): 548–69; Jasmin Lorch and Bettina Bunk,

"Gender Politics, Authoritarian Regime Resilience, and the Role of Civil Society in Algeria and Mozambique," *SSRN Electronic Journal*, 2016, https://doi.org/10.2139/ssrn.2863764; Frank C. Thames, "Women's Legislative Representation in Authoritarian Regimes," *SSRN Electronic Journal* (July 2017), https://doi.org/10.2139/ssrn.3001247.

134. Valentine M. Moghadam, "Democratization and Women's Political Leadership in North Africa," *Journal of International Affairs* 68, no. 1 (2014): 59–78; Aili Mari Tripp, *Seeking Legitimacy: Why Arab Autocracies Adopt Women's Rights* (Cambridge: Cambridge University Press, 2019).

135. Fatima Sadiqi and Moha Ennaji, "The Feminization of Public Space: Women's Activism, the Family Law, and Social Change in Morocco," *Journal of Middle East Women's Studies* 2, no. 2 (April 2006): 86–114.

136. Francesco Cavatorta and Emanuela Dalmasso, "Liberal Outcomes Through Undemocratic Means: The Reform of the *Code de Statut Personnel* in Morocco," *Journal of Modern African Studies* 47, no. 4 (December 2009): 496.

137. Richard E. Matland and Donley T. Studlar, "The Contagion of Women Candidates in Single-Member District and Proportional Representation Electoral Systems: Canada and Norway," *Journal of Politics* 58, no. 3 (August 1996): 707–33; Gregory D. Schmidt and Kyle L. Saunders, "Effective Quotas, Relative Party Magnitude, and the Success of Female Candidates: Peruvian Municipal Elections in Comparative Perspective," *Comparative Political Studies* 37, no. 6 (August 2004): 704–34.

138. Gregory D. Schmidt, "The Election of Women in List PR Systems: Testing the Conventional Wisdom," *Electoral Studies* 28, no. 2 (June 2009): 190–203.

139. Michael Herb, *The Wages of Oil: Parliaments and Economic Development in Kuwait and the UAE* (Ithaca, NY: Cornell University Press, 2014).

140. Sean L. Yom, "Jordan: The Ruse of Reform," *Journal of Democracy* 24, no. 3 (2013): 127–39; "Women Lost Out, with Only 1 Scoring Win in Recent Elections," *Arab Times*, https://www.arabtimesonline.com/news/women-lost-out-with-only-1-scoring-win-in-recent-elections/.

141. Stockemer, "Women's Parliamentary Representation"; Sarah Sunn Bush, "International Politics and the Spread of Quotas for Women in Legislatures," *International Organization* 65, no. 1 (January 2011): 103–37; Gretchen Bauer and Jennie E. Burnet, "Gender Quotas, Democracy, and Women's Representation in Africa: Some Insights from Democratic Botswana and Autocratic Rwanda," *Women's Studies International Forum* 41 (November 2013): 103–12.

142. Kristen Kao et al., "Female Representation and Legitimacy: Evidence from a Harmonized Experiment in Jordan, Morocco, and Tunisia," *American Political Science Review* 118, no. 1 (2024): 495–503.

3. NAVIGATING POWER

1. Jason Seawright and John Gerring, "Case Selection Techniques in Case Study Research: A Menu of Qualitative and Quantitative Options," *Political Research Quarterly* 61, no. 2 (June 2008): 294–308.

2. Freedom House, "Anxious Dictators, Wavering Democracies: Global Freedom Under Pressure," 2016, https://freedomhouse.org/sites/default/files/FH_FITW_Report_2016.pdf.

3. Relying on country experts' coding, Fish and Kroenig have generated a measure of legislative power for 158 countries since 2005. This indicator counts the presence or absence, in each country case, of thirty-two investigator-defined attributes ("powers") of legislative assemblies; M. Steven Fish and Matthew Kroenig, *The Handbook of National Legislatures: A Global Survey* (Cambridge: Cambridge University Press, 2011).

4. Gary King, Robert O. Keohane, and Sidney Verba, *Designing Social Inquiry: Scientific Inference in Qualitative Research* (Princeton, NJ: Princeton University Press, 2021).

5. Paul Maurice Esber, "Citizen Wayn? The Struggle of Parliament in Contemporary Jordan," *Middle East Law and Governance* 13, no. 3 (June 2021): 294–313.

6. Lisa Blaydes, *Elections and Distributive Politics in Mubarak's Egypt* (Cambridge: Cambridge University Press, 2010); Jennifer Gandhi, *Political Institutions Under Dictatorship* (Cambridge: Cambridge University Press, 2008); Xiaobo Lü, Mingxing Liu, and Feiyue Li, "Policy Coalition Building in an Authoritarian Legislature: Evidence from China's National Assemblies (1983–2007)," *Comparative Political Studies* 53, no. 9 (August 2020): 1380–416.

7. Melanie Manion, *Information for Autocrats: Representation in Chinese Local Congresses* (Cambridge: Cambridge University Press, 2015); Marwa Shalaby and Abdullah Aydogan, "Elite-Citizen Linkages and Issue Congruency Under Competitive Authoritarianism," *Parliamentary Affairs* 73, no. 1 (January 1, 2020): 66–88; Rory Truex, *Making Autocracy Work: Representation and Responsiveness in Modern China*. Cambridge Studies in Comparative Politics (New York: Cambridge University Press, 2016).

8. Paul Schuler, "Position Taking or Position Ducking? A Theory of Public Debate in Single-Party Legislatures," *Comparative Political Studies* 53, no. 9 (August 2020): 1493–524; Scott Williamson and Beatriz Magaloni, "Legislatures and Policy Making in Authoritarian Regimes," *Comparative Political Studies* 53, no. 9 (August 2020): 1525–43.

9. Carles Boix and Milan W. Svolik, "The Foundations of Limited Authoritarian Government: Institutions, Commitment, and Power-Sharing in Dictatorships," *Journal of Politics* 75, no. 2 (April 2013): 300–316; Ben Noble, "Authoritarian Amendments: Legislative Institutions as Intraexecutive Constraints in Post-Soviet Russia," *Comparative Political Studies* 53, no. 9 (August 2020): 1417–54.

10. Matthew Charles Wilson and Josef Woldense, "Contested or Established? A Comparison of Legislative Powers Across Regimes," *Democratization* 26, no. 4 (May 2019): 585–605.

11. Anne Meng, *Constraining Dictatorship: From Personalized Rule to Institutionalized Regimes* (New York: Cambridge University Press, 2020); Ken Ochieng' Opalo, *Legislative Development in Africa: Politics and Postcolonial Legacies* (Cambridge: Cambridge University Press, 2019); Ken Ochieng' Opalo, "Constrained Presidential Power in Africa? Legislative Independence and Executive Rule Making in Kenya, 1963–2013," *British Journal of Political Science* 50, no. 4 (October 2020): 1341–58.

12. E. J. Karmel, "Designing Decentralization in Jordan: Locating the Policy Among the Politics," *Middle East Law and Governance* 14, no. 2 (2021): 155–84.

13. Marwa Shalaby and Scott Williamson, "Executive Compliance with Parliamentary Powers Under Authoritarianism: Evidence from Jordan," *Governance* 37, no. 4 (2024): 1163–82.

14. Personal interview, Amman, 2018.

15. Rainer Grote, "Parliaments in the MENA Region: Between Timid Reform and Regression. A Comparative Survey," *Middle East Law and Governance* 13, no. 3 (June 2021): 252–71.

16. Hamad Albloshi, "Kuwait's National Assembly: Roles and Dynamics," in *Monograph Series: The Shura Council in the Persian Gulf* (Durham, United Kingdom, and Doha, Qatar: The Shura Councils in the Persian Gulf Monograph Series, no. 1, 2019), https://www.qu .edu.qa/static_file/qu/research/Gulf%20Studies/documents/Monograph%20Shura%20 Councils%201%20Kuwait%20Hamad%20H.%20Albloshi.pdf.

17. Jill Crystal, *Oil and Politics in the Gulf: Rulers and Merchants in Kuwait and Qatar* (Cambridge: Cambridge University Press, 1990).

18. The regime dissolved the parliament and suspended the constitution twice: between 1976 and 1981 and from 1986 to 1992.

19. Cabinet members are ex officio members with the same voting rights as elected members.

20. Abdullah Al-Remaidhi and Bob Watt, "Electoral Constituencies and Political Parties in Kuwait: An Assessment," *Election Law Journal: Rules, Politics, and Policy* 11, no. 4 (December 2012): 518–28.

21. Nathan Brown, *Moving Out of Kuwait's Political Impasse*, Carnegie Endowment for International Peace, 2007, https://carnegieendowment.org/research/2007/06/moving-out-of-kuwaits -political-impasse?lang=en.

22. Each member has the right to propose an amendment to the bill, even if the proposed bill was already forwarded to the specialized committee. Legislators then decide whether to consider the proposed amendment and, subsequently, whether to forward the amended text to the legislative and legal affairs committee for review, which is followed by a second deliberation session on the proposed bill. The emir has thirty days to veto the bill, and in case the bill is vetoed by the emir, the bill should pass if it obtains a two-third majority from the legislature (Albloshi, "Kuwait's National Assembly") and the decision is published in the National Assembly's Official Gazette (Law No. 12, 1963).

23. Abdeslam Maghraoui, "Monarchy and Political Reform in Morocco," *Journal of Democracy* 12, no. 1 (2001): 80.

24. For more information on the king's veto power, see https://carnegieendowment.org/research /2011/06/the-new-moroccan-constitution-real-change-or-more-of-the-same?lang=en.

25. A summary report provided by the Ministry of Human Rights and Relation with the Parliament, 187–88, https://www.mcrpsc.gov.ma/العلاقات-مع-البرلمان/التشريع/القوانين-المصادق-عليها /?codeSession=81#loisapp_page=1. Three of the twenty passed bills are related to the new gender-based violence law.

26. The bylaws of the 2012 Moroccan lower chamber: http://www.chambredesrepresentants .ma/sites/default/files/loi/reglement.interieur2012_1.pdf.

27. Driss Maghraoui, "Constitutional Reforms in Morocco: Between Consensus and Subaltern Politics," *Journal of North African Studies* 16, no. 4 (December 2011): 679–99.

28. Raphaël Lefèvre, "Balancing Act: Islamism and the Monarchy in Morocco," *Journal of North African Studies* 18, no. 4 (September 2013): 626–29.

29. Ameen Mashagbeh and Abdulazeez Alnowidi, "Parties and Parliamentary Experiences in Jordan and Morocco," Alquds Center for Political Studies, 2016, https://www.alqudscenter.org/index.php?l=en&pg=UFVCTElDQVRJTo5T&id=2325.

30. The Jordanian Parliament was suspended from 1974 to 1977 after the Rabat Arab League summit's decision that the Palestine Liberation Organization (PLO) was the only legitimate representative body of the Palestinian people. With half of the seats representing Palestinians, King Hussein seized the opportunity and dissolved the Parliament. A National Consultative Council soon replaced the Parliament with nominal powers.

31. Julia Choucair, *Illusive Reform: Jordan's Stubborn Stability* (Washington, DC: Carnegie Endowment for International Peace, 2006).

32. The National Consultative Council (NCC), established in 1977, comprised sixty members responsible for discussing laws with the king but was never granted the power to legislate or introduce bills.

33. Laurie A. Brand, *Women, the State, and Political Liberalization: Middle Eastern and North African Experiences* (New York: Columbia University Press, 1998).

34. Jordanian Elections Committee, http://www.entikhabat.jo/Public/DefaultAr.aspx.

35. Mona Christophersen, "Jordan's 2013 Elections: A Further Boost for Tribes," Norwegian Centre for Conflict Resolution (NOREF), 2013, https://www.files.ethz.ch/isn/162496/3cfcb191c3644dd32cdaoc2c3431d149.pdf.

36. Unlike their counterparts in Egypt, Syria, and Tunisia, the Jordanian monarchy did not repress the Islamists. Yet they are fragmented and split into four different movements that are hard to differentiate between on issues or ideology; see Jillian Schwedler, "Jordan: The Quiescent Opposition" (Washington, DC: Wilson Center, 2015), https://www.wilsoncenter.org/article/jordan-the-quiescent-opposition. However, this relationship was transformed because of the disagreement on the 1994 peace agreement with Israel and the ensuing changes to the electoral system.

37. The political parties' law is also known as Law No. 32. It defines a party as "a political organization made up of Jordanian members per the constitution and political participation regulations. Parties should have specific goals related to political, economic, and social affairs and operate by legitimate and peaceful means." Islamist parties were allowed for the first time to participate in elections, and they formed the Islamic Action Front Party (IAF) in December 1992. The Jordanian Parliament's official website is http://www.parliament.jo/en/.

38. Ibtissam Al-Attiyat, Musa Shteiwi, and Suleiman Sweiss, *Building Democracy in Jordan: Women's Political Participation, Political Party Life, and Democratic Elections* (Stockholm, Sweden: International Institute for Democracy and Electoral Assistance and the Arab NGO Network for Development, 2005).

39. Personal interview, Amman, 2018.

40. Sean L. Yom, "Jordan: The Ruse of Reform," *Journal of Democracy* 24, no. 3 (2013): 127–39.

41. The Jordanian Parliament's official website is http://www.parliament.jo.

42. Curtis R. Ryan, "Deja Vu All Over Again? Jordan's 2010 Elections," *Foreign Policy*, November 15, 2010, https://foreignpolicy.com/2010/11/15/deja-vu-all-over-again-jordans-2010-elections/.

43. Personal interview, Amman, 2018.

44. King Abdullah established the Independent Election Committee in 2012 after the dissolution of Jordan's Sixteenth Parliament in response to massive protests across Jordan demanding fraud-free elections and an end to the nepotism and vote buying that dominated Jordan's past few elections.

45. Omar Obeidat, "New Lower House Includes 74 New Faces," *Jordan Times*, September 24, 2016, http://www.jordantimes.com/news/local/new-lower-house-includes-74-new-faces.

46. Laurie A. Brand and Fayez Hammad, "Identity and the Jordanian Elections," *Foreign Policy*, January 17, 2013, https://foreignpolicy.com/2013/01/17/identity-and-the-jordanian-elections/; Ellen Lust-Okar, "Elections Under Authoritarianism: Preliminary Lessons from Jordan," *Democratization* 13, no. 3 (June 2006): 456–71.

47. Ellen M. Lust-Okar, "The Decline of Jordanian Political Parties: Myth or Reality?," *International Journal of Middle East Studies* 33, no. 4 (2001): 545–69.

48. The first female minister, In'am Al Mufti, was appointed in 1979 as the minister of social development. Later, the king appointed several women to the Senate: Layla Sharaf (1989), Naila Rasdhan (1993), Subhieh Al Ma'ani and Rima Khalaf (1997), and May Abul Samen (2003). Also, the first female judge in Jordan was appointed in 1996.

49. Personal interview, Amman, 2018.

50. In contrast, women were absent from the municipal elections even though women were granted the right to vote and stand for municipal elections in 1982.

51. Abla Amawi, "Against All Odds: Women Candidates in Jordanian Elections," in *From Patriarchy to Empowerment*, ed. Valentine M. Moghadam (Syracuse, NY: Syracuse University Press, 2007), 40–57.

52. The establishment of the Jordanian National Commission for Women (JNCW) in 1992—under the auspices of Princess Basma—marks one of the most significant milestones for state feminism in Jordan. The JNCW aimed to promote women's issues and integrate women into decision-making. Even though JNCW was initially established as a nongovernmental organization, the organization enjoyed "royal leadership," often acting as the mouthpiece for the regime.

53. Gehan Abou-Zeid, "The Arab Region: Women's Access to the Decision-Making Process Across the Arab Nation," in *Women, Quotas and Politics*, ed. Drude Dahlerup (New York: Routledge, 2006), 179–204.

54. Law No. 11 of 2003 on women's parliamentary quota law, http://www.parliament.jo.

55. Amal Dagestani and Musa Shteiwi, "The Jordanian Woman and Political Participation" (Amman, Jordan: CES, Center for Strategic Studies, University of Jordan, 1994); Husayn Abu Rumman, *Qirra'a Awaliyya fil-Intikhabat al-Niyabiyya al-Urduniyya: A Preliminary Reading of Jordan's Parliamentary Elections, Civil Society Issues* (Amman, Jordan: New Jordan Center for Studies, 2003); Husayn Abu Rumman, "The Women's Quota in Jordan: Crowning Three Decades of Support for Female Political Participation," in *The Arab Quota Report: Selected Case Studies* (Stockholm, Sweden: International Institute for Democracy

and Electoral Assistance, 2007), http://iknowpolitics.org/en/2011/09/arab-quota-report
-selected-case-studies. Women were elected based on the percentage of votes received in
their respective constituencies rather than the total number of votes acquired (the 2003
amended election law for the House of Deputies).

56. Ibtesam Alatiyat and Hassan Barari, "Liberating Women with Islam? The Islamists and
Women's Issues in Jordan," *Totalitarian Movements and Political Religions* 11, no. 3–4 (September 2010): 359–78.

57. Yasmeen Tabbaa, "New Spaces, More Politics? Women, Tribes, and Quotas in Jordan,"
Working Paper (Amman, Jordan: Center for Strategic Studies, 2009).

58. Personal interview, Amman, 2018.

59. In the 2003 elections, Jordan was divided into three electoral divisions and twelve governorates: Northern Jordan, Central Jordan, and Southern Jordan. Northern Jordan (Irbid,
Jarash, Ajlun, and Mafraq) has fourteen districts and is allocated thirty seats. Central Jordan (Al-Zarqa, Al-Balqa, Ma'daba, and Amman) has eighteen districts and is allocated
fifty seats. Finally, Southern Jordan (Karak, Maan, Al-Tufayla, and Aqaba) has thirteen
districts and twenty-three seats. In addition, there are six gender quota seats and twelve
ethnic quota seats.

60. Additionally, a 20 percent women's quota in municipal councils was introduced in early
2007.

61. The election commission calculates the percentage of votes obtained by the total number of votes cast in their constituency; women with the highest percentage of votes are
declared elected if no governorate obtains more than one reserved seat for women.

62. "Jordan's 2013 Parliamentary Elections at a Glance," *Impatient Bedouin*, January 23, 2013,
http://impatientbedouin.com/jordans-2013-parliamentary-elections-at-a-glance/.

63. The first female is Mariam Lozi (Amman, Fifth District), who won 3,631 votes, acquiring
the most votes in the three-member district. The second female who won under the single
nontransferable vote system was Wafaa Bani Mustafa (Jarash North, First District), who
won 3,989 or 7.66 percent of the votes. Bani Mustafa was an independent Islamist who
acquired a quota seat in the Sixteenth Parliament.

64. Personal interview, Amman, 2017.

65. Alaa Zuhheir Al-Rawashdeh, Asmaa Ribhi Al Arab, and Ali Mohammad Ali Al-Shboul,
"Difficulties Prevent Jordanian Women Participation in Political Life in Light of Some
Social Variables," *Asian Social Science* 8, no. 10 (August 2012): 208–22; Muna Ayoub Yousef
El Waked and Kholood Fawaz Al-Zoby, "The Challenges Hindering Jordanian Women
from Political Participation from the Perspective of the Female Graduate Students at the
University of Jordan," *Psychology and Education Journal* 58, no. 5 (2021): 1762–69, http://
psychologyandeducation.net/pae/index.php/pae/article/view/5590.

66. Brand and Hammad, "Identity and the Jordanian Elections."

67. Personal interview, Amman, 2018.

68. Personal interview, Amman, 2018.

69. The first Kuwaiti legislative council was established in 1938 following a massive campaign
spearheaded by wealthy merchants across the country. The council lasted only six months,

dissolving after disputes between the ruler and the merchants; see Crystal, *Oil and Politics in the Gulf.*

70. Michael Herb, *The Wages of Oil: Parliaments and Economic Development in Kuwait and the UAE* (Ithaca, NY: Cornell University Press, 2014), 14.

71. Oil exports constitute over 95 percent of the country's export revenues and 60 percent of its gross domestic product; see OPEC, "Organization of the Petroleum Exporting Countries," 2015, http://www.opec.org/opec_web/en/.

72. Ghanim Alnajjar, "The Challenges Facing Kuwaiti Democracy," *Middle East Journal* 54, no. 2 (Spring 2000): 242–58.

73. The role of the merchant's class was clear in the creation of the first Shura Council in 1921 and the Legislative Council of 1938.

74. Crystal, *Oil and Politics in the Gulf.*

75. Kuwait's first legislative council was elected by a restricted electorate in 1938. This council was dissolved within five months and was soon replaced by another legislative body. The 1939 Assembly lasted only for a few months because of legislative deadlock that occurred between the emir and the wealthy merchants/council members; see Ibrahim Dashti and Ramzy Salama, "The Amendment of the Electoral Constituencies: A Critical Phase in Promoting the Democratic Experience in Kuwait," Research and Data Unit of the Kuwaiti National Assembly, 2004 (Arabic); Ibrahim Dashti, "Women's Political Participation," Research and Data Unit of the Kuwaiti National Assembly, 2005.

76. Herb, *The Wages of Oil.*

77. Simple majority vote required; if two candidates receive an equal number of valid votes, the polling committee draws lots and the winner is declared.

78. Mary Ann Tétreault, "A State of Two Minds: State Cultures, Women, and Politics in Kuwait," *International Journal of Middle East Studies* 33, no. 2 (May 2001): 203–20.

79. Shafeeq N. Ghabra, "Balancing State and Society: The Islamic Movement in Kuwait," *Middle East Policy* 5, no. 2 (May 1997): 58–72.

80. Ghabra, "Balancing State and Society," 61–62.

81. Introducing changes to the electoral process was deemed a direct violation of Article 80 of the constitution, which stipulates that the legislative branch should solely determine the size and boundaries of the electoral districts. To overcome this constitutional hiccup, the emir's decree was soon submitted to the newly elected parliament for approval. Kuwait's Fifth Legislative Assembly—elected in 1981 and comprised of predominantly Islamist, tribal, and progovernment members—promptly ratified the royal decree, which enforced a flawed electoral system.

82. Decree No. 99/1980 was implemented in the 1981, 1985, 1992, 1996, 1999, 2003, and 2006 elections.

83. Al-Remaidhi and Watt, "Electoral Constituencies and Political Parties in Kuwait."

84. Alnajjar, "The Challenges Facing Kuwaiti Democracy."

85. Jane Kinninmont, *Kuwait's Parliament: An Experiment in Semi-democracy* (London: Chatham House, 2012).

86. Dashti and Salama, "The Amendment of the Electoral Constituencies."

87. Muhamad S. Olimat, "Women and Politics in Kuwait," *Journal of International Women's Studies* 11, no. 2 (2009): 199–212, https://vc.bridgew.edu/jiws/vol11/iss2/13; Muhamad S. Olimat, "Women and the Kuwaiti National Assembly," *Journal of International Women's Studies* 12, no. 3 (2011): 76–95, https://vc.bridgew.edu/jiws/vol12/iss3/6; Muhamad S. Olimat, "Arab Spring and Women in Kuwait," *Journal of International Women's Studies* 13, no. 5 (2012): 180–94. According to the Constitution of Kuwait, the Legislative Assembly can be only dissolved by either the emir or the Supreme Court. However, new elections must be called within two months of the dissolution; otherwise, the dissolution would be deemed unconstitutional.

88. Mary Ann Tétreault, *Stories of Democracy: Politics and Society in Contemporary Kuwait* (New York: Columbia University Press, 2000).

89. Alnajjar, "The Challenges Facing Kuwaiti Democracy."

90. Mazen K. Gharaibeh and Basel M. Al-Eideh, "Granting Kuwaiti Women the Right to Vote: The Impact on the Parliament's Composition and Political Streams (A Field and Analytical Study)," *Journal of the Social Sciences* 34, no. 2 (2006): 13–36.

91. MEED, "Reformists Suffer Election Defeat," *MEED: Middle East Economic Digest*, 2003, https://www.meed.com/reformists-suffer-election-defeat/.

92. Increased allegations of government corruption have created overwhelming discontent among citizens. For instance, the Orange Movement and the Alliance made significant gains in the Eleventh Assembly due to their successful campaigns to eradicate corruption; see Emily Regan Wills, "Democratic Paradoxes: Women's Rights and Democratization in Kuwait," *Middle East Journal* 67, no. 2 (April 2013): 173–84; Al-Remaidhi and Watt, "Electoral Constituencies and Political Parties in Kuwait."

93. Although tribal primaries were prohibited under Acts No. 9/1998 and No. 5/2005 (Article 31), they were still practiced under the new electoral law as tribes managed to control at least two of the five national districts.

94. Corey Flintoff, "Women Take Their Place in Kuwait's Parliament," NPR, 2009, http://www.npr.org/templates/story/story.php?storyId=104340287.

95. Kinninmont, *Kuwait's Parliament.*

96. Herb, *The Wages of Oil.*

97. Wills, "Democratic Paradoxes."

98. Olimat, "Women and the Kuwaiti National Assembly."

99. Haya al-Mughni and Mary Ann Tétreault, "Political Actors Without the Franchise: Women and Politics in Kuwait," in *Monarchies and Nations: Globalisation and Identity in the Arab States in the Gulf,* ed. Paul Dresch and James Piscatori (London: I. B. Tauris, 2005), 203–21.

100. Kuwait's Law 24 of 1962 governing the activity of associations gives the Ministry of Social Affairs and Labor complete control over voluntary associations; see Munira A. Fakhro, "Gender, Politics and the State in the Gulf Region," *Middle East Policy* 5, no. 3 (1997): 166–70.

101. Fakhro, "Gender, Politics and the State in the Gulf Region."

102. World Economic Forum, *Global Gender Gap Report* (Geneva, Switzerland: World Economic Forum, 2015), https://www3.weforum.org/docs/GGGR2015/cover.pdf.

103. Michele Dunne, "Women's Political Participation in the Gulf: A Conversation with Activists Fatin Bundagji (Saudi Arabia), Rola Dashti (Kuwait), Munira Fakhro (Bahrain),"

Carnegie Endowment for International Peace, August 12, 2008; Al-Rawashdeh et al., "Difficulties Prevent Jordanian Women Participation in Political Life."

104. Yagoub Yousif Al-Kandari and Ibrahim Naji Al-Hadben, "Tribalism, Sectarianism, and Democracy in Kuwaiti Culture," *Digest of Middle East Studies* 19, no. 2 (October 2010): 268.

105. Al-Kandari and Al-Hadben, "Tribalism, Sectarianism, and Democracy in Kuwaiti Culture," 272.

106. Anh Nga Longva, "Nationalism in Pre-Modern Guise: The Discourse on Hadhar and Badu in Kuwait," *International Journal of Middle East Studies* 38, no. 2 (May 2006): 171.

107. Ghabra, "Balancing State and Society."

108. Ghabra, "Balancing State and Society."

109. Brown, *Moving Out of Kuwait's Political Impasse.*

110. There are four main Islamist streams in the Kuwaiti National Assembly: the Islamic Constitutional Movement (ICM), the National Islamist Alliance, the Justice and Peace Alliance, and the Islamic Salafi Alliance. The ICM and the Islamic Salafi Alliance are both Sunni blocs, whereas the National Islamist Alliance and the Justice and Peace Alliance are Shi'ite blocs. Although the ICM and the Salafi Alliance tend to be mostly anti-regime, the other Islamist groups are mostly pro-regime.

111. Marwa Shalaby, "Women's Political Representation in Kuwait: An Untold Story," James A. Baker III Institute for Public Policy, 2015, http://www.bakerinstitute.org/research/womens -political-representation-kuwait/.

112. Personal interview, Kuwait City, 2023.

113. Personal interview, Kuwait City, 2023.

114. Safa al-Hashem was elected in July 2013. Representing the third district, she succeeded in winning 2,036 votes and became the only female MP in Kuwait's Fourteenth Legislative Chamber. She previously won a seat in the December 2012 elections, which was revoked and replaced by the 2013 legislative session.

115. Yuree Noh and Marwa Shalaby, "Kuwaitis Voted Saturday. Opposition Gains Send a Strong Signal About the Economy," *Washington Post*, November 29, 2016, https://www.washing tonpost.com/news/monkey-cage/wp/2016/11/29/kuwaitis-voted-saturday-opposition -gains-send-a-strong-signal-about-the-economy/; "Emir of Kuwait Dissolves Parliament," Aljazeera, October 17, 2016, https://www.aljazeera.com/news/2016/10/17/emir-of-kuwait -dissolves-parliament/.

116. Yasmina Sarhrouny, "Kuwait: Citizens' Perceptions of Women in Politics," *National Democratic Institute for International Affairs* 1, no. 1 (2007): 1–28.

117. Personal interview, Kuwait City, 2023.

118. James N. Sater, "Parliamentary Elections and Authoritarian Rule in Morocco," *Middle East Journal* 63, no. 3 (July 1, 2009): 381–400.

119. Inmaculada Szmolka, "Party System Fragmentation in Morocco," *Journal of North African Studies* 15, no. 1 (March 2010): 13–37.

120. Maghraoui, "Monarchy and Political Reform in Morocco."

121. Guilain Denoeux and Abdeslam Maghraoui, "King Hassan's Strategy of Political Dualism," *Middle East Policy* 5, no. 4 (January 1998): 106.

122. In the 1993 elections, the total number of representatives was 333. Two hundred twenty-two candidates were elected in single-member constituencies by a simple plurality vote. The remaining 111 representatives were selected by indirect ballot. In 1997, the number of representatives elected via direct voting increased to 325.

123. Personal interview, Rabat, 2020.

124. Personal interview, Rabat, 2020.

125. Matt Buehler, "The Threat to 'Un-Moderate': Moroccan Islamists and the Arab Spring," *Middle East Law and Governance* 5, no. 3 (2013): 231–57.

126. Driss Lagrin, "The Quota System and the Reality of Women's Political Participation in Morocco," Civil Dialogue News, 2009, https://www.ahewar.org/debat/show.art.asp?aid =165619.

127. James N. Sater, "Changing Politics from Below? Women Parliamentarians in Morocco," *Democratization* 14, no. 4 (August 2007): 723–42; Sater, "Parliamentary Elections and Authoritarian Rule in Morocco."

128. James Liddell, "Gender Quotas in Clientelist Systems: The Case of Morocco's National List," *Al-Raida Journal* 126–27 (2009): 79–86.

129. Michael J. Willis, "Political Parties in the Maghrib: Ideology and Identification. A Suggested Typology," *Journal of North African Studies* 7, no. 3 (September 2002): 1–28; Miquel Pellicer and Eva Wegner, "Socio-Economic Voter Profile and Motives for Islamist Support in Morocco," *Party Politics* 20, no. 1 (January 2014): 116–33; Matt Buehler, "Continuity Through Co-Optation: Rural Politics and Regime Resilience in Morocco and Mauritania," *Mediterranean Politics* 20, no. 3 (September 2, 2015): 364–85.

130. Moulay Driss El-Maarouf, Mourad el Fahli, and Jerome Kuchejda, "Morocco," in *KAS Democracy Report 2009*, ed. Habil Karsten Grabow et al., Parties and Democracies Vol. II, Konrad Adenauer Stiftung, 2009, https://www.kas.de/en/single-title/-/content/kas -demokratiereport-2009, 257–68.

131. Buehler, "The Threat to 'Un-Moderate.'"

132. Marwa Shalaby, "The Islamists Are Back in Morocco: How Did They Do It?," *Washington Post*, 2016, https://www.washingtonpost.com/news/monkey-cage/wp/2016/10/20/the -islamists-are-back-in-morocco-how-did-they-do-it/.

133. Buehler, "The Threat to 'Un-Moderate.'"

134. Fatima Sadiqi and Moha Ennaji, "The Feminization of Public Space: Women's Activism, the Family Law, and Social Change in Morocco," *Journal of Middle East Women's Studies* 2, no. 2 (April 2006): 86–114.

135. Personal interview, Rabat, 2020.

136. Francesco Cavatorta and Emanuela Dalmasso, "Liberal Outcomes Through Undemocratic Means: The Reform of the *Code de Statut Personnel* in Morocco," *Journal of Modern African Studies* 47, no. 4 (December 2009): 487–506; Aili Mari Tripp, *Seeking Legitimacy: Why Arab Autocracies Adopt Women's Rights* (Cambridge: Cambridge University Press, 2019).

137. Michael L. Ross, "Oil, Islam, and Women," *American Political Science Review* 102, no. 1 (February 2008): 107–23.

138. Hanane Darhour and Drude Dahlerup, "Sustainable Representation of Women Through Gender Quotas: A Decade's Experience in Morocco," *Women's Studies International Forum* 41 (November 2013): 132–42.

139. The two women were Badia Skalli from the Socialist Union of Popular Forces (USFP) and Latifa Bennani-Smires from the Istiqlal Party.

140. Lura Morton, "Women in Parliament: A Study of Issue-Specific Female Coalition Building in Morocco," Independent Study Project (ISP) Collection, 2018, https://digitalcollections .sit.edu/isp_collection/2836.

141. Abderrafie Zaanoun, "The Impact of the Quota System on Women Parliamentary Representation in Morocco: A Series of Reforms or a Regressive Path?," *Arab Reform Initiative*, April 14, 2022, https://www.arab-reform.net/publication/the-impact-of-the-quota-system -on-women-parliamentary-representation-in-morocco-a-series-of-reforms-or-a-regressive -path/.

142. James N. Sater, "Reserved Seats, Patriarchy, and Patronage in Morocco," in *The Impact of Gender Quotas*, ed. Susan Franceschet, Mona Lena Krook, and Jennifer M. Piscopo (New York: Oxford University Press, 2012).

143. Personal interview, Rabat, 2020.

144. Anouk Lloren, "Gender Quotas in Morocco: Lessons for Women's Descriptive and Symbolic Representation," *Representation* 50, no. 4 (October 2014): 527–38.

145. Zaanoun, "The Impact of the Quota System on Women Parliamentary Representation in Morocco."

146. Personal interview, Rabat, 2020.

147. Darhour and Dahlerup, "Sustainable Representation of Women Through Gender Quotas."

148. Liddell, "Gender Quotas in Clientelist Systems," 79.

149. Hanane Darhour and Drude Dahlerup, *Double-Edged Politics on Women's Rights in the MENA Region* (New York: Springer, 2020).

4. COMING TO POWER

1. Daniela Giannetti, Andrea Pedrazzani, and Luca Pinto, "Personal Ambitions, Expertise and Parties' Control: Understanding Committee Assignment in the Italian Chamber of Deputies," *Parliamentary Affairs* 72, no. 1 (January 2019): 119–40.

2. Note that women joined the Kuwaiti parliament for the first time in 2009.

3. Pedro Riera and Francisco Cantú, "Determinants of Legislative Committee Membership in Proportional Representation Systems," *Party Politics* 24, no. 5 (September 2018): 524–35; Malcolm Shaw, "Parliamentary Committees: A Global Perspective," *Journal of Legislative Studies* 4, no. 1 (March 1998): 225–51; Ann Towns, "Understanding the Effects of Larger Ratios of Women in National Legislatures: Proportions and Gender Differentiation in Sweden and Norway," *Women and Politics* 25, no. 1–2 (October 2008): 1–29.

4. Ella Prihatini, "Explaining Gender Gaps in Indonesian Legislative Committees," *Parliamentary Affairs* 74 (2019): 206–29.

5. Ingvar Mattson and Kaare Strøm, "Parliamentary Committees," in *Parliaments and Majority Rule in Western Europe*, ed. Herbert Döring (Mannheim, Germany: Mannheim Centre for European Social Research, 1995), 249–307.

6. Shane Martin and Tim A. Mickler, "Committee Assignments: Theories, Causes and Consequences," *Parliamentary Affairs* 72, no. 1 (January 2019): 77–98.

7. Giannetti et al., "Personal Ambitions, Expertise and Parties' Control."

8. Erik Damgaard, "How Parties Control Committee Members," in *Parliaments and Majority Rule in Western Europe*, ed. Herbert Döring (New York: St. Martin's, 1995), 308–24.

9. Kaare Strøm, "Parliamentary Committees in European Democracies," *Journal of Legislative Studies* 4, no. 1 (March 1998): 21–59.

10. David R. Mayhew, *Congress: The Electoral Connection* (New Haven, CT: Yale University Press, 1974); Rainbow Murray and Réjane Sénac, "Explaining Gender Gaps in Legislative Committees," *Journal of Women, Politics and Policy* 39, no. 3 (July 2018): 310–35.

11. Riera and Cantú, "Determinants of Legislative Committee Membership in Proportional Representation Systems."

12. Gary W. Cox and Mathew D. McCubbins, *Setting the Agenda: Responsible Party Government in the U.S. House of Representatives* (New York: Cambridge University Press, 2005); Keith Krehbiel, Kenneth A. Shepsle, and Barry R. Weingast, "Why Are Congressional Committees Powerful?," *American Political Science Review* 81, no. 3 (September 1987): 929–45; Richard F. Fenno, *Congressmen in Committees*. The Study of Congress Series (Berkeley, CA: Institute of Governmental Studies Press, 1995).

13. Diana Z. O'Brien, "Gender and Select Committee Elections in the British House of Commons," *Politics and Gender* 8, no. 2 (June 2012): 178–204.

14. Gary W. Cox and Mathew D. McCubbins, *Legislative Leviathan: Party Government in the House*. California Series on Social Choice and Political Economy (Berkely: University of California Press, 1993); Cox and McCubbins, *Setting the Agenda*; Forrest Maltzman, *Competing Principals: Committees, Parties, and the Organization of Congress* (Ann Arbor: University of Michigan Press, 1997); Robert Darcy, "Women in the State Legislative Power Structure: Committee Chairs," *Social Science Quarterly* 77, no. 4 (1996): 888–98.

15. See, for example, Ana Espírito-Santo and Edalina Rodrigues Sanches, "Who Gets What? The Interactive Effect of MPs' Sex in Committee Assignments in Portugal," *Parliamentary Affairs* 73, no. 2 (April 2020): 450–72; Hilde Coffé and Katia Schnellecke, "Female Representation in German Parliamentary Committees: 1972–2009," 7th ECPR General Conference, September 4–7, 2013, Bordeaux, France; Martin Baekgaard and Ulrik Kjaer, "The Gendered Division of Labor in Assignments to Political Committees: Discrimination or Self-Selection in Danish Local Politics?," *Politics and Gender* 8, no. 4 (December 2012): 465–82; Robert Pekkanen, Benjamin Nyblade, and Ellis S. Krauss, "Electoral Incentives in Mixed-Member Systems: Party, Posts, and Zombie Politicians in Japan," *American Political Science Review* 100, no. 2 (May 2006): 183–93; Sabri Ciftci, Walter Forrest, and Yusuf Tekin, "Committee Assignments in a Nascent Party System: The Case of the Turkish Grand National Assembly," *International Political Science Review* 29, no. 3 (June 2008): 303–24; Roseanna Michelle Heath, Leslie A. Schwindt-Bayer, and Michelle M. Taylor-Robinson,

"Women on the Sidelines: Women's Representation on Committees in Latin American Legislatures," *American Journal of Political Science* 49, no. 2 (April 2005): 420.

16. Pekkanen et al., "Electoral Incentives in Mixed-Member Systems," 189; Riera and Cantú, "Determinants of Legislative Committee Membership in Proportional Representation Systems." Distributive committees include the following areas: construction, transportation, trade and industry, agriculture, local affairs, house budget, and telecommunications. High-policy posts include finance, foreign affairs, legal affairs, defense, cabinet, tax, and basic policy. Public goods committees include environment, science, labor, social affairs, education, youth, and house management; see Pekkanen et al., "Electoral Incentives in Mixed-Member Systems."

17. O'Brien, "Gender and Select Committee Elections in the British House of Commons"; Pamela Pansardi and Michelangelo Vercesi, "Party Gatekeeping and Women's Appointment to Parliamentary Committees: Evidence from the Italian Case," *Parliamentary Affairs* 70, no. 1 (January 2017): 62–83.

18. Pekkanen et al., "Electoral Incentives in Mixed-Member Systems."

19. In a similar vein, committees can be classified as influential, technical and foreign affairs, social issues, and women's issues committees; see Tiffany D. Barnes, "Women's Representation and Legislative Appointments: The Case of the Argentine Provinces," *Revista Uruguaya de Ciencia Política* 23, no. 2 (2014): 135–63; Leslie A. Schwindt-Bayer, *Political Power and Women's Representation in Latin America* (New York: Oxford University Press, 2010); Heath et al., "Women on the Sidelines." Others have also categorized committees into major, issue, and burden committees; see Francisco Javier Aparicio and Joy Langston, "Committee Leadership Selection Without Seniority: The Mexican Case," *Centro de Investigación y Docencia Económicas (CIDE), División de Estudios Políticos* 217 (2009), https://citeseerx.ist.psu.edu/document?repid=rep1&type=pdf&doi=abbca3d68329936a00b f9065c98c6e781c19ccf6. Other studies have classified committees according to vertical and horizontal dimensions; see Nina C. Raaum, Lauri Karvonen, and Per Selle, "The Political Representation of Women: A Bird's Eye View," in *Women in Nordic Politics—Closing the Gap*, ed. Lauri Karvonen and Per Selle (Dartmouth, MA: Dartmouth Publishing, 1995), 25–58; Baekgaard and Kjaer, "The Gendered Division of Labor in Assignments to Political Committees."

20. Strøm, "Parliamentary Committees in European Democracies."

21. There are committees within the upper house in Jordan and Morocco, but I only focus on the lower chamber.

22. Amer Beni Amer, *Final Report on the Performance of the 17th Parliament During the Second Ordinary Session of 2015*, Hayat Center, Rased, 2015, http://www.hayatcenter.org/uploads/2018 /01/20180121122243ar.pdf.

23. This analysis includes only committees that have the power to report on bills and offer recommendations, either permanent/standing or temporary. Standing and permanent committees are used interchangeably because they refer to the same type of committee. Thus, we excluded committees that form for investigation and/or fact-checking purposes, such as an investigation of issues raised about the public money committee in Kuwait (2009) and the second investigatory parliamentary committee formed by the Ministry of Agriculture in Jordan (2010).

24. Author's interview with a female deputy from the secular Nida Tunis party, July 2017, Tunis, Tunisia. Personal interview, Tunis, 2017.

25. The Bylaws of the 2012 Moroccan House of Representatives, https://www.chambredes representants.ma/sites/default/files/reglementinterieur27.11.2013.pdf.

26. Legislators with no political bloc or parliamentary group affiliations are assigned as members in permanent committees upon their request and preference, limited to the seats assigned by the office.

27. The Bylaws of the 2013 Jordanian House of Representatives, https://representatives.jo /EBV4.0/Root_Storage/AR/EB_HomePage/النظام_الداخلي.pdf.

28. The Bylaws of Kuwait's House of Representatives (2009), http://www.kna.kw/clt-html5 /run.asp?id=2025.

29. Devin K. Joshi and Rakkee Thimothy, "Long-Term Impacts of Parliamentary Gender Quotas in a Single-Party System: Symbolic Co-Option or Delayed Integration?," *International Political Science Review* 40, no. 4 (September 2019): 591–606.

30. Anne Marie Goetz, "Women's Political Effectiveness: A Conceptual Framework," in *No Shortcuts to Power: African Women in Politics and Policy Making*, ed. Anne Marie Goetz and Shireen Hassim (London: Zed, 2003), 40.

31. Lena Wängnerud, "Women in Parliaments: Descriptive and Substantive Representation," *Annual Review of Political Science* 12, no. 1 (June 2009): 51–69.

32. Heath et al., "Women on the Sidelines."

33. Barnes, "Women's Representation and Legislative Appointments."

34. Hege Skjeie, "The Rhetoric of Difference: On Women's Inclusion Into Political Elites," *Politics and Society* 19, no. 2 (June 1991): 233–63.

35. Schwindt-Bayer, *Political Power and Women's Representation in Latin America.*

36. Darcy, "Women in the State Legislative Power Structure: Committee Chairs."

37. Sue Thomas, *How Women Legislate* (New York: Oxford University Press, 1994).

38. Yann P. Kerevel and Lonna Rae Atkeson, "Explaining the Marginalization of Women in Legislative Institutions," *Journal of Politics* 75, no. 4 (October 2013): 980–92; Baekgaard and Kjaer, "The Gendered Division of Labor in Assignments to Political Committees."

39. Baekgaard and Kjaer, "The Gendered Division of Labor in Assignments to Political Committees."

40. Kerevel and Atkeson, "Explaining the Marginalization of Women in Legislative Institutions."

41. Marwa M. Shalaby and Laila Elimam, "Arab Women in the Legislative Process," Sada, Washington, DC: Carnegie Endowment for International Peace, 2017, https://carnegie endowment.org/sada/2017/04/arab-women-in-the-legislative-process?lang=en; Marwa M. Shalaby and Laila Elimam, "Women in Legislative Committees in Arab Parliaments," *Comparative Politics* 53, no. 1 (October 2020): 139–67.

42. Kendall D. Funk, Laura Morales, and Michelle M. Taylor-Robinson, "The Impact of Committee Composition and Agendas on Women's Participation: Evidence from a Legislature with Near Numerical Equality," *Politics and Gender* 13, no. 2 (June 2017): 253–75.

43. King Abdullah of Jordan dissolved the parliament in 2012 after the Arab uprisings, and a new election law was introduced in June 2012.

44. Morocco does not have a stand-alone women's committee. It currently falls under the social sectors committee (see appendix A for more details).

45. Safa al-Hashem resigned from her seat in early 2014, leaving a single female legislator in the lower chamber.

46. Marwa Shalaby, "Women's Political Representation and Authoritarianism in the Arab World," Project on Middle East Political Science, 2016, https://pomeps.org/womens-political -representation-and-authoritarianism-in-the-arab-world; Mala Htun, "Women and Democracy," in *Constructing Democratic Governance in Latin America*, 2nd ed., ed. Jorge I. Domínguez and Michael Shifter (Baltimore: Johns Hopkins University Press, 2003), 200–220.

47. Winnie Byanyima, "Politics, Good Governance and Gender: The Experience of Three African Countries," in *Fifth Global Forum on Re-Inventing Government*, November 3–7, 2003, Mexico City, Mexico.

48. Youth and sports committees, as well as special needs committees, which are temporary, are included in the social affairs category for Kuwait. As shown in table 4.1, these committees have persisted throughout the last three legislative sessions of the lower chamber. Morocco's standing social issues committee includes youth and sports, disability, and social affairs.

49. Fernando Bizzarro, Allen Hicken, and Darin Self, "The V-Dem Party Institutionalization Index: A New Global Indicator (1900–2015)," *SSRN Electronic Journal*, 2017, https://doi .org/10.2139/ssrn.2968265; Fernando Bizzarro, John Gerring, Carl Henrik Knutsen et al., "Party Strength and Economic Growth," *World Politics* 70, no. 2 (April 2018): 275–320; Lars Pelke, "Party Institutionalization, Authoritarian Regime Types, and Women's Political Equality," *Contemporary Politics* 27 (April 2021): 461–86; Magnus B. Rasmussen and Carl Henrik Knutsen, "Party Institutionalization and Welfare State Development," *British Journal of Political Science* 51, no. 3 (July 2021): 1203–29.

50. The data collection process and analysis aimed to capture the membership in each legislative assembly as accurately as possible; however, the total numbers vary due to resignations, by-elections, government appointments, and/or the deaths of some members.

51. Schwindt-Bayer, *Political Power and Women's Representation in Latin America*.

52. Scott A. Frisch and Sean Q. Kelly, "A Place at the Table: Women's Committee Requests and Women's Committee Assignments in the U.S. House," *Women and Politics* 25, no. 3 (March 2003): 1–26; Mercedes Mateo Díaz, *Representing Women? Female Legislators in West European Parliaments*, ECPR Monographs Series (Colchester, United Kingdom: ECPR Press, 2005).

53. Karen Beckwith, "Numbers and Newness: The Descriptive and Substantive Representation of Women," *Canadian Journal of Political Science* 40, no. 1 (March 2007): 27–49.

54. Barnes, "Women's Representation and Legislative Appointments"; Hilde Coffé, Catherine Bolzendahl, and Katia Schnellecke, "Parties, Issues, and Power: Women's Partisan Representation on German Parliamentary Committees," *European Journal of Politics and Gender* 2, no. 2 (June 2019): 257–81.

55. Frisch and Kelly, "A Place at the Table"; Pansardi and Vercesi, "Party Gatekeeping and Women's Appointment to Parliamentary Committees."

56. Prihatini, "Explaining Gender Gaps in Indonesian Legislative Committees"; Pansardi and Vercesi, "Party Gatekeeping and Women's Appointment to Parliamentary Committees."

57. Vicky Randall, *Women and Politics: An International Perspective*, 2nd ed. (Chicago: University of Chicago Press, 1987).

58. Jean Yule, "Women Councillors and Committee Recruitment," *Local Government Studies* 26, no. 3 (September 2000): 31–54.

59. Data on vice president (VP) and reporter positions in Morocco's 2012 legislature are missing. Also, the VP positions did not exist in the Jordanian lower chamber until 2013. There are no VP positions in the Kuwaiti legislature.

60. A female legislator from the socialist team served as the president of the social committee for two consecutive terms in 2007.

61. Acknowledging the unequal representation of women in leadership positions, the internal bylaws of the Moroccan legislature were modified in 2013 (that came into effect in the 2016 session), stipulating that women should be granted at least one-third of leadership positions within all political institutions; however, the law never specified the "type" of leadership position. It is still unclear whether this change will advance female leadership in top positions, especially in more influential committees.

62. Personal interview, Amman, 2018.

63. Personal interview, Amman, 2018.

64. Personal interview with a former female legislator in the Moroccan Lower Chamber, Rabat, 2020.

65. Personal interview, Amman, 2018.

66. Personal interview, Amman, 2016.

67. Personal interview, Amman, 2018.

68. Personal interview, Amman, 2018.

69. Nichole M. Bauer, *The Qualifications Gap: Why Women Must Be Better Than Men to Win Political Office* (Cambridge: Cambridge University Press, 2020), 4.

70. Personal interview with a former female legislator in the Jordanian Lower Chamber, Amman, 2018.

71. Personal interview with a female legislator in the Moroccan Lower Chamber, Rabat, 2020.

72. Personal interview, Amman, 2016.

5. DISCERNING THE LINK BETWEEN DESCRIPTIVE AND SUBSTANTIVE REPRESENTATION

1. Fiona Mackay, "'Thick' Conceptions of Substantive Representation: Women, Gender and Political Institutions," *Representation* 44, no. 2 (July 2008): 125–39.

2. Daniel Höhmann, "When Do Female MPs Represent Women's Interests? Electoral Systems and the Legislative Behavior of Women," *Political Research Quarterly* 73, no. 4 (2019): https://doi.org/10.1177/1065912919859437.

3. Allen Hicken and Erik Martinez Kuhonta, eds., *Party System Institutionalization in Asia: Democracies, Autocracies, and the Shadows of the Past* (Cambridge: Cambridge University Press, 2014), 573.

4. Aldo F. Ponce and Susan E. Scarrow, "Party Institutionalization and Partisan Mobilization," *Government and Opposition* 58 (February 2022): 745–64.

5. Fernando Bizzarro et al., "Party Strength and Economic Growth," *World Politics* 70, no. 2 (April 2018): 275–320.

6. Elin Bjarnegård, *Gender and Politics: Explaining Male Dominance in Parliamentary Representation*. Gender and Politics Series (London: Palgrave Macmillan, 2013).

7. Tiffany D. Barnes, *Gendering Legislative Behavior: Institutional Constraints and Collaboration* (New York: Cambridge University Press, 2016), 3.

8. Susan J. Carroll, *Women as Candidates in American Politics* (Bloomington: Indiana University Press, 1994), 15.

9. Philip Norton, "Introduction: Parliament Since 1960," in *Parliamentary Questions*, ed. Mark Franklin and Philip Norton (New York: Clarendon, 1993), 1–22.

10. Karen Bird, "Gendering Parliamentary Questions," *British Journal of Politics and International Relations* 7, no. 3 (August 2005): 353–70.

11. Christian B. Jensen, Sven-Oliver Proksch, and Jonathan B. Slapin, "Parliamentary Questions, Oversight, and National Opposition Status in the European Parliament: Parliamentary Questions," *Legislative Studies Quarterly* 38, no. 2 (May 2013): 259–82; Matti Wiberg, "Parliamentary Questioning: Control by Communication," *Parliaments and Majority Rule in Western Europe* (1995): 179–222.

12. Shane Martin, "Parliamentary Questions, the Behaviour of Legislators, and the Function of Legislatures: An Introduction," *Journal of Legislative Studies* 17, no. 3 (September 2011): 259–70; Shane Martin, "Using Parliamentary Questions to Measure Constituency Focus: An Application to the Irish Case," *Political Studies* 59, no. 2 (June 2011): 472–88.

13. Edmund Malesky and Paul Schuler, "Nodding or Needling: Analyzing Delegate Responsiveness in an Authoritarian Parliament," *American Political Science Review* 104, no. 3 (August 2010): 482–502.

14. Eduardo Alemán, Juan Pablo Micozzi, and Margarita M. Ramírez, "The Hidden Electoral Connection: Analysing Parliamentary Questions in the Chilean Congress," *Journal of Legislative Studies* 24, no. 2 (April 2018): 227–44.

15. Bjørn Erik Rasch, "Opposition Parties, Electoral Incentives and the Control of Government Ministers: Parliamentary Questioning in Norway," in *Parlamente, Agendasetzung und Vetospieler*, ed. Steffen Ganghof, Christoph Hönnige, and Christian Stecker (Wiesbaden, Germany: VS Verlag für Sozialwissenschaften, 2009), 199–214.

16. Amer Beni Amer, *Final Report on the Performance of the 17th Parliament During the Second Ordinary Session of 2015*, Hayat Center, Rased, 2015, http://www.hayatcenter.org/uploads/2018/01/20180121122243ar.pdf.

17. Marwa Shalaby and Abdullah Aydogan, "Elite-Citizen Linkages and Issue Congruency Under Competitive Authoritarianism," *Parliamentary Affairs* 73, no. 1 (January 1, 2020): 66–88.

18. Sandra Grey, "Numbers and Beyond: The Relevance of Critical Mass in Gender Research," *Politics and Gender* 2, no. 4 (December 2006): 492–502.

19. Martin, "Parliamentary Questions, the Behaviour of Legislators, and the Function of Legislatures"; Martin, "Using Parliamentary Questions to Measure Constituency Focus."

20. The bylaws of the 2012 Jordanian Lower Chamber: http://www.chambredesrepresentants .ma/sites/default/files/loi/reglement.interieur2012_1.pdf.

21. Abdo I. Baaklini, Guilain Denoeux, and Robert Springborg, *Legislative Politics in the Arab World: The Resurgence of Democratic Institutions* (Boulder, CO: Lynne Rienner, 1999); Eva Wegner, *Islamist Opposition in Authoritarian Regimes: The Party of Justice and Development in Morocco*. Religion and Politics (Syracuse, NY: Syracuse University Press, 2011).

22. Personal interview, Rabat, 2020.

23. Personal interview, Rabat, 2020.

24. The Comparative Agendas Project was initiated by Bryan Jones and Frank Baumgartner in 1993 as the U.S. policy agenda. See appendix B for the detailed codebook.

25. Frank R. Baumgartner and Bryan D. Jones, *Agendas and Instability in American Politics*. American Politics and Political Economy Series (Chicago: University of Chicago Press, 1993); Frank R. Baumgartner, Bryan D. Jones, and John Wilkerson, "Comparative Studies of Policy Dynamics," *Comparative Political Studies* 44, no. 8 (August 2011): 947–72; Laura Chaqués Bonafont and Anna M. Palau Roqué, "Comparing Law-Making Activities in a Quasi-Federal System of Government: The Case of Spain," *Comparative Political Studies* 44, no. 8 (August 2011): 1089–119; Alper T. Bulut, "Measuring Political Agenda Setting and Representation in Turkey: Introducing a New Approach and Data Set," *Party Politics* 23, no. 6 (November 2017): 717–30; Bryan D. Jones and Frank R. Baumgartner, "Representation and Agenda Setting," *Policy Studies Journal* 32, no. 1 (February 2004): 1–24; Gert-Jan Lindeboom, "Public Priorities in Government's Hands: Corresponding Policy Agendas in the Netherlands?," *Acta Politica* 47, no. 4 (October 2012): 443–67.

26. Four graduate-level researchers coded the parliamentary data. The coders received extensive training and worked with researchers at the Policy Agendas Project headquarters at the University of Texas, Austin. We had 94 percent intercoder reliability.

27. The list of topics of the comparative agenda categories were slightly modified to better fit the MENA context. For example, the Law, Crime, and Family Issues category was divided into two: (1) Law and Crime and (2) Women, Child, and Family. Similarly, a Corruption category was added to the codebook (see appendix B).

28. According to the official parliament reports, there were 9,583 oral questions posed between 2011 and 2016 in Morocco's lower chamber. Two hundred seven questions were withdrawn, and roughly seven hundred questions were asked by teams and thus excluded from the analysis. During the same session, about 23,077 written questions were posed. In this chapter, I focus only on oral questions.

29. Karen Celis, "Substantive Representation of Women: The Representation of Women's Interests and the Impact of Descriptive Representation in the Belgian Parliament (1900–1979)," *Journal of Women, Politics and Policy* 28, no. 2 (July 2006): 85–114.

30. The speaker, Jasim Al-Kharafi, and the elected minister, Rudan al-Rudan, did not pose any questions in 2009. Marzuq al-Ghanim (the speaker) and Khalf al-Anzi (reelected from 2009) did not ask questions in 2013.

31. The coding scheme distinguishes between policy and nonpolicy areas. All nonpolicy bills and questions were coded under a "government operations" category not included in the multivariate analysis in the following section.

32. Malesky and Schuler, "Nodding or Needling"; Rory Truex, "The Returns to Office in a 'Rubber Stamp' Parliament," *American Political Science Review* 108, no. 2 (May 2014): 235–51; Rory Truex, *Making Autocracy Work: Representation and Responsiveness in Modern China*. Cambridge Studies in Comparative Politics (New York: Cambridge University Press, 2016).

33. There are four main Islamist streams in the Kuwaiti National Assembly: the Islamic Constitutional Movement (ICM), the National Islamist Alliance, the Justice and Peace Alliance, and the Islamic Salafi Alliance. The ICM and the Islamic Salafi Alliance are both Sunni blocs, whereas the National Islamist Alliance and the Justice and Peace Alliance are Shi'ite blocs. While the ICM and the Salafi Alliance tend to be anti-regime, the other two Islamist groups are mostly pro-regime.

34. Omar Obeidat, "New Lower House Includes 74 New Faces," *Jordan Times*, September 24, 2016, http://www.jordantimes.com/news/local/new-lower-house-includes-74-new-faces.

35. See chapter 4 for more information on committee assignments' rules and procedures across the three cases.

36. Leslie A. Schwindt-Bayer, "Still Supermadres? Gender and the Policy Priorities of Latin American Legislators," *American Journal of Political Science* 50, no. 3 (July 2006): 570–85; Sven-Oliver Proksch and Jonathan B. Slapin, "Parliamentary Questions and Oversight in the European Union," *European Journal of Political Research* 50, no. 1 (January 2011): 53–79.

37. Committee assignments may change from one round to another within the same legislative session; therefore, each MP is treated as an individual observation across rounds or quarters. For example, although there are only fifty MPs in the Kuwaiti assembly, we have two hundred observations for the entire 2009 session, given the changes in the committee assignments across the four quarters. In Morocco, MPs maintain their committee assignment and can only join one committee. In Jordan, multiple committee assignments are allowed.

38. I do not include controls for the districts' characteristics in Morocco and Kuwait. Sixty of the sixty-seven female legislators are elected via national lists in Morocco. Thus, elected quota women's political mandate is not based on a geographical representation or constituency. In Kuwait, there are only five electoral districts, and tribal candidates dominate the fourth and fifth districts. Women were never able to get elected for these districts, which leaves minimal variation in district characteristics for our analysis.

39. J. Scott Long, *Regression Models for Categorical and Limited Dependent Variables*. Advanced Quantitative Techniques in the Social Sciences 7 (Thousand Oaks, CA: Sage, 1997).

40. In 2013–2016, Jordan's Lower House had twenty permanent committees with eleven members each, as well as several investigation committees. Investigatory committees are excluded from our analysis for consistency and to ensure the comparability of the results across sessions and cases.

41. The coefficient for the women and family category is rather inflated in table 5.6 given the very small number of questions posed in this area.

42. Morocco has only nine permanent committees, and members are only allowed to be members of one committee. Parties are proportionally represented across committees.

43. There were ten permanent and seven temporary committees in Kuwait's 2009–2011 legislature. Several investigation committees were excluded from the analysis.

44. Personal interview with a female legislator, Rabat, February 2020.

45. Personal interview with a former female legislator, Rabat, 2020.

46. Höhmann, "When Do Female MPs Represent Women's Interests?," 2.

47. Personal interview, Amman, 2018.

48. Personal interview, Amman, 2019.

CONCLUSION

1. Author's interview with a former female deputy in the Jordanian lower chamber, March 2018, Amman, Jordan.

2. Susan J. Carroll, *Women as Candidates in American Politics* (Bloomington: Indiana University Press, 1994).

3. Suen Wang, "Do Women Always Represent Women? The Effects of Gender Quotas on Substantive Representation," *Political Behavior* 45, no. 4 (July 2022): 1979–99.

4. Barbara Geddes, Joseph Wright, and Erica Frantz, "Autocratic Breakdown and Regime Transitions: A New Data Set," *Perspectives on Politics* 12, no. 2 (June 2014): 313–31.

5. Daniel Pemstein, Kyle L. Marquardt, Eitan Tzelgov, et al., "The V-Dem Measurement Model: Latent Variable Analysis for Cross-National and Cross-Temporal Expert-Coded Data," *SSRN Electronic Journal*, 2019, https://doi.org/10.2139/ssrn.3395892.

6. Daniela Donno and Anne-Kathrin Kreft, "Authoritarian Institutions and Women's Rights," *Comparative Political Studies* 52, no. 5 (April 2019): 720–53.

7. Susan D. Hyde and Nikolay Marinov, "Which Elections Can Be Lost?," *Political Analysis* 20, no. 2 (2012): 191–210.

8. Donno and Kreft, "Authoritarian Institutions and Women's Rights," 720–53.

9. My goal is not to establish a causal link between party institutionalization and the three outcomes in model C.1. This analysis aims to show the presence of a correlation between my three outcomes and the party institutionalization index.

10. Denise M. Walsh, *Women's Rights in Democratizing States: Just Debate and Gender Justice in the Public Sphere* (Cambridge: Cambridge University Press, 2011).

11. Valeriya Mechkova and Amanda B. Edgell, "Substantive Representation, Women's Health, and Regime Type," *Comparative Political Studies* 57, no. 14 (2024): 2449–81.

12. Gretchen Bauer and Jennie E. Burnet, "Gender Quotas, Democracy, and Women's Representation in Africa: Some Insights from Democratic Botswana and Autocratic Rwanda," *Women's Studies International Forum* 41 (November 2013): 103–12.

13. Donno and Kreft, "Authoritarian Institutions and Women's Rights."

14. Michael Bernhard et al., "Parties, Civil Society, and the Deterrence of Democratic Defection," *Studies in Comparative International Development* 55, no. 1 (March 2020): 1–26.

15. Personal interview, Kuwait City, 2023.

16. Marwa Shalaby and Scott Williamson, *How Parliaments Matter: Policy and Opposition in the Middle East's Authoritarian Legislatures* (unpublished manuscript, 2023).

17. Gretchen Bauer, "'Let There Be a Balance': Women in African Parliaments," *Political Studies Review* 10, no. 3 (September 2012): 370–84.

18. Miki Caul Kittilson, *Challenging Parties, Changing Parliaments: Women and Elected Office in Contemporary Western Europe*. Parliaments and Legislatures (Columbus: Ohio State University Press, 2006).

19. Rainbow Murray, Mona Lena Krook, and Katherine A. R. Opello, "Why Are Gender Quotas Adopted? Party Pragmatism and Parity in France," *Political Research Quarterly* 65, no. 3 (September 2012): 529–43.

20. Andrew Reynolds, "Women in the Legislatures and Executives of the World: Knocking at the Highest Glass Ceiling," *World Politics* 51, no. 4 (July 1999): 547–72.

21. Yeşim Arat, "Democratic Backsliding and the Instrumentalization of Women's Rights in Turkey," *Politics and Gender* 18, no. 4 (December 2022): 911–41.

22. Lihi Ben Shitrit, "Authenticating Representation: Women's Quotas and Islamist Parties," *Politics and Gender* 12, no. 4 (December 2016): 781–806; Janine Astrid Clark and Jillian Schwedler, "Who Opened the Window? Women's Activism in Islamist Parties," *Comparative Politics* 35, no. 3 (April 2003): 293.

23. Katrine Beauregard, "Partisanship and the Gender Gap: Support for Gender Quotas in Australia," *Australian Journal of Political Science* 53, no. 3 (July 2018): 290–319; Ronald Inglehart and Pippa Norris, *Rising Tide: Gender Equality and Cultural Change Around the World* (New York: Cambridge University Press, 2003); Mona Lena Krook and Diana Z. O'Brien, "The Politics of Group Representation: Quotas for Women and Minorities Worldwide," *Comparative Politics* 42, no. 3 (March 2010): 253–72; Ana Catalano Weeks and Jonathan Homola, "How Can We Measure Women's Substantive Representation," *Comparative Politics Newsletter* 32, no. 2 (2022): 16–21, https://www.comparativepoliticsnewsletter.org/wp-content/uploads/2022/12/APSA-CP_32_2_Dec_2022.pdf.

24. Sergei Guriev and Daniel Treisman, "Informational Autocrats," *Journal of Economic Perspectives* 33, no. 4 (November 2019): 100–127.

25. Shireen Hassim, "Perverse Consequences? The Impact of Quotas for Women on Democratization in Africa," in *Political Representation*, ed. Ian Shapiro et al. (New York: Cambridge University Press, 2010), 211–35.

26. Bauer and Burnet, "Gender Quotas, Democracy, and Women's Representation in Africa," 110.

27. Edmund Malesky and Paul Schuler, "Nodding or Needling: Analyzing Delegate Responsiveness in an Authoritarian Parliament," *American Political Science Review* 104, no. 3 (August 2010): 482–502; Rory Truex, *Making Autocracy Work: Representation and Responsiveness in Modern China*. Cambridge Studies in Comparative Politics (New York: Cambridge University Press, 2016).

28. Joan Acker, "From Sex Roles to Gendered Institutions," *Contemporary Sociology* 21, no. 5 (September 1992): 565–69.

29. Christopher F. Karpowitz, Tali Mendelberg, and Lauren Mattioli, "Why Women's Numbers Elevate Women's Influence, and When They Do Not: Rules, Norms, and Authority in Political Discussion," *Politics, Groups, and Identities* 3, no. 1 (January 2015): 150.

30. Bruno Castanho Silva, Danielle Pullan, and Jens Wäckerle, "Blending in or Standing Out? Gendered Political Communication in 24 Democracies," *American Journal of Political Science* (June 8, 2024), https://doi.org/10.1111/ajps.12876.

31. Marwa M. Shalaby and Laila Elimam, "Women in Legislative Committees in Arab Parliaments," *Comparative Politics* 53, no. 1 (October 2020): 139–67.

32. Louise Chappell, "Comparing Political Institutions: Revealing the Gendered 'Logic of Appropriateness,'" *Politics and Gender* 2, no. 2 (June 2006): 223–35.

33. Lyn Kathlene, "Power and Influence in State Legislative Policymaking: The Interaction of Gender and Position in Committee Hearing Debates," *American Political Science Review* 88, no. 3 (September 1994): 560–76; Cindy Simon Rosenthal, *When Women Lead: Integrative Leadership in State Legislatures* (New York: Oxford University Press, 1998).

34. Sandra Grey, "Does Size Matter? Critical Mass and New Zealand's Women MPs," *Parliamentary Affairs* 55, no. 1 (January 2002): 19–29.

35. Personal interview, Kuwait City, 2023.

36. Yvonne Galligan, Sara Clavero, and Marina Calloni, *Gender Politics and Democracy in Post-Socialist Europe* (Farmington Hills, MI: Barbara Budrich, 2007).

37. Personal interview, Kuwait City, 2023.

38. Beth Reingold, "Women as Officeholders: Linking Descriptive and Substantive Representation," in *Political Women and American Democracy*, ed. Christina Wolbrecht, Karen Beckwith, and Lisa Baldez (Cambridge: Cambridge University Press, 2008), 158.

39. Daniel Höhmann, "When Do Female MPs Represent Women's Interests? Electoral Systems and the Legislative Behavior of Women," *Political Research Quarterly* 73, no. 4 (2019): https://doi.org/10.1177/1065912919859437.

40. Kathleen Bawn and Michael F. Thies, "A Comparative Theory of Electoral Incentives: Representing the Unorganized Under PR, Plurality and Mixed-Member Electoral Systems," *Journal of Theoretical Politics* 15, no. 1 (January 2003): 5–32; John M. Carey and Matthew Soberg Shugart, "Incentives to Cultivate a Personal Vote: A Rank Ordering of Electoral Formulas," *Electoral Studies* 14, no. 4 (December 1995): 417–39; Santiago Olivella and Margit Tavits, "Legislative Effects of Electoral Mandates," *British Journal of Political Science* 44, no. 2 (April 2014): 301–21.

41. Marwa Shalaby, "Women's Political Representation and Authoritarianism in the Arab World," Project on Middle East Political Science, 2016, https://pomeps.org/womens-political-representation-and-authoritarianism-in-the-arab-world.

42. Mounah Abdel-Samad and Lindsay J. Benstead, "Do Islamist Parties Help or Hinder Women? Party Institutionalization, Piety and Responsiveness to Female Citizens," *Digest of Middle East Studies* 31, no. 4 (October 2022): 293–318.

43. Reingold, "Women as Officeholders."

44. UN Women, *Regional Analysis on the Implementation of UNSCR 1325 in the Arab States* (New York: UN Women, 2015), 54, https://mlkrook.org/pdf/UNWROAS_2015.pdf; Organisation for Economic Co-operation and Development and Center of Arab Woman for Training and Research, *Women in Public Life: Gender, Law and Policy in the Middle East and North Africa* (Paris: OECD Publishing, 2014), 135, https://doi.org/10.1787/9789264224636-en.

45. Lindsay J. Benstead, "Do Female Local Councilors Improve Women's Representation?," *Journal of the Middle East and Africa* 10, no. 2 (April 3, 2019): 95–119.

BIBLIOGRAPHY

Abdelgawad, Hala, and Mazen Hassan. "Women in the Egyptian Parliament: A Different Agenda?" *Review of Economics and Political Science* 8, no. 6 (October 2019): 558–76. https://www.emerald.com/insight/content/doi/10.1108/reps-06-2019-0076/full/html.

Abdel-Samad, Mounah, and Lindsay J. Benstead. "Do Islamist Parties Help or Hinder Women? Party Institutionalization, Piety and Responsiveness to Female Citizens." *Digest of Middle East Studies* 31, no. 4 (October 2022): 293–318.

AbuKhalil, As'ad. "Gender Boundaries and Sexual Categories in the Arab World." *Feminist Issues* 15, no. 1–2 (March 1997): 91–104.

Abu Rumman, Husayn. *Qirra'a Awaliyya fil-Intikhabat al-Niyabiyya al-Urduniyya: A Preliminary Reading of Jordan's Parliamentary Elections, Civil Society Issues*. Amman, Jordan: New Jordan Center for Studies, 2003.

——. "The Women's Quota in Jordan: Crowning Three Decades of Support for Female Political Participation." In *The Arab Quota Report: Selected Case Studies*. Stockholm, Sweden: International Institute for Democracy and Electoral Assistance, 2007. http://iknowpolitics.org/en/2011/09/arab-quota-report-selected-case-studies.

Abou-Zeid, Gehan. "In Search of Political Power: Women in Parliament in Egypt, Jordan, and Lebanon." In *Women in Parliament: Beyond Numbers*, edited by Azza Karam, 43–54. Stockholm, Sweden: International Institute for Democracy and Electoral Assistance, 1998.

——. "The Arab Region: Women's Access to the Decision-Making Process Across the Arab Nation." In *Women, Quotas and Politics*, edited by Drude Dahlerup, 179–204. New York: Routledge, 2006.

Acker, Joan. "From Sex Roles to Gendered Institutions." *Contemporary Sociology* 21, no. 5 (September 1992): 565–69.

Adams, S. Kimberly. "The Significant Influence of Proportional Representation and Democratization on the Share of Female Parliamentarians in Middle Eastern and North African (MENA) Countries." *International Journals of Arts and Sciences* 11, no. 1 (2018): 237–52.

Ahmed, Leila. *Women and Gender in Islam: Historical Roots of a Modern Debate*. New Haven, CT: Yale University Press, 1993.

Alatiyat, Ibtesam, and Hassan Barari. "Liberating Women with Islam? The Islamists and Women's Issues in Jordan." *Totalitarian Movements and Political Religions* 11, no. 3–4 (September 2010): 359–78.

Alatiyat, Ibtesam, Musa Shteiwi, and Suleiman Sweiss. *Building Democracy in Jordan: Women's Political Participation, Political Party Life, and Democratic Elections*. Stockholm, Sweden: International Institute for Democracy and Electoral Assistance and the Arab NGO Network for Development, 2005.

Albloshi, Hamad. "Kuwait's National Assembly: Roles and Dynamics." In *Monograph Series: The Shura Council in the Persian Gulf*. Durham, United Kingdom, and Doha, Qatar: The Shura Councils in the Persian Gulf Monograph Series, no. 1, 2019. https://www.qu.edu.qa/static_file/qu/research/Gulf%20Studies/documents/Monograph%20Shura%20Councils%201%20Kuwait%20Hamad%20H.%20Albloshi.pdf.

Albrecht, Holger. "The Nature of Political Participation." In *Political Participation in the Middle East*, edited by Ellen Lust-Okar and Saloua Zerhouni, 15–32. Boulder, CO: Lynne Rienner, 2008.

Alemán, Eduardo, Aldo F. Ponce, and Iñaki Sagarzazu. "Legislative Parties in Volatile, Nonprogrammatic Party Systems: The Peruvian Case in Comparative Perspective." *Latin American Politics and Society* 53, no. 3 (2011): 57–81.

Alemán, Eduardo, Juan Pablo Micozzi, and Margarita M. Ramírez. "The Hidden Electoral Connection: Analysing Parliamentary Questions in the Chilean Congress." *Journal of Legislative Studies* 24, no. 2 (April 2018): 227–44.

Alexander, Amy C., and Christian Welzel. "Islam and Patriarchy: How Robust Is Muslim Support for Patriarchal Values?" *International Review of Sociology* 21, no. 2 (July 2011): 249–76.

Al-Kandari, Yagoub Yousif, and Ibrahim Naji Al-Hadben. "Tribalism, Sectarianism, and Democracy in Kuwaiti Culture." *Digest of Middle East Studies* 19, no. 2 (October 2010): 268–85.

Alnajjar, Ghanim. "The Challenges Facing Kuwaiti Democracy." *Middle East Journal* 54, no. 2 (Spring 2000): 242–58.

Al-Rasheed, Madawi. *A Most Masculine State: Gender, Politics and Religion in Saudi Arabia*, vol. 43. New York: Cambridge University Press, 2013.

Al-Rawashdeh, Alaa Zuhheir, Asmaa Ribhi Al Arab, and Ali Mohammad Ali Al-Shboul. "Difficulties Prevent Jordanian Women Participation in Political Life in Light of Some Social Variables." *Asian Social Science* 8, no. 10 (August 2012): 208–22.

Al-Remaidhi, Abdullah, and Bob Watt. "Electoral Constituencies and Political Parties in Kuwait: An Assessment." *Election Law Journal: Rules, Politics, and Policy* 11, no. 4 (December 2012): 518–28.

Al-Sabah, Meshal. *Gender and Politics in Kuwait: Women and Political Participation in the Gulf*. London: I. B. Tauris, 2013.

Al Shalabi, Jamal, and Tareq Al-Assad. "Political Participation of Jordanian Women." *Égypte/ Monde Arabe* 3, no. 9 (2012): 211–30. https://doi.org/10.4000/ema.3033.

Al Subhi, Ahlam Khalfan, and Amy Erica Smith. "Electing Women to New Arab Assemblies: The Roles of Gender Ideology, Islam, and Tribalism in Oman." *International Political Science Review* 40, no. 1 (January 2019): 90–107.

Amawi, Abla. "Against All Odds: Women Candidates in Jordanian Elections." In *From Patriarchy to Empowerment*, edited by Valentine M. Moghadam, 40–57. Syracuse, NY: Syracuse University Press, 2007.

Angrist, Michele Penner. *Party Building in the Modern Middle East*. Seattle: University of Washington Press, 2006.

Angrist, Michele. "War, Resisting the West, and Women's Labor: Toward an Understanding of Arab Exceptionalism." *Politics and Gender* 8, no. 1 (March 2012): 51–82.

Aparicio, Francisco Javier, and Joy Langston. "Committee Leadership Selection Without Seniority: The Mexican Case." *Centro de Investigación y Docencia Económicas (CIDE), División de Estudios Políticos* 217 (2009). https://citeseerx.ist.psu.edu/document?repid=rep1&type=pdf&doi=abbca3d68329936a00bf9065c98c6e781c19ccf6.

Arat, Yeşim. "Democratic Backsliding and the Instrumentalization of Women's Rights in Turkey." *Politics and Gender* 18, no. 4 (December 2022): 911–41.

Ayata, Ayşe Güneş, and Fatma Tütüncü. "Critical Acts Without a Critical Mass: The Substantive Representation of Women in the Turkish Parliament." *Parliamentary Affairs* 61, no. 3 (July 2008): 461–75.

Baaklini, Abdo I., Guilain Denoeux, and Robert Springborg. *Legislative Politics in the Arab World: The Resurgence of Democratic Institutions*. Boulder, CO: Lynne Rienner, 1999.

Baekgaard, Martin, and Ulrik Kjaer. "The Gendered Division of Labor in Assignments to Political Committees: Discrimination or Self-Selection in Danish Local Politics?" *Politics and Gender* 8, no. 4 (December 2012): 465–82.

Banducci, Susan A., Todd Donovan, and Jeffrey A. Karp. "Minority Representation, Empowerment, and Participation." *Journal of Politics* 66, no. 2 (May 2004): 534–56.

Barnes, Tiffany D. *Gendering Legislative Behavior: Institutional Constraints and Collaboration*. New York: Cambridge University Press, 2016.

——. "Women's Representation and Legislative Appointments: The Case of the Argentine Provinces." *Revista Uruguaya de Ciencia Política* 23, no. 2 (2014): 135–63.

Barnett, Carolyn, Alexandra Blackman, and Marwa Shalaby. "Gender Stereotypes in Autocracies: Experimental Evidence from Morocco." *Journal of Politics* (forthcoming). https://www.journals.uchicago.edu/doi/10.1086/733000.

Barnett, Carolyn, and Marwa Shalaby. "Success Beyond Gender Quotas: Gender, Local Politics, and Clientelism in Morocco." GLD Working Paper. Program on Governance and Local Development, University of Gothenburg, 2021. https://gunet.sharepoint.com/sites/sy-grp-gld---external-communications/Shared%20Documents/Forms/AllItems.aspx?id=%2Fsites%2Fsy%2Dgrp%2Dgld%2D%2D%2Dexternal%2Dcommunications%2FShared%20

Documents%2FPDFs%2ofor%2owebsite%2o%28external%29%2FGLD%2oWorking%
2oPaper%2oSeries%2FWP%2048%2Fgld%2Dworking%2Dpaper48%2Epdf&parent
=%2Fsites%2Fsy%2Dgrp%2Dgld%2D%2D%2Dexternal%2Dcommunications%2FSh
ared%2oDocuments%2FPDFs%2ofor%2owebsite%2o%28external%29%2FGLD%2o
Working%2oPaper%2oSeries%2FWP%2048&p=true&ga=1.

Bauer, Gretchen. "'Let There Be a Balance': Women in African Parliaments." *Political Studies Review* 10, no. 3 (September 2012): 370–84.

Bauer, Gretchen, and Jennie E. Burnet. "Gender Quotas, Democracy, and Women's Representation in Africa: Some Insights from Democratic Botswana and Autocratic Rwanda." *Women's Studies International Forum* 41 (November 2013): 103–12.

Bauer, Nichole M. *The Qualifications Gap: Why Women Must Be Better Than Men to Win Political Office.* Cambridge: Cambridge University Press, 2020.

Baumgartner, Frank R., and Bryan D. Jones. *Agendas and Instability in American Politics.* American Politics and Political Economy Series. Chicago: University of Chicago Press, 1993.

Baumgartner, Frank R., Bryan D. Jones, and John Wilkerson. "Comparative Studies of Policy Dynamics." *Comparative Political Studies* 44, no. 8 (August 2011): 947–72.

Bawn, Kathleen, and Michael F. Thies. "A Comparative Theory of Electoral Incentives: Representing the Unorganized Under PR, Plurality and Mixed-Member Electoral Systems." *Journal of Theoretical Politics* 15, no. 1 (January 2003): 5–32.

Beauregard, Katrine. "Partisanship and the Gender Gap: Support for Gender Quotas in Australia." *Australian Journal of Political Science* 53, no. 3 (July 2018): 290–319.

Beckwith, Karen. "Numbers and Newness: The Descriptive and Substantive Representation of Women." *Canadian Journal of Political Science* 40, no. 1 (March 2007): 27–49.

——. "Plotting the Path from One to the Other." In *Representation*, edited by Maria C. Escobar-Lemmon and Michelle M. Taylor-Robinson, 19–40. New York: Oxford University Press, 2014.

Beckwith, Karen, and Kimberly Cowell-Meyers. "Sheer Numbers: Critical Representation Thresholds and Women's Political Representation." *Perspectives on Politics* 5, no. 3 (September 2007): 553.

Bektas, Eda, and Esra Issever-Ekinci. "Who Represents Women in Turkey? An Analysis of Gender Difference in Private Bill Sponsorship in the 2011–15 Turkish Parliament." *Politics and Gender* 15, no. 4 (December 2019): 851–81.

Belschner, Jana. "Electoral Engineering in New Democracies: Strong Quotas and Weak Parties in Tunisia." *Government and Opposition* 57, no. 1 (January 2022): 108–25.

Ben Shitrit, Lihi. "Authenticating Representation: Women's Quotas and Islamist Parties." *Politics and Gender* 12, no. 4 (December 2016): 781–806.

Beni Amer, Amer. *Final Report on the Performance of the 17th Parliament During the Second Ordinary Session of 2015.* Hayat Center, Rased, 2015. http://www.hayatcenter.org/uploads/2018/01/20180121122243ar.pdf.

Benstead, Lindsay J. "Do Female Local Councilors Improve Women's Representation?" *Journal of the Middle East and Africa* 10, no. 2 (April 3, 2019): 95–119.

——. "Why Quotas Are Needed to Improve Women's Access to Services in Clientelistic Regimes." *Governance* 29, no. 2 (April 2016): 185–205.

Benstead, Lindsay J., Amaney A. Jamal, and Ellen Lust. "Is It Gender, Religiosity, or Both? A Role Congruity Theory of Candidate Electability in Transitional Tunisia." *Perspectives on Politics* 13, no. 1 (March 2015): 74–94.

Benstead, Lindsay, and Ellen Lust. "Why Do Some Voters Prefer Female Candidates? The Role of Perceived Incorruptibility in Arab Elections." In *Gender and Corruption: Historical Roots and New Avenues for Research*, edited by Helena Stensöta and Lena Wängnerud, 83–104. New York: Palgrave Macmillan, 2018.

Bernhard, Michael, Allen Hicken, Christopher M. Reenock, and Staffan I. Lindberg. "Institutional Subsystems and the Survival of Democracy: Do Political and Civil Society Matter?" *SSRN Electronic Journal*, 2015. https://doi.org/10.2139/ssrn.2613824.

——. "Parties, Civil Society, and the Deterrence of Democratic Defection." *Studies in Comparative International Development* 55, no. 1 (March 2020): 1–26.

Bill, James A., and Robert Springborg. *Politics in the Middle East*, 4th ed. The HarperCollins Series in Comparative Politics. New York: HarperCollins, 1994.

Bird, Karen. "Gendering Parliamentary Questions." *British Journal of Politics and International Relations* 7, no. 3 (August 2005): 353–70.

Bizzarro, Fernando, John Gerring, Carl Henrik Knutsen et al. "Party Strength and Economic Growth." *World Politics* 70, no. 2 (April 2018): 275–320.

Bizzarro, Fernando, Allen Hicken, and Darin Self. "The V-Dem Party Institutionalization Index: A New Global Indicator (1900–2015)." *SSRN Electronic Journal*, 2017. https://www.v-dem.net/media/publications/v-dem_working_paper_2017_48.pdf.

Bjarnegård, Elin. *Gender and Politics: Explaining Male Dominance in Parliamentary Representation*. Gender and Politics Series. London: Palgrave Macmillan, 2013.

Bjarnegård, Elin, and Pär Zetterberg. "How Autocrats Weaponize Women's Rights." *Journal of Democracy* 33, no. 2 (April 2022): 60–75.

Blackman, Alexandra Domike, and Marlette Jackson. "Gender Stereotypes, Political Leadership, and Voting Behavior in Tunisia." *Political Behavior* 43, no. 3 (2021): 1037–66.

Blaydes, Lisa. *Elections and Distributive Politics in Mubarak's Egypt*. Cambridge: Cambridge University Press, 2010.

Boix, Carles, and Milan W. Svolik. "The Foundations of Limited Authoritarian Government: Institutions, Commitment, and Power-Sharing in Dictatorships." *Journal of Politics* 75, no. 2 (April 2013): 300–316.

Bonafont, Laura Chaqués, and Anna M. Palau Roqué. "Comparing Law-Making Activities in a Quasi-Federal System of Government: The Case of Spain." *Comparative Political Studies* 44, no. 8 (August 2011): 1089–119.

Brancati, Dawn. "Democratic Authoritarianism: Origins and Effects." *Annual Review of Political Science* 17, no. 1 (May 2014): 313–26.

Brand, Laurie A. *Women, the State, and Political Liberalization: Middle Eastern and North African Experiences*. New York: Columbia University Press, 1998.

Brand, Laurie A., and Fayez Hammad. "Identity and the Jordanian Elections." *Foreign Policy*, January 17, 2013. https://foreignpolicy.com/2013/01/17/identity-and-the-jordanian-elections/.

Bratton, Kathleen A. "Critical Mass Theory Revisited: The Behavior and Success of Token Women in State Legislatures." *Politics and Gender* 1, no. 1 (2005): 97–125.

Brown, Nathan. *Moving Out of Kuwait's Political Impasse.* Carnegie Endowment for International Peace, 2007. https://carnegieendowment.org/research/2007/06/moving-out-of-kuwaits-political -impasse?lang=en.

Brown, Nathan J. *When Victory Is Not an Option: Islamist Movements in Arab Politics.* Ithaca, NY: Cornell University Press, 2012.

Brownlee, Jason. *Authoritarianism in an Age of Democratization.* Cambridge: Cambridge University Press, 2007.

Buehler, Matt. "Continuity Through Co-Optation: Rural Politics and Regime Resilience in Morocco and Mauritania." *Mediterranean Politics* 20, no. 3 (September 2, 2015): 364–85.

——. "The Threat to 'Un-Moderate': Moroccan Islamists and the Arab Spring." *Middle East Law and Governance* 5, no. 3 (2013): 231–57.

Bulut, Alper T. "Measuring Political Agenda Setting and Representation in Turkey: Introducing a New Approach and Data Set." *Party Politics* 23, no. 6 (November 2017): 717–30.

Bush, Sarah Sunn. "International Politics and the Spread of Quotas for Women in Legislatures." *International Organization* 65, no. 1 (January 2011): 103–37.

Bush, Sarah Sunn, and Eleanor Gao. "Small Tribes, Big Gains: The Strategic Uses of Gender Quotas in the Middle East." *Comparative Politics* 49, no. 2 (January 2017): 149–67.

Bush, Sarah Sunn, and Pär Zetterberg. "Gender Quotas and International Reputation." *American Journal of Political Science* 65, no. 2 (April 2021): 326–41.

Byanyima, Winnie. "Politics, Good Governance and Gender: The Experience of Three African Countries." In *Fifth Global Forum on Re-Inventing Government.* November 3–7, 2003, Mexico City, Mexico.

Canon, David T., and Richard A. Posner. *Race, Redistricting, and Representation: The Unintended Consequences of Black Majority Districts.* Chicago: University of Chicago Press, 1999.

Carey, John M., and Matthew Soberg Shugart. "Incentives to Cultivate a Personal Vote: A Rank Ordering of Electoral Formulas." *Electoral Studies* 14, no. 4 (December 1995): 417–39.

Carroll, Susan J., ed. *The Impact of Women in Public Office.* Bloomington: Indiana University Press, 2001.

——. *Women as Candidates in American Politics.* Bloomington: Indiana University Press, 1994.

Casal Bértoa, Fernando. "Political Parties or Party Systems? Assessing the 'Myth' of Institutionalisation and Democracy." *West European Politics* 40, no. 2 (March 2017): 402–29.

Casal Bértoa, Fernando, Zsolt Enyedi, and Martin Mölder. "Party and Party System Institutionalization: Which Comes First?" *Perspectives on Politics* 22, no. 1 (March 2024): 194–212.

Castanho Silva, Bruno, Danielle Pullan, and Jens Wäckerle. "Blending in or Standing Out? Gendered Political Communication in 24 Democracies." *American Journal of Political Science* (June 8, 2024), https://doi.org/10.1111/ajps.12876.

Caul, Miki. "Women's Representation in Parliament: The Role of Political Parties." *Party Politics* 5, no. 1 (January 1999): 79–98.

Cavatorta, Francesco, and Emanuela Dalmasso. "Liberal Outcomes Through Undemocratic Means: The Reform of the *Code de Statut Personnel* in Morocco." *Journal of Modern African Studies* 47, no. 4 (December 2009): 487–506.

Cavatorta, Francesco, and Lise Storm, eds. *Political Parties in the Arab World: Continuity and Change.* Edinburgh, United Kingdom: Edinburgh University Press, 2018.

Celis, Karen. "Substantive Representation of Women: The Representation of Women's Interests and the Impact of Descriptive Representation in the Belgian Parliament (1900–1979)." *Journal of Women, Politics and Policy* 28, no. 2 (July 2006): 85–114.

Celis, Karen, Sarah Childs, Johanna Kantola, and Mona Lena Krook. "Rethinking Women's Substantive Representation." *Representation* 44, no. 2 (July 2008): 99–110.

Chaney, Elsa M. *Supermadre: Women in Politics in Latin America.* Latin American Monographs 50. Austin: University of Texas Press, 1979.

Chappell, Louise. "Comparing Political Institutions: Revealing the Gendered 'Logic of Appropriateness.'" *Politics and Gender* 2, no. 2 (June 2006): 223–35.

Charrad, Mounira M. "Kinship, Islam, or Oil: Culprits of Gender Inequality?" *Politics and Gender* 5, no. 4 (December 2009): 546.

——. *States and Women's Rights: The Making of Postcolonial Tunisia, Algeria, and Morocco.* Berkeley: University of California Press, 2001.

Charrad, Mounira M., and Amina Zarrugh. "Equal or Complementary? Women in the New Tunisian Constitution After the Arab Spring." *Journal of North African Studies* 19, no. 2 (March 2014): 230–43.

Chaturvedi, Neilan S., and Orlando Montoya. "Democracy, Oil, or Religion? Expanding Women's Rights in the Muslim World." *Politics and Religion* 6, no. 3 (September 2013): 596–617.

Childs, Sarah. *New Labour's Women MPs: Women Representing Women.* London: Routledge, 2004.

Childs, Sarah, and Mona Lena Krook. "Should Feminists Give Up on Critical Mass? A Contingent Yes." *Politics and Gender* 2, no. 4 (December 2006): 522–30.

Choucair, Julia. *Illusive Reform: Jordan's Stubborn Stability.* Washington, DC: Carnegie Endowment for International Peace, 2006.

Christophersen, Mona. "Jordan's 2013 Elections: A Further Boost for Tribes." Norwegian Centre for Conflict Resolution (NOREF), 2013. https://www.files.ethz.ch/isn/162496/3cfcb191c3644 dd32cdaoc2c3431d149.pdf.

Ciftci, Sabri, Walter Forrest, and Yusuf Tekin. "Committee Assignments in a Nascent Party System: The Case of the Turkish Grand National Assembly." *International Political Science Review* 29, no. 3 (June 2008): 303–24.

Clark, Janine A., and Francesco Cavatorta, eds. *Political Science Research in the Middle East and North Africa*, vol. 1. New York: Oxford University Press, 2018.

Clark, Janine Astrid, and Jillian Schwedler. "Who Opened the Window? Women's Activism in Islamist Parties." *Comparative Politics* 35, no. 3 (April 2003): 293.

Clayton, Amanda. "How Do Electoral Gender Quotas Affect Policy?" *Annual Review of Political Science* 24, no. 1 (May 11, 2021): 235–52.

Clayton, Amanda, Cecilia Josefsson, Robert Mattes, and Shaheen Mozaffar. "In Whose Interest? Gender and Mass–Elite Priority Congruence in Sub-Saharan Africa." *Comparative Political Studies* 52, no. 1 (January 2019): 69–101.

Clayton, Amanda, and Pär Zetterberg. "Quota Shocks: Electoral Gender Quotas and Government Spending Priorities Worldwide." *Journal of Politics* 80, no. 3 (July 2018): 916–32.

Coffé, Hilde, Catherine Bolzendahl, and Katia Schnellecke. "Parties, Issues, and Power: Women's Partisan Representation on German Parliamentary Committees." *European Journal of Politics and Gender* 2, no. 2 (June 2019): 257–81.

Coffé, Hilde, and Katia Schnellecke. "Female Representation in German Parliamentary Committees: 1972–2009." 7th ECPR General Conference, September 4–7, 2013, Bordeaux, France.

Coppedge, Michael, John Gerring, Carl Henrik Knutsen et al. "V-Dem [Country–Year/Country–Date] Dataset vii.i." Varieties of Democracy (V-Dem) Project, 2021.

Coppedge, M., J. Gerring, S. I. Lindberg et al. "V-Dem Codebook v6." Varieties of Democracy (V-Dem) Project, 2016.

Coppedge, M., J. Gerring, S. I. Lindberg et al. "V-Dem Codebook v9." Varieties of Democracy (V-Dem) Project, 2019.

Coppedge, M., J. Gerring, S. I. Lindberg et al. "V-Dem Country-Year Dataset v9." Varieties of Democracy (V-Dem) Project, 2019.

Cox, Gary W., and Mathew D. McCubbins. *Legislative Leviathan: Party Government in the House*. California Series on Social Choice and Political Economy. Berkely: University of California Press, 1993.

——. *Setting the Agenda: Responsible Party Government in the U.S. House of Representatives*. New York: Cambridge University Press, 2005.

Crowley, Jocelyn Elise. "When Tokens Matter." *Legislative Studies Quarterly* 29, no. 1 (February 2004): 109–36.

Crystal, Jill. *Oil and Politics in the Gulf: Rulers and Merchants in Kuwait and Qatar*. Cambridge: Cambridge University Press, 1990.

Dagestani, Amal, and Musa Shteiwi. "The Jordanian Woman and Political Participation." Amman, Jordan: CES, Center for Strategic Studies, University of Jordan, 1994.

Dahlerup, Drude. "From a Small to a Large Minority: Women in Scandinavian Politics." *Scandinavian Political Studies* 11, no. 4 (December 1988): 275–98.

——. "Women in Arab Parliaments: Can Gender Quotas Contribute to Democratization?" *Al-Raida Journal* 126, no. 27 (2009): 28–38.

——, ed. *Women, Quotas and Politics*. Routledge Research in Comparative Politics 10. London: Routledge, 2006.

Damgaard, Erik. "How Parties Control Committee Members." In *Parliaments and Majority Rule in Western Europe*, edited by Herbert Döring, 308–24. New York: St. Martin's, 1995.

Darcy, Robert. "Women in the State Legislative Power Structure: Committee Chairs." *Social Science Quarterly* 77, no. 4 (1996): 888–98.

Darhour, Hanane. "L'Autonomisation politique des femmes: Les implications de l'usage du gender quotas dans le Parlement Marocain." Unpublished PhD diss., University of Sidi Mohammed Ben Abdellah, Morocco, 2008.

Darhour, Hanane, and Drude Dahlerup. *Double-Edged Politics on Women's Rights in the MENA Region*. New York: Springer, 2020.

——. "Sustainable Representation of Women Through Gender Quotas: A Decade's Experience in Morocco." *Women's Studies International Forum* 41 (November 2013): 132–42.

Dashti, Ibrahim. "Women's Political Participation." Research and Data Unit of the Kuwaiti National Assembly, 2005.

Dashti, Ibrahim, and Ramzy Salama. "The Amendment of the Electoral Constituencies: A Critical Phase in Promoting the Democratic Experience in Kuwait." Research and Data Unit of the Kuwaiti National Assembly, 2004. Arabic.

David, Assaf, and Stefanie Nanes. "The Women's Quota in Jordan's Municipal Councils: International and Domestic Dimensions." *Journal of Women, Politics and Policy* 32, no. 4 (October 2011): 275–304.

Denoeux, Guilain, and Abdeslam Maghraoui. "King Hassan's Strategy of Political Dualism." *Middle East Policy* 5, no. 4 (January 1998): 104–30.

Diamond, Larry Jay. "Thinking About Hybrid Regimes." *Journal of Democracy* 13, no. 2 (2002): 21–35.

Dix, Robert H. "Democratization and the Institutionalization of Latin American Political Parties." *Comparative Political Studies* 24, no. 4 (January 1992): 488–511.

Dodson, Debra L., and Susan J. Carroll. *Reshaping the Agenda: Women in State Legislatures*. New Brunswick: Eagleton Institute of Politics, Rutgers, State University of New Jersey, 1991.

Dodson, Debra L., Susan J. Carroll, Ruth B. Mandel, Katherine E. Kleeman, Ronnee Schreiber, and Debra Liebowitz. *Voices, Views, Votes: The Impact of Women in the 103rd Congress*. Center for the American Woman and Politics (CAWP). New Brunswick: Eagleton Institute of Politics, Rutgers, State University of New Jersey, 1995.

Donno, Daniela, Sara Fox, and Joshua Kaasik. "International Incentives for Women's Rights in Dictatorships." *Comparative Political Studies* 55, no. 3 (March 2022): 451–92.

Donno, Daniela, and Anne-Kathrin Kreft. "Authoritarian Institutions and Women's Rights." *Comparative Political Studies* 52, no. 5 (April 2019): 720–53.

Donno, Daniela, and Bruce Russett. "Islam, Authoritarianism, and Female Empowerment: What Are the Linkages?" *World Politics* 56, no. 4 (July 2004): 582–607.

Doumato, Eleanor Abdella, and Marsha Pripstein Posusney, eds. *Women and Globalization in the Arab Middle East: Gender, Economy, and Society*. Boulder, CO: Lynne Rienner, 2003.

Driss El-Maarouf, Moulay, Mourad el Fahli, and Jerome Kuchejda. "Morocco." In *KAS Democracy Report 2009*, edited by Habil Karsten Grabow et al. Parties and Democracies Vol. II. Konrad Adenauer Stiftung, 2009. https://www.kas.de/en/single-title/-/content/kas-demokratiereport -2009, 257–68.

Dunne, Michele. "Women's Political Participation in the Gulf: A Conversation with Activists Fatin Bundagji (Saudi Arabia), Rola Dashti (Kuwait), Munira Fakhro (Bahrain)." Carnegie Endowment for International Peace, August 12, 2008.

El-Helou, Margaret. "Women and Parliamentary Elections in Lebanon." In *Arab Women and Political Participation*, edited by Hussein Abu Rumman, 200–220. Amman, Jordan: al-Urdon al-Jadid Research Centre, 2000.

Esber, Paul Maurice. "Citizen Wayn? The Struggle of Parliament in Contemporary Jordan." *Middle East Law and Governance* 13, no. 3 (June 2021): 294–313.

Espírito-Santo, Ana, and Edalina Rodrigues Sanches. "Who Gets What? The Interactive Effect of MPs' Sex in Committee Assignments in Portugal." *Parliamentary Affairs* 73, no. 2 (April 2020): 450–72.

Fakhro, Munira A. "Gender, Politics and the State in the Gulf Region." *Middle East Policy* 5, no. 3 (1997): 166–70.

Fallon, Kathleen M., Liam Swiss, and Jocelyn Viterna. "Resolving the Democracy Paradox: Democratization and Women's Legislative Representation in Developing Nations, 1975 to 2009." *American Sociological Review* 77, no. 3 (June 2012): 380–408.

Fenno, Richard F. *Congressmen in Committees*. The Study of Congress Series. Berkeley, CA: Institute of Governmental Studies Press, 1995.

Fish, M. Steven. "Islam and Authoritarianism." *World Politics* 55, no. 1 (October 2002): 4–37.

Fish, M. Steven, and Matthew Kroenig. *The Handbook of National Legislatures: A Global Survey*. Cambridge: Cambridge University Press, 2011.

Flintoff, Corey. "Women Take Their Place in Kuwait's Parliament," NPR, 2009. https://www.npr.org/2009/05/20/104340287/women-take-their-place-in-kuwaits-parliament.

Forman-Rabinovici, Aliza, and Udi Sommer. "Can the Descriptive-Substantive Link Survive Beyond Democracy? The Policy Impact of Women Representatives." *Democratization* 26, no. 8 (November 2019): 1513–33.

Franceschet, Susan, Mona Lena Krook, and Jennifer M. Piscopo, eds. *The Impact of Gender Quotas*. New York: Oxford University Press, 2012.

Freedom House. "Anxious Dictators, Wavering Democracies: Global Freedom Under Pressure." 2016. https://freedomhouse.org/sites/default/files/FH_FITW_Report_2016.pdf.

Frisch, Scott A., and Sean Q. Kelly. "A Place at the Table: Women's Committee Requests and Women's Committee Assignments in the U.S. House." *Women and Politics* 25, no. 3 (March 2003): 1–26.

Funk, Kendall D., Laura Morales, and Michelle M. Taylor-Robinson. "The Impact of Committee Composition and Agendas on Women's Participation: Evidence from a Legislature with Near Numerical Equality." *Politics and Gender* 13, no. 2 (June 2017): 253–75.

Galligan, Yvonne, Sara Clavero, and Marina Calloni. *Gender Politics and Democracy in Post-Socialist Europe*. Farmington Hills, MI: Barbara Budrich, 2007.

Gandhi, Jennifer. *Political Institutions Under Dictatorship*. Cambridge: Cambridge University Press, 2008.

Gandhi, Jennifer, and Ellen Lust-Okar. "Elections Under Authoritarianism." *Annual Review of Political Science* 12, no. 1 (June 2009): 403–22.

Gandhi, Jennifer, Ben Noble, and Milan Svolik. "Legislatures and Legislative Politics Without Democracy." *Comparative Political Studies* 53, no. 9 (August 2020): 1359–79.

Geddes, Barbara. *Paradigms and Sand Castles: Theory Building and Research Design in Comparative Politics*. Ann Arbor: University of Michigan Press, 2003.

——. "What Do We Know About Democratization After Twenty Years?" *Annual Review of Political Science* 2, no. 1 (June 1999): 115–44.

Geddes, Barbara, Joseph Wright, and Erica Frantz. "Autocratic Breakdown and Regime Transitions: A New Data Set." *Perspectives on Politics* 12, no. 2 (June 2014): 313–31.

——. *How Dictatorships Work: Power, Personalization, and Collapse.* Cambridge: Cambridge University Press, 2018.

Gehlbach, Scott, and Philip Keefer. "Investment Without Democracy: Ruling-Party Institutionalization and Credible Commitment in Autocracies." *Journal of Comparative Economics* 39, no. 2 (June 2011): 123–39.

Ghabra, Shafeeq N. "Balancing State and Society: The Islamic Movement in Kuwait." *Middle East Policy* 5, no. 2 (May 1997): 58–72.

——. "Kuwait and the Dynamics of Socio-economic Change." *Middle East Journal* 51 (1997): 358–72.

Gharaibeh, Mazen K., and Basel M. Al-Eideh. "Granting Kuwaiti Women the Right to Vote: The Impact on the Parliament's Composition and Political Streams (A Field and Analytical Study)." *Journal of the Social Sciences* 34, no. 2 (2006): 13–36.

Giannetti, Daniela, Andrea Pedrazzani, and Luca Pinto. "Personal Ambitions, Expertise and Parties' Control: Understanding Committee Assignment in the Italian Chamber of Deputies." *Parliamentary Affairs* 72, no. 1 (January 2019): 119–40.

Goetz, Anne Marie. "Women's Political Effectiveness: A Conceptual Framework." In *No Shortcuts to Power: African Women in Politics and Policy Making,* edited by Anne Marie Goetz and Shireen Hassim, 29–80. London: Zed, 2003.

Goulding, Kristine. "Unjustifiable Means to Unjustifiable Ends: Delegitimizing Parliamentary Gender Quotas in Tunisia." *Al-Raida Journal* 126–27 (2009): 71–78.

Grey, Sandra. "Does Size Matter? Critical Mass and New Zealand's Women MPs." *Parliamentary Affairs* 55, no. 1 (January 2002): 19–29.

——. "Numbers and Beyond: The Relevance of Critical Mass in Gender Research." *Politics and Gender* 2, no. 4 (December 2006): 492–502.

Grote, Rainer. "Parliaments in the MENA Region: Between Timid Reform and Regression. A Comparative Survey." *Middle East Law and Governance* 13, no. 3 (June 2021): 252–71.

Guriev, Sergei, and Daniel Treisman. "Informational Autocrats." *Journal of Economic Perspectives* 33, no. 4 (November 2019): 100–127.

Hamid, Shadi. *Islamic Exceptionalism: How the Struggle Over Islam Is Reshaping the World.* New York: St. Martin's, 2016.

Hassim, Shireen. "Perverse Consequences? The Impact of Quotas for Women on Democratization in Africa." In *Political Representation,* edited by Ian Shapiro, Susan C. Stokes, Elisabeth Jean Wood, and Alexander S. Kirshner, 211–35. New York: Cambridge University Press, 2010.

Hatem, Mervat F. "Economic and Political Liberation in Egypt and the Demise of State Feminism." *International Journal of Middle East Studies* 24, no. 2 (May 1992): 231–51.

Heath, Roseanna Michelle, Leslie A. Schwindt-Bayer, and Michelle M. Taylor-Robinson. "Women on the Sidelines: Women's Representation on Committees in Latin American Legislatures." *American Journal of Political Science* 49, no. 2 (April 2005): 420.

Henríquez, María José, and Tatiana Rein-Venegas. "The Resignification of the Chilean Dictatorship's International Discourse: Decolonisation, Religious Tolerance and Women's Rights." *Women's Studies International Forum* 82 (September 2020): 102389.

Herb, Michael. *The Wages of Oil: Parliaments and Economic Development in Kuwait and the UAE.* Ithaca, NY: Cornell University Press, 2014.

Hicken, Allen, and Erik Martinez Kuhonta, eds. *Party System Institutionalization in Asia: Democracies, Autocracies, and the Shadows of the Past.* Cambridge: Cambridge University Press, 2014.

———. "Shadows from the Past: Party System Institutionalization in Asia." *Comparative Political Studies* 44, no. 5 (May 2011): 572–97.

Hinnebusch, Raymond A. "Political Parties in MENA: Their Functions and Development." *British Journal of Middle Eastern Studies* 44, no. 2 (April 2017): 159–75.

Höhmann, Daniel. "When Do Female MPs Represent Women's Interests? Electoral Systems and the Legislative Behavior of Women." *Political Research Quarterly* 73, no. 4 (2019): https://doi.org/10.1177/1065912919859437.

Htun, Mala. "Women and Democracy." In *Constructing Democratic Governance in Latin America*, 2nd ed., edited by Jorge I. Domínguez and Michael Shifter, 200–220. Baltimore: Johns Hopkins University Press, 2003.

Htun, Mala, Marina Lacalle, and Juan Pablo Micozzi. "Does Women's Presence Change Legislative Behavior? Evidence from Argentina, 1983–2007." *Journal of Politics in Latin America* 5, no. 1 (April 2013): 95–125.

Htun, Mala, and S. Laurel Weldon. "The Civic Origins of Progressive Policy Change: Combating Violence Against Women in Global Perspective, 1975–2005." *American Political Science Review* 106, no. 3 (August 2012): 548–69.

Huntington, Samuel P. *Political Order in Changing Societies.* New Haven, CT: Yale University Press, 1968.

Hyde, Susan D., and Nikolay Marinov. "Which Elections Can Be Lost?" *Political Analysis* 20, no. 2 (2012): 191–210.

Inglehart, Ronald, and Pippa Norris. *Rising Tide: Gender Equality and Cultural Change Around the World.* New York: Cambridge University Press, 2003.

International IDEA. *Gender Quotas Database.* 2020. www.idea.int/data-tools/data/gender-quotas.

Inter-Parliamentary Union (IPU). "Women in National Parliaments." Inter-Parliamentary Union, September 2017. http://archive.ipu.org/wmn-e/arc/classif010917.htm.

———. "Women in National Parliaments." Inter-Parliamentary Union, February 2019. http://www.ipu.org/wmn-e/classif.htm.

———. "Women in National Parliaments." Inter-Parliamentary Union, October 2019. http://archive.ipu.org/wmn-e/world.htm.

———. "Women in National Parliaments." Inter-Parliamentary Union, September 2021. https://www.ipu.org/women-in-politics-2021.

Janda, Kenneth. *Political Parties: A Cross-National Survey.* New York: Free Press, 1980.

Jensen, Christian B., Sven-Oliver Proksch, and Jonathan B. Slapin. "Parliamentary Questions, Oversight, and National Opposition Status in the European Parliament: Parliamentary Questions." *Legislative Studies Quarterly* 38, no. 2 (May 2013): 259–82.

Jones, Bryan D., and Frank R. Baumgartner. "Representation and Agenda Setting." *Policy Studies Journal* 32, no. 1 (February 2004): 1–24.

Jones, Mark P. "Gender Quotas, Electoral Laws, and the Election of Women: Lessons from the Argentine Provinces." *Comparative Political Studies* 31, no. 1 (February 1998): 3–21.

——. "Legislator Gender and Legislator Policy Priorities in the Argentine Chamber of Deputies and the United States House of Representatives." *Policy Studies Journal* 25, no. 4 (December 1997): 613–29.

Joseph, Suad, and Susan Slyomovics, eds. *Women and Power in the Middle East.* Philadelphia: University of Pennsylvania Press, 2001.

Joshi, Devin K., and Rakkee Thimothy. "Long-Term Impacts of Parliamentary Gender Quotas in a Single-Party System: Symbolic Co-Option or Delayed Integration?" *International Political Science Review* 40, no. 4 (September 2019): 591–606.

Kao, Kristen, Ellen Lust, Marwa Shalaby, and Chagai M. Weiss. "Female Representation and Legitimacy: Evidence from a Harmonized Experiment in Jordan, Morocco, and Tunisia." *American Political Science Review* 118, no. 1 (2024): 495–503.

Karam, Azza. "Women in Politics Beyond Numbers." IDEA: Stockholm, 1998. https://www.idea .int/publications/catalogue/women-parliament-beyond-numbers.

Karmel, E. J. "Designing Decentralization in Jordan: Locating the Policy Among the Politics." *Middle East Law and Governance* 14, no. 2 (2021): 155–84.

Karpowitz, Christopher F., Tali Mendelberg, and Lauren Mattioli. "Why Women's Numbers Elevate Women's Influence, and When They Do Not: Rules, Norms, and Authority in Political Discussion." *Politics, Groups, and Identities* 3, no. 1 (January 2015): 149–77.

Kathlene, Lyn. "Power and Influence in State Legislative Policymaking: The Interaction of Gender and Position in Committee Hearing Debates." *American Political Science Review* 88, no. 3 (September 1994): 560–76.

Kerevel, Yann P., and Lonna Rae Atkeson. "Explaining the Marginalization of Women in Legislative Institutions." *Journal of Politics* 75, no. 4 (October 2013): 980–92.

Khalil, Andrea. "Tunisia's Women: Partners in Revolution." *Journal of North African Studies* 19, no. 2 (March 2014): 186–99.

King, Gary, Robert O. Keohane, and Sidney Verba. *Designing Social Inquiry: Scientific Inference in Qualitative Research.* Princeton, NJ: Princeton University Press, 2021.

Kinninmont, Jane. *Kuwait's Parliament: An Experiment in Semi-democracy.* London: Chatham House, 2012.

Kittilson, Miki Caul. *Challenging Parties, Changing Parliaments: Women and Elected Office in Contemporary Western Europe.* Parliaments and Legislatures. Columbus: Ohio State University Press, 2006.

Koss, Daniel. *Where the Party Rules: The Rank and File of China's Communist State.* Cambridge: Cambridge University Press, 2018.

Krehbiel, Keith, Kenneth A. Shepsle, and Barry R. Weingast. "Why Are Congressional Committees Powerful?" *American Political Science Review* 81, no. 3 (September 1987): 929–45.

Krook, Mona Lena. *Quotas for Women in Politics: Gender and Candidate Selection Reform Worldwide.* New York: Oxford University Press, 2009.

Krook, Mona Lena, and Diana Z. O'Brien. "The Politics of Group Representation: Quotas for Women and Minorities Worldwide." *Comparative Politics* 42, no. 3 (March 2010): 253–72.

Kunovich, Sheri, and Pamela Paxton. "Pathways to Power: The Role of Political Parties in Women's National Political Representation." *American Journal of Sociology* 111, no. 2 (2005): 505–52.

Lagrin, Driss. "The Quota System and the Reality of Women's Political Participation in Morocco." Civil Dialogue News, 2009. https://www.ahewar.org/debat/show.art.asp?aid=165619.

Lefèvre, Raphaël. "Balancing Act: Islamism and the Monarchy in Morocco." *Journal of North African Studies* 18, no. 4 (September 2013): 626–29.

Levitsky, Steven, and Lucan Way. "The Rise of Competitive Authoritarianism." *Journal of Democracy* 13, no. 2 (2002): 51–65.

Liddell, James. "Gender Quotas in Clientelist Systems: The Case of Morocco's National List." *Al-Raida Journal* 126–27 (2009): 79–86.

Lindberg, Staffan I., Nils Düpont, Masaaki Higashijima et al. "Codebook Varieties of Party Identity and Organization (V-Party) V2." Varieties of Democracy (V–Dem) Project, 2022.

Lindeboom, Gert-Jan. "Public Priorities in Government's Hands: Corresponding Policy Agendas in the Netherlands?" *Acta Politica* 47, no. 4 (October 2012): 443–67.

Linz, Juan J., and Alfred C. Stepan. *Problems of Democratic Transition and Consolidation: Southern Europe, South America, and Post-Communist Europe.* Baltimore: Johns Hopkins University Press, 1996.

Lloren, Anouk. "Gender Quotas in Morocco: Lessons for Women's Descriptive and Symbolic Representation." *Representation* 50, no. 4 (October 2014): 527–38.

Loidolt, Bryce, and Quinn Mecham. "Parliamentary Opposition Under Hybrid Regimes: Evidence from Egypt: Parliamentary Opposition Under Hybrid Regimes." *Legislative Studies Quarterly* 41, no. 4 (November 2016): 997–1022.

Long, J. Scott. *Regression Models for Categorical and Limited Dependent Variables.* Advanced Quantitative Techniques in the Social Sciences 7. Thousand Oaks, CA: Sage, 1997.

Longva, Anh Nga. "Nationalism in Pre-Modern Guise: The Discourse on Hadhar and Badu in Kuwait." *International Journal of Middle East Studies* 38, no. 2 (May 2006): 171.

Lorch, Jasmin, and Bettina Bunk. "Gender Politics, Authoritarian Regime Resilience, and the Role of Civil Society in Algeria and Mozambique." *SSRN Electronic Journal*, 2016. https://doi.org/10.2139/ssrn.2863764.

Lovenduski, Joni, and Pippa Norris. "Westminster Women: The Politics of Presence." *Political Studies* 51, no. 1 (March 2003): 84–102.

Lü, Xiaobo, Mingxing Liu, and Feiyue Li. "Policy Coalition Building in an Authoritarian Legislature: Evidence from China's National Assemblies (1983–2007)." *Comparative Political Studies* 53, no. 9 (August 2020): 1380–416.

Lührmann, Anna, Nils Düpont, Masaaki Higashijima et al. "V-Party Dataset V1." V-Dem Institute, 2020. https://doi.org/10.23696/VPARTYDSV1.

Lührmann, Anna, Marcus Tannenberg, and Staffan I. Lindberg. "Regimes of the World (RoW): Opening New Avenues for the Comparative Study of Political Regimes." *Politics and Governance* 6, no. 1 (2018): 60–77. https://doi.org/10.17645/pag.v6i1.1214.

Lust, Ellen. "Competitive Clientelism in the Middle East." *Journal of Democracy* 20, no. 3 (2009): 122–35.

Lust, Ellen, and Lindsay J. Benstead. "Is the Future Female? Lessons from a Conjoint Experiment on Voter Preferences in Six Arab Countries." *Comparative Political Studies* 57, no. 14 (2024): 2376–413.

Lust, Ellen, and David Waldner. "Parties in Transitional Democracies: Authoritarian Legacies and Post-Authoritarian Challenges in the Middle East and North Africa." In *Parties, Movements, and Democracy in the Developing World*, edited by Nancy Bermeo and Deborah J. Yashar, 157–89. Cambridge Studies in Contentious Politics. Cambridge: Cambridge University Press, 2016.

Lust-Okar, Ellen. "The Decline of Jordanian Political Parties: Myth or Reality?" *International Journal of Middle East Studies* 33, no. 4 (2001): 545–69.

——. "Elections Under Authoritarianism: Preliminary Lessons from Jordan." *Democratization* 13, no. 3 (June 2006): 456–71.

——. *Structuring Conflict in the Arab World: Incumbents, Opponents, and Institutions.* Cambridge: Cambridge University Press, 2005.

Lust-Okar, Ellen, and Amaney Ahmad Jamal. "Rulers and Rules: Reassessing the Influence of Regime Type on Electoral Law Formation." *Comparative Political Studies* 35, no. 3 (April 2002): 337–66.

Mackay, Fiona. "'Thick' Conceptions of Substantive Representation: Women, Gender and Political Institutions." *Representation* 44, no. 2 (July 2008): 125–39.

Magaloni, Beatriz. "Credible Power-Sharing and the Longevity of Authoritarian Rule." *Comparative Political Studies* 41, no. 4–5 (April 2008): 715–41.

——. *Voting for Autocracy: Hegemonic Party Survival and Its Demise in Mexico.* Cambridge: Cambridge University Press, 2006.

Magaloni, Beatriz, and Ruth Kricheli. "Political Order and One-Party Rule." *Annual Review of Political Science* 13, no. 1 (May 2010): 123–43.

Maghraoui, Abdeslam. "Monarchy and Political Reform in Morocco." *Journal of Democracy* 12, no. 1 (2001): 73–86.

Maghraoui, Driss. "Constitutional Reforms in Morocco: Between Consensus and Subaltern Politics." *Journal of North African Studies* 16, no. 4 (December 2011): 679–99.

Mainwaring, Scott, ed. *Party Systems in Latin America: Institutionalization, Decay, and Collapse.* New York: Cambridge University Press, 2018.

——. *Rethinking Party Systems in the Third Wave of Democratization: The Case of Brazil.* Stanford, CA: Stanford University Press, 1999.

Mainwaring, Scott, and Timothy Scully, eds. *Building Democratic Institutions: Party Systems in Latin America.* Stanford, CA: Stanford University Press, 1995.

Mainwaring, Scott, and Edurne Zoco. "Political Sequences and the Stabilization of Interparty Competition: Electoral Volatility in Old and New Democracies." *Party Politics* 13, no. 2 (March 2007): 155–78.

Malesky, Edmund, and Paul Schuler. "Nodding or Needling: Analyzing Delegate Responsiveness in an Authoritarian Parliament." *American Political Science Review* 104, no. 3 (August 2010): 482–502.

———. "The Single-Party Dictator's Dilemma: Information in Elections Without Opposition." *Legislative Studies Quarterly* 36, no. 4 (November 2011): 491–530.

Maltzman, Forrest. *Competing Principals: Committees, Parties, and the Organization of Congress.* Ann Arbor: University of Michigan Press, 1997.

Manion, Melanie. *Information for Autocrats: Representation in Chinese Local Congresses.* Cambridge: Cambridge University Press, 2015.

Mansbridge, Jane. "Quota Problems: Combating the Dangers of Essentialism." *Politics and Gender* 1, no. 4 (December 2005): 622–38.

———. "Should Blacks Represent Blacks and Women Represent Women? A Contingent 'Yes.'" *Journal of Politics* 61, no. 3 (August 1999): 628–57.

Martin, Shane. "Parliamentary Questions, the Behaviour of Legislators, and the Function of Legislatures: An Introduction." *Journal of Legislative Studies* 17, no. 3 (September 2011): 259–70.

———. "Using Parliamentary Questions to Measure Constituency Focus: An Application to the Irish Case." *Political Studies* 59, no. 2 (June 2011): 472–88.

Martin, Shane, and Tim A. Mickler. "Committee Assignments: Theories, Causes and Consequences." *Parliamentary Affairs* 72, no. 1 (January 2019): 77–98.

Mashagbeh, Ameen, and Abdulazeez Alnowidi. "Parties and Parliamentary Experiences in Jordan and Morocco." Alquds Center for Political Studies, 2016. https://www.alqudscenter.org/index.php?l=en&pg=UFVCTElDQVRJTo5T&catID=21&id=2325.

Mateo Díaz, Mercedes. *Representing Women? Female Legislators in West European Parliaments.* ECPR Monographs Series. Colchester, United Kingdom: ECPR Press, 2005.

Matland, Richard E. "Enhancing Women's Political Participation: Legislative Recruitment and Electoral Systems." In *Women in Parliament: Beyond Numbers*, edited by Julie Ballington and Azza Karam, 93–111. Stockholm, Sweden: International Institute for Democracy and Electoral Assistance, 2005.

Matland, Richard E., and Donley T. Studlar. "The Contagion of Women Candidates in Single-Member District and Proportional Representation Electoral Systems: Canada and Norway." *Journal of Politics* 58, no. 3 (August 1996): 707–33.

Mattson, Ingvar, and Kaare Strøm. "Parliamentary Committees." In *Parliaments and Majority Rule in Western Europe*, edited by Herbert Döring, 249–307. Mannheim, Germany: Mannheim Centre for European Social Research, 1995.

Mayhew, David R. *Congress: The Electoral Connection.* New Haven, CT: Yale University Press, 1974.

Mechkova, Valeriya, and Ruth Carlitz. "Gendered Accountability: When and Why Do Women's Policy Priorities Get Implemented?" *European Political Science Review* 13, no. 1 (February 2021): 3–21.

Mechkova, Valeriya, and Amanda B. Edgell. "Substantive Representation, Women's Health, and Regime Type." *Comparative Political Studies* 57, no. 14 (2024): 2449–81.

MEED. "Reformists Suffer Election Defeat." *MEED: Middle East Economic Digest*, 2003. https://www.meed.com/reformists-suffer-election-defeat/.

Meng, Anne. *Constraining Dictatorship: From Personalized Rule to Institutionalized Regimes.* New York: Cambridge University Press, 2020.

Miller, Michael K. "Democratic Pieces: Autocratic Elections and Democratic Development Since 1815." *British Journal of Political Science* 45, no. 3 (July 2015): 501–30.

——. "Elections, Information, and Policy Responsiveness in Autocratic Regimes." *Comparative Political Studies* 48, no. 6 (May 2015): 691–727.

Moghadam, Valentine M. "Democratization and Women's Political Leadership in North Africa." *Journal of International Affairs* 68, no. 1 (2014): 59–78.

——. *Modernizing Women: Gender and Social Change in the Middle East*, 3rd ed. Boulder, CO: Lynne Rienner, 2013.

Moghadam, Valentine M., and Fatemeh Haghighatjoo. "Women and Political Leadership in an Authoritarian Context: A Case Study of the Sixth Parliament in the Islamic Republic of Iran." *Politics and Gender* 12, no. 1 (March 2016): 168–97.

Morton, Lura. "Women in Parliament: A Study of Issue-Specific Female Coalition Building in Morocco." Independent Study Project (ISP) Collection, 2018. https://digitalcollections.sit .edu/isp_collection/2836.

Muasher, Marwan. "The Path to Sustainable Political Parties in the Arab World." Sada. Washington, DC: Carnegie Endowment for International Peace, 2013. https://carnegieendowment .org/posts/2013/11/the-path-to-sustainable-political-parties-in-the-arab-world?lang=en.

Mughni, Haya al-. *Women in Kuwait: The Politics of Gender*. London: Saqi, 1993.

Mughni, Haya al-, and Mary Ann Tétreault. "Political Actors Without the Franchise: Women and Politics in Kuwait." In *Monarchies and Nations: Globalisation and Identity in the Arab States in the Gulf*, edited by Paul Dresch and James Piscatori, 203–21. London: I. B. Tauris, 2005.

Murray, Rainbow, Mona Lena Krook, and Katherine A. R. Opello. "Why Are Gender Quotas Adopted? Party Pragmatism and Parity in France." *Political Research Quarterly* 65, no. 3 (September 2012): 529–43.

Murray, Rainbow, and Réjane Sénac. "Explaining Gender Gaps in Legislative Committees." *Journal of Women, Politics and Policy* 39, no. 3 (July 2018): 310–35.

National Democratic Institute. "Final Report on the Moroccan Legislative Elections." 2007. http://www.ndi.org/files/2316_ma_report_electionsfinal_en_051508_1.pdf.

National Democratic Institute. "International Observation Mission Morocco November 2011: Preliminary Election Statement." 2011. https://www.ndi.org/sites/default/files/Morocco -Preliminary-Statement-112611-ENG.pdf.

Noble, Ben. "Authoritarian Amendments: Legislative Institutions as Intraexecutive Constraints in Post-Soviet Russia." *Comparative Political Studies* 53, no. 9 (August 2020): 1417–54.

Noh, Yuree, and Marwa Shalaby. "Kuwaitis Voted Saturday. Opposition Gains Send a Strong Signal About the Economy." *Washington Post*, November 29, 2016. https://www.washingtonpost .com/news/monkey-cage/wp/2016/11/29/kuwaitis-voted-saturday-opposition-gains-send -a-strong-signal-about-the-economy/.

——. "Who Supports Gender Quotas in Transitioning and Authoritarian States in the Middle East and North Africa?" *Comparative Political Studies* 57, no. 14 (2024): 2313–47.

Norris, Pippa. "Why Do Arab States Lag the World in Gender Equality?" *SSRN Electronic Journal*, 2009. https://papers.ssrn.com/sol3/papers.cfm?abstract_id=1474820.

Norris, Pippa, and Joni Lovenduski. *Political Recruitment: Gender, Race, and Class in the British Parliament*. New York: Cambridge University Press, 1995.

Norton, Philip. "Introduction: Parliament Since 1960." In *Parliamentary Questions*, edited by Mark Franklin and Philip Norton, 1–22. New York: Clarendon, 1993.

Obeidat, Omar. "New Lower House Includes 74 New Faces." *Jordan Times*, September 24, 2016. http://www.jordantimes.com/news/local/new-lower-house-includes-74-new-faces.

O'Brien, Diana Z. "Gender and Select Committee Elections in the British House of Commons." *Politics and Gender* 8, no. 2 (June 2012): 178–204.

Olimat, Muhamad S. "Arab Spring and Women in Kuwait." *Journal of International Women's Studies* 13, no. 5 (2012): 180–94.

——. "Women and the Kuwaiti National Assembly." *Journal of International Women's Studies* 12, no. 3 (2011): 76–95. https://vc.bridgew.edu/jiws/vol12/iss3/6.

——. "Women and Politics in Kuwait." *Journal of International Women's Studies* 11, no. 2 (2009): 199–212. https://vc.bridgew.edu/jiws/vol11/iss2/13.

Olivella, Santiago, and Margit Tavits. "Legislative Effects of Electoral Mandates." *British Journal of Political Science* 44, no. 2 (April 2014): 301–21.

Opalo, Ken Ochieng'. "Constrained Presidential Power in Africa? Legislative Independence and Executive Rule Making in Kenya, 1963–2013." *British Journal of Political Science* 50, no. 4 (October 2020): 1341–58.

——. *Legislative Development in Africa: Politics and Postcolonial Legacies*. Cambridge: Cambridge University Press, 2019.

OPEC. "Organization of the Petroleum Exporting Countries." 2015. http://www.opec.org/opec_web/en/.

Organisation for Economic Co-operation and Development. "Women in Business: Policies to Support Women's Entrepreneurship Development in the MENA Region." OECD, 2012. https://www.oecd.org/en/publications/women-in-business_9789264179073-en.html.

Organisation for Economic Co-operation and Development and Center of Arab Woman for Training and Research. *Women in Public Life: Gender, Law and Policy in the Middle East and North Africa*. Paris: OECD Publishing, 2014. https://doi.org/10.1787/9789264224636-en.

Osborn, Tracy L. *How Women Represent Women: Political Parties, Gender, and Representation in the State Legislatures*. New York: Oxford University Press, 2012.

Panebianco, Angelo. *Political Parties: Organization and Power*. Cambridge Studies in Modern Political Economies. Cambridge: Cambridge University Press, 1988.

Pansardi, Pamela, and Michelangelo Vercesi. "Party Gatekeeping and Women's Appointment to Parliamentary Committees: Evidence from the Italian Case." *Parliamentary Affairs* 70, no. 1 (January 2017): 62–83.

Papada, Evie, David Altman, Fabio Angiolillo et al. "Defiance in the Face of Autocratization. Democracy Report 2023." *Democracy Report*, 2023. https://www.v-dem.net/documents/29/V-dem_democracyreport2023_lowres.pdf.

Paxton, Pamela, and Melanie Hughes. *Women, Politics, and Power: A Global Perspective*. Thousand Oaks, CA: Sage, 2014.

Pedersen, Mogens N. "The Dynamics of European Party Systems: Changing Patterns of Electoral Volatility." *European Journal of Political Research* 7, no. 1 (March 1979): 1–26.

Pekkanen, Robert, Benjamin Nyblade, and Ellis S. Krauss. "Electoral Incentives in Mixed-Member Systems: Party, Posts, and Zombie Politicians in Japan." *American Political Science Review* 100, no. 2 (May 2006): 183–93.

Pelke, Lars. "Party Institutionalization, Authoritarian Regime Types, and Women's Political Equality." *Contemporary Politics* 27 (April 2021): 461–86.

Pellicer, Miquel, and Eva Wegner. "Socio-Economic Voter Profile and Motives for Islamist Support in Morocco." *Party Politics* 20, no. 1 (January 2014): 116–33.

Pemstein, Daniel, Kyle L. Marquardt, Eitan Tzelgov et al. "The V-Dem Measurement Model: Latent Variable Analysis for Cross-National and Cross-Temporal Expert-Coded Data." *SSRN Electronic Journal*, 2019. https://doi.org/10.2139/ssrn.3395892.

Phillips, Anne. *The Politics of Presence.* New York: Oxford University Press, 1995.

Pitkin, Hanna Fenichel. *The Concept of Representation.* Berkeley: University of California Press, 1969.

Poguntke, Thomas, Susan E. Scarrow, Paul D. Webb et al. "Party Rules, Party Resources and the Politics of Parliamentary Democracies: How Parties Organize in the 21st Century." *Party Politics* 22, no. 6 (November 2016): 661–78.

Ponce, Aldo F., and Susan E. Scarrow. "Party Institutionalization and Partisan Mobilization." *Government and Opposition* 58 (February 2022): 745–64.

Prihatini, Ella. "Explaining Gender Gaps in Indonesian Legislative Committees." *Parliamentary Affairs* 74 (2019): 206–29.

Proksch, Sven-Oliver, and Jonathan B. Slapin. "Parliamentary Questions and Oversight in the European Union." *European Journal of Political Research* 50, no. 1 (January 2011): 53–79.

Quota Project. *Global Database of Quotas for Women*, 2021. www.quotaproject.org.

Raaum, Nina C., Lauri Karvonen, and Per Selle. "The Political Representation of Women: A Bird's Eye View." In *Women in Nordic Politics—Closing the Gap*, edited by Lauri Karvonen and Per Selle, 25–58. Dartmouth, MA: Dartmouth Publishing, 1995.

Randall, Vicky. *Women and Politics: An International Perspective.* 2nd ed. Chicago: University of Chicago Press, 1987.

Randall, Vicky, and Lars Svåsand. "Party Institutionalization in New Democracies." *Party Politics* 8, no. 1 (January 2002): 5–29.

Randjbar-Daemi, Siavush, Eskandar Sadeghi-Boroujerdi, and Lauren Banko. "Introduction to Political Parties in the Middle East: Historical Trajectories and Future Prospects." *British Journal of Middle Eastern Studies* 44, no. 2 (April 2017): 155–58.

Rasch, Bjørn Erik. "Opposition Parties, Electoral Incentives and the Control of Government Ministers: Parliamentary Questioning in Norway." In *Parlamente, Agendasetzung und Vetospieler*, edited by Steffen Ganghof, Christoph Hönnige, and Christian Stecker, 199–214. Wiesbaden, Germany: VS Verlag für Sozialwissenschaften, 2009.

Rasmussen, Magnus B., and Carl Henrik Knutsen. "Party Institutionalization and Welfare State Development." *British Journal of Political Science* 51, no. 3 (July 2021): 1203–29.

Reingold, Beth. "Women as Officeholders: Linking Descriptive and Substantive Representation." In *Political Women and American Democracy*, edited by Christina Wolbrecht, Karen Beckwith, and Lisa Baldez, 128–47. Cambridge: Cambridge University Press, 2008.

Resta, Valeria. "Leftist Parties in the Arab Region Before and After the Arab Uprisings: 'Unrequited Love'?" In *Political Parties in the Arab World*, edited by Francesco Cavatorta and Lise Storm, 21–48. Edinburgh, United Kingdom: Edinburgh University Press, 2018.

Reynolds, Andrew. "Women in the Legislatures and Executives of the World: Knocking at the Highest Glass Ceiling." *World Politics* 51, no. 4 (July 1999): 547–72.

Reynolds, Andrew, Ben Reilly, and Andrew Ellis. *Electoral System Design: The New International IDEA Handbook*. Handbook Series. Stockholm, Sweden: International Institute for Democracy and Electoral Assistance, 2005.

Riera, Pedro, and Francisco Cantú. "Determinants of Legislative Committee Membership in Proportional Representation Systems." *Party Politics* 24, no. 5 (September 2018): 524–35.

Rizzo, Helen, Abdel-Hamid Abdel-Latif, and Katherine Meyer. "The Relationship Between Gender Equality and Democracy: A Comparison of Arab Versus Non-Arab Muslim Societies." *Sociology* 41, no. 6 (December 2007): 1151–70.

Rizzo, Helen Mary. *Islam, Democracy, and the Status of Women: The Case of Kuwait*. Middle East Studies. New York: Routledge, 2005.

Rosenthal, Cindy Simon. *When Women Lead: Integrative Leadership in State Legislatures*. New York: Oxford University Press, 1998.

Ross, Michael L. "Does Oil Hinder Democracy?" *World Politics* 53, no. 3 (April 2001): 325–61.

——. "Oil, Islam, and Women." *American Political Science Review* 102, no. 1 (February 2008): 107–23.

Rule, Wilma. "Why Women Don't Run: The Critical Contextual Factors in Women's Legislative Recruitment." *Western Political Quarterly* 34, no. 1 (March 1981): 60.

Ryan, Curtis R. "Deja Vu All Over Again? Jordan's 2010 Elections." *Foreign Policy*, November 15, 2010. https://foreignpolicy.com/2010/11/15/deja-vu-all-over-again-jordans-2010-elections/.

Sabbagh, Amal. "Overview of Women's Political Representation in the Arab Region: Opportunities and Challenges." *Arab Quota Report: Selected Case Studies*, 2007. https://www.idea.int/sites/default/files/publications/the-arab-quota-report-selected-case-studies.pdf.

Sadiqi, Fatima, and Moha Ennaji. "The Feminization of Public Space: Women's Activism, the Family Law, and Social Change in Morocco." *Journal of Middle East Women's Studies* 2, no. 2 (April 2006): 86–114.

Salhi, Zahia Smail. "Algerian Women, Citizenship, and the 'Family Code.'" *Gender and Development* 11, no. 3 (November 2003): 27–35.

Sanbonmatsu, Kira. "Political Parties and the Recruitment of Women to State Legislatures." *Journal of Politics* 64, no. 3 (August 2002): 791–809.

Sandberg, Eve, and Kenza Aqertit. *Moroccan Women, Activists, and Gender Politics*. Lanham, MD: Lexington Books, 2017.

Sarhrouny, Yasmina. "Kuwait: Citizens' Perceptions of Women in Politics." *National Democratic Institute for International Affairs* 1, no. 1 (2007): 1–28.

Sartori, Giovanni. *Parties and Party Systems: Volume 1: A Framework for Analysis*. Cambridge: Cambridge University Press, 1976.

Sassoon, Joseph. *Anatomy of Authoritarianism in the Arab Republics.* Cambridge: Cambridge University Press, 2016.

Sater, James N. "Changing Politics from Below? Women Parliamentarians in Morocco." *Democratization* 14, no. 4 (August 2007): 723–42.

——. "Parliamentary Elections and Authoritarian Rule in Morocco." *Middle East Journal* 63, no. 3 (July 1, 2009): 381–400.

——. "Reserved Seats, Patriarchy, and Patronage in Morocco." In *The Impact of Gender Quotas,* edited by Susan Franceschet, Mona Lena Krook, and Jennifer M. Piscopo. New York: Oxford University Press, 2012.

Sawi, Ali. "State of Parliament in the Arab States." *SSRN Electronic Journal,* 2018. https://papers.ssrn.com/sol3/papers.cfm?abstract_id=3294968.

Schedler, Andreas. "The Menu of Manipulation." *Journal of Democracy* 13, no. 2 (2002): 36–50.

——. "The Nested Game of Democratization by Elections." *International Political Science Review* 23, no. 1 (January 2002): 103–22.

——. *The Politics of Uncertainty: Sustaining and Subverting Electoral Authoritarianism.* New York: Oxford University Press, 2013.

Schmidt, Gregory D. "The Election of Women in List PR Systems: Testing the Conventional Wisdom." *Electoral Studies* 28, no. 2 (June 2009): 190–203.

Schmidt, Gregory D., and Kyle L. Saunders. "Effective Quotas, Relative Party Magnitude, and the Success of Female Candidates: Peruvian Municipal Elections in Comparative Perspective." *Comparative Political Studies* 37, no. 6 (August 2004): 704–34.

Schuler, Paul. "Position Taking or Position Ducking? A Theory of Public Debate in Single-Party Legislatures." *Comparative Political Studies* 53, no. 9 (August 2020): 1493–524.

Schwedler, Jillian. "Jordan: The Quiescent Opposition." Washington, DC: Wilson Center, 2015. https://www.wilsoncenter.org/article/jordan-the-quiescent-opposition.

Schwindt-Bayer, Leslie A. "Making Quotas Work: The Effect of Gender Quota Laws on the Election of Women." *Legislative Studies Quarterly* 34, no. 1 (February 2009): 5–28.

——. *Political Power and Women's Representation in Latin America.* New York: Oxford University Press, 2010.

——. "Still Supermadres? Gender and the Policy Priorities of Latin American Legislators." *American Journal of Political Science* 50, no. 3 (July 2006): 570–85.

Seawright, Jason, and John Gerring. "Case Selection Techniques in Case Study Research: A Menu of Qualitative and Quantitative Options." *Political Research Quarterly* 61, no. 2 (June 2008): 294–308.

Shalaby, Marwa. "The Islamists Are Back in Morocco: How Did They Do It?" *Washington Post,* 2016. https://www.washingtonpost.com/news/monkey-cage/wp/2016/10/20/the-islamists-are-back-in-morocco-how-did-they-do-it/.

——. "Support for Gender Quotas and Perceived Corruption in Developing Democracies: Evidence from Lebanon." In *Corruption and Informal Practices in the Middle East and North Africa.* Corruption and Anti-Corruption Studies. New York: Routledge, 2019.

——. "Women's Political Representation and Authoritarianism in the Arab World." Project on Middle East Political Science, 2016. https://pomeps.org/womens-political-representation-and-authoritarianism-in-the-arab-world.

——. "Women's Political Representation in Kuwait: An Untold Story." James A. Baker III Institute for Public Policy, 2015. https://www.bakerinstitute.org/sites/default/files/2015-09/import/WRME-pub-PoliRep-Kuwait-091515.pdf.

Shalaby, Marwa, and Abdullah Aydogan. "Elite-Citizen Linkages and Issue Congruency Under Competitive Authoritarianism." *Parliamentary Affairs* 73, no. 1 (January 1, 2020): 66–88.

Shalaby, Marwa M., and Laila Elimam. "Arab Women in the Legislative Process." Sada. Washington, DC: Carnegie Endowment for International Peace, 2017. https://carnegieendowment.org/sada/2017/04/arab-women-in-the-legislative-process?lang=en.

——. "Examining Female Membership and Leadership of Legislative Committees in Jordan." In *Double-Edged Politics on Women's Rights in the MENA Region*, edited by Hanane Darhour and Drude Dahlerup, 231–55. Cham, Switzerland: Palgrave Macmillan, 2020.

——. "Women in Legislative Committees in Arab Parliaments." *Comparative Politics* 53, no. 1 (October 2020): 139–67.

Shalaby, Marwa, and Scott Williamson. "Executive Compliance with Parliamentary Powers Under Authoritarianism: Evidence from Jordan." *Governance* 37, no. 4 (2024): 1163–82.

——. *How Parliaments Matter: Policy and Opposition in the Middle East's Authoritarian Legislatures*. Unpublished manuscript, 2023.

Shaw, Malcolm. "Parliamentary Committees: A Global Perspective." *Journal of Legislative Studies* 4, no. 1 (March 1998): 225–51.

Sika, Nadine, and Yasmin Khodary. "One Step Forward, Two Steps Back? Egyptian Women Within the Confines of Authoritarianism." *Journal of International Women's Studies* 13, no. 5 (2012): 91–100.

Skjeie, Hege. "The Rhetoric of Difference: On Women's Inclusion Into Political Elites." *Politics and Society* 19, no. 2 (June 1991): 233–63.

Škrabáková, Katarína. "Islamist Women as Candidates in Elections: A Comparison of the Party of Justice and Development in Morocco and the Muslim Brotherhood in Egypt." *Die Welt Des Islams* 57, no. 3–4 (October 2017): 329–59.

Stockemer, Daniel. "Women's Parliamentary Representation: Are Women More Highly Represented in (Consolidated) Democracies Than in Non-Democracies?" *Contemporary Politics* 15, no. 4 (December 2009): 429–43.

Storm, Lise. "Parties and Party System Change." In *Political Change in the Middle East and North Africa: After the Arab Spring*, edited by Szmolka Inmaculada Szmolka, 63–88. Edinburgh, United Kingdom: Edinburgh University Press, 2017.

——. *Party Politics and Prospects for Democracy in North Africa*. Boulder, CO: Lynne Rienner, 2014.

Strøm, Kaare. "Parliamentary Committees in European Democracies." *Journal of Legislative Studies* 4, no. 1 (March 1998): 21–59.

Studlar, Donley T., and Ian McAllister. "Does a Critical Mass Exist? A Comparative Analysis of Women's Legislative Representation Since 1950." *European Journal of Political Research* 41, no. 2 (March 2002): 233–53.

Svolik, Milan W. *The Politics of Authoritarian Rule*. Cambridge: Cambridge University Press, 2012.

Swers, Michele L. "Are Women More Likely to Vote for Women's Issue Bills Than Their Male Colleagues?" *Legislative Studies Quarterly* 23, no. 3 (August 1998): 435.

———. *The Difference Women Make: The Policy Impact of Women in Congress.* Chicago: University of Chicago Press, 2002.

Szmolka, Inmaculada. "Party System Fragmentation in Morocco." *Journal of North African Studies* 15, no. 1 (March 2010): 13–37.

———. "Political Change in North Africa and the Arab Middle East: Constitutional Reforms and Electoral Processes." *Arab Studies Quarterly* 36, no. 2 (2014): 128.

Tabbaa, Yasmeen. "New Spaces, More Politics? Women, Tribes, and Quotas in Jordan." Working Paper. Amman, Jordan: Center for Strategic Studies, 2009.

Tajali, Mona. "Protesting Gender Discrimination from Within: Women's Political Representation on Behalf of Islamic Parties." *British Journal of Middle Eastern Studies* 44, no. 2 (April 2017): 176–93.

Tam, Waikeung. "Do Female Legislators Have Different Policy Priorities Than Their Male Colleagues in an Undemocratic/Semi-Democratic Legislature? The Case of Hong Kong." *Journal of Legislative Studies* 23, no. 1 (January 2017): 44–70.

Tate, Katherine. *Black Faces in the Mirror: African Americans and Their Representatives in the U.S. Congress.* Princeton, NJ: Princeton University Press, 2004.

Tavana, Daniel L., and Erin York. "Cooptation in Practice: Measuring Legislative Opposition in an Authoritarian Regime." Preprint. Open Science Framework, November 2020. https://osf.io/preprints/osf/fjdw5_v1.

Taylor-Robinson, Michelle M., and Roseanna Michelle Heath. "Do Women Legislators Have Different Policy Priorities Than Their Male Colleagues? A Critical Case Test." *Women and Politics* 24, no. 4 (January 2003): 77–101.

Teo, Terence K. "Inequality Under Authoritarian Rule." *Government and Opposition* 56, no. 2 (April 2021): 201–25.

Teorell, Jan, Stefan Dahlberg, Sören Holmberg, Bo Rothstein, Anna Khomenko, and Richard Svensson. "The Quality of Government Standard Dataset, Version Jan16." University of Gothenburg: The Quality of Government Institute, 2016. http://www.qog.pol.gu.se doi:10.18157/QoGStdJan16.

Tétreault, Mary Ann. "A State of Two Minds: State Cultures, Women, and Politics in Kuwait." *International Journal of Middle East Studies* 33, no. 2 (May 2001): 203–20.

———. *Stories of Democracy: Politics and Society in Contemporary Kuwait.* New York: Columbia University Press, 2000.

Thames, Frank C. "Women's Legislative Representation in Authoritarian Regimes." *SSRN Electronic Journal* (July 2017). https://doi.org/10.2139/ssrn.3001247.

Thomas, Sue. *How Women Legislate.* New York: Oxford University Press, 1994.

Thomas, Sue, and Susan Welch. "The Impact of Gender on Activities and Priorities of State Legislators." *Political Research Quarterly* 44, no. 2 (June 1991): 445–56.

Towns, Ann. "Understanding the Effects of Larger Ratios of Women in National Legislatures: Proportions and Gender Differentiation in Sweden and Norway." *Women and Politics* 25, no. 1–2 (October 2008): 1–29.

Tripp, Aili Mari. "Do Arab Women Need Electoral Quotas?" *Foreign Policy*, January 19, 2012. https://foreignpolicy.com/2012/01/19/do-arab-women-need-electoral-quotas/.

———. "How African Autocracies Instrumentalize Women Leaders." *Politics and Gender* 20, no. 1 (2024): 217–22.

———. "Legislative Quotas for Women: Implications for Governance in Africa." In *African Parliaments*, edited by M. A. Mohamed Salih, 48–60. New York: Palgrave Macmillan, 2005.

———. *Seeking Legitimacy: Why Arab Autocracies Adopt Women's Rights.* Cambridge: Cambridge University Press, 2019.

Tripp, Aili Mari, and Alice Kang. "The Global Impact of Quotas: On the Fast Track to Increased Female Legislative Representation." *Comparative Political Studies* 41, no. 3 (March 2008): 338–61.

Truex, Rory. "Authoritarian Gridlock? Understanding Delay in the Chinese Legislative System." *Comparative Political Studies* 53, no. 9 (August 2020): 1455–92.

———. *Making Autocracy Work: Representation and Responsiveness in Modern China.* Cambridge Studies in Comparative Politics. New York: Cambridge University Press, 2016.

———. "The Returns to Office in a 'Rubber Stamp' Parliament." *American Political Science Review* 108, no. 2 (May 2014): 235–51.

United Nations Development Programme (UNDP). *Human Development Report, 2005.* New York: UNDP, 2005. https://hdr.undp.org/content/human-development-report-2005.

UN Women. *Regional Analysis on the Implementation of UNSCR 1325 in the Arab States.* New York: UN Women, 2015. https://mlkrook.org/pdf/UNWROAS_2015.pdf.

Valdini, Melody Ellis. *The Inclusion Calculation: Why Men Appropriate Women's Representation.* New York: Oxford University Press, 2019.

Verge, Tània, and Maria de la Fuente. "Playing with Different Cards: Party Politics, Gender Quotas and Women's Empowerment." *International Political Science Review* 35, no. 1 (January 2014): 67–79.

Waked, Muna Ayoub Yousef El, and Kholood Fawaz Al-Zoby. "The Challenges Hindering Jordanian Women from Political Participation from the Perspective of the Female Graduate Students at the University of Jordan." *Psychology and Education Journal* 58, no. 5 (2021): 1762–69. http://psychologyandeducation.net/pae/index.php/pae/article/view/5590.

Walsh, Denise M. *Women's Rights in Democratizing States: Just Debate and Gender Justice in the Public Sphere.* Cambridge: Cambridge University Press, 2011.

Wang, Suen. "Do Women Always Represent Women? The Effects of Gender Quotas on Substantive Representation." *Political Behavior* 45, no. 4 (July 2022): 1979–99.

Wängnerud, Lena. "Testing the Politics of Presence: Women's Representation in the Swedish Riksdag." *Scandinavian Political Studies* 23, no. 1 (March 2000): 67–91.

———. "Women in Parliaments: Descriptive and Substantive Representation." *Annual Review of Political Science* 12, no. 1 (June 2009): 51–69.

Weeks, Ana Catalano, and Jonathan Homola. "How Can We Measure Women's Substantive Representation." *Comparative Politics Newsletter* 32, no. 2 (2022): 16–21. https://www.comparativepoliticsnewsletter.org/wp-content/uploads/2022/12/APSA-CP_32_2_Dec_2022.pdf.

Wegner, Eva. *Islamist Opposition in Authoritarian Regimes: The Party of Justice and Development in Morocco.* Religion and Politics. Syracuse, NY: Syracuse University Press, 2011.

Welborne, Bozena. "On Their Own? Women Running as Independent Candidates in the Middle East." *Middle East Law and Governance* 12, no. 3 (September 2020): 251–74.

——. "The Strategic Use of Gender Quotas in the Arab World." William and Kathy Hybl Democracy Studies Fellowship Paper. Washington, DC: IFES, 2010. https://aceproject.org/ero-en/regions/africa/MZ/ifes-the-strategic-use-of-gender-quotas-in-the.

Welborne, Bozena C., and Gail J. Buttorff. "Gender Quotas in the Arab World—20 Years On." *Digest of Middle East Studies* 31, no. 4 (October 2022): 340–58.

Wiberg, Matti. "Parliamentary Questioning: Control by Communication." *Parliaments and Majority Rule in Western Europe* (1995): 179–222.

Williamson, Scott, and Beatriz Magaloni. "Legislatures and Policy Making in Authoritarian Regimes." *Comparative Political Studies* 53, no. 9 (August 2020): 1525–43.

Willis, Michael J. "Political Parties in the Maghrib: Ideology and Identification. A Suggested Typology." *Journal of North African Studies* 7, no. 3 (September 2002): 1–28.

Wills, Emily Regan. "Democratic Paradoxes: Women's Rights and Democratization in Kuwait." *Middle East Journal* 67, no. 2 (April 2013): 173–84.

Wilson, Matthew Charles, and Josef Woldense. "Contested or Established? A Comparison of Legislative Powers Across Regimes." *Democratization* 26, no. 4 (May 2019): 585–605.

World Bank. *Capabilities, Opportunities and Participation: Gender Equality and Development in the Middle East and North Africa Region.* Washington, DC: World Bank, 2011.

——. *Opening Doors: Gender Equality and Development in the Middle East and North Africa.* Washington, DC: World Bank, 2013. https://documents1.worldbank.org/curated/en/338381468279877854/pdf/Main-report.pdf.

World Economic Forum. *Global Gender Gap Report.* Geneva, Switzerland: World Economic Forum, 2015. https://www3.weforum.org/docs/GGGR2015/cover.pdf.

Wright, Joseph. "Do Authoritarian Institutions Constrain? How Legislatures Affect Economic Growth and Investment." *American Journal of Political Science* 52, no. 2 (April 2008): 322–43.

Wylie, Kristin N. *Party Institutionalization and Women's Representation in Democratic Brazil.* Cambridge: Cambridge University Press, 2018.

Yadav, Vineeta, and Bumba Mukherjee. *The Politics of Corruption in Dictatorships.* New York: Cambridge University Press, 2016.

Yardımcı-Geyikçi, Şebnem. "Party Institutionalization and Democratic Consolidation: Turkey and Southern Europe in Comparative Perspective." *Party Politics* 21, no. 4 (July 2015): 527–38.

Yom, Sean L. "Jordan: The Ruse of Reform." *Journal of Democracy* 24, no. 3 (2013): 127–39.

Yule, Jean. "Women Councillors and Committee Recruitment." *Local Government Studies* 26, no. 3 (September 2000): 31–54.

Zaanoun, Abderrafie. "The Impact of the Quota System on Women Parliamentary Representation in Morocco: A Series of Reforms or a Regressive Path?" *Arab Reform Initiative*, April 14, 2022. https://www.arab-reform.net/publication/the-impact-of-the-quota-system-on-women-parliamentary-representation-in-morocco-a-series-of-reforms-or-a-regressive-path/.

INDEX

power and role of, 6, 11, 20, 23–24, 51, 52, 62, 68; with women and committee assignments, 66, 109–10. *See also* party institutionalization

parties, political: authoritarian, 4, 10–13, 43; banning of, 20, 55, 66, 107; ban on formation of, 80; branches, 58, 64, 65, 170; comparative, 21, 22, 180, 181; competition and, 63; democracies and role of, 7, 10; formation of, 55, 77, 79–80, 98; ideology, 52, 61, 134, 169, 182; with illusion of freedom and pluralism, 55; interests of women and, 12, 64, 144, 145, 146, 163, 169, 175; with inter-party competition, 6, 57; Islamist, 54, 55, 56; Jordan, 20, 55–56, 66, 70–71, 79–80, 82–84, 107, 127, 132, 145, 158–59, 244n37; Kuwait with political groups instead of, 77, 107, 158, 181, 249n110, 259n33; with legislative behavior and power of women, 4; MENA region with party systems and, 53–56; Morocco, 62, 66, 67, 71, 99–104, 107, 127, 145, 158, 170, 251n139; nonregime, 10, 11; opposition, 55, 101, 103, 116; PI, political power of women and authoritarian, 10–13; with policy preferences, 63, 180, 185; role of, 60–61, 63, 175–76; ruling, 8, 10, 13, 27, 58, 62; single, 54, 230n43; "strength" and institutionalization, 217n9; targeting weaknesses of, 70; women and political representation in MENA with PI and, 60–66; youth, 83

partisanship, 10, 49, 111, 127, 144

"partly free" countries, 6, 19, 71

party institutionalization (PI): absence of, 56, 158; authoritarian parties, political power of women and, 10–13; authoritarian regimes and cross-national models of, 176–79; autocracies and micro-level effects of, 22, 138; collaboration and, 144–45; complexity and, 12, 52, 57, 64; defined, 5; depth of, 11, 12, 52, 63, 64, 65, 221n64; descriptive representation, women and, 13, 52; elements of, 238n90; female representation and, 19; index, 58–59, 59, 67; individual, 6, 11, 14, 22, 46, 56–58, 61,

173, 177–78; influence of, 51–53; Jordan, 20, 60, 66, 72, 73; Kuwait, 59–60, 72, 73, 145; in MENA, 56–60, 60; Morocco, 20, 52, 59, 66, 72–73, 73; power with, 109, 175; PSI and, 11; regime and, 6; rights of women in autocracies influenced by, 177, 205–6; scope of, 11, 12, 52, 63, 64, 175, 221n64; substantive representation and, 13, 22, 44, 52, 62, 157–68, 169, 173–76, 180; Tunisia and, 13, 44; variable, 132, 163, 165, 178; women and political representation in MENA with parties and, 60–66; women with committee membership and, 126–35

"Party Institutionalization, Authoritarian Regime Types, and Women's Political Equality" (Pelke), 232n69

"Party Institutionalization in New Democracies" (Randall and Svåsand), 238n90

Party of Progress and Socialism (PPS), Morocco, 101, 103

party system institutionalization (PSI), 22, 23, 53, 54; absence of, 101; individual PI and, 6, 11, 56–57; MENA and, 58

party systems: MENA region with parties and, 53–56; single, 54

patriarchy, 32–33, 61, 94, 185; gender norms and, 28; gender roles and, 35–36; public, 38; with sharia-based laws, 103

Paxton, Pamela, 61

Pelke, Lars, 222n73, 232n69

Personal Status Code (CPS), Tunisia, 39

physical attacks, 185

PI. *See* party institutionalization; individual parties' institutionalization

PII. *See* V-Dem party Institutionalization Index

Pitkin, Hannah, 46–47

PJD. *See* Justice and Development Party

pluralism, 55, 100, 102

Poisson count model, 159

Policy Agendas Project, 258n26

policy change, 48, 109, 185

policy preferences, 9, 15, 53, 183; electoral system and, 186; gender differences and, 48;

also descriptive representation; substantive representation

research: on authoritarian institution structure and outcomes, 7, 8; gender and authoritarian politics, 21, 69, 184–87; on legislative behavior of women, 48; on women in politics in established democracies, 5–6, 48–49

rights: economic, 13, 38, 51, 102, 180; human, 7, 9, 243n25; individual freedoms and, 79

rights, of women, 100, 179; advancing, 28–29, 51; in autocracies influenced by PI, *177, 205–6*; autocrats with, 8, 15; suppression of, 28; voting, 38, 40, 84, 85, 93, 245n50

RNI. *See* National Rally of Independents

role congruity theory, 32

"rubber stamp" bodies, 74

Rudan, Rudan al-, 259n30

rules and procedures, of parliamentary committees, 113–17

ruling-party institutionalization, 10, 13, 27, 62

Rwanda, 180

Sabah al-Salim al-Sabah (Emir of Kuwait) (1965–1977), 89–90

Sadat, Anwar, 39, 230n46

Salafis, 98, 127, 158, 249n110, 259n33

Saud, Yehya al-, 1–2

Saudi Arabia, 222n78, 231n51; Shura Council, 40, 223n88; women in workforce, 36

scope conditions, 175–76

secret voting, 113, 116, 139

sectarianism, tribalism and, 95

"service deputies," 91

sexism, 2, 187

sex ratios, male-female population, 34

Sharaf, Layla, 245n48

sharia-based laws, patriarchy with, 103

Sheikh Jaber al-Ahmad al-Jaber al-Sabah (Emir of Kuwait) (1977–2006), 91

Shura councils, 40, 223n88, 247n73

single nontransferable vote (SNTV, one-person-one-vote), 68, 80–83, 85–87, 93, 97, 246n63

Skalli, Badia, 251n139

Skalli, Nouzha, 103

Škrabáková, Katarína, 62

SNTV. *See* single nontransferable vote

Social Affairs Committees, 124–27, 129, *130*, 131–33, 135, 137–38, 141

social identity theory, 32

Socialist Union of Popular Forces (USFP), Morocco, 67, 99–103, 251n139

social sectors committee, Morocco with, 255n44

social welfare, 49, 94, 111, 145, 153, 155, 157

sociocultural explanations, for representation in MENA, 28–33

Spain, 98

STATA, 160

state legislatures, U.S., 110, 119

stereotypes, gender, 32–33, 111, 118, 140

Storm, Lisa, 56

structural explanations, for representation in MENA, 34–38

sub-Saharan Africa, 49, 50, 180, 230n49

substantive representation, 17, 23, 69, 127, 184, 187; comparative perspective, 46–50; gender quotas and, 10, 21, 144; influence and, 5; interests of women and, 53, 145; Morocco and, 68, 102; numerical and, 50; party ideology and, 182; PI and, 13, 22, 44, 52, 62, 157–68, 169, 173–76, 180; PQs and, 18, 145

Svåsand, Lars, 238n90

symbolic representation, 47

Syria, 74, 222nn78–79, 244n36

systemness, PI and, 57, 238n90

Thomas, Sue, 48

transparency, 101, 141, 173

Transportation Committees, 119, 125, 126, 137

tribalism, 82, 95

tribal systems, with political power of women, 28, 29

tribes: Bedouin populations, 87, 90, 95; in Jordan, 28, 80; in Kuwait, 96–97

Tunisia, 51, 222nn78–79, 231n51; Arab uprisings, 39, 56; constitution, 231n56, 231n61; as electoral autocracy, 74; gender, religion

GPSR Authorized Representative: Easy Access System Europe, Mustamäe tee 50, 10621 Tallinn, Estonia, gpsr.requests@easproject.com

www.ingramcontent.com/pod-product-compliance
Lightning Source LLC
Chambersburg PA
CBHW022138020426
42334CB00015B/956